Pragmatic and Semantic Aspects of Early Language Development

by
Ernst L. Moerk, Ph.D.
Department of Psychology
California State University, Fresno

University Park Press
Baltimore • London • Tokyo

UNIVERSITY PARK PRESS

International Publishers in Science and Medicine
Chamber of Commerce Building
Baltimore, Maryland 21202

Copyright © 1977 by University Park Press

Typeset by Action Comp Co., Inc.

Manufactured in the United States of America
by Universal Lithographers, Inc., and The Optic Bindery Incorporated

Library of Congress Cataloging in Publication Data

Moerk, Ernst L.
Pragmatic and semantic aspects of early language development.
Includes index.
1. Children—Language.   2. Psycholinguistics.   3. Languages—
Physiological aspects.   4.   Nonverbal communication.   5.   Language and
languages—Study and teaching.   I. Title.
P118.M64   401′.9   77-5394
ISBN 0-8391-1118-5

Contents

Preface / ix

chapter one / TOPICS AND AIMS / 1

Terms and Topics in Theoretical Perspective / 1
Meaning and semantics / 2. Functions and pragmatics / 6.
Communication, speech, and language / 8.
Aims of the Study / 10
Overall explanatory sufficiency and theoretical integration / 10.
Diachronic/epigenetic synthesis / 13. Deliberation and equilibration of
contrasting approaches / 15.
Summary and Conclusion / 25

**chapter two / BIOLOGICAL BASES FOR LANGUAGE
DEVELOPMENT / 27**

Theoretical Positions / 27
Relevant Anatomical and Functional Facts / 34
Peripheral organs and their innate functions / 34. Central
characteristics of the human organism and their effects / 36. Global,
innate functions and their implications for cognitive and language
development / 42.
Summary and Conclusion / 52

**chapter three / PERCEPTUAL, MOTOR AND COGNITIVE
ANTECEDENTS OF LANGUAGE
DEVELOPMENT / 55**

Theoretical Background / 55
Controversies / 55. Methodological considerations / 58. Range of
antecedents / 58.
Functions / 59
Information exchange / 59. Development of vocalization / 64.
Increasing attentional capacities / 65. Increasing ability to discriminate
fine differences and to attend to distinctive features / 67.
Generalization, classification, and abstraction / 69. Hierarchies of
classification / 69. Functional equivalence / 70. Relations / 71.
Transformations / 71. Imagery and iconic representation / 72.

Imitation / 74. Increasing perspectivism /75 . Distancing
functions / 76. Learning and memory development / 76. Association
of sound patterns with other experiences / 79. Meaningfulness of
communication / 80.

Development of Meaning before Language / 81
Literature on the development of meaning / 81. Concept
development / 83. Discrepancies between the concepts of the child
and adult / 84.

Preverbal Structures Encountered and Assimilated by the Child / 89
Spatial structures / 92. Temporal structures / 93. Action
structures / 93. Interaction structures / 93. Embedded
structures / 94. Opportunities for acquisition of these structures / 97.

**chapter four / INVOLVEMENT OF INNATE PROPENSITIES AND
ACQUIRED COGNITIVE SKILLS IN LANGUAGE
ACQUISITION AND LANGUAGE BEHAVIOR / 99**

Information Exchange / 101
Information exchange with the inanimate environment /102.
Information exchange with the animate-social environment / 104.
Effect of the complexity of the social environment / 104.

Imitation / 105

Temporal Patterns of Behavior / 107

Transformations / 110

**Primitive Generalizations, Classifications, and Functional
Equivalence / 111**

Symbolic Representation and Use of Words / 115

Specific Concepts and Meanings / 119
Expressive function / 121. Directive function / 122. Referential
function / 123.

**Parallels Between the Syntax of Nonverbal Behavior and the Structures
of Verbal Behavior / 135**
Act-sentence / 136. Concatenating of actions—coordinating and
subordinating of clauses / 137. Overlapping of behavior episodes—
embedding of clauses / 138. Differentiated combinations of cognitive
structures and sentence constituents / 138. Problem of word order / 144.

Summary and Conclusion / 146

**chapter five / NONVERBAL MEANS OF MESSAGE TRANSMISSION
AND THEIR RELATIONSHIPS TO THE FORM AND
CONTENT OF VERBAL MESSAGES / 149**

Theoretical Perspective / 149
Formulation of the problem / 149. Kindred conceptualizations of
communication / 151. Relationships between reality, its human
representation, and various forms of human behavior / 152. Concise
outline of man's multidimensional communicative space / 159.

Characteristics of Children's Multichannel Communication / 167
Theoretical perspective / 167. Factual research on the
interdependencies between behavior setting and expressed
message / 170. Nonverbal communication and its relationship to
verbal communication during childhood / 183. Relationships of all
nonverbal means of message transmission to verbal means and to
communication efficiency / 190.
Summary and Conclusion / 200

**chapter six / VERBAL CHANNEL OF COMMUNICATION AND
INSTRUCTIONAL ASPECTS OF VERBAL
INTERACTION / 203**

Scope of the Inquiry / 203
Cognitive/learning aspects of language acquisition / 204. Motivational
aspects of language acquisition / 205.
Delimitation of the Topics / 207
Age period under investigation and the speed of language
acquisition / 207. Sources of input and their importance for language
learning / 208.
**Overall Approaches in Research on Language Input and Language
Learning / 214**
Approaches to data collection or data generation / 215. Theoretical
orientations underlying the diverse methodological decisions / 220.
Formal Aspects of Language Instruction and Language Learning / 226
Forms and structures of interactions / 226. Adaptations of adult speech
to the child's linguistic level / 230. Specific training techniques
employed by adults (verbal encoding of shared perceptions and
conceptualizations; utilization of rhythmic and rhyming characterizations
of language; modeling and imitation and some teaching/learning
processes involved in them; question and answer interactions and their
training functions; interactional/instructional potential of incomplete
sentences; maternal correction of children's utterance) / 236.
Conclusions / 254.
Dynamic Aspects of Dyadic Interactions / 256.
Theoretical perspective of the problem / 257. Kindred
conceptualizations of the dynamics of language acquisition (utilitarian/
operant function; cognitive operant function; interaction/communication
intrinsic motivations; multiple motivational variables) / 261.

Summary and Conclusion / 277

REFERENCES CITED / 279
INDEX / 317

Preface

Several books and many articles are currently appearing on aspects of language development. Almost all of them transcend purely grammatical descriptions and are aimed more at semantic and pragmatic analyses. If another volume is added to this rapidly expanding literature, the question may be asked what it has to offer to justify its publication. The main contributions of this volume are twofold. The first derives directly from the course of development of the research endeavor in general. After the field of psycholinguistics had been defined in the 1950's and had received an important theoretical impetus during the 1960's, another revolution of the axis that ties theoretical formulations to factual evaluations occurred during the first part of the 1970's. Many specific phenomena have been elaborated during the last few years: the relationships between cognition and language have been explored; the functions of language have again attracted the attention of several investigators; nonverbal communication has been considered; and language training has been observed in the home and used with considerable success in therapy despite its minimal contact with the general field of developmental psycholinguistics. A rich array of factual information consequently has been established in the various fields, and important theoretical conceptualizations can be found in diverse sources. What is needed now, and is attempted in this volume, is the integration of this wealth of data and ideas so that a more unified picture of the language-learning child can be established.

It is hoped that in this manner the book will contribute to establishing bridges and to abolishing artificial and inappropriate dividing lines. The specialist interested in the training of language skills will find chapters on their biological and cognitive bases that may guide his training endeavors; he will also be shown how the most efficient trainers of language skills (normal middle-class mothers) proceed with their instruction. Investigators concerned primarily with sensorimotor and cognitive bases of language will find detailed reminders showing that sociocultural and interpersonal aspects are of great importance, as emphasized by Russian authors and American behaviorists, respectively. Brain specialists will be reminded of the vast range of psychological variables, and psychologists will be referred to the profound and overriding effects of anatomical and neurological aspects.

A second justification for this book arises from the writer's own course of development. After having been raised and educated in central Europe, he moved to the United States. Having been and still remaining an admirer of Konrad Lorenz and European ethologists, he has become a defender of some ideas in Skinner's *Verbal Behavior.* Having been trained in the schools of H. Rohracher, H. Hess, and A. Luchsinger, who accorded special attention to anatomical and physiological bases of language and speech, a fact reflected especially in Chapter Two of this book, he has learned in the United States to pay equally close attention to the external and social determinants of "speech acts" or "verbal behavior." Because of these manifold intellectual roots, the book represents an integration in a second sense: The often contrasting theoretical approaches, generally treated elsewhere as mutually exclusive, are here critically scrutinized and applied toward an overall understanding of language development.

Equally as manifold as the roots and the references is the indebtedness of the writer. Valuable insights have been gained from the Russian tradition, as expressed in the studies of Vygotsky, Luria, and Leontiev. Thoughts of Eastern-European authors, such as Slama-Cazacu or authors from the Prague school, have been incorporated, whereas the conceptualizations and findings of Central/Western European and Anglo-Saxon writers form the backbone of the presentation. The history-minded reader will recognize traces of Humboldtian and nineteenth century thinking and will be able to follow trends including those of the near future, i.e., the late 1970's. This indebtedness is fully evident from the extensive list of references.

It is also customary to list a large number of persons who actively contributed in one way or another to the production of the book. The writer would be very happy to follow this tradition if he could. But, as a matter of fact, the work on the present book was primarily one of lonely labor, the obstacles were many and unexpected, and the help received was rare indeed. A graduate seminar held at California State University, Fresno, provided a welcome opportunity to test and improve conceptualizations. One of the main contributions was made by our department chairman, Dr. Wayne Holder, who was very considerate in scheduling a heavy teaching load in a manner that left time for research work. A more direct impact was made by my wife, Claudia, who spent many hours checking and rechecking the progressively refined versions of the manuscript to discover and eliminate Germanisms in style and who shared in the more monotonous tasks of checking the references and reference lists. After the months and years of lonely work on this project, it was a pleasant surprise to obtain intensive and enthusiastic support from University Park Press in the final stages of the production of this book. This enthusiasm and efficiency revived my flagging spirits and contributed greatly toward bringing a long and arduous project to a pleasant and enjoyable conclusion. While acknowledging this support wherever it was provided, I want to reserve my most warmly felt appreciation for our three-and-a-half-year old daughter. She reacted with admirable patience and understanding to my delay tactics when she asked for the hundredth time, "Can you now play with me, Vato?" and I replied once again, "A little later, my love." Whatever Kirstin had to miss in parent-child interaction because of my work on this book, I hope that other children gain in enriched and optimal stimulation as the lasting fruits of this endeavor.

Pragmatic and Semantic Aspects of Early Language Development

chapter
one
Topics
and Aims

TERMS AND TOPICS IN THEORETICAL PERSPECTIVE

Whether measured in number of publications or in the productivity of new ideas and new approaches, the field of developmental psycholinguistics is currently very active and productive. This almost feverish activity suggests that the prevalent ideas and systems are not yet seen as satisfactory and that various authors approach the field with somewhat different perspectives. It appears advisable, therefore, that this book should begin with a short sketch of the overall perspective which will represent the underlying framework. Since it is only intended to present a brief sketch of the general outlook, historical and theoretical remarks are combined in a less than systematic manner. More extensive treatments of the history (Aaronson, 1976; Blumenthal, 1970) as well as of theoretical problems (Stemmer, 1973; Vetter and Howell, 1971) are found in the literature.

The most basic elements of the framework to be followed should be and are found in the title of every book. The terms *pragmatic* and *semantic aspects* probably will evoke a responsive cord in all persons actively involved in the field of early language development, though the response may not in all cases be a positive one. While the choice of these terms fulfills on that account a communicative function, it also entails considerable hazards. Both terms are currently employed very often, in many different contexts, and for various purposes. It can be expected, therefore, that a semantic features analysis would show profound differences in the various uses to which they are put. Along Wittgensteinian lines, by equating meaning with its uses, Bouveresse (1974: 382) spoke of "the more or less complete disappearance of the semantic-pragmatic distinction." If this assertion were accepted at face value, then the present title and many similar

1

ones in the field would be more redundant than informative. Bates (1976a) goes one step further in attempting to decide which of these two aspects is more basic and which can be derived from the other. She states, "logically and ontogenetically all of semantics and syntactics are derived ultimately from pragmatics ..." (1976: 425–426). In other words, as spelled out in later chapters, one encounters the common chicken-egg problem here: Certainly, interactions with social partners lead to concepts; but how could an infant or any person interact with social partners if his acts were not already meaningful responses to certain incoming or internally arising stimuli? The newborn infant's orienting response is, in a certain sense, a meaningful question about the meaning of a noticed stimulus. The infant's spontaneous cry is a meaningful expression of his state and is understood by his parents in this manner. Similarly, his social smiles even at the age of a few weeks are meaningful reactions to meaningful stimulus complexes, i.e., human faces. Considering this evidence one could with equal or even with more justification argue that, logically and ontogenetically, all of pragmatics and of the syntax of behavior is derived from semantics, since meaningless behavior would be unstructured, chaotic, and socially dysfunctional.

The solution of this argument probably cannot be found in the realm of ontogeny alone, but rests in the fields of genetics and evolution. As Piaget (1971) has argued convincingly, heredity provides both specific information and regulatory mechanisms. What Piaget calls information in this context is equivalent to one aspect of meaning; what he calls regulatory mechanisms leads to social interactions, i.e., pragmatics, among many other things. The details of these roots and relationships are explored in later sections and chapters. In this book, *contents* or *products* refer to meaning aspects, and *functions* pertain to the realm of pragmatics. Not only is the justification of the subdivision into semantics and pragmatics controversial, the meaning of each term and the implications of its use for psychological research on first-language acquisition are wide open for debate. To establish a common frame of reference, at least for the present study, a brief attempt at describing and clarifying the implications of these terms is first provided.

Meaning and Semantics

As is generally known, during recent times linguists have largely excluded semantics from their domain by arguing that this topic is too unwieldy, including in principle the study of man's entire world view (Katz and Fodor, 1963). Oettinger (1972) still referred to the "semantic wall," suggesting that no opening has yet been found to breach it. Neither has the idea of "semantic features" nor the controversy surrounding this term contributed much to the clarification of this domain.

In contrast to the linguists' eschewing of this topic, a large number of philosophers have been intensively preoccupied with it. A long lineage could be established from antiquity through the Middle Ages and the more modern times to Frege, Tarski, Carnap, and Suppes. Various collaterals are marked by the names of Susan Langer, Charles Morris, and Ludwig Wittgenstein and his followers in the area of so-called natural language philosophy. Frege's distinction between *meaning* and *reference*, approximating the ideas currently expressed by the terms *intension* versus *extension,* is presupposed as an important source of disambiguation in all the following sections. The concern of Charles Morris or Ludwig Wittgenstein with the meaningful and practical uses of language is already expressed in the choice of this book's title and is encountered throughout the book.

The principal features of the concepts *meaning* and *semantics*, however, are derived from other areas, namely, developmental psychology and the study of early speech use. Recent advances in these fields provide the bases. Research on language acquisition has come a long way since the early work of Brown and associates on distributional phenomena of child speech. Most investigators have now arrived at the study of the whole child, almost in the manner of Tiedemann (1787) and Preyer (1882), both of whom dealt with "the mind of the child" (*die Seele des Kindes*); i.e., they have (re)turned unashamedly to a mentalistic approach. New terms such as *cognition* or *conceptual development* are employed, and Piaget's and others' experimental and observational methods are relied upon, but the amount of inference from the data to the theoretical interpretations is, however, large in all cases. This turn of the *Zeitgeist* has enormously enriched the study of language acquisition, but it has also endangered it in the sense amply illustrated by the earlier antimentalistic diatribes of observationally oriented psychologists. It is hoped that the resulting enrichment can be demonstrated throughout the body of this book. Whether the conceptual fuzziness that is often a concomitant of "mentalistic" discussions has been sufficiently avoided, will have to be left to the judgment of the reader. It is accepted almost as a matter of fact that it cannot currently be completely eschewed.

Since it is admitted that a somewhat hazardous approach has been chosen, a few words may be required to justify this choice, besides the general allusion to its rich potential: The wealth of research in the field of cognitive development published since the breakthrough of Piaget's theoretical approach, first in Europe and since the 1950's also in the United States, is self-evident. A vast array of factual information and systematic theoretical interpretation of data is, therefore, readily available to the investigator who wants to explore how the young child forms his conceptualizations and communicates them verbally. If the term *communication* is taken in its broadest sense as *information transmission,* it follows that all behavior, i.e., also that shown in psychological experiments or during observation sessions, communicates something about the child's conceptual ordering of his world (see Orne, 1973). This source of established evidence is, therefore, almost inexhaustible.

The second great advantage of the mentalistic or cognitive approach to the study of any behavior, and therefore also of language development, is more conceptual. In referring to the *meaning* of a specific stimulus complex for a child, the child's responses over a certain time period and over a variety of situations are integrated. This stands in contrast to the preoccupation with merely one type of stimulus-response sequence. Formulated somewhat facetiously, it could be said with justification that a cognitive approach is more behavioral, that is, it includes more behavior, than a behavioristic approach. The currently ubiquitous artifact, the computer, which is known inside and outside and can therefore be "understood" more easily, can serve to clarify the point. Theoretically, one could talk with ease about stimulus-response sequences when describing the computer's function. Everybody, however, refers to computer programs, thereby implicitly acknowledging that this mentalistic approach conveys much more information about the "behavior" of the computer in its present and potential aspect than stimulus-response descriptions do. This is readily accepted in the field of computer sciences, since everybody is aware that nothing mentalistic is involved in the terminology. The wealth of information conveyed in naming a computer program can always and easily be proved by running a wide variety of tasks through the computer and checking to see if it "behaves" according to the program. This is routinely done in the testing of specific programs. Theoretically, the social scientist could also "run" a child, or a rat for that matter, whose *concept* or *meaning* he* has described, through a wide variety of situations that involve the concept in question, and he could check the accuracy of his description of the child's behavioral program. If, for example, a child's concept of *dog* would include the feature "dangerous animal," this could be shown quite easily in a wide variety of behavior settings. To demonstrate all the features of a concept is undoubtedly more difficult in practice, but it could be based upon the same simple methodological principle. The advantage of the baby-biographical approach, with the child's own parents as observers, is immediately obvious when the mentalistic method is considered from this perspective. Almost nobody can have as much behavioral evidence about a specific child than the concerned and attentive caregiver. If this caregiver is in addition trained and masters the basic tools of science, then he will be best able to describe the child's program, i.e., his conceptual system. It therefore may be no accident that child-language researchers have returned not only to the mentalistic interpretation of child behavior but also to the method of the baby-biography (see Bloom, 1970; Bowerman, 1974; Greenfield and Smith, 1976; Halliday, 1975).

The best description, though not yet quantification, of this conceptualization of meaning can be given in matrix-algebra terms. The meaning of a concept or of any other stimulus could be shown in a response matrix whose two dimensions are time and situational variety. In matrix algebra a single number, D, the determinant of a matrix, is employed to represent the generalized variance in the set of tests. Similarly, when the philosopher/linguist/psychologist talks about the *meaning* of an object or word, he attempts to give just such a generalized determination. When he talks about the *extension* of a term, he refers to the temporal dimension since elements of the set are encountered across a temporal continuum. When he refers to *semantic features* or the *intension* of a concept, he refers to the variety of situational specifications that this concept has undergone. Wittgenstein probably aimed at something similar in his famous dictum that meaning is use; only the variance in use over time and situations needs perhaps to be emphasized somewhat more than it was done by Wittgenstein.

In accordance with this belief in the value of the cognitive approach, which is implied though not usually justified in recent publica-

---

*Gender-specific pronouns are used throughout this book for the sake of clarity and simplicity only. They are not meant to be exclusionary.

tions on child language development, a cognitive-semantic approach is followed in the present study. Such a cognitive orientation, which is largely rooted in Piaget's system, implies that the study of language development can and has to be extended over the period before the first signs of language appear. Since concepts can be inferred only if they are expressed, i.e., communicated in the wider sense, the emphasis on early cognitive development is combined here with an emphasis on early communicative development, which at this time has to be nonverbal. The infant's information transmission is directed toward both the inanimate and the animate environment. An intense concern with the situation or the context of communicative behavior is, therefore, theoretically required, namely, a wide variety of stimuli have to be considered when the communicative response of the child is explored. As soon as the attention centers upon the animate environment, which is predominantly the human environment but includes anthropomorphized pet animals, the pragmatic aspect of language development becomes the center of attention. This second element of the title therefore has to be considered more carefully.

Functions and Pragmatics

An astonishing phenomenon is evident when the current interest in the pragmatic aspects of language is considered: Skinner (1957) attempted an incursion into the field of "verbal behavior" and was fiercely attacked by Chomsky (1959). Palermo (1970, 1976) defected from the behavioristic line, and even one of its stalwarts, Staats, has become silent. It would appear that, of the major investigators in the field, only Braine is supporting the factual/behavior-oriented position. At the same time the *pragmatic* approach is becoming highly fashionable and many authors emphasize the principle of *speech acts*. It almost appears as if the proponents of these newer approaches were not aware that *pragmatics* and *acts* are only the Greek and Latin terms, respectively, for *behavior*. When Wittgenstein, whose contribution is just now becoming appreciated in publications on language development, insisted on language as a social institution and on language use as intersubjective *behavior* [sic], he employed almost the same words as Skinner. His famous pronouncement that "to understand the meaning of an expression requires to see how it is used" evidently aims toward an operational behavioral definition of *meaning*.

Since the functional aspect of language is emphasized in connection with the pragmatic approach, it should be remembered that functional analyses are the goal of behavioristic research. The most basic principle of behavioristic approaches, that the response is a function of one or several stimuli together with the learning history of the organism, is of course functional. This functional/behavioristic orientation is not only prevalent in the field of early language development, it is perhaps even more prevalent in the burgeoning field of sociolinguistics, as can be seen in many of the publications of Hymes, Gumperz, and others.

The main goal of the above paragraph is not and could not be the analysis of the complex trends in psychological research over the period referred to, nor the comparison of various psychological systems. Much more time and space would be required for either of these goals. These brief remarks serve mainly as a notice to the reader that the term *pragmatics* does have to include, and does include in the present study, many features that are conventionally referred to by the term *behavioristic*. These features stand out especially in Chapter Six, when language training and learning and the informational and motivational feedback provided by parents are discussed.

When Charles Morris defined pragmatics as "the relation of signs to interpreters" (1946:217), his intention, however, was broader than is mostly conceived today. He specified that pragmatics also included the origins of signs. If the origins of language are included in the definition of pragmatics, then the anatomical, neurological, and overall biological aspects of language need to be considered under this domain as well. This broad definition is employed here, especially in Chapter Two. Although most obvious in Chapter Two, this biological aspect of pragmatics can be discovered in many other contexts. As seen in Chapters Three and Four, the description of the child's cognitive development is profoundly influenced by Piaget's thinking. It is also known that Piaget tied the development of knowledge to the whole process of embryogenesis or, more generally, to biology, as it is most precisely expressed in the title of one of his latest books. Since language is tied to cognition and cognition to biology, the pragmatic concerns with the origins of signs are also encountered in Chapters Three and Four. In Chapter Five, when verbal communication is related to other preverbal channels of communication and to basic biological interactions with the environment, this last feature of the concept pragmatics is encountered again.

The two most widely used and at the same time least clear terms of the title have been explicated above, and the overall range of the project has thereby been sketched out. The other elements of the title are treated in a much briefer way, with the expectation that a common frame of reference can be more easily presupposed in respect to them. The term *development* is employed more in the continental European tradition that can be characterized by the term *epigenesis.* Heinz Werner's work (1940), or the contributions collected by Harris (1957), reflect this approach closely. Piaget's essay on "development and learning" (1964) is especially relevant, since so much of the present book builds upon Piaget's thinking. Development here is seen neither as predominantly guided by genetic factors, which were perhaps emphasized too much by Gesell in the Anglo-Saxon realm, nor by mere learning, as the extreme behaviorists would have it. An integration of both factors leading to qualitative new phenomena, i.e., epigenesis in all behavior and also in communicative behavior, is partly described and partly presupposed.

Communication, Speech, and Language

One last remark of clarification and delimitation of the topics to be covered is required in respect to the topic of *language.* After Saussure's distinction between *langue* and *parole,* which was reflected in the recently predominant competence-performance dichotomy, much use and probably misuse have been made of this differentiation. Since the present approach is based upon psychological principles, almost nothing will be found of the formal structural models that were in vogue during the 1960's. It has been pointed out often enough by many writers that every corpus of data can be described in many formal ways. It also becomes more generally accepted that by far not enough evidence is currently available to decide whether any of these formal descriptions really comes close to a description of human competence. Finally, critics of Chomsky's system (e.g., Hiorth, 1974) have pointed out that Chomsky's entire terminology was chosen incorrectly. Chomsky clearly dealt with the realm of *la langue,* at least as long as he made his constructive contributions to linguistic theory, and tried to provide a parsimonious and optimal description of the linguistic system. In this realm neither the term *competence* nor that of *performance* can be applied with any justification. Chomsky's "systematic ambiguity," namely, whether he aimed at a linguistic-descriptive or psychological explanatory theory, may have been systematic, but it nevertheless was a precarious linguistic performance that misled many readers and apparently often the author of this dichotomy himself. Performance, which should be the first object of study when psychological explanatory theories are envisaged, was eschewed, and minute scientific investigation of human rule-governed behavior was replaced by pseudoexplanation and mere naming. Evidently, the term *competence* explains equally as much or as little as the terms *intelligence, instinct, fate,* or even *predestination.*

After the habitual subdivision of the semantic field of the English term *language* has been questioned, it can be briefly specified how the term is used in the present context: In compliance with the principles of factual scientific investigation, the material for any conclusions will be the behavioral products of the child. Most of these products are systematically similar to each other so that they provide evidence of rules which underlie their production. Such rule-governed behavior is not only found in language but also in nonverbal communication and in nonverbal behavior generally. To understand the development of rule-governed language behavior, it is first necessary to understand other forms of rule-governed behavior, especially rule-governed nonverbal communicative behavior. It is therefore suggested repeatedly that the infant may have developed preverbal "language systems" whose study is most important for the understanding of language development *per se.* In this sense the term *language* is used more broadly than is customary in much of the previous literature. On the other hand, little attempt is made to speculate on what the encompassing system of linguistic competence may be that underlies the child's language products. As is sometimes suggested in the literature, the child may not even have such an encompassing rule system, and specific types of productions may follow rules that are not connected with many other rules. As seen especially in Chapters Five and Six, many of the linguistic productions of the child seem to be governed by rules referring to extralinguistic contexts and the presuppositions of both communication partners, and much less by considerations of linguistic correctness or even wellformedness. What has been recently labeled as *communicative competence* reflects this aspect of the rules that govern the child's verbal behavior and therefore his verbal products. In this manner language behavior is broadly intergrated into other aspects of rule-governed behavior. These are studied by psychologists, ethologists, and some linguists, who see in language more than a system of spoken or written forms (Chafe, 1970; Pike, 1954, 1955, 1959; Rommetveit, 1968).

The manner of this integration probably could be best described as a strongly nativistic-epigenetic colored cognitive-learning theoretical frame of reference. Predominant shaping influences of this framework can be named (in alphabetical order and not in order of importance): A. Bandura, K. Bühler, K. Lorenz, J. Piaget, and L. Wittgenstein. In respect to factual findings, the strong influence of contemporary American-English psycholinguistic research is evident throughout the text and the reference section.

AIMS OF THE STUDY

Overall Explanatory Sufficiency and Theoretical Integration

In the process of delimiting the domain of the present investigation, several of the aims and goals have been indirectly referred to. It may prove helpful to summarize these goals more concisely. Such a summary provides two advantages. It facilitates the evaluation of whether a sufficiently broad variety of mechanisms has been included which could account for language acquisition. It also permits the reader to judge, when he studies the next chapters, whether all the objectives have been accomplished or at least explored in detail.

Since the basic goal is to explain language development in its totality, it is not enough to describe specific singular aspects which, though necessary for language acquisition, are not sufficient for its explanation. Also, what is or should be meant by the term *sufficiency*, as applied to language acquisition, has to be considered. Would minimal sufficiency be adequate, or must overdetermining phenomena be explored? As Chomsky, Lenneberg, and others have often argued, almost all children acquire language in spite of a wide range of intellectual capacities and environmental conditions. Since it can be taken for granted that not all of these children encounter the same cognitive and environmental preconditions, it must be concluded that normal language development is highly overdetermined. Antecedents which may account for a large amount of the variance in the language skills of one group of children may contribute nothing at all in the case of another widely different group. The first task, therefore, is to describe and explore a wide range of antecedents whose contribution to language acquisition can be demonstrated or at least argued plausibly. The next and more complex task is to show which combinations of these diverse antecedents lead to language skills. It would be even better if one could demonstrate quantitatively which systematic combinations of antecedent skills lead to quicker language acquisition and to a higher level of ultimate language skills. Some very crude "experiments of nature," i.e., children who lack one or even more sensory functions or who grow up in very deprived environmental conditions, can be and have been studied to demonstrate the effects of specific gaps in the antecedents. If the currently widely employed early language training programs are better described and compared regarding their effects upon overall language level and specific language skills, more insights into the optimal combinations for language training and learning will be gained. At present a less ambitious goal had to be chosen, that of accounting for a wide range of antecedents that can be considered not only as sufficient for language acquisition but also as representing alternate avenues for the attainment of this skill. This account contains redundant elements, i.e., elements that reinforce and possibly accelerate the effect of other elements, whose absence, however, would not seriously interfere with language acquisition.

Within this overall goal specific subgoals can be stated: Instead of attempting to explain merely the structure of early language, the functioning of human children is explored. Instead of concentrating upon language only, a wide variety of communicative functions and their interdependencies are studied. Since communication and not only verbal language is the object of investigation, no lower limit exists for the age period which can be subjected to the study. The domain is not only broadened to include nonverbal social communication but also to consider information exchange generally. The infant could not communicate his concept of an object to his social partner if he had not earlier explored objects by means of sensorimotor processes. To describe the meaning of the linguistic expression that he employs, one has to explore the meaning he has formed during this precommunicative information intake. All these above-mentioned extensions of the domain can be brought together under one heading: The goal of the study is to transcend a particularistic fixation upon mere language in order to include in a holistic approach the entire child together with his inanimate and animate environment.

One further consequence of this functional and holistic approach follows logically. Instead of synchronic considerations of language skills, which are still encountered in much of the literature, such as R. Brown's (1973) stages of language development, a diachronic approach is advocated and employed. This diachrony pertains not to

the historical development of one specific language but to the ontogenetic establishment of one person's language skills. It scarcely can
be doubted, and it is implicitly accepted in most publications on
language development, that the earlier levels of language skills profoundly affect the form that the later levels will take. The same necessarily applies to the still earlier levels of preverbal communication
skills and to the preceding and simultaneous construction of knowledge
about the world. Whereas the advisability of long-term diachronic
investigations of first-language acquisition is clearly perceived, it
could not be realized in the present study for the entire age period
during which language development proceeds. The main attention is
therefore devoted to the earlier ages during which the foundations for
all later acquisitions are laid.

From the various points made above, it follows that the overall
manner or approach of the present study could be characterized as
integrative: An integration of a wide variety of subfields in the area of
child development is aimed at, an integration of the ideas derived
from various schools of thought is attempted, and a bridging of the
inheritance-environment controversy is envisaged. It is evident from
even a cursory consideration of the publications appearing during the
last two decades in the domain of developmental psycholinguistics
that theses and antitheses have been prevalent. Hegel has expounded
in detail that such dichotomic approaches appear to be a basic principle of human thinking. Yet little chance of mutual fertilization and
of a viable offspring exists if the twain never meet. Now that representatives of both extreme positions have had their say, it appears
that the time for a synthesis or integration has arrived. In fact, the
Piagetian term *equilibration* would better fit the goal of the present
study than the words *synthesis* or *integration*. The opposing theses
are not to be combined; rather, respective positions have to be weighed
and balanced in the elaboration of a more complex explanation. It is
hoped that the result of the present labor will be seen not as an eclec-
tic compilation of the findings from opposing fields but as a new
product in the epigenetic sense.

An attempt is made here to break through superficial terminological differences of frozen theoretical positions and to explore profound or basic communalities that underlie various scientific approaches. Communalities have to exist, since all schools refer to the
same reality, namely, the developing child. Consequently, their
denotata must be largely similar and the extensions of their concepts
must overlap. If the overall set of extensions is so similar, the overall

set of intensions also must reflect this communality. Though the sections are subdivided according to particular topics, all the following chapters represent a search for communalities. Moreover, a double type of integration is sought. First, the specific topics are viewed in a diachronic/epigenetic perspective to show the broad trends of development of these functions. Then the various approaches and theories are compared, contrasted, and finally integrated not only within but also across chapters.

Diachronic/Epigenetic Synthesis

In the title of Chapter Two, Biological Bases for Language Development, the logical emphasis is placed upon the word *bases* and upon the earliest stages of development. In accordance with Piaget's long-established approach and the thinking found in several of the most recent publications in developmental psycholinguistics, the chapters explore how these bases, both in their contentive and functional perspectives, lead to qualitatively new developments. Considerable attention is devoted to the study of the relationships between biological structures and the functions directly attributable to these structures on the one hand, and those functions that are more remotely derived from the original structures because of a complex conflux of many other influences, on the other hand. Whereas the primordial importance of innate structures as well as their continuing multiple impacts are emphasized, it will become increasingly evident in the course of the exposition that no specific innate linguistic structures are needed to explain language acquisition.

Chapter Three, Perceptual, Motor, and Cognitive Antecedents of Language Development, is specifically devoted to the discussion of the preverbal period. It presents information on many and, it is hoped, most of the functions and conceptualizations that arise from the interaction of genetic bases and environmental givens. The gradual developments of these functions and their products, i.e., single conceptualizations or meanings and complex conceptual structures and the understanding of relationships, are described. The specific links between these preverbal and the later verbal phenomena are then explicated in Chapter Four.

The complexity of the relationships to be handled in Chapter Four is reflected by its somewhat cumbersome title, Involvement of Innate Propensities and Acquired Cognitive Skills in Language Acquisitions and Language Behavior. This chapter is central to the entire argument of the present study since it represents the conceptual and temporal bridge between the preverbal and the verbal periods. As the word *involvement* in the title suggests, causal relationships are throughout implied, though often only antecedent-consequent relationships can be factually proved. Slight suggestions of causality and expositions on the psychological plausibility of the links often have to suffice instead of fully established causal evidence. This last fact makes the argument often precarious, and it is foreseen that some of the specific links that are suggested will be found not to apply to all children or even not to apply at all. Whereas a comprehensive and hypothesis-creating approach has been chosen, finality could not be envisaged at the present state of science in this field.

Chapter Five, Nonverbal Means of Message Transmission and Their Relationships to the Form and Content of Verbal Messages, encompasses once again preverbal phenomena but leads fully into the period of verbal behavior. It therefore could be considered as an explication and extension to verbal behavior of one specific aspect of Chapter Four. This topic is treated separately since message transmission is probably the most characteristic aspect of language behavior. After the range of the discussion is expanded in Chapters Three and Four to encompass a wide range of functions and to attain a sufficiently broad scope in the purview of language antecedents, a gradual narrowing can be observed in the last two chapters of the book. Chapter Five deals only with communication, and Chapter Six is devoted exclusively to varying aspects of verbal communication. The underlying theme of Chapter Five is the sometimes asserted and often only implied contention that the preverbal infant has established a relatively effective nonverbal "language" before he begins to acquire verbal language. His task therefore is relatively easy when he begins to cope with the linguistic givens of his environment. He needs only to translate his established conceptual and communicative system into a new code. That he does this very gradually and economically is demonstrated in Chapter Five.

Finally, in Chapter Six, some systematic research results, incidental remarks, and theoretical statements of many and diverse authors are reported on how adults interact verbally with their children and how they train them thereby in linguistic skills. Both aspects of this aim are expressed in the title, Verbal Channel of Communication and Instructional Aspects of Verbal Interactions. Teaching, rehearsal, and testing strategies, as well as techniques to motivate the child to attend to the material of instruction, are described. Even though the chapter spans the age period between around two and five years, the evidence for some of the conclusions is still quite sparse and of doubtful generalizability. All available data are derived from very small samples of children, from brief sections of verbal interactions, or from too-homogeneous cultural backgrounds. Although preliminary, these findings should help to dispel the currently fashionable summary condemnations of the learning theoretical approach to language acquisition. In contrast, they should demonstrate that such considerations have to constitute a fundamental aspect of any explanation of first-language acquisition, though it is only one aspect among many others. Some of the specific findings also should disprove several often-repeated assertions that parents neither correct nor reward their children's linguistic mistakes and trials, respectively. The entire chapter therefore should fulfill an important function for the second major aim of this book, the integration of contributions from different fields of study. The first goal, the diachronic presentation of processes and products, provides the connecting theme from the discussion of perinatal phenomena in Chapter Two to the interactional phenomena at the age of five years, as referred to in Chapter Six.

Deliberation and Equilibration of Contrasting Approaches

The double word-play in this title is chosen to emphasize the goal of the present section and of the entire book. It is the intention to consider and weigh well, Latin *deliberare*, the various theories and approaches and to balance, Latin *equilibrare*, the contribution of each carefully. In both verbs the Latin word *libra* (scales) forms the root. This metaphor symbolizes two aspects: first, that all elements of the equation are needed to attain the balance and that therefore none can be eliminated from the consideration; and second, that the integration has to be equitable, and full justice should be done to the valuable contributions of the various opposing or parallel but unrelated approaches.

Though it lies somewhat in the control of the writer of a book how encompassing he wants to be, the situation is quite different in respect to this second, more ambitious goal, i.e., to integrate the approaches of the various schools. The representatives of these schools and the critical general reader will judge how closely this goal is approximated. The last section of Chapter One shows how this integration is conceived and planned. It explores how each single chapter is related to various approaches in the field of developmental psycholinguistics and how seemingly contradictory approaches represent complementary and necessary contributions to the understanding of specific topics.

What Is Biological in Speech and Language? It could appear that the discussion of biological bases of language development as attempted in Chapter Two would present itself as most easily amenable to an integrative approach. The pertinent factual evidence can be established by means of the methods of the natural sciences, such as neurology, biology, biochemistry, or biophysics. Since these methods are relatively highly developed, the results should be only minimally subjected to doubt and controversy. In addition, the biological-neurological basis for language is probably quite universal in contrast to the highly varied cultural influences that contribute to language acquisition. This too should permit the formulation of general laws.

The actual situation is quite different. After the controversy that flared up since Chomsky's publication of his nativistic conceptions, it need not be emphasized that we are very far from a convergence of ideas in this field. Whether it was Chomsky's (1959) attack against Skinner (1957), or the argument of R. Wells (1969) and of the philosophers represented in Morton (1970b) against Chomsky (1966), contrasts are much more apparent than are avenues for agreement and integration. Fortunately, research is conducted on a more sophisticated level than these fashionable philosophical controversies would suggest. Lorenz (1965, 1969) published several profound explorations on the relationship between innate bases and learning. In addition to these, Piaget's (1971) book on the relationship between biological aspects generally and the establishment of knowledge has prepared the ground for an integration of these two aspects in the specific area of language development. Though certainly less well known in the Anglo-Saxon literature than Chomsky's barren misconceptions and his shifting positions, Lorenz's and Piaget's publications, which are the fruits of life-long interest in research on biological phenomena, are conceptually and scientifically much more fertile. These authors analyze how innate bases and learning/cognition are the indispensable dual aspects of every adaptation to a changing environment and how both these aspects are complexly related. Similar considerations have been reflected during the most recent years in much of the literature that traces the development of language back to preverbal and neonatal functions. Bruner's (1974/75, 1975) publications may be the most representative examples, since they combine Piagetian and European conceptualizations with those derived from his own work in the United States. The ideas of Lorenz, Piaget, or Bruner do not need to be and could not be presented within the confines of Chapter Two. In contrast, they are presupposed and immediately incorporated into the specific discussions on language development.

In addition to these conceptual clarifications, valuable factual findings from diverse areas of brain research have been published during the recent decades. Those most relevant for the understanding of the phenomenon *language* in its species specificity and the phenomena of *communication* and *conceptualization*, which are common to many species, are briefly referred to. Whereas these references are intended as reminders for psychologists and as anchor points for discussions in later chapters, they necessarily lack the breadth and depth that a specialist in any of these areas would expect. In putting communication and conceptualization into wider cross-species perspectives, man's species-specific characteristics that lead from genetic potential, in interaction with cultural givens, to cognitive and linguistic skills stand out in clearer contrast. Such a contrast highlights the manifold aspects of the human condition that contribute to and are necessary for language development.

Which Functions Contribute to Speech Acquisition? The integrative task for Chapter Three, dealing with the perceptual, motor, and cognitive antecedents of language development, is conceptually not formidable. All these variables have been explored in psychological research, and contrasts in theoretical orientation between the various groups who concentrate upon individual topics are not very profound. Through the influence of Piaget on American psychology, Berlyne's (1965) attempt at translating Piaget's system in learning theoretical terms, or Bruner's many attempts to evaluate Piaget's ideas experimentally, a genuine cognitive learning theoretical approach has developed in the United States. Miller, Galanter, and Pribram's (1960) book was one of the first milestones in this recent achievement. Bruner's extensive publications were aimed in a similar direction, and more recently Gagné (1968) has systematically developed these ideas.

The more formidable task is that of a judicious selection of all those variables that may be important antecedents, including only those variables and excluding all irrelevant ones. Therefore, an encompassing and well elaborated theory of the relationship among learning, cognitive development in general, and language development in particular would be required. It need not be emphasized that such a theory does not exist yet. The task, however, is not overwhelming if one considers the description of antecedents as hypotheses and is aware that some of these hypotheses will have to be adjusted in accordance with future research findings. During the last decades, valuable groundwork has been done concerning these questions. One of the earliest attempts of this kind is that of Slobin (1966). Bever's (1970) justifiably well known discussions of "the cognitive basis for linguistic structures" provide considerable refinements of this approach. Olson (1970), McNamara (1972), Moerk (1973), and Slobin (1973) have continued the constructive exploration of this topic. From a somewhat different perspective, Sinclair has attempted for several years to explore the contributions that Piaget's research on cognitive development could make to the understanding of language development. Morehead and Morehead (1974) and Moerk (1975a), while still adhering to Piaget's system, have greatly expanded the range of cognitive antecedents. Moerk (in preparation-b) has concentrated recently not so much on a content but a process approach, attempting to show how the processes described by Piaget can account for language acquisition. Any review of some of the most recent literature on language development (Bowerman, 1974, 1976; Bruner, 1974/75, 1975; Dore, 1974; Ryan, 1974) shows that such a cognitive-Piagetian approach is now almost generally accepted.

Anyone willing to delve below superficial terminological differences would find analogical conceptualizations in Staats' (1971) and Osgood's (1971) discussions of language development and language functioning, respectively. Whenever cognitively oriented psychologists search for what they call *strategies* of language learning and retention, they often could just as well be using the term *learning set*. Generalizations, overgeneralizations, and lack of differentiation are not only explored in the realm of learning psychology, but they are equally important in the study of the meaning of children's words. Older and several more detailed longitudinal studies have reported the fact that some words vanish for certain periods from the vocabulary of language-learning children and have to be reacquired thereafter. The parallels between this phenomenon and forgetting and relearning are quite evident. Many more specific similarities between the learning approach to human development and the various cognitive interpretations of this same process could be described. Piaget (1964) has provided a cogent analysis of the relationships between learning and cognition and their complementary functions, and he has thereby contributed to the integration of these two perspectives.

When the diverse antecedents of language are discussed in Chapter Three, it is not attempted to differentiate sharply among them according to the theoretical system which contributed most to their elucidation and exploration. This does not appear necessary, since all these systems are judged as dealing roughly with phenomena on the same level of abstraction, i.e., the level of theoretical constructs, independent of whether they are defined in learning-theoretical or cognitive terminology.

What Routes Lead from Potential to Product?   While the main task in Chapter Three is the judicious selection and the encompassing description of the diverse antecedent phenomena, the main task of their integration to account for language acquisition is reserved for Chapter Four. Two levels of accomplishment are conceivable in this attempt. On a first level, the whole set of phenomena encountered in language is matched with the entire set of functions that have been described as language antecedents without attempting the pairing of specific members of both sets. The relatedness between antecedents and consequences can be demonstrated through developmental continuities and intermediate levels in the epigenetic process. This approach is easier considering the state of the research, since the psychological development of children during the first two years of life is comparatively well explored and since a good overall estimate can be made of what the necessary psychological processes underlying verbal behavior are.

The more difficult and more sophisticated approach would consist of specific one-to-one, many-to-one, or one-to-many matchings of functions involved in language behavior and preverbal developments. To attain this goal, experimental analyses would be needed that indicate specifically which type of functions are involved in specific linguistic acts. Linguistic performance would need to be fully understood on the basis of psychological processes. As is widely known, a study of linguistic performance was eschewed by Chomsky and his immediate followers. Psychologists attempting to assess the transformative model in psychological experiments have obtained equivocal and contradictory results, and these endeavors have been largely discontinued during the last few years. Many of the recently applied language-training programs contain sections intended to enhance general learning and cognitive skills, which are assumed to be conducive to language learning and performance. The programs, their procedures, and their results, however, are still too insufficiently described to allow confident inferences of which types of cognitive training enhance specific types of linguistic performance. Because of this lack of progress in the more experimental-theoretical as well as the practical analyses of language acquisition and training, this higher, scientifically more satisfactory level of precise matching cannot yet be attained. In the terms of Heinz Werner's "orthogenetic law," the present approach is still a global-diffuse one with only partial attempts at differentiation. Only a very preliminary attempt toward hierarchic integration of the diverse elements can be made at this time. While it is hoped that the relations between overall preverbal skills and their products, i.e., language skills, are traced quite clearly and comprehensibly in the discussions of Chapter Four, the higher level of analytical matching as just described has to await further advances in experimental analyses of language performance.

Support for the differentiation of specific skills and for their matching comes from various sources. The most important ones are the recent cognitively oriented approaches to language acquisition, such as Bloom's (1970, 1973), Bowerman's (1974, 1976), Bruner's (1975), and many others that are referred to throughout this book. From a cross-species perspective, Premack (1975) has provided an example of a different type of analytical approach. By describing diverse species' physiological and intellectual capacities and relating these to their natural communicative systems and their ability to learn an artificial language, Premack approximated a pairing of cognitive and communicative functions. Siklossy (1975) has attempted to "teach" a computer a language and has thereby partially succeeded in formalizing the processes that might be involved in the task of language acquisition. Approaches to automatic translation also may contribute some valuable information toward the goal of functionally analyzing language-like processes. The primary and the most valid contributions, however, have to come from the minute study of first-language acquisition. It is hoped that the wide range of hypotheses and their relatively clear specification in Chapters Three and Four will stimulate studies aimed at substantiating or refuting the proposed matchings and continuities.

What Forms Do the Products Take? Chapter Five, with its discussion of nonverbal means of message transmission and their relationships to the form and content of verbal messages, represents a more detailed study of one of the continuities leading from preverbal to verbal communicative behavior. Since the topic is relatively restricted, the task is at least theoretically less complex. A survey of the relevant literature shows, however, that large gaps exist. In contrast to the relatively extensive studies of nonverbal communication of adults and the recent intensive analyses of the nonverbal interactions of young infants and their mothers (Kaye, 1977; D. N. Stern, 1975), the data are sparse just for the period that is critical for the present concern. Bates' (1976a, b) studies on the pragmatics of language development include some longitudinal observations and anecdotal reports on nonverbal aspects. The recent communicational analyses of early verbal products as structurally and functionally complete messages (Bloom, 1973; Dore, 1975; Menzel and Johnson, 1975; Rodgon, 1976; Ryan, 1974) follow the same theoretical approach and provide some supporting data. The rediscovery of K. Bühler's (1934) insight into the completeness of even one-word utterances as far as their message character is concerned, combined with the recently available electronic means to record on videotape situational contexts and nonverbal behaviors together with acoustic messages, promises to lead soon to a more complete description and explanation of the phenomena of multichannel communication. When this multichannel communication in early childhood is better understood, then its function for language acquisition will become clearer.

Additional support in this endeavor comes from two further fields: One is the ethological and ecological exploration of animal and human behavior (e.g., Hinde, 1972). In ecological studies, special emphasis is placed upon information exchange and social communication. Since the context dependency of nonverbal messages is perceived more easily than that of verbal messages, the multichannel nature of nonverbal communication has been described and understood more fully in ethological investigations. These insights can be relatively easily transferred to the beginnings of a verbal communication. The other source of valuable direction is the research on artificial sign languages, such as American Sign Language, that is performed by Bellugi (1975) and her associates. When the structural complexity of sign language as a whole and the communicative function of specific nonverbal gestures are better understood, then the structure and functions of spontaneous preverbal gestures so commonly used by infants can be better clarified.

Though the gaps in the data will be obvious in reading Chapter Five, a high degree of continuity exists in respect to the theoretical account of the involved developments. Verbal elements are incorporated into preverbal messages (partly described in Chapters Three and Four) as soon as verbal tools are mastered and when these verbal utterances fulfill the communicative goals more effectively. Since message exchange and communication are the central concepts, the multichannel nature of the message and its dependency upon situational and communicational context provide no conceptual hurdles. Examples of the phenomena are provided, and the rationale of the approach is spelled out. Detailed factual substantiation has to await future intensive and extensive studies.

How and Why Does the Child Learn His Specific Mother Tongue? With the reference to verbal utterances in Chapter Five, one element is therefore included whose appearance has not yet been followed in detail. In Chapters Two to Four the antecedents of language are described in a manner that is intended to apply to all languages. Since each child acquires his mother tongue, another phenomenon has to be explored to explain language development fully. This is the teaching of the culture-specific code that occurs at various levels of awareness in most of the interactions between adult and child. These instructional activities are described in Chapter Six. As in every instructional setting, two aspects are conveniently differentiated, one pertaining to the conveying of information about the topic of concern and the other pertaining to the arousal and maintenance of the attention and motivation of the learner. Because of the negative attitude against the application of learning principles to language development, an attitude very pervasive during the last decades, positive findings are sparse on both topics, and misleading overgeneralizations from a few specific observations and prejudices abound. One well supported finding is that the language which mothers employ in conversation with their children is simpler and better fit for acoustical and grammatical analysis than that employed by adult communication partners. Few other principles, however, are generally reported and acknowledged. Valuable beginnings were made by Friedlander and associates (1970, 1972) and by the group around Baldwin (Baldwin, 1973; Baldwin and Baldwin, 1973). Yet it is only during the last two to three years that more substantial results have been reported (Cross, 1975, 1977; Moerk, 1974a, 1975c, 1976a, b; Snow, 1975, 1976). Though most of the specific evidence still has to be collected, even the general finding that mothers adapt their speech to their children's level implies a profound theoretical reorientation. It clearly refutes the earlier argument propounded by some linguists that speech input is so complex and chaotic that no child could learn his first language from this input. The evidence concerning the extreme simplification, situation-adaptedness, and repetitiveness of maternal speech suggests strongly that the child can in fact acquire his language skills on this basis, given all the previously discussed cognitive skills he has already mastered.

The recent findings of Cross, Moerk, and Snow and her associates have also contributed greatly to demonstrate *how* the child is acquiring his language skills and *how* his mother is teaching them. The conceptual basis for these recent explorations into the dyadic interactions between mothers and their children has already existed for some time. Bell (1968) refuted the previous misconception that the direction of effects in mother-child interactions always goes from the mother to the child. Bell emphasized in contrast the effects of the child upon the mother. Moerk (1972) employed a more complex conceptualization whereby he described the circular verbal interactions between mothers and children. Similar principles have been propounded recently by Lewis and associates (Lewis and Freedle, 1973; Lewis and Lee-Painter, 1974). With the recent publications of Moerk (1976a, b) the description of feedback cycles, subroutines, and the differentiation between informational and motivational feedback have been incorporated into the study of first-language training and learning. Based upon the long tradition of American learning psychology and the established skills in analyzing and describing processes of learning, the road to a more complete description of the learning processes that lead to first-language competence should not be too long or too difficult anymore. Since the emphasis in this entire book is on the child's activity in his forming and testing of hypotheses and his formulating of rules, the contrast between the classical learning approach and the linguists' description of rule systems is overcome in this approach.

The second topic pertaining to the question of language learning has been even more neglected. Remarks on the motivational factors involved in first-language instruction and learning are dispersed in much of the literature. Most of these remarks, however, are barely substantiated, and some of them are obviously misleading. The climate generated by Chomsky's attack on Skinner's sketch of the acquisition of "verbal behavior" still appears to predominate, and any specific discussion of reinforcement for verbal learning is taboo. This writer's experience with the publication of two of his articles on the topic of motivation seems to show that the denial of reinforcement is one of those scientific laws that has never been established but is nonetheless severely enforced in the manner of political laws by the community of editors and reviewers. Since it is commonly accepted in other fields of learning psychology that motivational factors can and often do have important effects upon the speed of learning and upon retention of learned materials, motivational variables in language acquisition need to be considered in an encompassing approach to language acquisition. Although the factually established evidence is still sparse, theoretical considerations about the motivations involved in language acquisition go back more than one hundred years. A brief presentation of these theoretical questions and some factual data (Leonard, 1975; Moerk, 1976a; Whitehurst, 1972) may open up the topic at least for objective and serious discussion. It also should contribute to a terminological and theoretical clarification and integration. More specifically, the following discussions should demonstrate that widely contradictory theoretical approaches are prevalent in the field of first-language acquisition, coexisting peacefully only because of terminological differences which obscure the contrasts. Since Aristotle's *organon* approach to language, the functions of language have been stressed by a wide variety of philosophers and factual investigators. K. Bühler emphasized this aspect in 1934, making explicit references to Aristotle, and his tripartite categorization of functions became almost part of the consensus in psycholinguistics. Nonpsychologists usually talk about the intention the child has when he is engaging in verbal behavior. Halliday (1975) has even worked out a system of the developmental functions of language. Though finer differences may exist in the intension of the terms and more profound ones in the connotations they elicit, it cannot be denied that the basic conceptualizations conveyed by the socio- and psycholinguistic concept of *functions* and by Skinner's *operant function* are similar. If language is employed functionally to attain extralinguistic goals, then the attainment of these goals represents the "reinforcement" for verbal behavior. The above-described psycholinguistic consensus is consequently almost identical to Skinner's approach, though the latter is still commonly regarded as completely unacceptable to cognitively oriented child-language investigators. Since two contradictory statements, namely, that Skinner's operant function is at best a very minor phenomenon and that functional uses of language are commonplace and of great importance, cannot be simultaneously true, a logical and factual evaluation of these two dominant approaches appears required to arrive at a more concordant view.

SUMMARY AND CONCLUSION

It would appear that the range of topics discussed in the following chapters represents a broad enough basis to cover all the necessary routes that lead to language. After a survey of the biological roots and their cognitive-behavioral and social consequences in Chapter Two, a wide range of antecedents that develop during infancy is discussed in Chapter Three. Chapter Four suggests how these antecedents become transformed into and applied in language behavior. Chapter Five follows the transition from nonverbal to verbal communication in detail, tracing how verbal elements are fitted organically into preverbal communicative structures. The continuity between preverbal and verbal functions thereby becomes highly conspicuous. Finally, Chapter Six details the processes of verbal training and learning. Whereas Chapters Two to Five deal mainly with phenomena of the first two years of life, Chapter Six follows the establishment of the linguistic system during the entire preschool period. The description is necessarily less detailed and molecular for this long time span than it could be for the more intensively studied periods. Many of the cognitive refinements that appear only during this period and that interact with linguistic training/learning could not be mentioned.

In the overall discussion of linguistic phenomena, semantic and structural aspects are treated more extensively than phonetic and phonological ones. Linguists also may find that many of their important distinctions have not been treated in full detail. The present approach is neccessarily more molar and comparable to the psychologist's exploration of the development of locomotory skills and not to the physiologist's description of the movement of individual muscle groups or muscles. It is hoped that investigators with more molecular interests will find in the following chapters many suggestions and points from where they can branch off in the pursuit of their own specific topics and that their more particular findings will largely complement the present overall outline.

chapter
two

Biological Bases for Language Development

THEORETICAL POSITIONS

It is broadly asserted that the main difference between all other animals and man lies in the latter's development of a highly complex system of symbolization and language. The biological basis for this evolutionary new acquisition is generally presumed to lie in the structure and function of the brain. Attention therefore could be centered upon this organ when the innate bases for language development are discussed.

Such an approach, however, could be construed as a serious reason against including a chapter on innate bases in a book of the present format. Even if such a chapter were long and detailed, no more could be accomplished than a summary of a point of view and of a few facts regarding the functions of the brain and their complex effects upon language development. To deal fully with this complex topic and to summarize most of the important and relevant research would demand a team of writers and volumes of writing.

Furthermore, in spite of the extensive literature on brain structures, functions, and development, the currently existing knowledge is by far not detailed enough to support or refute on a neurological basis the nativistic claims made recently by Chomsky (1965, 1966) and McNeill (1970a, b), or even to explain the acquisition of language generally. These two strands of scientific research and argument, neurological brain research and psycholinguistic speculations or investigations, coexist side by side without any real meeting point that could lead to mutual fertilization and clarification. Since a solution of

27

the question is not possible at present, its discussion may appear unwarranted.

In spite of this substantive argument against the inclusion of the present chapter, the arguments for at least a short analysis of this problem prevail. The first reason is related to the *Zeitgeist*, or the currently predominant trends and controversies in scientific thinking. Beginning with the early publications of Chomsky, and especially after the appearance of his books, *Aspects of the Theory of Syntax* and *Cartesian Linguistics*, the controversy is too much in the open to be passed by without a short factual evaluation. These same ideas were adopted by McNeill (1970a, b) and propagated vigorously. A similar trend is encountered in many of the publications on this topic. A tendency toward a nativistic stance is found also in the field of intelligence and intelligence testing. More generally it appears that American psychology is, after half a century of uncritical environmentalism, turning to a premature and uncritical acceptance of factually unsupported nativistic postulates. Therefore, a critical consideration of some approaches and data may lead to a more balanced stance.

The second argument for the inclusion of this topic is logical-developmental. This argument was forcefully presented by Lorenz (1965): Since all the causal chains of development begin with hereditary information, which is transmitted through the genes, the logical first task is to clarify this blueprint of the developing organism. The next question follows necessarily: "What are the causal chains which begin at the blueprint given in the genome and which end up, by devious and often highly regulative routes, by producing adapted structure ready to function?" (Lorenz, 1965: 43).

According to this argument the developmental scientist would have to begin his investigation at the level of genes and chromosomes if he were a geneticist, at the moment of conception if he were an embryologist, or at least at the moment of birth. He would then study what the specific structures and functions were at these starting points, which serve as prerequisites for later changes. Finally, he would explore step by step how the inborn structures interact with environmental influences leading to altered and more complex structures and functions.

Evidence is quickly accumulating to show that even in man many specific functions and competences appear at the moment of birth or shortly afterwards. These functions have profound effects not only upon early behavior but also upon the acquisition of new structures that in turn affect later overt behavior. Piaget (1952) sketched out the processes of how higher forms of intelligence develop from inborn reflexes. More recent evidence comes from the perceptual research of Fantz (1958, 1961), Watson (1966), and many others.

This argument as expounded by Lorenz, as well as common-sense considerations, makes it clear that the innate components of a living system and, therefore, of behavior come temporally and logically first. That the "innate" can only be defined negatively as propounded by Wells (1970) is therefore not correct. One could reverse the argument of Wells and define "learned" negatively as what is not innate. Although this approach would be more consistent with facts of nature where learning is slowly added to or superimposed upon innate patterns, it still would not be a productive definition. Positive definitions for both "learned" and "innate" characteristics appear to provide a better and more operational methodology that in turn leads to more definite results.

That such positive approaches to the question of what is innate are possible has been broadly demonstrated by European ethologists. Lorenz (1965), Tinbergen (1952), and Hediger (1961) are only the best known of them. Detailed and exact descriptions of the structures and functions of the various organs and especially the sophisticated deprivation experiments of some of these ethologists have demonstrated feasible approaches to this topic.

The final reason for the inclusion of the topic is again logical, but this time related to the delimitation of the topic of the book. The title of this book contains the promise that the pragmatic aspects of language development would be dealt with. Morris (1946: 219) defined pragmatics in the following way: "Pragmatics is that portion of semiotics which deals with the origin, uses, and effects of signs within the behavior in which they occur." Uses and effects of language are discussed in several of the following chapters. The origins, however, are necessarily in part neurophysiological, derived and related to innate characteristics. To cover fully the topic of pragmatics, these origins have to be included even if the available evidence is preliminary and cannot be summarized exhaustively.

Three approaches to the exploration of innate basis of any behavior and therefore also of language behavior are possible and are encountered in the literature: As argued by Fodor, Bever, and Garret (1974), every empiricist implicitly accepts many inborn principles.

Innate properties lead the organism to perceive stimuli, to integrate many elements of stimuli in the perception of an object, and to classify the specific object as a member of a specific set of objects. Transfer of learning happens only to other members of this set and not to members of other sets that have one or a few stimuli in common with the object used during training. Lorenz (1969) argued in a similar manner that only innate biological mechanisms can explain why reinforcements function as such, or why the organism increases the probability of his response after it has experienced positive reinforcement. According to this argument it is a truism that innate bases exist for all behavior. If nothing more can be said about it, these bases could be neglected without great loss in research on learning. American learning psychology has followed just this course during most of the last fifty years.

The opposite approach recently has been chosen by Chomsky and has been propounded in a more or less identical manner by McNeill. Chomsky postulates a "language acquisition device" which is, according to most of his statements, innate. He defines this device in detail in *Aspects of the Theory of Syntax* (1965: 30). He states that a child who is capable of language learning must have:

1. A technique for representing input signals
2. A way of representing structural information about these signals
3. Some initial delimitation of a class of possible hypotheses about language structure
4. A method for determining what each such hypothesis implies with respect to each sentence
5. A method for selecting one of the (presumably, infinitely many) hypotheses that are allowed by (3) and are compatible with the given primary linguistic data

Immediately after this enumeration of the postulated characteristics of the language acquisition device, Chomsky admits "that the assumption about innate capacity is extremely strong." He spells out the functioning of this device in more detail in the following passage, which was coauthored with G. S. Miller (Chomsky and Miller, 1963: 276–277):

A practical language-learning device would have to incorporate strong assumptions about the class of potential grammars that a natural language can have. Presumably the device would have available an advance specification of the general form that a grammar might assume and also some procedure to decide whether a particular grammar is better than some alternative grammar on the basis of the sample input. Moreover, it would have to have certain phonetic capacities for recognizing and producing sentences and it would need to have some method, given one of the permitted grammars, to determine the structural description of any arbitrary sentence. All this would have to be built into the device in advance before it could start to learn a language. To imagine that an adequate grammar could be selected from the infinitude of conceivable alternatives by some process of pure induction on a finite corpus of utterances is to misjudge completely the magnitude of the problem.

In addition to postulating this strong hypothesis about innate capacities, the authors also stress that, according to their point of view, pure induction could not explain the acquisition of language. A final quote from Chomsky (1965:33) demonstrates even more clearly how his nativistic position has led him to an antilearning approach. "His [the child's] knowledge of the language, as this is determined by his internalized grammar, goes far beyond the presented linguistic data and is in no sense an 'inductive generalization' from these data."

Chomsky's nativism already has been often and profoundly criticized from a philosophical-theoretical point of view as evident in the books edited by Cowan (1970), Hook (1969), and Morton (1970b). Geschwind's remark best expresses the scientific sterility of this approach: "The fact that somebody comes along and says, 'Oh I believe that language has a biological basis' is too easy a way out; between you and me, we can all say that and then disregard it, it's a familiar trick." One point has not yet been elaborated in this controversy, and it would deserve an extended analysis: This strong nativistic assumption stands in contrast to everything that is known about the capacities of the infant and young child. Although recent research has fostered an appreciation of the infant's capacities, this detailed knowledge of the abilities and limitations of the infant has demonstrated clearly that under no stretch of the imagination could the infant perform the following feats: to maintain simultaneously a considerable number of complex hypotheses; to evaluate them on the basis of data; and to select the one best fitting to these data. At a minimum, these capacities, however, would be required by the theory of Chomsky. Although scientific prudence would require that strong assumptions are supported by strong evidence, Chomsky's assumptions are in conflict with all the evidence that has been amassed in developmental research on infancy and early childhood. They therefore cannot be taken seriously as a psychological language acquisition model.

The third approach to the study of innate bases has been alluded to already in two of the above quotations. Geschwind protested against the practice of only asserting biological bases and disregarding them immediately afterward instead of demonstrating them in actual research on language development. Lorenz referred more precisely to the "causal chains" and the "devious and highly regulated routes" that lead from the innate based to final language performance. Only this type of exploration and elucidation of the links between physiology and performance can contribute new insights. This survey sketches out these links as far as possible. The same principle has been followed by Piaget. He demonstrated how cognitive development originates from the stage of reflexes and evolves organically through the interaction of the innate bases with environmental aliments into the cognitive structures of the adolescent and adult.

Any complex developmental analysis of these processes would demonstrate consistently that end products are multiply determined. Only rarely is it the case that one or a few conditions are necessary and sufficient for the explanation of the final structure. Furthermore, transformations and changes in underlying structure and in surface form are often encountered in the course of development. It would probably be misleading, therefore, to restrict one's search for antecedents of language to the realm of behaviors that are closely related to language. Aside from the fact that each investigator would define the phrase *related to language* differently, several considerations require a broad approach in order to include all or at least most of the conditions that may be necessary, conducive, and sufficient for language acquisition: First, language comes into existence only between one and two years of age, i.e., after the child has already learned to cope effectively with many aspects of his environment. Since no single plausible predecessor of this skill can be specified in the prelingual period, it has to be concluded that it is a product of the confluence of many factors. The involvement of acoustic and vocal organs in the normal development of spoken language, of cognitive skills in the conceptualization and formulation of the message, and of a desire to communicate are the most obvious prerequisites for language development. Since the terms *cognitive skills* and *need for verbal communication* represent only broad categories of phenomena, finer differentiations have to be made.

Cognition not only provides the necessary designata for the signs of language (Morris, 1938), it is much more intrinsically involved in language acquisition. The formulation of correct syntactic structures presumes the formation of word classes, of rules for the combination of words into phrases and of phrases into sentences. A wide variety of cognitive functions must be involved in these processes (Moerk, 1973, 1975a). Therefore, the use of one term, *cognition*, may easily obscure the variety of antecedents that enter into the process of rule-governed speech or the comprehension of speech.

The same problem is encountered in connection with the "communicative function of language." Research on nonverbal communication (Hinde, 1972) has demonstrated that many messages are communicated even by adults in nonverbal channels. Since most higher vertebrates live at least during certain periods in social groups, they have developed specific and complex means of communication. Recent ethological research has provided impressive evidence of this communicative effectiveness (Lorenz, 1966; Washburn and DeVore, 1961). In contrast to this similarity in communicative behavior across many species of higher vertebrates, the research of the Gardners (1969) with the chimpanzee Washoe has demonstrated that, in spite of intensive training, this communicative competence only leads to very rudimentary linguistic skills. The only partial success of the Gardners is underscored by the almost complete failure of the Kellogs (1933) and the Hayes (1951). These experiments provide an impressive example of the influence of a seemingly superficial variable on the development of the rudiments of language. The last two groups of authors relied on the vocal channel while the Gardners used American Sign Language. An interaction of communicational intent plus competence and the specific channel in which communication skills are trained seems to have led to the contrasting outcomes. If the reports of Fouts (1973) are substantiated through ongoing studies that their young chimpanzees proceed much faster and much further in their linguistic skills than those studied previously, another variable, an innately programmed critical period, may have to be postulated as a contributing factor.

These examples derived from subhuman vertebrates and also from man demonstrate that a desire to communicate alone does not lead to language development. Only if other variables are added does it contribute to a large extent in the acquisition of language. That it presents a necessary condition is seen in the case of autistic children, who show very little desire to communicate and consequently do not acquire language skills.

The above considerations provide a first impression of some variables that may interact in the acquisition of language skills. A graphic outline of this multidetermination is presented in Figure 4.2 (Chapter Four). An analysis of some of the more important innate bases is attempted in the next sections. First, anatomical structures and functions that are most obviously involved in language are discussed; then bases are analyzed whose involvement is more indirect and can be less easily demonstrated, though highly probable or logically necessary. According to this plan, the more peripheral organs and their inborn functions are first focused upon. Next are summarized central structures whose involvement in language performance is proved through a wide range of research results. Finally analyzed are global structures, functions, and their consequences that still need to be explored in more detail but seem necessary for a complete account of language acquisition.

RELEVANT ANATOMICAL AND FUNCTIONAL FACTS

Peripheral Organs and Their Innate Functions

A detailed anatomical description of individual organs is not presented here. It can be found in relevant works in the fields of anatomy and it was excellently presented for psychologists and linguists in the work of Lenneberg (1967). In this chapter only species-specific innate bases for language acquisition are discussed.

Vocal Mechanisms   Lenneberg (1967) summarized the evidence that the facial muscles, the oral cavity, and the larynx of man are structurally different and more refined than those of closely related animals. This refined structural arrangement allows for the production of finely differentiated sound patterns that are necessary for effective communication of a multitude of diverse contents. Lieberman (1967, 1968) presented evidence that structural mechanisms directly related to the production of speech are present at birth and that generally the vocal mechanism is preprogrammed to acquire speech. In the course of evolution this preprogramming may have been a very basic and important root for the development of language. It can be generally concluded, from these and other sources (Kelemen, 1949), that the vocal tract of mankind is especially well prepared for sound production. Both Lieberman and Kelemen have stressed the structural restrictions of the larynx in animals with regard to the same function. In contrast, it is generally observed that the human infant starts to be vocally active in a wide variety of ways and remains interested in exercising his vocal skills especially during the first years of language development (Weir, 1962). In this respect the differences between the human baby and the higher apes are pronounced as documented by the Kellogs (1933). Many early studies as summarized by Irwin (1948) have shown that the infant starts "training" his vocal skills from the age of two to three months and that he expands his sound repertoire considerably during the first half year of life. None of the higher apes is as prone to babble and chatter.

Acoustic Mechanisms   Not only are the vocal mechanisms innately programmed for the acquisition of phonemic skills, the ears are also especially structured for voice reception. It has been shown that the range of human voice production coincides with the optimal range of auditory perception. The special sensitivity for these frequencies allows the child and adult to differentiate fine contrasts in the perceptions of spoken words. How early this structural fittedness produces effects was demonstrated by several authors. Eisenberg (1967) reported that the human neonate responds differentially to patterned sound stimuli which are approximately in the range of the human voice. Wolff's (1966) observations proved that, already at the age of two weeks, the voice is more effective in arresting crying than other vocal stimuli. While this later preference may already be learned, it is evident that it must be based upon the fine discriminatory ability of the infant for acoustic stimuli in the range of the human voice. Such fine differentiation specifically for adult phonemic categories was recently demonstrated by Eimas and his associates (1971). Their infant subjects, ranging in age from one to four months, differentiated synthetic speech sounds better when they came from different adult phonemic categories than when they were from the same category. That this interest in the human voice together with the readiness of the vocal apparatus of the infant for functioning leads early to a first kind of vocal communication was supported by Stone and Church (1968) as well as by Freedman, Loring, and Martin (1967). They reported "babbling dialogues" between the mother and her infant beginning from the second month of life and continuing until the infant was quite proficient in verbal communication. That the infant, at the age of around six months, is more responsive to his mother's voice than to that of a stranger was established by Kagan and Lewis (1965). This finding indicates that the frequency characteristics of the signal are analyzed in a very sophisticated way.

This evidence proves that the infant is acoustically well prepared to acquire language. This equipment consists of mechanisms which produce early a special sensitivity for sounds that are produced by the human vocal apparatus. This sensitivity predisposes the child to attend to his mother's voice and to notice fine differences in her voice patterns. The special endowment in both the vocal and acoustic modality soon produces vocal interaction habits which later change in form, but which are strong and persistent enough to become semiautonomous motives.

Relevance of the Innate Characteristics of the Peripheral Organs for Language Development   The relevance of the above-discussed functions for language development is accepted by most scientists (Allport, 1924; Mowrer, 1954; Staats and Staats, 1963). Lenneberg (1966) and McNeill (1970b) have argued, however, that babbling shows little or no relationship to later language behavior. Berko and Brown (1960) also claimed that the phonetic structure begins to develop only after the babbling period has come to an end. These assertions stand in direct contrast to the evidence on acoustic development that has recently been gathered. The solution to this controversy will have to await further detailed longitudinal and cross-sectional studies. However, even if the child should perceive sounds differentially and produce them for some time before concentrating upon the phonemes of his mother tongue, this would only demonstrate that the tie between innate functions and acquired characteristics is less close and immediate. Such a conclusion would be fully in agreement with the hypotheses proposed in the present analysis. Since it is not intended in this book to follow the acquisition of phonetic skills, the developments from innate propensity to correct discrimination and enunciation is not studied in detail but is only discussed briefly in Chapter Three.

Central Characteristics of the Human Organism and Their Effects

The word *central* in the above subtitle has to be interpreted more as "functionally central" and not so much as central in a spatial sense. The implications of the size, the specific structures, and the functions of the brain are analyzed in this section. Because of the brain's complexity and the practical difficulties in studying its functions, the relationships between specific brain phenomena and language acquisition and performance are only little understood. It is impossible, therefore, to spell out in detail the "causal chains" that lead from innate structures and physiological function to actual language behavior. Only general outlines and broad relationships, substantiated as far as possible, can be given. Furthermore, no attempt is made either to summarize all the research on the relations between language and the brain or to delve into the existing controversies. Many specific as well as comprehensive and excellent publications have appeared on this topic. The reader is referred to Penfield and Roberts (1959), Salzinger and Salzinger (1967), or to the short and precise survey by Geschwind (1970) for a more comprehensive study of anatomical facts and problems.

General Size and Capacity of the Brain   Nearly all authors agree that the brain of the human species is superior in size and structural complexity as compared to the brain of other species. A possible exception to this rule may be the dolphin (*Tursiops truncatus*) (Lilly, 1967). This superiority applies to absolute size when compared to our nearest ancestors, the higher apes, as well as to the ratio of brain weight to spinal cord weight (apes = 15.1; man = 55.1) or the ratio between the association areas and the sensory areas. Jerison (1973), in using a somewhat more complex method of calculating his "encephalization quotient," could again demonstrate that this superiority applies also to actual brain size in relation to body size. The encephalization quotient of the rhesus monkey is 2.09; of the chimpanzee, 2.48; and of *Homo sapiens*, 7.39 (female) and 7.79 (male). Besides weight and size, the internal structure also reveals many differences. Most visible is the number of convolutions of the cortex, which result in an enlargement of the surface of the brain. Several finer species-specific structures of the human brain have been described in comparative brain research. They are briefly discussed below.

The implications of this difference in brain structure and size are also quite generally agreed upon. The human brain has a much greater capacity for the storage and processing of information than that of all other species as far as currently known. This capacity affects all areas of cognition and, consequently, also language acquisition. It has been repeatedly argued, for example, that the acquisition of labels for concepts and percepts requires an enormous increase of storage capacity. The storage of word sequences leading to the abstraction of patterns and the learning of grammatical rules as recently suggested by Braine (1971a, b) require even more storage potential, which is only furnished in the enlarged brain of the human species. Some more specific relations between memory development and language acquisition are discussed in Chapter Three.

More important than the storage capacity *per se* may be another consequence of the increase in size and complexity of the human brain: The human brain not only has a larger number of neurons, but these neurons are interconnected with each other in a very complex network. Specific centers of the cortex are connected with each other and with centers of the brain stem by many fiber tracts. Many well defined areas of the brain principally serve an integrating function between several or many of the other centers. These anatomical interconnections between brain centers and groups of neurons result in combinatorial possibilities whose number is for all practical purposes infinite. These interconnections could be the anatomical substratum of the productivity and generativity of behavior generally and especially of language behavior.

While the implications of this network of interconnections in the brain are broad and fascinating, too little is known about them at present that could contribute to the explanation of language development. More attention has been focused on specific structures of the brain and their functions.

Hemisphere Dominance   A fascinating and broadly investigated topic in the area of brain research is the phenomenon of the dominance of one hemisphere of the human brain. An engrossing account of this field has been recently provided by Dimond and Beaumont (1974). This dominance in respect to learned behavior appears, according to most research findings, to be almost species-specific for man (Geschwind, 1970). The small number of species investigated, and the fact that bird songs, which are partially learned, are unilaterally controlled, preclude, however, a final judgment regarding this specificity. The implications of this dominance for general cognitive and language development are still a matter of controversy, though Geschwind's research (Geschwind, 1965, 1970, 1972) as well as the studies of Sperry, as summarized in Sperry and Gazzaniga (1967), have already contributed much evidence. It has been shown that, in addition to the dominance of the left hemisphere, the functions of both hemispheres are finely differentiated and specialized. These topics are presented in detail in two recent issues of the journal *Brain and Language* (1974, Vol. 1(4); 1975 Vol. 2(2)) and cannot be repeated here.

From the developmental point of view, the relatively slow establishment of this dominance is of great interest, since it is in contrast to Wada's (1974) discovery of a structural asymmetry between both hemispheres even in the six-month-old fetus. This asymmetry is, consequently, established anatomically before birth though it is only slowly realized functionally (Geschwind, 1974). Lenneberg (1967), in summarizing data from various studies, could demonstrate that functionally a near equipotentiality between both hemispheres exists until the age of two years. In fifty percent of the children who sustain lesions of the left hemisphere during these first two years of life, language development proceeds without any interruptions. In the other fifty percent it is somewhat delayed but not substantially interfered with. It seems, therefore, that a lesion of the left hemisphere during this early period induces the right hemisphere to take over the functions of language. Functional rigidification proceeds only slowly as evident from other studies: Though a considerable degree of language skills is established before left/right asymmetries in motor behavior are consolidated, severe lesions of the left hemisphere up to the age of ten to fifteen years still result in a takeover of the language functions by the right hemisphere. Dichotic listening studies as summarized by Satz et al. (1975) and by Porter and Berlin (1975) lead to similar conclusions: Significant ear asymmetry is not found in children younger than nine years, and the magnitude of the differences reaches a plateau at age eleven. An interesting contrast between early innate structural/anatomical differentiation and prolonged functional openness is encountered in this instance. Detailed histological/developmental studies accompanied by parallel behavioral investigations are needed to shed light upon the questions opened up by these discrepancies.

W. Hess (1962) considered it significant that, through the localization of dominant language functions in one hemisphere only, the speed of neuronal transmissions between single centers can be considerably increased. The high speed and precision of language functions, of course, have to be based upon physiological and anatomical correlates, which would be found in the differentiation of the hemispheres (Semmes, 1968). It has been recently demonstrated, however (Butler and Norrsell, 1968; Gazzaniga and Sperry, 1967; Levy, 1974), that at least in some cases the minor hemisphere functions successfully, even if more slowly, in language comprehension and production. While the prenatal anatomical differentiation of the hemispheres demonstrates the innate bases of language, the evidence for the recuperation of language functions and especially the last-mentioned discovery concerning their multiple control are impressive proof of the multiplicity of the routes leading from innate givens to realized functions.

Specific Brain Structures and the Problem of Localization of Language Functions   Much research exists concerning the localization of brain functions generally and the localization of language centers specifically. The broad range of the available findings was comprehensively surveyed by Penfield and Roberts (1959) and summarized in a shorter form by Lenneberg (1967) and Campbell (1970). Many of the well established facts, therefore, are well known and need not be repeated here. Though many controversies remain unsolved regarding the specificity of localization, little doubt exists concerning the fact that some localization is found in the brain. As for language centers, Lenneberg (1967) concluded from his review of the relevant research, and especially from the work of Penfield and Roberts, that at best a statistical relationship can be assumed between specific language functions and specific centers when a wide variety of patients are studied. This relative degree of indeterminacy, however, does not preclude clear localization of language functions for the individual adult. Geschwind (1970) places more stress on this well determined relationship on the individual level. Differences among individuals can be demonstrated to be partly a consequence of the developmental history of the individual, often consisting of early lesions which led to a displacement of the function to other areas.

More relevant to the question about the innateness of language structures is the species specificity of some of the structures. If it can be demonstrated that other species do not have certain structures or have them only in a rudimentary form, and if the same structures are involved in language functions, then this is relatively clear evidence for such structural-functional relationships. Geschwind (1965) provides several strong arguments for such species-specific innate language bases. His most important point is that only the human brain has an "association area of association areas" located anatomically in the angular gyrus and the posterior temporoparietal region. This area would make it possible for the individual to make intermodal and multimodal associations. The argument for such a species-specific structure is supported by behavioral findings as summarized by Geschwind (1964, 1965). Geschwind demonstrated that intermodal associations are acquired much faster and with greater ease by human subjects than by any of the higher apes or by other animals on phylogenetically lower levels. In the developmental domain, Aronson and Rosenbloom (1971) provided evidence that even thirty-day-old infants perceive within a common auditory-visual space.

Their subjects became visibly distressed when they observed their mother speaking to them while her voice was displaced in space.

Consequences of this structural innovation in the human brain are easily imaginable although they are not yet fully proved. The acquisition of a concept of an object requires the association of many of the specific characteristics of this object into one complex whole. This object concept is probably stored on the enactive, iconic, and symbolic levels. Evidence of this triple storage can be found in various types of aphasia, where, for example, the symbolic function has been lost but the object still can be recognized and handled correctly. Although animals may have an enactive and iconic representation for objects, the symbolic representation is probably new or at least much more pronounced for the human species.

This structural innovation in the human brain, by providing an immense and finely structured association network, may be the necessary basis also for the complex interrelations of the human cultural and social system. Objects and events are classified and the resulting classes are again fitted into a hierarchy of classes. The same principle also applies to the labels of language. In addition to this hierarchical classification, including many sets and subsets of vocabulary items, words are also related structurally in syntactic form as evident in sentences. This combination of influences, the anatomical basis and the cultural product of this basis, when they converge upon the child who grows up in his family, may constitute two of the most profound and pervasive causes of language development.

Other species-specific structures have been mentioned in the literature. Geschwind (1965) argued that Wernicke's area, which is intimately involved in language comprehension, is fully developed only in the human cortex while apes have it only in a rudimentary form. Penfield and Roberts (1959) proposed that only man possesses areas in the motor cortex devoted to vocalization, and Konorski, as quoted by Thorpe (1967), pointed out that there is nothing exactly comparable in other species to the arcuate bundle in the brain of man which connects the posterosuperior part of the temporal lobe and runs to the lateral frontal region. This structure is seen as the neurological basis of imitation, which in turn is indispensable for normal language learning. Luria (1965) also postulated uniqueness of functioning in the human brain based on differences in the degree of development of structures.

Since much less research on functional localization in children exists, definite conclusions cannot be drawn. The evidence that children recover more quickly and more completely from extensive brain damage, which has destroyed part or all of their language centers, suggests that localization is less rigid at younger ages. A conclusion such as this implies that localization could at least in part be a consequence of "learning" or the way in which brain structures are used. The influence of only gradual maturation, however, cannot be ruled out since the brain has been shown to mature physiologically up to the age of eighteen years. The possibility that environmental influences affect the functional rigidification of these structures is herewith given. This conclusion also helps to partly explain the lack of complete congruence found between centers and functions in the patients of Penfield and Roberts. Since a statistical correlation was found, however, it has to be concluded that there are at least some predispositions in the human brain to process and store certain language functions in specific areas.

At present, too little is known of the functions of many structurally distinct areas of the central nervous system to delineate all of the structures that constitute innate bases for language acquisition and function. The above summary, even if it is brief, suggests specifically that innate predispositions toward specialization within each hemisphere exist, but at the same time considerable flexibility, at least during the early years of childhood, remains. Even if specific brain structures can be shown to contribute differentially to language acquisition and performance, Lashley's theory of mass action is still partially applicable. Language involves so many complex functions that a more or less global involvement of the brain in language behavior has to be assumed.

Comparative research regarding the question of localization of language functions is impossible as long as animals do not speak a language. If the current attempts to teach the higher apes language systems should be successful, fascinating new areas of comparative research following the model of Penfield and Roberts or the ablation studies of Milner (1962) would open up.

Global, Innate Functions and Their Implications for Cognitive and Language Development

Orienting Reflex The orienting reflex, which is important for cognitive development, is functional at birth. Its functional readiness was demonstrated in the visual as well as in the acoustic field (Spears and Hohle, 1967). This orienting reflex leads to the infant's first "orientation" or information intake. Recent research (Fantz, 1958, 1965) on the perceptual development of the infant has shown that this information is analyzed, restructured, and stored in a highly differentiated manner.

Three important principles are attested to by the orienting reflex. The first is that active orientation toward outside stimuli leads to active information intake. These two aspects of activity are encountered in principle, even though not in their specific form, in many later processes during childhood and adulthood. The infant searches out and actively tries to "assimilate" new stimuli, as observed by Piaget (1952); he is very interested in sounds and soon shows special attention to novel sound patterns, as demonstrated by Friedlander (1970). On a more global level a "curiosity drive" or "exploratory drive" of the child is described in much of the pertinent recent literature. This active exploratory drive leads immediately and necessarily to the second important function, the function of question-answer interaction with the environment. The orienting reflex and the resulting information intake which follows are very similar in their informational structure to that of a question-answer interaction. Novel and discrepant stimuli generally lead to the "question" and the assimilation of the stimuli provides the "answer." This questioning does not appear merely in connection with this reflex. Francis (1969) found evidence that negative, interrogative, and imperative expressional markers are present in intonation patterns starting from the early neonatal days. This quest for information continues in the toddler stage in the form of exploratory behavior. The toddler also obtains information from the human environment by pointing to objects and uttering sounds with interrogative intonations. The infant's *what* and *why* questions, the adolescent's search for information, or the scientist's quest for knowledge are all examples of the same principle.

A continuity of question-answer principles from birth to adulthood and a similarity of the cognitive functions are suggested by these considerations. They also demonstrate that transformational operations are performed by the infant shortly after birth and that the infant, therefore, has ample time and opportunity to train transformations before he ever begins to form or even to comprehend verbal transformations. Piaget (1952) has shown how the infant engages in many kinds of sensorimotor transformations during his first two years of life. These are discussed in a later chapter. Here it is of importance that the structure of some of these transformations, principally the one embodied in the orienting reflex, already exists at birth and is, therefore, probably inborn. This leads to the third important function, the primal incorporation of the cause-effect principle: The observations concerning the functions of the orienting reflex seem to provide some first cues regarding the development of another very basic cognitive principle, namely, causality. If the newborn reacts to a stimulus by searching for its source, he demonstrates an inborn conception of effect-cause relationship. The probable implications of this very early appearing behavioral structure for later language structure is discussed presently.

Functions of the Sensory Organs   When considering the functions of the sensory apparatus, a general underlying principle has to be formulated first: Sensory organs are structured to register or be affected by stimuli from the environment. Since all sensory organs are functional soon after birth, the experience of being affected is very global for the infant. Also, when the infant actively searches for new stimulation, the cause-effect relationship between the stimulus source and sensation is continuously experienced as he becomes acquainted with objects and their qualities. Banging to produce sounds or kicking and shaking to produce movements of a suspended mobile are some of the more obvious pertinent behaviors. Any establishment of an if—then relationship, however, is equally relevant: "If I put this object in my mouth, then it feels ..." In the social situation, discussed in detail later on in this book, the infant has to be pronouncedly passive in situations of being fed and being taken care of generally. The consistent reactions of the infant to these experiences of being cared for are easily observable and broadly described in the literature. It is consequently evident that these situations are somehow registered by the nervous system and are soon recognized by the infant. This described encounter encompasses two constituents which are related to each other through a basic form of transformation: the experience of being affected plus the growing awareness of objective, external causes.

Consequence of These Functions

Mastery of Transformations   A transformation connecting passive and active experiences is, therefore, often observed by the child. In the frequently repeated and uniform daily routines of caring for the child, the opportunity to learn this transformation is continuously encountered. With only three meals per day, the infant has approximately one thousand learning trials during his first year of life. Such a number of trials is impressive and leads to learning even in many of the lower and less intelligent organisms.

It is not only the feeding situation that leads to an understanding of this transformation. As soon as the infant actively starts to manipulate his environment around the second half of the first year of life, he can become acquainted with the active form through his own behavior. When the infant touches his hands or feet he simultaneously receives an active and passive sensation, that of touching as well as that of being touched. When he begins to study the results of his activities at the age of around one year (Piaget, 1952), he shows that he is fully aware of the transformation taking place between his intentional acts and the outcomes of these acts. The number of oppportunities to experiment with these transformations is practically unlimited, and the normal, healthy, and active infant makes good use of these almost unlimited opportunities.

Learning about Causality   When one considers the processes involved in these activitites, it becomes evident that the infant once again encounters the principle of causality. This time it is experienced somewhat differently: While the infant first encountered the effect and searched by means of the orienting reflex for the cause, he himself is now often the cause which produces the effect through his motor activities. Specific modalities of the effect are differentiated. They, as well as the structures which are involved in these behaviors, are discussed in later chapters.

Conclusions Drawn from the Principles Involved in Sensory Functions   From the analysis of the above-discussed interactions, it can be concluded that the infant becomes familiar with transformations on a preverbal level. In this aspect, therefore, psycholinguists such as Chomsky (1965) and McNeill (1966) seem to be correct: The infant has an understanding of transformations when he acquires language. Therefore, he will probably master more easily transformations that he encounters in the verbal material. It seems, however, unnecessary to postulate that the knowledge of such linguistic structures or rules has to be inborn, if the child searches for them at the age of approximately two years. In contrast, the above-mentioned developmental data make it plausible that the child has acquired these principles; that he could acquire them is based in turn upon innate functions. It is, however, also clear that the discussed innate principles serve only as building blocks for transformations and are qualitatively different from the results of their functions. It will be the task of future research to demonstrate in detail how the resulting cognitive structures affect the search and the acquisition of linguistic structures. Some preliminary considerations and data are summarized later when more of the innate foundations have been discussed.

In the above analysis of how the sensory and motor structures of the child automatically lead to cognitive structures, the principle of causality was encountered twice. These phenomena are not only relevant to the controversy of whether the notion of causality is innate or learned (Immanuel Kant versus John Locke), they also provide some first clues of which cognitive structures later will be reflected in syntactic structures. In the child's reflexive and voluntary activities, he continuously encounters effects and discovers that not only he himself but also other persons can cause effects to happen. These effects are mostly produced by actions upon objects. Besides the actions and the objects, the persons involved in carrying out the actions as well as the specific characteristics of the situation will impress themselves upon the infant. Evidence of the storage of traces of these structures in the brain are found in the expectations of the infant or in the surprise shown when an expectation does not materialize. The exact parallel between these cognitive structures and the later appearing linguistic subject-action-object structure can only be mentioned at this point; it is analyzed in detail later in the book.

Principle of Serial Order and Temporal Patterns   One of the most general principles of behavior and perception is that they are arranged in temporal sequence. While the brain stem regulates a large variety of functions simultaneously, and while several processes can be taking place simultaneously on a preconscious level in the cortex, full consciousness seems to be restricted to one main content per time unit. Sensory and motor organs are structured in such a way that they can perform only one function at a time. If more complex situations arise, the elements have to be analyzed in temporal sequence and the relevant responses are again produced in a similar temporal sequence. This basic principle of functioning applies even more specifically to later language behavior which requires complete conscious involvement. A detailed discussion of the principle of serial order has been presented by Lashley (1951). Gibson (1963) and Berlyne (1969) have demonstrated in their own research and through the survey of the literature that the attention span of the infant is very narrow. The younger the child, the more restricted the attention span appears to be, that is, the more he has to concentrate upon only one aspect of the situation, while he either neglects other aspects or deals with them in temporal sequence.

Much evidence for temporal structures has been provided in the early work of Piaget and by many recent publications. They are found first in the reflexes which become functional during the later months of prenatal development. The hand-to-mouth movements, the sucking reflex, and the rhythmic sequence of sucking—swallowing—breathing are some examples of the more complex reflex chains which are found in the neonate (Kravitz and Boehm, 1971; Wolff, 1966). Bruner (1969) described the increasing coordination which occurs during the first half year of life in the reach—grasp—retrieve—mouth sequence. This sequence becomes more flexible during the second six months, a fact which makes it also accessible to transformations, such as deletions, permutations, or more specific morphological changes. The development of structured behavior during the first two years of life is described most extensively by Piaget (1952). It is also analyzed in more detail in the next chapter. The correspondences between nonverbal temporal structures and verbal temporal structures are demonstrated in Chapter Four.

A further inborn species-specific trait which may have had an enormous impact upon language development phylogenetically and which still must have a profound impact upon every child is man's upright gait.

Bipedalism and Its Consequences The fact that the human species became fully bipedal was a decisive step in anthropogenesis and still has strong influences in ontogenesis. Man's upright gait leaves the hands free for tool use and tool production. Recent archeological, prehistorical, and anthropological research suggests that man's brain evolved by means of an alloplastic process, which Weston LaBarre (1954) called "evolution by prosthesis." This term signifies that man began to use amplifiers of his capacities which in turn led to selection pressures and an increase in brain weight, size, and complexity (Campbell, 1970). Thorpe (1974), in a critical analysis of the theories on what caused the increase in man's brain size, was more prone to postulate "man's culture" as a major factor. Since "culture" has its broadest base in technological achievements and the production of artifacts, and since the most primitive form of culture and tradition consists of handing down experience in the use of those technological achievements to younger generations, tools are an essential cause of culture and therewith also of the increase in brain size.

Whenever objects are used as tools, and even more when tools are produced, the handled object must leave more than a merely fleeting impression, soon to be forgotten. In contrast, to be effectively used it must be fully cognized in all important aspects. Through prolonged use it becomes known in even more detail. This activity with and upon objects leads to a differentiated representation of the object and to its embedding in a large association network. The same process can be observed in every infant during his first two years of life. By means of his activity he becomes well acquainted with certain objects, their functions, and a few persons who are an especially interesting type of object. Piaget (1952), in his discussion of the development of the *object* concept, demonstrated that the infant recognizes these objects, i.e., has stored information about them.

Evidence for the importance of the hand in the cognitive exploration of the world still can be found in the vocabulary of many languages. The roots of the English words *handling*, *manipulating*, or *grasping* are evident. The same phenomenon is found in other languages. The importance of sensory processes generally is mirrored in words such as *insight*, *intuition*, or *to see* for *understanding*. Furthermore, it is generally observed that the first words which the child acquires are words for very well known persons or objects and for a few well known actions. A relatively clear causal chain from innate structures, to derived function, to cognitive analysis, and linguistic encoding can be discerned in this case.

Based upon his experiences, the infant also would search for linguistic means to combine the sign for an action and for the object of the action. This establishment of syntactic structures is further analyzed in Chapters Four and Six.

If the above considerations lead to the reaffirmation of some form of a "language acquisition device," it also becomes clear that such a device develops by means of the preverbal experiences and communications of the child and, therefore, does not need to be inborn.

The discussion of some of the inborn bases from which specific functions in early infancy derive has led directly to the analysis of cognitive acquisitions during the first year of life. These acquisitions are analyzed more comprehensively in Chapter Three. At present, further central and global innate characteristics of the human organism which appear to have effects on language development are discussed.

Prolonged Dependency of the Infant in a Complex Social and Cultural Environment   One of the important characteristics which distinguishes man from other species is his prolonged and profound dependency upon his social environment during infancy and childhood. Its impacts upon human cognitive development and the transmission of civilization have been broadly discussed by philosophers, biologists, and psychologists alike. At present, only those aspects which seem to be most relevant for language acquisition are mentioned.

Need for Communication with Adults   Since the infant remains dependent upon adults for such a long time, the fulfillment of his needs also depends upon adults. While these needs are basic and easily communicable through instinctual means during early infancy, they become more differentiated and new means of communication are needed at later stages of development. In the case of the young infant who receives all his nourishment through breast feeding, a mere hunger cry will be sufficient to bring him his mother and the needed nourishment. When food and drink are ingested separately, the situation becomes more complex, but it can still be solved through instinctual means by all animals. As soon as the child has to choose between, for example, orange juice or milk, the use of referential communication becomes a prerequisite for communicating his needs successfully. Generally, with the increasing need to convey complex and differentiated messages, the message-generating system must become more sophisticated. The experience the child has of being able to communicate his intention successfully may represent a powerful motive for the acquisition of language skills. The Sterns (1907) observed this phenomenon and postulated a "language-shortage" (*Sprachnot*) to account for the child's struggle to communicate his intentions and for many of the creative productions resulting from this search. Learning theorists used a similar argument.

Effects of the Man-made Environment   During his prolonged dependency the infant and child grows up in a man-made environment. Its effect is already evident in a simple situation, as when the child has to make a choice between orange juice or milk. Even this simple predicament is typically human. An infinite number of similar but more complex choice situations are encountered in every home. Since the young child mostly does not have the means to attain his goals without help, he has to convey his preferences to an adult.

The influence of the artificiality of the environment, however, goes much deeper. All the man-made properties of this environment represent a human interpretation of the natural environment. From simple tools, to objects of play, to the decorating of objects, and up to the social rules and regulations, the child is completely surrounded by human interpretations. In contrast to the offspring of animals the child encounters symbolically transformed objects in his play. The young animal can wrestle with his litter mates or play with the prey brought home by its parents. All the objects of play are equivalent to the objects of the animal's later more serious activity. The child, by contrast, encounters "manufactured" shapes, colors, sounds, model trains, model animals, or toy weapons; he skims through picture books with his mother, and later engages in active fantasy after being exposed to fairy tales or myths. A close look at this sequence, and the play objects which were mentioned approximately in the sequence in which they appear in the course of child development, bespeaks a very interesting principle. A gradual process of "distancing" or increasing "symbolization" seems to be built into the play activities of the child and the objects he uses. This distancing progresses systematically until it attains the level of real language. It begins with the child's encounter with shapes, colors, and sounds which are explored as mere sensory impressions; then it advances to toys, which are only one step removed from the real object, by virtue of size and weight; it reaches a higher level in pictures, which are already symbols for the real objects; and it attains the final degree of remoteness in stories, which represent real or even imaginary objects through the signs of language only.

Lengthy and systematic investigations would be needed to analyze in detail the processes of how the social environment reshapes the world for the child. Little research exists on this topic besides the persuasive hypotheses of Leontiev (1959, 1970). If, however, the basic principle of this argument is accepted, then it follows logically that the prolonged dependency of the child must contribute to the development of a symbolic system in a human environment, which always consists of man-made and largely symbolic structures.

Vocal Nature of the Human Environment   The human environment is not only symbolic but also extremely vocal. All human infants, even those born deaf, begin by producing sounds in the course of the normal activation of their vocal apparatus. The acoustic feedback provided by the infant's own voice, and even more the feedback provided by the social environment, first lead in hearing children to the circular processes of babbling—listening—babbling. Later, speaking becomes one of the most persistent habits, as seen in all normal children and in adults. The "babbling dialogues" as described by Stone and Church (1968), the experimental research of Rheingold (1956, 1959), children's monologues as investigated by Piaget, Vygotsky, Luria et al., the broadly observed monologues of mothers (Moerk, 1972), and the adult's compulsion to converse when in company, all provide evidence for the strength of this habit.

As stated previously, this loquacity is specific for the species man and in contrast to the behavior of other primates. Most higher apes are quite reticent, and little vocal interaction is observed between mothers and their offspring (Kellog and Kellog, 1933). Only monkeys and birds are equally prone to "chatter," and in both groups a system of vocal communication has been developed.

Structure of Adult Behavior When the infant interacts with and observes adults in his environment, he learns yet another necessary principle, which must have important consequences for language development. The acts of adults are not chaotic but well structured and again represent a human interpretation of the environment. Through observation and imitation, the infant not only learns to perform specific acts, but he also comes to comprehend the general underlying structures of this behavior. The structures of adult behavior are usually in the form of subject—action, or subject—action—object. Consequently, before the infant even starts pronouncing his first words, he has observed thousands and probably tens of thousands of examples of such structured action. These actions are salient for the infant because they are connected with human activities that continuously provide him with the satisfaction of his needs. Therefore, he will be especially attentive whenever they are performed in front of him. When the infant begins to act in a similar way during the first half year of life, he can produce these structures by himself *ad libitum*. Abstractions of basic structures from varying acts appear around the same time as described in detail by Piaget. As the infant consequently will be very familiar with these structures, it would be expected that he would try to structure the verbal presentation of his environment in the same or at least in a similar way. These parallels of nonverbal and verbal structures are analyzed in detail in a later part of the book. At present, it needs only to be demonstrated how the universal primary group experience (Sebald, 1968) subjects the child to universally observed structures and processes which in turn lead to universal cognitive structures. Since language is a symbolic representation of cognitively interpreted experience, it is to be expected that those same universal structures will also appear in language behavior.

Child's Imitation   While the child is observing the verbal and nonverbal behavior of adults, and while he learns about its structure, he also begins to imitate these adults. The theories of imitation have a long history ranging from Freud to Miller and Dollard, to the reformulations of Mowrer (1952, 1958), to the systematic investigation of Bandura et al. (1963). Those controversies about the causes of imitation need not be repeated in the present discussion, since only the fact that children imitate is important. At first, nonverbal imitation will allow infants, by means of their own actions, to experience how behavior is structured. The imitation of the verbal behavior of adults will lead first to the selection of the sound patterns of the mother tongue, then to single words, and later to the acquisition of the complete adult language skills. It would be impossible or at least a good deal more difficult for the child to master those structures if he would not live for such a long period of time in close intimacy with and proximity to significant adults whom he can imitate.

Much of the behavior of adults is based upon their own social and symbolic propensities. This symbolic behavior encompasses abbreviated acts, leads to pure gestures, and reaches its peak in verbal activity. When imitating these behaviors, the child, nearly necessarily, has to acquire symbolic behavior and finally also language behavior.

SUMMARY AND CONCLUSION

This last discussion has seemingly strayed far from the general topic of the innate bases of language behavior. It has, however, led directly to social and symbolic behavior. Since species-specific, i.e., innate, traits of man lead to this prolonged dependency, which involves a prolonged subjection to symbolic models, learning of symbolic behavior is necessary in such a situation. Even in a comparatively simple social system such as that of ants or birds, the behavior of one member serves as a signal for the behavior of another member or the entire group. Very soon even the abbreviated form of the original behavior can serve as the signal. This has been generally observed by ethologists under the term *ritualization* (Lorenz, 1966). The same phenomenon was also found in the research conducted on rats in the laboratory (Mowrer, 1960). A "law of minimum effort" or minimum action makes higher animals and especially human beings inveterate users of signals, symbols, and signs. The larger the number of messages that have to be signified, the more complex the signifying systems have to become. Man not only has complex messages to encode, but he also has the vocal, acoustic, and optical organs which represent flexible and sensitive means for encoding and decoding. Communication and storage of these signals and signal systems in the brain have resulted in the complex man-made environment with its traditions, its culture, and its language. The infant being born into this environment is forced because of his nature to remain intimately bound to it for one to two decades. The basic propensities which once led to the creation of this symbolic system in interaction with the product of this natural inclination, i.e., the symbolic system which surrounds the child, have to lead to the development of language as observed in each normal child. Since language is multiply overdetermined, only severe defects can completely interfere with its development. That an optimal environment is needed to assure its optimal development, is proved by the linguistic difficulties of culturally deprived children on the one hand and the biographies of outstanding writers and poets on the other.

From the above discussion, it could be concluded that nearly all of language is based upon inborn potentials and species-specific traits. This is true in a trivial sense because nothing could develop for which no inborn potential existed. Such a conclusion, however, is a tautology and does not provide any new insight. Since only broad potentials and predispositions for language could be demonstrated as inborn, the specific realizations of the predispositions have to be accounted for through learning. The next chapters demonstrate how these traits develop and lead to language acquisition while the child interacts with his environment generally and especially with his human environment.

chapter
three

Perceptual, Motor, and Cognitive Antecedents of Language Development

THEORETICAL BACKGROUND

Controversies

The evidence surveyed in the last chapter led to the rejection of the nativistic hypothesis in its strong form and to its acceptance in the weak form. The innate structures and tendencies for behavior and perception interact with environmental givens and result in cognitive and behavioral structures. These cognitive and behavioral structures are in turn the basis of language development. What needs to be demonstrated in this chapter is how these structures develop before the infant acquires language and in which respects they provide the bases for specific language structures. Before approaching this task, the problem is first briefly reformulated and stated in terms that are familiar from many controversies in the literature. In this way, the present approach is related to the theoretical positions taken by other investigators.

McNeill (1970c) formulated and analyzed the same question in his discussion of the roots of linguistic universals. He defined as *strong universals* phenomena that are directly based upon innate linguistic capacities and wherein no cognitive principles intervene. He labeled as *weak universals* those that are based upon universal cognitive structures, while *erratic universals* would be those that can be based upon either innate linguistic or antecedent cognitive structures. Chomsky and McNeill relied largely upon strong universals. Lenneberg (1967) was somewhat contradictory and therefore confusing to his readers. On page one of his principal publication (Lenneberg, 1967) he wrote: "A major objective of this monograph is to show that reason, discovery, and intelligence are concepts that are as irrelevant for an explanation of the existence of language as for the existence of bird songs or the dance of bees." Later conclusions seem to contradict this programmatic announcement. On page 374 he wrote: "Language is the manifestation of species-specific cognitive propensities[;] ... cognitive function is a more basic and primary process than language, and ... the dependence-relationship of language upon cognition is incomparably stronger than vice versa." And again on page 377: "In other words, universal grammar is of a unique type, common to all men, and it is entirely the by-product of peculiar modes of cognition based upon the biological constitution of the individual." On the preceding page, however (p. 376), he argued that, "If language is an aspect of a fundamental, biologically determined process, it is not scientifically profitable to look for a cause of language development in the growing child...." And he stated, "...language-readiness is a state of latent language structure." He finished this same chapter (chapter nine) and with it his book with the following statement (p. 394): "However, there are many reasons to believe that the processes by which the realized, outer structure of a natural language comes about are deeply-rooted, species-specific, innate properties of man's biological nature." These last statements probably induced Teuber (1967) to label Lenneberg's stand as a "radically nativistic view of language" and to equate his position with that of Chomsky. It is not clear from the above quotes what Lenneberg's exact position is. If language is a consequence of cognitive functions, then it would have to depend to a large extent upon learning and intellectual processes, with the exception of those cognitive elements which are postulated as inborn in a Cartesian sense (see Chomsky's *Cartesian Linguistics*, 1966). Lenneberg does not seem to postulate such innate knowledge, since he refers only to "cognitive propensities" or "of cognition based upon the biological constitution of the individual." In order that his constitution be developed into functional cognitive structures, much learning would have to occur. This was demonstrated by Lenneberg himself in chapters seven and eight of his book.

In contrast to this unclear position of Lenneberg, Slobin (1966), Lakoff and Ross (1967), Fillmore (1968), McCawley (1968), Olson (1970), Schlesinger (1971a), McNamara (1972), and Moerk (1973) lean unambiguously toward a semantic interpretation of deep structures and consequently toward a cognitive interpretation of language structures and principles. Most of the contributors to *Biological, Social, and Linguistic Factors in Psycholinguistics* (Morton, 1970b) presented a similar view. The most prolific representatives of this cognitive approach are probably Bruner (1967, 1974) and Sinclair-de Zwart (1971, 1973). Bruner is strongly influenced by and Sinclair-de Zwart is a close associate and disciple of Piaget. Both their interpretations of language development are, therefore, rooted to a large part in Piaget's work. Piaget himself repeatedly expressed the conviction that language acquisition and performance can be explained on the basis of cognitive development; however, he has done little research that is specifically related to this question. The links between his theories and the facts of language development still need to be spelled out. Ryan (1974) and Moerk (1975a) have recently presented detailed and encompassing analyses of these relations.

In spite of this high level of agreement among all these authors, the evidence supporting these assumptions has not yet been comprehensively described. To attain this goal it has to be shown how specific learning processes and specified cognitive functions and structures are based upon innate roots, how they change during the preverbal period, and how they grade into language skills. In this endeavor, areas will be found where an abundance of unconnected evidence exists, evidence which only needs integration and application to the problem of language acquisition. By contrast, other areas will be conspicuous through a dearth of data, or the data will be so widely dispersed in the literature and will appear so unrelated that their integration seems difficult, if not impossible, for one person. Consequently, some inferences will have to remain tentative or hypothetical until they can be clarified by future investigations specifically designed to test these hypotheses.

In this chapter, functions, cognitive structures, and semantic developments are defined as possible antecedents of language that appear before the child has acquired any language skills or while his language skills are still less complex than his nonverbal performances. Yet not all functions and skills that precede language are summarized but only those which appear to be potentially relevant for later language acquisition and behavior. The next chapter explicates how these nonverbal antecedents reappear in the same or a parallel and derived form in the verbal behavior of children. At the present time, close similarity between functions as well as the continuity of the developmental curve of each function are taken as suggestive evidence for cause-effect relationships until experimental research provides the crucial evidence for this causal connection.

Methodological Considerations

From a methodological viewpoint, deprivation experiments which are not possible with human beings would provide the most decisive tool to produce convincing answers. Some questions probably can be decided through a study of unplanned, accidental "deprivation experiments" of nature or of society. If the child is born without a specific structure and function that is hypothesized as a necessary prerequisite for or at least as highly conducive to later language acquisition, or if his environment impedes his acquisition of such a function, then the effect of this deprivation on language acquisition can be studied. Research on the language development of the deaf and of severely deprived children falls into this category. A second approach for the evaluation of the hypotheses suggested in this and the following chapters would be enrichment experiments. If children are trained to be especially proficient in certain skills which are postulated as antecedents of language, and if they later prove to be quicker and more proficient in their language development, the postulated connection would appear to be supported. This latter approach is based upon the principle of concomitant variation, $y = f(x)$.

Range of Antecedents

Since language behavior is a very complex activity, only a large variety and a complex network of antecedents can be expected to account for most or all forms of language behavior. The antecedents must cover as wide a range of phenomena as language itself encompasses. General functions, their resultant specific concepts or meaning, and their structural arrangements have to be dealt with. Meanings cannot be amorphous but have to be delimited and, therefore, structured. That early meanings are still very functional can be seen in the verbal definitions of preschoolers. Functions, concepts, and structures are, consequently, closely interrelated. They seem to represent the most basic aspects of behavior, cognition, and also of language development. For ease of discussion, they are described separately, though their intimate interrelatedness often becomes evident.

First, specific functions which appear before language behavior, and which seem to be instrumental for language acquisition, are analyzed. Functions related to specific sensory organs, as well as those tied more to central and global organs such as the brain, are analyzed separately. Second, specific elements of meaning, consisting of specific concepts and of relationships among concepts which the child acquires during the first two years of life, are summarized. Stress is laid on dimensions and polarities of meaning and on the distinctive features characterizing them. Finally, specific structures of nonverbal behavior, as well as the regular transformations of these structures, are analyzed to see if and how they compare with later appearing language structures and transformations.

FUNCTIONS

A wide variety of specific functions develop before the onset of verbal behavior. Many of them are necessarily and logically related to the child's later language performance and are therefore pertinent to the present discussion. A broad range of topics have to be discussed, and they do not always have a clearly established relationship to one another. In order to structure the following discussion somewhat along logical lines, the global function of communication exchange is discussed first, then specific functions involved in this communication exchange are studied with respect to later language development. Finally, it is demonstrated how these functions integrate in meaningful communication. The specific concepts communicated are then summarized in the third main section of this chapter.

Information Exchange

A very basic principle of all living beings on higher phylogenetic levels is that almost all of their waking life consists of information exchange with the environment. That this function rests upon inborn bases was demonstrated in Chapter Two under the discussion of the orienting reflex. Two kinds of information exchange have to be differentiated: 1) the exchange with the inanimate environment, which consists of the intake and output of signals; and 2) the exchange with the animate environment, which is, for the child, primarily the human environment, and is transacted mainly on the symbolic level.

In both instances the overt form of the stimuli serves as a signifier for some underlying meaning and is interpreted as such. The following discussion demonstrates that close similarities exist between both forms of information exchange. Developmental evidence suggests that Trevarthen (1974) is correct in arguing that intersubjectivity is primary and that dealings with the physical world are based on it. Information exchange with the inanimate environment is, however, more ubiquitous, though its relationship to language development is more indirect, and it is summarized briefly before the more complex topic of social communication is approached.

Information Exchange with the Inanimate Environment   The physical structure of the human organism, which is the basis for the first kind of information exchange, was briefly sketched in the preceding chapter. Since sensory and motor organs are functional from birth on, the normal infant cannot avoid receiving information from his environment. The sensory organs record stimuli and the infant himself produces messages by means of his motor behavior. Since his motor behavior often directly affects his environment, he receives immediate feedback. Since the physical environment is omnipresent, the infant gains information about it whenever he is awake and alert.

Many refinements of both sensory and sensorimotor feedback functions occur during the early months and years after birth, yet the basic principle remains the same: The organism has to continue to exchange information with the physical environment as long as it is alive.

Structures of the Exchanged Information   It is evident almost immediately with the first acts of information exchange that the information either incoming or outgoing is structured in some way and is perceived as structured. The term *information* itself implies structure because complete entropy does not contain information. Recent research on the perceptual development of children has shown that they do not experience their environment as "buzzing, blooming confusion" as was thought previously. Motor behavior is also structured since birth, and the structures soon become quite complex as shown in the work of Piaget, Bruner, and many later investigators.

Social Communication   Basic for and immanent to the design of the human organism is also the information transmission between the child and the social environment. The human newborn is completely dependent upon the care of adults in his social group, and without this close and continuous care he would not survive even for a few days. To meet the needs of the newborn effectively, adults have to be able to discern these needs. This discrimination is based upon the at least minimally adequate expression of these needs by the infant. The expressive function of communication is inborn and can be found from birth on as reflexive-instinctual crying which expresses a general form of excitement. Soon, however, the communication of the infant becomes more differentiated, approaching stepwise the end state of linguistic communication.

Differentiation of Communicative Functions During the first year two developments can be discerned resulting in the directive and referential functions. The crying of the infant always contains a directive function for the mother (Moss, 1973); it attains the same function for the child as soon as he recognizes the temporal if-then sequence of cry and wish-fulfillment. Then his requests are expressed with an awareness of the goal and the necessary means to reach these goals (Piaget, 1952; Bates, Camaioni, and Volterra, 1975). A similar situation is found in the transition from the grasping reflex to directed and coordinated grasping and reaching, when the child communicates with the inanimate environment. As soon as the infant differentiates goals, which necessarily must be diverse, differentiated referential behavior begins to develop. This referential behavior is first indicated in the active scanning, searching, and directed reaching. The reaching soon changes to pointing in accordance with the law of minimum action as discussed in the previous chapter. Pointing, however, is the first step toward ostensive definition (Olson, 1970). It is common enough knowledge that this ostensive definition is one of the most common means used by children for the acquisition of new vocabulary. The same principle is found in the behavior of adults when they attempt to teach children unfamiliar words. These principles, however, are discussed in more detail in Chapter Six.

These three functions—the expressive, directive, and referential— are identical to those functions which have been postulated for adult language. They were recently analyzed by Hymes (1967) and Jakobson (1960). The same or very similar formulations have, however, already been used by K. Bühler (1934) and even in the nineteenth century by W. von Humboldt. From the above discussion it becomes evident why these functions are so basic and universal in language. The human infant is a fully dependent organism with many different needs. His developing memory together with fine discrimination abilities lead therefore necessarily to a change from the original primitive and global expressive function to the directive and finally to the referential function. The human environment represents a conducive and supporting factor for this change.

Research spanning more than one century as well as common experience provides evidence that the infant soon starts to communicate more than just his basic needs when he begins smiling, cooing, and babbling. These "messages" have important effects not only upon the adult caregivers but also upon the dyadic relationship developing between the infant and the adult. Evidence stemming mainly from clinical and ethological/experimental (Stern, 1975) research proves that infants can perceive adults early as sources of messages and that even very young infants are responsive to fine nuances in adult behavior. This information transmission often proceeds even though both parties are not fully aware of it, as when children acquire fears from their parents, fears of which the parents often are themselves unaware.

Differentiation of Communication Contents   Besides the change in the functions of communication from reflexive to intentional and referential, the messages become differentiated into finer categories. The differentiation of emotions and of their expressions has been extensively analyzed by previous investigators (Bridges, 1932; Freedman, Loring and Martin, 1967). The wants and needs of the infant become more varied, and specific means to express each one are discovered. Finally, the objects or classes of objects in the environment are endowed with relatively stable characteristics and functions, and this in turn necessitates specific means of reference for each object or each category. Piaget (1952) described a very similar phenomenon as increasing accommodation of the child. Even casual observation suggests that the one-year-old infant and his caregiver communicate in a relatively differentiated way intentionally and effectively although the infant has not yet acquired even the rudiments of language. Later, adult words are added and used by the infant for the encoding of the intended messages; however, words are also created spontaneously, the so-called private words which children use to express something whenever labels from the adult language are not yet available (Ausubel and Sullivan, 1970; Bruner, 1972a).

In this process another important phenomenon appears that may be decisive for language development. It was already observed by Tiedemann in the eighteenth century and reaffirmed by Trevarthen (1974). During the second half of the first year of life, at the latest, the infant begins to communicate with his social environment about the inanimate environment; i.e., objects become items of common interest between mother and infant and therefore also items of communication. This type of communication must have a strong impact upon the development of the referential function, as recently demonstrated in minute detail by Bates, Camaioni, and Volterra (1975).

Differentiation of Communication Channels   A fact which has been heretofore often neglected seems to be important for the full understanding of communicative performance and of language acquisition: Nonverbal communication either in the form of crying patterns, gestures, or facial expressions does not completely stop when verbal forms of communication appear. Rather, the nonverbal communication continues to fulfill important, even if changed and diminishing, functions in overall communication throughout life. A similar but more restricted reliance upon several media is found also in apes, as pointed out by Campbell (1970). Casual adult conversation too would be seriously deficient in communication content and efficiency without these nonverbal messages. Hall, Birdwhistle, Hinde, and Meharabian have explored these paralinguistic functions in extensive publications. Bernstein discussed similar phenomena in his description of "public language," which is used mainly in lower-class backgrounds.

Since children as well as adults have at their disposal several media of communication, the functions of these channels are soon differentiated. The preponderance of the various media changes in the course of development, and the verbal channel usurps nearly fully the referential function. The expressive function continues to be performed mostly by nonverbal channels, while several channels are combined to convey directive messages. A fine analysis of these interrelationships is provided in Chapter Five.

The basis for this communication in various channels lies largely in the structure and function of the human body. All the sensory organs of the infant are functioning from birth on. They already constitute six or more different media for information intake. The infant also uses his motor organs in a wide variety of ways, from gross motor activities to fine muscle coordinations, such as in facial expressions and vocal play, to a combination of several of these forms. In this way he conveys his wishes, feelings, and other experiences to the human caregivers through crying, facial expressions, gestures, gestures accompanied by vocal and facial expressions, and through vocal sequences with various intonations. Finally he uses the means of human speech. In each of these modalities several finer differentiations can be observed; with human speech this differentiability is almost infinite.

Furthermore, even for a single sensory organ, such as the acoustic modality, several modes of communication reception can be differentiated: The tone of voice becomes "meaningful" to the infant relatively early; he can also finely differentiate familiar from strange voices as demonstrated by Friedlander (1970). Even nonhuman sound sources can have exciting or soothing effects (Steinschneider, 1967) upon the infant. He also discriminates adult intonation patterns as evident in his imitation of them. Finally, verbal messages are finely differentiated, and they become the modality most important for future communicative progress.

A similar fine or even finer differentiation in the visual modality was explored by the widely known recent work in perceptual development (Fantz, 1965; Fantz, Ordy, and Udelf, 1968; Gibson, 1963; B. White, 1971; White and Held, 1966). Recognition of patterns precedes the discrimination of subtle facial expressions, and these skills are further refined in the course of perceptual development (E. J. Gibson, 1969a, b; J. J. Gibson, 1966).

Development of Vocalization

It is not intended to survey all the existing evidence on the development of vocalization, since this has recently been done well by Menyuk (1971). Only a short summary of the most pertinent points is presented.

Sound production, which appears immediately at birth in the form of crying, is based upon an innate tendency. For the first one or two months it remains the most prominent form of vocalization. However, changes can be observed even in this innate form of vocalization. Murai (1960) demonstrated that the average duration of single crying sounds approaches four hundred milliseconds, which is approximately the length of a consonant-vowel-consonant sequence as it is later found in syllables. Even the intonation contour of the infant cry is similar to the intonation contour which appears later in babbling. Both contours consist of frequencies which first rise and then fall (Lieberman, 1967). During the first few months of life, negative, interrogative, and imperative expressional markers are also differentiated in the infant's intonational patterns. At the age of around two months, the first cooing sounds can be observed, and they shade gradually into the generally observed babbling. During this cooing stage, as well as later during the babbling stage, an increasing variety of sounds and sound patterns have been recorded by various investigators (see Menyuk, 1971). Frequent changes in the sounds used and exercised are generally reported. It appears that during this time a large array of vocal skills is developed by the infant. Babbling dialogues arise in which the child responds to sounds of others by repeating his own sounds. From around six months on, the influence of the language used by surrounding adults becomes increasingly evident in the infant's own babbling. Imitation of fundamental frequencies of individual sounds, as well as of intonation patterns, was detected by Lieberman (1967), Fry (1966), and Olson (1968), respectively. A similar imitation combining nonhuman and human sound models is encountered in onomatopoetic words, which are employed frequently in infant speech. Onomatopoetic words, through their close phonetic tie to the denotatum or sound source, fulfill the reference function of language in a most simple and obvious form. All this would suggest a continuity from preverbal to verbal vocalizations. Brown (1957) suggested the term *babbling drift* for this phenomenon.

In contrast to the above reports, Bever (1961) and other investigators reported pronounced changes in the vocalization patterns of infants around the end of the first year. Jakobson (1962) even concluded that a qualitative gap exists between the babbling of the infant and his real language utterances. These assertions seem to point toward important changes and discontinuities at a time when the infant begins to produce utterances voluntarily in contrast to the more involuntary babbling of the preverbal period.

In spite of this one conflict in the interpretation of the data, a general pattern can be abstracted from the existing evidence: The infant begins to vocalize immediately at birth, and these vocalizations change during the first year of life in accordance with the maturation of central and peripheral structures as well as through environmental influences. An approximation, even if it does not proceed continuously, to adult language is observable, and many adult vocal patterns are anticipated in the babbling of the preverbal infant. While a few sounds and sound combinations are learned only during early or even middle childhood, the main work of tuning the vocal organ to the harmonies of the mother tongue is completed early in infancy.

Increasing Attentional Capacities

Attention is commonly defined as a selective emphasis on certain stimuli and experiences with the simultaneous suppression of other possible contents of consciousness. A finer differentiation of this phenomenon leads to three components (Jeffrey, 1968): an alerting or arousal component, a receptor orienting component, and an internal cue selection component. If this triple distinction is followed in detail, differential courses of the development would have to be charted for attention in various sensory modalities. While the internal cue selection component is a central processing characteristic, probably similar for most sensory modalities, differences in the arousal component and the receptor orienting component have to be expected when various sensory modalities are studied. This is especially important for the acoustic modality in contrast to other modalities, because the infant is much more passively subjected to acoustic stimuli as compared to, for example, visual or haptic experiences. Any sound within the hearing range of the infant will impinge upon his ears and cannot easily be avoided. Since many of these acoustical stimuli are salient for the infant, much involuntary attention optimizing the perception of the stimulus, therefore, would have to be excepted in this modality.

As mentioned in the preceding chapter the acoustic organs are functional immediately at birth and the infant reacts to acoustic stimuli with an orienting response. If the studies of Eimas et al. (1971) are supported by future research, then it will also have to be concluded that acoustical stimuli involve the internal cue selection component very early. Otherwise it could not be explained how infants from the age of one month on would be able to differentiate sounds categorically in accordance with phoneme boundaries. From the evidence that is currently available, one therefore has to conclude that, at least in the acoustic realm, the attentional capacities are functioning on a high level of differentiation already during the neonatal period. Similarly high levels of attentional performance in the visual realm have been demonstrated in many experiments conducted by Kagan and associates (e.g., Kagan and Lewis, 1965).

During the course of the first year, the orienting reactions of the infant become more complex and his interest span increases (Gibson, 1963; Steinschneider, 1967). While during the first weeks of life attention is more passive, the infant being "stuck" with a stimulus (Bruner, 1969), around five to six weeks of age he shifts to active exploratory scanning (Wolff, 1965). Specific evidence for this progress in attentional development is mentioned later in connection with the discussion of acoustic development and sound discrimination.

A very important qualitative addition to the process of attending emerges at approximately eight to nine months of age (Kagan and Klein, 1973). Around this time the infant begins to compare his internal schemata or cognitive structures with the perceptual schemata he encounters, and the weight of attentional behavior shifts more toward the internal component and toward hypothesis testing. This shift is extremely important for cognitive development generally (e.g., the development of the object concept) and equally for language development. It is known from studies on comprehension that sometime between seven and nine months of age infants begin to understand the first words; i.e., they compare stored traces of sound complexes and the associated meaning with incoming acoustic stimulus complexes. That this type of attending is a necessary prerequisite for language functioning is self-evident.

Independent of whether it is in the visual or acoustical realm, most research has demonstrated that stimuli pertaining to human beings are of special interest to the infant and that he attends longer to those than to most other experiences. Evidence for the prolonged attention given to the human voice as compared to other sound sources was provided by Friedlander (1970). Turnure's (1971) results suggested also that infants between the ages of three and six to nine months become increasingly attentive to the human voice. That this attention leads to fine discriminations and learning is seen from the studies analyzed below. In the normal primary group situation the infant, of course, has ample opportunity to attend to and to study human voice patterns. Specific evidence of this high level of attention has been provided in the discussion of the imitation of individual sounds and intonation patterns in the previous section. More specific discussions of imitation are presented in the following sections and chapters of this book.

Increasing Ability to Discriminate
Fine Differences and to Attend to Distinctive Features

Communication has as a prerequisite a relatively fine discrimination ability on the part of the communicating subject. Some of the evidence on the development of this ability has been already mentioned in the section on information exchange. Here it needs to be stressed that these fine discrimination abilities of the infant are used in a wide variety of situations for an equally wide variety of stimuli. To master this information load in an effective way, the information processing system has to abstract early a smaller array of "distinctive features." These distinctive features and the resulting differentiations have been proved in the visual realm by Gibson (1963, 1969a, b) and in the acoustic realm by Lewis and Goldberg (1969). Preliminary developmental studies exist on distinctive features in the phonetic realm (Jakobson, 1941; see the review by Eimas et al., 1971). That the infant uses acoustic features in an astonishingly differentiated way was shown in the experiments conducted by Friedlander (1970). In these experiments the infant was able to differentiate the natural voice of the mother from her distorted voice and both types of voices from that of strangers. This one study on voice recognition shows that the infant uses a graded approach, i.e., a variety of features, by which to judge the familiarity of voices. Recent research by Boyd (1975) and Culp and Boyd (1975) demonstrated that even two-month-old infants can differentiate the voice of the mother from that of strangers, as well as differing intonation patterns, and even changes in sound patterns resulting from slight changes in content of a heard passage. Around seven months of age the infant is also able to discriminate the intonation patterns of the human voice, such as a threatening or a questioning intonation. Shortly after the age of seven months most children come to understand the first simple verbal commands.

By integrating the data from older observational studies and from recent experimental research, clear lines of development become evident: The infant is attentive to sounds and differences in auditory stimulation from the moment of birth on (Kearsley, 1973). At around one month of age he discriminates between sounds pertaining to different phonemic categories but not between those differing by the same amount but pertaining to the same adult phonemic category. By the age of two months, he discriminates the voice of his mother from that of strangers and even the first stanza of a poem from the second one. Between the third and seventh month (Bühler and Hetzer, 1928) he reacts meaningfully to friendly and unfriendly intonation patterns, and after the age of seven months he reacts meaningfully to the content of the message and not only to its intonation.

Though the recent interest in receptive language development is barely five years old, the evidence that has been accumulated is nevertheless impressive. It is also strong enough to suggest that a continuous development leads the infant from innate acoustic functions to the mastery of complex stimulus patterns and to their meaningful interpretation. At this point the topic has to be taken up again when early language performance is discussed in the next chapters.

Generalization, Classification, and Abstraction

The development of the ability to discriminate and the reliance upon distinctive features lead necessarily to the acquisition of further functions, namely, classification and generalization (Berlyne, 1965, 1970; Piaget, 1952). The development of generalizations is based upon the ability to abstract common characteristics from a multitude of stimuli and to build classes of objects, all of which elicit a common response. Living beings are so structured that their range of behavior is smaller than their range of sensitivity. Therefore, they can react only with a relatively small variety of behaviors to an immensely large number of distinct stimuli. The living system, therefore, has to rely upon response generalizations to groups of stimuli in order to act efficiently. This requirement is even more pressing for the young infant because his response repertoire is smaller than that of the adult. As is commonly known, generalized response tendencies exist since birth (Berlyne, 1965). They have been described by Piaget (1952) as tendencies toward assimilation. However, as long as the child is not able to make distinctions among various stimulus complexes, no real generalizations of his behavior can occur. As discrimination proceeds in several sensory channels, generalization has to proceed in just as many channels. Consequently, the child creates first the class of objects generally, then classes of visually perceived objects, classes of sounds and sound patterns, such as the above discussed phonemes, the friendly voice, the angry voice, or the familiar voice. He also learns to differentiate question intonations from affirmative ones, and finally sound patterns representing words. Carroll (1964a, b) has elaborated in detail and from a more encompassing perspective that classifications are formed phylogenetically and ontogenetically long before the advent of language.

Hierarchies of Classification

Classes are broken down into subclasses or combined into superordinate classes leading to hierarchies of classifications. As Heidbreder (1958) has suggested, the infant's manipulation of objects must lead him to an understanding of "thingness" or "substance." This understanding would result in one of the most comprehensive concepts or classes. More experience in this manipulation will then lead to a subdivision of the "object class" into several and finally many different groups of objects. A similar process is observed in regard to the class of "events." Events are subdivided into actions, caused by human beings, movements without visible human agents, and volitional states of want and desire, which are not yet translated into actions. The attempts of the infant to assimilate every object to its inborn action-schemes are soon altered by experience, so that he develops in the course of the sensorimotor period many specific action-schemes. Similar hierarchies could be demonstrated in many other areas, such as in the various perceptual modalities, in social relations, or in the breakdown of the global class of communication into several distinct means of communicating.

Functional Equivalence

Abstraction consists of what logicians and mathematicians call the "forming of an equivalence class." Two types of equivalence classes are formed by the infant. The first type leads to classification and hierarchies of classifications. When the infant produces one type of response to a variety of stimulus complexes, he demonstrates that he has established the functional equivalence of those stimulus complexes. The necessity of the establishment of such equivalences becomes perhaps even clearer if perceptual constancies are considered. In the case of almost all perceptions, a considerable range of variation is permissible before the receiver becomes consciously aware of those variations and stops producing the habitual equivalence response. These equivalence ranges allow for the differentiation of mere phonetic from phonemic variations in speech input.

The second type of equivalence class is of special importance for later language because it concerns functional equivalence of stimuli reaching the infant through various sense organs. On the basis of intermodal associations, discussed in Chapter Two, the infant establishes the equivalence between the mother's voice, her face, and the satisfactions which are proceeding from her. Similar equivalences are established among the various characteristics of the infant's toys, which orient the infant toward one and the same action. Of special importance in the life of the preverbal child are the equivalence judgments between the visual and acoustic modality, and the visual-acoustic and haptic modalities. These equivalences are intensively explored during the first two years of life in the sensorimotor circular processes. A very basic and profound knowledge of the equivalence of visual and acoustic stimuli is, therefore, built up by the infant long before he learns of the equivalences between words and perceived objects or actions. The impressiveness of these equivalences is best demonstrated when the infant employs sound symbolism in his onomatopoetic words. In addition to these roots of passive equivalence experiences, there probably also exist bases for active equivalence construction in the infant. The interest of the infant in his voice production, his voice play, as well as the early differentiation of his instinctual crying according to various needs has been broadly described. A similar phenomenon is even found on lower phylogenetic levels. The equivalence of a specific sound pattern to an experience of hunger, or of pain, or specifically in the case of animals, the equivalence of a warning call to a specific danger, is a common phenomenon. This same equivalence is also found in the vocal antecedents of the first words, *mama*, *baba*, which are expressions of satisfaction when eating. The infant trains another productive equivalence while he accompanies his play, his gestures, and soon his ostensive definitions with babbled sounds. A later chapter demonstrates that the mother does something similar in her monologues by describing her activities while caring for the infant. Such equivalences together with the equivalence found in onomatopoetic words may represent the links between animal sound production or echolalic behavior of infants and the speech of the child or adult.

Relations

The understanding of the above principles heralds a much more extended and profound development: the child's skill in dealing with relations. The equivalence relation applies already to stimuli as well as responses of a wide variety; yet many other relations in the environment of the child have been and still remain to be discovered. Relationships among objects in space are established during the early part of the sensorimotor period, likewise relationships between acts on the time continuum or between acts and their results. Cognitively differentiated relations in the social field between the infant and his caregivers are established very early. Generally, it can be stated that any meaningful activity and any adjustment to the natural and social environment require at least a preliminary understanding of a great manifold of relations as a prerequisite. These relations among the elements are meaningful, highly consistent, and structured.

Transformations

The insight into size and form constancies, as well as the understanding of constant as well as changing relations, implies a further cognitive principle: the principle of transformation. In the child's perceptual activity and motor acts, he frequently has to perform transformations to be able to produce the correct and adapted responses to the varied configurations of the stimuli. Piaget (1952, 1954) demonstrated many instances of transformations in the motor field during the period of sensorimotor development, such as when the infant adapts his reaching to changes in the perceptual data, or when he approaches a goal in a new way after his first attempt has failed. These phenomena become most apparent during stage four, the coordination of secondary schemas and their applications to new situations. Evidence for transformations of sensory input appears whenever the child recognizes objects whose form or size has changed due to changes in position, etc. This recognition shows that he has abstracted in a form of mental transformations from the altered attributes and has restored the "base structure" of the object in his mind. This function is found on an even more basic level in the field of visual perception. With every movement of the head or the eyes the images of objects on the retina also move, and the infant should perceive an almost unpredictable and chaotic whirl of objects and persons in space. However, as recent research has proved, early in his life the infant can differentiate between real movement of objects and the movement of the images of objects on the retina. In this case, the brain has to perform calculations and to transform the sensations into perceptions of static objects and the movements of the head. With these processes the infant transforms variable surface structures into stable base structures. In a contrasting manner, when he realizes his intentions by adapting his behavior to a changing and varied environment, he transforms base structures, i.e., his intentions and meanings, into surface structures.

Lenneberg (1967) has demonstrated convincingly that the essence of transformations goes back to the neonatal period, and Piaget (1970) has argued that even the most elementary knowledge is based upon transformations. Accordingly, it would have to be logically concluded, if it were not argued equally convincingly by linguistics (Chomsky, 1957), that transformations also play a profound role in language behavior.

Imagery and Iconic Representation

Imagery and representation are very closely related to language and to many of the functions which have been discussed here as antecedents of language. They therefore have been mentioned already in many of the previous sections and will continue to reappear in the surveys on the development of imitation, memory, and other functions. Since the topic is very broad, and in order to avoid extensive overlap with other sections, only a few of the main pertinent points are summarized here.

That imagery may be one of the most basic functions of vertebrates is suggested by the research on early imprinting. Imprinting upon the mother figure is found in many animal species soon after birth and has permanent effects. Both visual and acoustic imprinting may prove to be related to early differentiation of sound patterns as described above, but only the phenomenon of visual imprinting is considered here. Visual imprinting and recognition of the features of the parent must be based upon some form of iconic representation in the newborn animal. Though imprinting has not yet been demonstrated conclusively in the human infant, similar phenomena have been described. Carpenter and Stechler (1967) found that the two-week-old infant can differentiate a picture of the mother's face from other stimuli. Evidence for a similar early and fine differentiation of mirror images of the mother from those of other women was provided by Bower (1971) for infants younger than twenty weeks of age. These recent findings are partly in contrast to the descriptions of Lewis (1951) and Piaget (1952), who postulated that visual memory and recognition appear only shortly before the first birthday. Piaget demonstrated, however, what he called motor recognition or recognitory assimilation already for the third stage of the sensorimotor period (four to eight months). He suggested, therefore, a sequential development with motor representation appearing before iconic representation. This same sequential development has been extensively propagated by Bruner under the terms *enactive* and *iconic representation.* As commonly known from Bruner's descriptions, symbolic representation follows as the third and final stage in this development and is seen as the most characteristic aspect of language.

The discrepancy between the older and the more recent assertions probably can be explained by the fact that, in the recent studies that were quoted above, images or mirrors of the mother were used to test the child's iconic representation, while the earlier authors talked about object representation generally. Differences in saliency of these stimuli may have been the cause for the differential memorization. Ramsay and Campos (1975), for example, demonstrated that infants at the age of eight months are able to encode the features of toys well enough so that they can recognize the toys and differentiate them from other but similar ones. Fagan (1971) reported recognition of similar visual stimuli in five-month-old infants. Similar evidence can be derived from everyday experience with children, and it is also found in the research literature.

From a combination of the above data and interpretations it can be concluded that infants are able to represent experiences iconically as well as enactively soon after birth, namely, that they have the opportunity to train these forms of representation for several months before they master symbolic representation. It was pointed out in the preceding chapter how the social environment with the help of toys and pictures builds the bridge for the child to progress smoothly to this more abstract representation. Though it does not strictly belong to a discussion of antecedents of language, it may be important to keep in mind that many recent studies have demonstrated that iconic functions are still involved in linguistic performances of adults. In a similar manner, iconic features of discourse have been described by Jakobson as well as by Greenberg. Another close link between the iconic and the symbolic mode of representation has been mentioned in connection with the frequent onomatopoetic words of infants. This phenomenon and its iconic character have been discussed in detail by Lewis (1951). More research is needed to explore all the details of this relationship.

Imitation

The more enactive aspect of representation is seen in the phenomenon of imitation. Piaget (1952) has described how already during his stage three, from four to eight months of age, the infant is trying actively to imitate a large variety of phenomena. Stern and Stern (1907) and Lewis (1951) demonstrated imitation during the second month of life. Trevarthen (1974) and Moore and Meltzoff (1975) found evidence for the same behavior during the neonatal period. Imitation becomes more perfected during the ensuing months when the child begins to imitate new models as well as the rhythmic pattern of modeled sound sequences. It is significant that imitative behavior becomes most prominent after the ninth month and reaches its peak at the end of the first year (Luchsinger and Arnold, 1965; McCarthy, 1954). The close coincidence with the first stages of language development is self-evident. Around the child's first birthday, deliberate and rather accurate imitation is broadly observed. The models for this imitation may be present, but they can also be absent.

Although Lenneberg (1962) has proved through a case study that imitation and performance are not absolutely necessary for the acquisition of language, during the early stages imitation is normally one of the main tools of language acquisition. Its function and developmental curve are described in Chapter Six.

Increasing Perspectivism

The development of the awareness of thoughts and feelings of others is a relatively slow process. Precursors of this awareness are found in imitation. Piaget's daughter was able to imitate the temper tantrum exhibited by her visitor quite exactly and successfully. With this imitation she proved at least an awareness of behavior patterns of others. More evidence for this awareness appears between the first and second birthday of the infant. Piaget (1926) closely followed the decline in egocentrism and the increase of perspectivism in older children.

It is logically necessary for effective communication that the sender of a message evaluate the information requirement of the receiver both before and during the transmission of the information. Otherwise much redundancy would result, or, in the case where needed information is not transmitted, it would lead to gaps in the communication process. This development was explored partly by Piaget (1926) and Kohlberg et al. (1968) in connection with the controversy concerning "egocentric" or "private" speech. Further evidence in support of the slow pace of this development comes from Flavell et al. (1968). It was shown by the studies of Glucksberg and Krauss (1967) and Hess and Shipman (1965) that the stage of complete perspectivism is never completely reached by many persons, especially by those from cognitively deprived environments.

Some specific developments in this dimension during the first few years of life, as well as evidence that the child develops communicative perspectivism somewhat earlier than was suggested by previous investigators, are summarized in Chapter Five. The fact that mother and child communicate quite effectively even on the preverbal level also indicates that the child must encode at least minimally sufficient information to be understood by the mother. The apparent conflict between those conclusions is resolved when the contexts or the ecological conditions of the child are more fully considered in Chapter Five.

Distancing Functions

With the development of communication during the first year of life a further very important change in functions can be observed: The infant relies progressively more upon receptors for distant stimuli. This "distancing function" appears already in the transition from the main reliance upon the senses of touch, smell, and taste, evident in the mouthing of objects by the newborn, to reliance upon sight and sound. Through this process the child has to become aware that stimuli stand for something which is different from the stimuli themselves. While the experiences of touch, smell, and taste are based upon the actual encounter with the objects or parts of them, the senses of sight and sound rely only upon "signals," which stand for the real object. The infant has here his first encounter with "representational" meaning. He becomes aware that the stimuli do not always stand in an exact equivalence relationship to the objects and that there exists a certain arbitrariness of sensation—object relations. This must have developed as soon as the infant becomes aware of size and shape constancy in spite of changed stimulus configurations.

With the acquisition of language signs the child becomes more accustomed to this arbitrariness of the connection between signifier and signified though he speaks still mainly in the here and now. That the insight into the complete arbitrariness is only a gradual process is revealed by the age-old *physei-thesei* controversy, by the fact that children confound objects and labels, as well as by historical and anthropological evidence, such as killing in effigy, name spells, and by nominalistic tendencies in the sciences. Lewis (1937) and Werner and Kaplan (1963) have provided excellent and detailed accounts of this increase in decontextualization.

This slow development of insight into the arbitrariness of language signs may seem to stand in contradiction to the early development of this insight in connection with size and shape constancy of visual objects. This constancy is, however, not absolute either. Furthermore, it is found in many fields throughout the later stages of development that the same function can appear at different times in various media. Piaget's description of "vertical décalages" refers to a very similar phenomenon (Flavell, 1963; Moerk, 1975a).

Learning and Memory Development

Many questions are still unsolved regarding the nature of memory, its development, and its relation to intentional and incidental learning. Until recently it was generally reported that memory and with it learning are relatively poor during early infancy (Campbell and Spear, 1972). The parallel of memory development and of physiological changes in the brain, such as the progressive rate of myelinization, changes in the electroencephalogram patterns, or changes in the structure of nerve cells, are well explored and have been recently summarized by Campbell and Spear (1972). These physiological facts appear to be in close correspondence with the findings of the research on amnesia of childhood memories (Schachtel, 1947). They are, however, in absolute contrast to the recent evidence for the success of operant conditioning experiments during the first months of life as well as regarding the importance of early experience for the entire later development of man (e.g., Freud, Piaget) and animals (e.g., Lorenz, Scott). In his survey on learning in young infants, Stevenson (1972) concluded that, "when pleasant stimuli are used the neonate seems to be able to learn rather quickly." Since already at a few weeks of age the infant visually recognizes his mother, long-term storage of distinctive optical features has to be assumed. Recognition of the mother's voice already appears around the age of three months (Turnure, 1971) or earlier. Elkind (1967) has demonstrated that early sensorimotor coordinations are retained later in life. Similar evidence comes directly from language acquisition. Intonation patterns and pronunciation skills are required during the first year; the basic syntactic rules are acquired before the age of three years. Just for those early years, however, almost complete amnesia is found in adults concerning their childhood experiences.

At present, this paradox is not yet fully resolved. As Campbell and Spear pointed out, one of the main explanatory hypotheses could be derived from the phenomenon of reinstatement. Only those early acquired skills that are refreshed periodically are retained. Reinstatement or continuing exercise is obviously most prominent in language behavior. If continuing exercise does not occur, such as when the young child is moved to a different linguistic community, early acquired language skills cannot be recalled or employed in communication.

These phenomena point toward the possible importance of multistore memory models (Waugh and Norman, 1965). If there are clear differences between the short-term sensory storage, a short-term memory that is independent of specific sensory modalities, and one or several long-term memories (Greeno and Bjork, 1973), then the development of each of these functions should be studied developmentally. Braine (1971a, b) presented convincing arguments that such a hypothesis concerning several intermediate memory stores as contrasted to the permanent memory store could contribute to the understanding of the learning of syntactic rules. Similar support for multiple storage functions is found throughout the literature and has been mentioned repeatedly in the previous sections. The infant, for example, acquires the skills to differentiate phonemes, i.e., a sensory-specific capacity, long before the first syntactic structures appear in his speech or are understood. Also, the recognition, "understanding," and imitation of intonation patterns considerably precede those of syntactic structures or even of single words. In this connection the results of Rossi and Wittrock (1971) are also highly suggestive. They found that two-year-olds used mainly phonetic relationships in the form of rhyming items as a basis for remembering; three-year-olds used syntactic relationships for the same goal; and conceptual principles and serial position increasingly became the most decisive aspects for older children. This three-step developmental sequence corresponds closely to the three-to-four-level memory model discussed in the literature (e.g., Greeno and Bjork, 1973): the short-term memory storage used for phonemic features; the intermediate to long-term memory applied to syntactic properties; and the storage for "semantic and factual knowledge," which is virtually permanent.

Besides the processes of storage, those of rehearsal and retrieval are also of great importance to learning and in the application of learned principles when producing correct speech. Though it is known from a plethora of studies that children become more skilled in their rehearsal strategies, almost nothing is known about the rehearsal of language-related properties. The fact of babbling as overt rehearsal of phonetic information and the playful monologues of Weir's child in the crib (Weir, 1962) point toward phonetic and syntactic/morphological rehearsal. Several investigators reported also that young children are prone to imitate specifically the unknown words in a modeled utterance. Imitation also could be a form of overt rehearsal.

Practically no information exists even for the adult of how he retrieves the correct grammatical structures when he wants to encode a message. That this retrieval can be problematic is evident from the many truncated sentences and false starts heard during conference discussions. It is especially obvious in the difficulties and mistakes of persons learning to speak a foreign language. Children who are just learning their first language may have similar problems, as suggested by the many irregularities that are found in their speech, which make the writing of encompassing grammars even for speech at a narrow age level impossible. Since no evidence has been accumulated on this question, its importance for the understanding of the processes of language acquisition only can be remarked upon at present.

In conclusion, it has to be admitted that there are too many unknown elements to assert confidently that all necessary prerequisites, as far as storage processes are concerned, are developed when the infant begins to learn his first language. On the other hand, much evidence for early and long-term learning exists. It also has been fully demonstrated that the child struggles for several years to acquire even the basic language skills. What is known about the developing and changing storage processes in no way contradicts the conclusion that these language skills are slowly and lawfully acquired in some form of learning process.

Association of Sound Patterns with Other Experiences

The ability to store associations in memory is, of course, of utmost significance to language acquisition. Each steady association of a sound pattern with a nonacoustic experience is based upon memory. Many of these associations are simple and nonverbal. Instances of such associations are the conditioning of a dog to the sound of a bell or the infant's association of the voice of the mother and of other sounds with the feeding situation. In both these instances the sounds have attained some meaning, and this sound-meaning connection is, in principle, arbitrary. A similar phenomenon is encountered even in the case of most wild animals, when they learn to associate certain sounds with danger or with the presence of prey. These sounds are thenceforth used as signals for the real objects. Because these connections can be established between nearly any discriminable sound and any biologically meaningful object or experience, the function which these sounds perform approaches more that of a sign than that of a signal. Inborn mechanisms often may facilitate the establishment of such ties. The special responsiveness of the young infant to the human voice and equally to facial patterns was described above. It is commonly known that even the fetus during the last months of pregnancy reacts with strong movements to loud sounds, that the newborn shows defensive reactions to the same loud sounds, and that certain frequencies of the sound spectrum have soothing or disturbing qualities (Eisenberg, 1970; Steinschneider, 1967). The instinctual reactions of many lower animals to specific sound patterns, which are mostly species specific, are extensively described by ethological researchers. All these cases are evidence for a very basic function which could be translated as "certain sound patterns are meaningful." That much learning builds upon and supersedes this basic function is self-evident in the case of human language and it has been demonstrated also for bird songs (Burtt, 1967). That such an innate basis could and does help in the acquisition of language is suggested by the phenomenon of onomatopoesis (Werner and Kaplan, 1963). Its exact influence will have to be analyzed by future extensive research.

It is probable that future research will produce new insights into further cognitive functions and their relation to language acquisition. More pressing, however, is the need to analyze in minute detail how cognitive and language functions are linked developmentally. The goal of the present survey could not be an exhaustive summary of all the involved functions and even less of the exact connections. It was therefore intended to present a considerable array of functions whose early development is securely attested to and which are logically and/or demonstrably connected with verbal behavior. If much or even all of normal language acquisition can be accounted for even by this limited number of functions, then the completeness of the description is only of minor importance. It is the task in Chapter Four to exemplify in more detail some of those links between cognition and language.

Meaningfulness of Communication

Another principle has to be discussed first: Language as a semantic system is necessarily a means of communication, a tool to confer information from a sender to a receiver. This transmission of meaningful information presupposes an organism which conceives this meaning. Consequently, the child must have developed a certain array of meanings before he can begin to confer information intentionally to his human environment. Furthermore, meaning *per se* cannot be transmitted by the signs used in language. Rather, meaning is released in and reconstructed by the receiver after the receipt of information, as shown by Bransford, Barclay, and Franks (1972). To be released or reconstructed, the elements of meaning here to be known to the child when he decodes verbal statements (McNamara, 1972; Schank, 1972).

The following section explores how meaning develops before the appearance of the first-language products and what specific meanings can be inferred from the overt behavior of the child. The discussion proceeds very cautiously, and only elements of meaning for which clear and indisputable behavioral evidence exists are included. It is expected that more components of meaning will be discovered at comparably early ages when scientists begin to investigate this field intensively. The main concern here is to show that the infant develops an awareness of a considerable range of meanings before the appearance of language. A later section of this book compares these preverbal meanings with the first verbal statements, and parallels or the lack of them are discussed.

DEVELOPMENT OF MEANING BEFORE LANGUAGE

Literature on the Development of Meaning

A survey of the literature proves that the topic *meaning* had been seriously neglected during the last twenty-five years until approximately 1970, even when language development *per se* was studied. Even less attention has been paid to the preverbal development of meaning. The resultant lack of data prevents the presentation of a full account of this development. Results from scientific research, therefore, have to be supplemented by common-sense knowledge and experience to round out the presentation. Furthermore, hypotheses and well founded suggestions are sometimes included to break the ground for later, more systematic data collections.

In contrast to the recent neglect of meaning in the study of the antecedents of language, many of the older investigations on this topic (Ament, 1899; Leopold, 1939-1949; Kohler, 1929; Stern and Stern, 1907) describe developmental phenomena more encompassingly and, therefore, permit conclusions about the semantic development of their subjects.

Equal concern with the problem of meaning is found in one of the linguistic landmarks from the beginning of the century by Ogden and Richards (1923) entitled *The Meaning of Meaning*. These authors approached the problem of meaning from a linguistic and philosophical point of view and tried to differentiate the diverse uses of the term and to establish an agreed-upon conceptual domain for this term. The success of this attempt—or the lack of it—can be seen in the fact that the controversy about meaning is still unabated at present. This is especially pertinent to the psychological analysis of meaning.

An approach which is more psychological and which appeared more fruitful for the present goal is found in the work of G. Mead (1934), *Mind, Self, and Society*. A statement of Mead (1934:78) succinctly expresses the point of departure of the author, and it also defines the semantic scope of the term *meaning* as it is used in the present discussion: "Nature has meaning and implication but not indication by symbols ... Meanings are in nature, but symbols are the heritage of man." To clarify the following discussion a brief expansion should be added to this statement. Meaning results from the specific relationships of each species to things in nature. The young infant and child, therefore, probably perceives the *meaning* of objects rather than the objects *per se*. This conclusion was drawn by Church (1961) and is also supported by the "functional definitions" of the preschool child. Meaning is, therefore, established for each species in the course of evolution and is supplemented for the individual through learning about those relationships which are more variable in his environment. For each species different objects are meaningful. The extent of inherited versus learned meaning varies with each species, while the learned component is especially large in man because of his cultural heritage. Language plays one of the most important roles in the transmission and conservation of this culturally defined meaning. A similar though less prevalent process of acquisition of meanings during ontogenesis by means of imitation and learning also can be observed in many species lower than man, as is abundantly demonstrated by recent ethological research. It follows logically from G. Mead's point of view as well as from the preceding remarks that meaning in this sense is an integral part of living beings. It therefore can be discovered in the behavior of the child at birth, and its varieties increase rapidly even before the infant has become acquainted with the socially defined system of meanings as represented in language. A similar, pragmatic point of view in the discussion of meaning was proposed by Brown (1958a, b). He demonstrated that many of the meanings which later will be associated with verbal labels are developed through practical constraints of discrimination accuracy and communication efficiency. Carroll (1964a, b) explained meaning in a similar vein, and he followed the example of Mead by tracing the development of meaning back to its infrahuman origins. A more detailed analysis of the primacy of meaning was recently presented by

McNamara (1972), who also discussed, in support of his thesis, the recent psycholinguistic literature such as Olson (1970), McCawley (1968), Fillmore (1968), Lakoff and Ross (1967), and Slobin (1966).

Closest to the goal of the present discussion comes the short summary of Kaplan and Kaplan (1971) and that of Ervin-Tripp (1971). These authors argued convincingly that during the first two years of life, when the vocabulary of the child is still very constricted, a considerable number of concepts are developed. Many of these concepts or ideas appear long before the comprehension of the first word and even longer before the meaningful utterance of a word. The following discussion provides a summary of specific concepts that these authors inferred from the behavior of the preverbal child. This list is supplemented with other examples supported partly by casual observations of children and partly by systematic data collections.

Concept Development

The reader will have noticed that the entire literature on concept development was not even mentioned in the above outline. One reason for this is that practically all research in this field deals with subjects who are considerably older. A second but equally important reason is found in the fact that these investigations mostly dealt with experimental situations geared to ascertain which concepts of shape, form, size, etc., the child could produce in an artificial situation during a short-term encounter. The concepts acquired in everyday real life, however, seem to be very different. In laboratory experiments, the concepts which the organism develops spontaneously are almost fully neglected for the sake of a simplified experimental design. Motivational variables are largely eliminated in these studies. In contrast, in everyday life the infant or child encounters situations which are of the utmost biological, emotional, and social significance to him. Therefore, it has to be expected that he will be much more involved in categorizing, ordering, and interpreting these situations than any artificial laboratory assignments. This explanation is substantiated by the comparison of results of experiments on concept development and studies of the natural nonverbal and verbal behavior of children as described by Piaget (1952, 1954). Children prove through their everyday behavior that they have ordered their experiences into certain categories, i.e., have developed concepts, while they are still unwilling to conform to the expectations of the experimenter.

This note of precaution does not imply that the development of meaning cannot be studied objectively or even experimentally. It is asserted however, that the situations have to be ecologically significant to the subject and not only to the experimenter. How little stress is put upon this type of concept development can be seen from the fact that the term *concept* appears neither in the indices of the last two volumes of *Advances in Child Development and Behavior* (Reese, 1973, 1974) nor in the monumental volume of Stone, Smith, and Murphy (1973), *The Competent Infant*.

Discrepancies Between the Concepts of Child and Adult

One further precaution has to be kept in mind in the analysis of the development of meaning. The concepts of the infant and the child are probably only in very few cases exactly equivalent to the concepts of the adult. If the young child's concepts are described in terms taken from adult language, some semantic blurring necessarily has to be risked. Any verbal description of these concepts can be only an approximation of the concept held by the child. Furthermore, the extension of the semantic space covered by specific concepts is for a considerable time not clearly delimited (Anglin, 1975). Its borders must be considered to be in a state of flux until they are fixated by the acquisition of a label together with the acceptance of the delimitations socially defined by this label and reinforced by surrounding adults. This same principle was stressed by Hörmann (1967) and is amply documented by observations of how young children experiment with the use of their first labels. It was beautifully and poetically described by Chambers (1904:30):

> The child's intellectual landscape is like a meadow in a dense fog. Nearby objects are clear. Those next removed in distance are dim. Remote ones are in a light of mystery. Beyond that lies the great unknown. The child unquestionably perceives the world through a mental fog. But as the sun of experience rises higher and higher these boundaries are beaten back.

Since the infant has categorized the world in his own private way in his preverbal experience, the old categories will resist restructuring when he encounters the semantic organization of the adult world. The language categories as well as nonverbal encounters force the child to redefine his previously acquired meaningful structures and he arrives at new categories that enable him to communicate more effectively. A variety of examples of the sometimes crass dissimilarity of concepts held by children as compared to those held by adults was summarized by Lewis (1951). They were collected from the work of many authors who had studied children of various mother tongues.

Because of the constraints of verbal presentation, semantic development has to be described in temporal sequence. It is, however, not implied that the sequence of development is identical to the temporal sequence described here. The number of children upon which most reports have been based, and the instances in which the appearance of specific concepts was described in detail, are too few to establish any normative data. It also has to be expected that large individual differences in this respect will be found, caused by the variations in the social and physical environment of the children. Generally, all the acquisitions described below appear during the first year of life or latest during the first half of the second year, i.e., before the equivalent language labels are mastered by the child. It is also logically necessary that concepts develop before words; otherwise, the label supplied by adults could not be attached to any content and would remain a meaningless sound soon to be forgotten. The difficulty that even adults experience in learning a large number of nonsense syllables proves that the child learns his language in a meaningful way.

After all those precautions are duly taken into account, a description of the development of a meaningful world for the infant can be attempted. The general functional changes which lead to the development of meaning were already discussed above. It was argued that, in a social environment, the expressive function necessarily leads to the directive function. As requests are expressed in regard to specific satisfactions, the referential function is soon added to the directive function. These three main dimensions are further differentiated into many finer categories. Piaget (1952) described in detail how instinctual crying changes during the first few months to intentional crying, which is already directive. When needs and requests are later expressed with an awareness of the goal and the means to reach it, the referential function is implicated. Evidence for the use of this referential function can be clearly seen in the overt behavior of the child, when pointing partially replaces reaching and grasping. Finally, when the instinctual grasping and reaching, which previously served the expressive and directive function, lead to play and to an acquaintance with objects, the referential function becomes slowly independent of the directive function. During the sensorimotor explorations, reaching and grasping are supplemented by active experimentation leading to further autonomy of reference from instinctual means and needs.

The above-described differentiations can be efficiently summarized by means of the commonly employed feature notation. The communicational dimension is subdivided into ± expressive; ± directive; and ± referential. Through the child's interaction with the adult social environment the directive function soon leads to a subdivision into requests and rejections: ± directive, therefore, can be subdivided into ± request and ± rejection. During the course of the first year, an integration of the directive and the referential function results in an awareness of possession: ± possession.

The differentiation of emotions was already mentioned as implying a fine subdivision of the expressive function. According to the often quoted outline of the development of emotions by Bridges (1932), the following meaningful reaction can be differentiated: ± delight (two months), ± anger (three months), ± disgust (four months), ± fear (five months). Delight is again differentiated into ± elation (eight months) and ± affection (ten months). Finally, during the second year of life ± jealousy becomes apparent (Bridges, 1932). A recent critical evaluation of modern research on emotional development (Freedman et al., 1967) would alter this picture in small details without, however, detracting from the basic conclusion concerning the progressive differentiation of meaningful emotions.

The most important and extensive differentiation, however, appears with respect to the objective world, i.e., in the referential aspect. Recent research has demonstrated that the newborn and the young infant already can react specifically to stimuli emanating from human beings. Facial configurations (Fantz, 1965) and the human voice (Wolff, 1966, 1969) attract the infant's interest for a prolonged period and have soothing effects. These findings prove that the newborn has already developed the roots of a first and probably rudimentary meaning of ± human.

The appearance of stranger anxiety at around seven months indicates that the infant at this time differentiates between the caregiver and strange persons, bespeaking a concept of ± familiar. Around the same time the differentiation of ± female is developing (Kaplan and Kaplan, 1971). During the course of the first year of life the child discovers not only other persons in his environment but also himself. This leads to the concept of ± self.

It is evident from the sensorimotor behavior of the infant that he is very intent on discovering the objective world around him. The concept of ± object, consequently, is already established during the later part of the first year at the latest. Ball and Tronick (1971) as well as Bower (1971) in ingenious experiments demonstrated rudiments of an object concept already in infants ranging in age from two to eleven weeks. As objects are encountered in many specific forms, many sub-classes soon can be formed by the child. As soon as this concept of an object is established several other developments necessarily follow: Objects can be present or absent, resulting in a concept of ± presence. Objects also can vanish from existence, as when they are eaten, resulting in the experience ± existence. Stern (1930) provided evidence that the child at around nine months of age starts to differentiate absence from nonexistence. This ability is fully developed at twelve months of age. Bower (1967) provided reliable data supporting the observation of Stern that the infant really can differentiate between "absent but existent" and "absent plus nonexistent."

Objects are always arranged in a certain relationship in space. This may be a relationship between two objects, or between one object and the child himself or another person. An insight into this basic fact is clearly demonstrated by the child during the first year of life and it must lead to a first understanding of different locations in space: ± location in space, which implies a primordial understanding of space, ± space. Babska (1970) concluded from her research that space occupied by an object is even earlier seen by the child as a critical attribute than the specific visual characteristics of the object. This finding also supports the conclusion of the early development of spatial concepts.

Lewis already demonstrated in 1937 that the infant, since around the beginning of the second year of life, develops some first understanding of past and future. These two concepts, ± past and ± future, are fully established toward the end of this year. Similar evidence can be gained from the studies of Piaget (1952). While an understanding of the future probably develops from the first needs and expectations of the infant, the concept of the past is founded upon the actual experiences of the child and the storage function of the nervous system. The concept of ± quantity, which is encountered as ± amount, ± size, and ± number, is similarly based upon the inborn needs and capacities of the infant. He first may become aware of this experience when he wants more food; later, when he explores objects, he must become aware of their size. The understanding of ± number is basic but undifferentiated, as discussed by Miller (1956). Piaget has shown that this perception of number is for a long time not yet based upon the understanding of a true number concept.

The infant and child is foremost an active organism. In the process of his activity, he produces often or even most of the time some effects upon objects. He has to become aware, therefore, of the concept of ± agent from his own activity as well as from observing the acts of other persons. The broad range of reports on the infant's effectance motivation and on operant conditioning, for that matter, shows that the child early becomes aware of the contiguity between his acts and their effects. Piaget (1952, 1954) observed the appearance of this phenomenon between three and seven months. Many different agents exist in the environment of the child, a fact which leads to the overlearning of this concept. This overlearning also may be the reason why physical causality is often interpreted in an animistic way.

Logically and practically included in the concept ± agent is the concept ± action. When the child himself is engaging in activities, he is first only aware of the action and the object of the action but not fully of himself as initiator. As Piaget observed in his own children, the child between the ages of twelve and eighteen months studies closely the effects of his actions. Consequently, the child must develop the following new dimensions before he is one and a half years old and starts formulating more-word sentences: ± action, ± object of action, ± effect of action. Examples of these concepts can be seen in the "omnipotent" behavior described by the psychoanalytic school or in the "magicophenomenalistic" interpretations of causality described by Piaget.

The use of the term *action*, however, unjustifiably may force the child's conception into an adult mold. Evidence collected in the nineteenth century and by Freud, Werner, Piaget, Michotte, and others suggests that the child may more nearly establish a broad conception of "dynamics-movement-efficacy-action." This concept would include the innate attentive reaction to movements and other changes in stimulus characteristics, an undifferentiated complex of wish-intention-action, and an animistic interpretation of observed processes. Only later will specific subsets become differentiated and articulated.

The preceding survey on the meaningful dimensions that are differentiated by the infant during his first year or at the beginning of his second year of life can be taken only as a preliminary guide for further research. The data base is very small at present, but it is justifiable to conclude that the world of preverbal infant is meaningful and differentiated. Similar evidence for the period after the child has begun to combine words has been comprehensively summarized by Brown (1973). Cromer (1974) extended this argument with data from the entire preschool period and partly even from middle childhood. With recent research being concentrated upon this question, it can be confidently expected that the currently existing gaps in the factual evidence soon will be filled. The meaningful preverbal conceptualizations are to a large part not completely unconnected with one another, nor are their relationships chaotic. In contrast, the structure of the social and cultural environment together with the structure of the body of the child lead to structured perceptions and actions which necessarily must have equivalents in mental structures. These structures are discussed presently.

PREVERBAL STRUCTURES
ENCOUNTERED AND ASSIMILATED BY THE CHILD

Structure is an all-pervasive phenomenon in the experience of the infant as well as of the adult. The physical sciences have consistently shown that almost all of the physical environment is structured. During the course of evolution, the human organism has acquired structures that are finely adapted to the structures of the physical environment. As a consequence of these biological structures and their interaction with the structures of the environment, the behavior of adults is also always structured. It is even difficult to produce intentionally a prolonged sequence of completely unstructured behavior. Applied research has shown that airplane pilots cannot follow a completely random course in their attempt to avoid hostile missiles, but they soon follow a pattern in the alterations of their course. This imposition of patterns by the human organism is widely experienced by individuals riding a train or listening to a watch, for example. Gestalt psychology has discussed many of those and similar *Gestalten.* Similar phenomena are observed in the predilection of young children for rhymes and rhythmic activities, in the reduplication during the babbling period, and in many other behaviors. It can be concluded, consequently, that the infant not only observes structures in the physical environment as well as in the social environment, he also produces structures in his behavior, and he even will be prone to impute structures into unstructured sequences of events. In the case of the young infant the best evidence for such structures can be found in his structured acts. As the term *act* implies, structured units have a beginning and an end; single acts are of a relatively short duration; and several acts can be connected with each other in a longer behavioral sequence. Piaget (1952, 1954) has provided the earliest evidence for such structured sequences in his analysis of the infant's development during the sensorimotor stage. Barker and Wright (1955) encountered similar structures in their ecological research. They analyzed in detail how acts of shorter duration can be embedded between acts of longer duration and how they form super- and subordinate strings. From these descriptions of Barker and Wright, the similarity between structured behaviors and sentences with main and subordinate clauses becomes abundantly evident.

Detailed theoretical analyses of cognitive and behavioral structures were also presented by Miller, Galanter, and Pribram (1960). Yet only throughout the last few years have these structures of behavior attracted the attention of a larger number of scientists. Pribram and Tubbs (1967) and Bruner (1969) discussed the "syntax of behavior," and Osgood (1971) differentiated preverbal perceptual-motor behavior into semantics and syntactics. The largest amount of evidence was collected by Barker and Wright (1955) in the above-mentioned studies. Valuable observations were again presented recently by Bloom (1970) directly in connection with the study of language acquisition. Bloom was impressed by the parallels between linguistic and cognitive as well as environmental structures, and she concluded that her subjects encoded "what they know of the world of objects, events, and relations" by the use of linguistic structures. The recent work of Bruner (1971, 1973, 1974) has especially contributed much factual and theoretical clarification about the development of behavioral structures. Barker and Wright, furthermore, have developed an objective and reliable methodology for the analysis of the stream of behavior. This methodology was recently succinctly summarized by Barker (1968). Modern technology provides the necessary equipment in the form of film cameras or videotape units for an even more detailed exploration of behavioral structures. It appears, therefore, that the theoretical and the methodological prerequisites have been established for intensified research on structures of behavior. If the 1975 meeting of the Society for Research on Child Development provided a representational sample, then it can be concluded that investigators in the area of infancy have fully begun to utilize this leverage.

From the still incomplete data resulting from formal investigations and from common-sense knowledge, it is suggested that a hierarchy in structural complexity exists. The highest complexity would be found in the physical world, which includes the organism as part of this physical world. The complexity of the organism has to be sufficient to cope with the environmental complexity. The observable behavior produced by this same mechanism, however, seems to be very much simplified in its structural arrangement as compared to the surrounding physical structures. As much of behavior is based upon unnoticed, unknown, or subconscious processes, it can be concluded that the cognitive structures underlying the behavioral structures are even less complex. Evidence for such a conclusion can be found in the research of Piaget, who repeatedly found that his subjects could find the correct solution to problems without being able to explain what procedures they had used.

Verbal structures as expressed in everyday language in most cases appear to be even simpler than the underlying cognitive structures. This assumption is most pertinent to the child who is trying to learn his first language. Evidence to support this conclusion comes from general observations, the analyses of Brown and collaborators, and from specific statements of Bloom (1970). Bloom found, for example, that the noun-noun structures which she often encountered in the verbal behavior of her subjects expressed five different semantic relationships. Her suggestion concerning "reduction transformations" refers to the same principle. A similar linguistic simplification is found in the one-word sentence, in the omission of functors in the language of the two-year-old, or in the difficulty adults have in comprehending sentences with many embedded clauses. That the problem of adapting the linguistic system to the complexity of the observed phenomena transcends the realm of lay language can be generally found in scientific and especially in psychological research. Until very recently researchers felt obliged to resort mainly to univariate designs in their experiments, though they were fully aware that the actual situations were almost always much more complex. The mathematical tools were simply not yet available to develop designs that would be equally as complex as the real-life situation. A striking and more than superficial analogy is seen between the infant with his one-word sentence and the scientist with his univariate design.

It follows from the preceding discussions that structures are encountered on all levels of the environment-organism-symbol system continuum. Clear differences in the complexity between the environmental, behavioral, cognitive, and linguistic structures, however, have to be expected.

As discussed in Chapter Two, certain predilections for environmental structures, such as for the human face or the human voice, seem to be inborn. Inborn behavioral structures are encountered in the form of reflexes, which, like later babbling, follow clear temporal patterns. These inborn preferences and structures probably provide the basis for the behavioral and cognitive structures that develop later. How such a development could proceed was sketched out by Piaget (1952) when he showed how inborn reflexes and perceptual mechanisms lead to behavioral and cognitive schemas. The meaningful concepts of the infant, discussed in preceding sections of this chapter, would be the cognitive products of the interaction of environmental structures and inborn or acquired structures and functions.

The present section deals with a different type of structure that seems to be of special importance to the syntax of nonverbal behavior and later to the syntax of verbal behavior. The structures of single concepts could be defined as elementary since they cannot be easily and readily subdivided into subunits and restructured so that the relationships between the units are altered. In contrast they seem to be subject to the laws of topological geometry. The structures discussed in the following section are, by contrast, much more variable, and, consequently, their elements can be easily rearranged and lead to transformed structures. Such arrangements can be observed in the physical and social environment and are later reproduced in the behavior and the cognitive structures of the infant and adult. Several categories of structures seem to be differentiable, as discussed below.

Spatial Structures

Under the category of spatial structures fall the structures that are constituted by the arrangements of objects in space. The furniture of the home together with the entire outlay of the house is one instance of this structure that the child experiences relatively early in his life. This structure is relatively stable, but other locative structures are much more flexible and changable, for example, persons moving around in the environment, objects being carried to or away from the child, or the infant himself being carried around or later moving around by himself. All these instances make the child familiar with locative structure and also immediately with the fact that continuous transformations are taking place within these locative structures.

Temporal Structures

Closely connected with the locative structures are other ones experienced under the same circumstances: the structural arrangements of events in time. In the child's own movements and in the movements of other persons the dimension of succession in time mostly will be very salient. The feeding situation, for example, which is of primary importance to the infant, is quite complex in its temporal structure. The rising feeling of hunger, subsequent hunger pangs, the mother's preparation for the feeding situation, the feeding itself, and the final experience of satisfaction are elements that recur so often in a relatively stable sequence that the infant quickly learns the association among the elements of these structures. In the already classical paper on temporal structures, Lashley (1951) concluded that any skilled motor act displays a syntax. Lenneberg (1971) discussed the vast literature on temporal aspects of behavior, and especially Bruner is wont in many of his publications to refer to the "syntax of behavior." It is securely established according to these sources that specific action structures appear early in life. The reader is referred to Chapter Two for a discussion of the inborn bases of these early appearing temporal structures.

Action Structures

Piaget (1952) has demonstrated in detail just how the infant becomes fully familiar during the sensorimotor period with the execution of structured acts of his own and of others as well as with their transformations. When the infant learns to combine means to reach some goals, he constructs complex spatiotemporal patterns. He also has to transform previously established structures as soon as he adapts his schemata to the requirements of new situations. The evolving of early skilled action is also described in the earlier mentioned publications of Bruner. He also provided an encompassing integration of the broad literature on this topic. For the present purpose a finer description of some of these structures is required.

Interaction Structures

Concomitantly with the development of the aforementioned structures, more complexity is necessarily added by the social environment.

The infant is mostly not acting in an unresponsive vacuum, but the adults are reacting to the infant. Complex interaction structures are therewith developed relatively early. The feeding situation is again a prime case of this interaction. Short games such as pat-a-cake would be further examples. Very often in these interactions with adults, parts of the inanimate physical environment are involved. This adds a further dimension to the complexity of these structures. Generally, it is evident that the infant is well oriented in these interactions and that he acts or reacts in an organized fashion to the variables of the situation. These consistent behaviors provide evidence for the development of cognitive structures, which are somehow in accordance, though probably not isomorphic, with the environmental and action structures.

Embedded Structures

Since the best example of the complexity of the resulting structures is found in the feeding situation, it is briefly analyzed here. The following structures are involved in feeding: 1) objects from the inanimate environment, their arrangement in space, and changes in this arrangement during the feeding situation; 2) adult human beings—in this case mainly the mother—who perform a series of well structured and consistently repeated acts in close proximity to the child and with direct effects upon the child; and 3) acts of the infant himself, which are also structured, because they represent a response to the structured environment or the structured acts of the mother. A complete episode in such an interaction, consequently, consists of many substructures which are incorporated into the larger act. Sequential arrangements, embeddings, and transformations in the temporal sequence or in the form of active-passive alternations occur regularly in this episode. It is improbable that the young infant is immediately aware of the entire sequence of this episode and of all its relationships. It has to be stressed, however, that this episode is repeated so often and for such a long time that much learning must and does take place. Evidence of some understanding of these relationships appears early in the infant's anticipations of consecutive acts, such as when he starts sucking as soon as the mother picks him up.

The constituent structures that make up the entire episode are most relevant for the present discussion. They are analyzed in the following section. One of the most basic structures occurring in the encounters of the infant with his environment is the structure *operation-object*. The dash in this formulation expresses the fact that the operation is aimed toward an object. This operation can be a physical act such as carrying the bottle, but it can also be a mental act such as recognizing the bottle, which in turn may be followed by the physical act such as reaching for and grasping the bottle. The term *operation* is used here in a wider sense than by Piaget. The category *operation-object* can be subdivided into three subcategories: 1) action upon an object; 2) perception of an object, which is, as especially Russian research has proved, an active analysis of the object; and 3) cognitive operations concerning an object. The parallel between this subdivision and the differentiation by Bruner of "enactive, iconic, and symbolic functioning" or of the sensorimotor, intuitive, and operational stages of Piaget is quite close. It is probable that also in the operations described above a temporal progression exists so that cognitive operations follow actions and perceptions, and contemplative perceptions follow the enactive sensorimotor processes. No distinct developmental stages in these three forms of operations are postulated, however. Perception at least of stimulus complexes is already evident during the early sensorimotor period, and the first signs of cognitive operations also appear at this stage in the form of representation, memory, or invention of new means to reach ends.

The basic structure of operation-object contains three aspects that are considered in the following sections: 1) the *object*, which is structured in itself and stands in structured relationships to other objects; 2) the various forms of *operations*, which can be performed on an even wider variety of objects; and 3) the *operator* or the source of the operations.

Several groups of structures can be differentiated in regard to objects: the first one is the structured relationship among several objects as discussed above in connection with locative relationships. This ordered relationship can be further differentiated into relations among inanimate objects, between objects and the child himself, between objects and other persons in the child's environment, and finally between two or several persons. Person-relationships in turn encompass two subgroups: relationships between the infant and others, and those among other persons irrespective of the child. The nature of the relationships can vary also. That the cognitive representation of locative relationships is later generalized upon other social relationships is evident from the use of terms such as *close relatives, close friends, distant acquaintances, opponents,* and many more. This generalization from locative to social relationships probably points to a temporal sequence in the cognitive mastery of these relationships. The same argument has been made convincingly for the generalization from locative to temporal relationships (H. Clark, 1973). The intimate connection between locative, temporal, and causal structures is discussed above and need not be repeated. In the beginning, the infant probably makes only vague differentiations among those groups of structures. Piaget's findings and those of more recent investigators (Brackbill, 1967; Bruner, 1973), however, provide evidence that most of these differentiations are made during the first two years of life.

Structures of the object itself can be best described under the heading *modifier-object*, which is also how they are generally expressed verbally. As soon as the infant learns to differentiate among objects according to color, form, or use, he proves that he is aware of some modifiers of these objects. When he starts arranging objects into classes in accordance with critical attributes, he already incorporates this lower level skill into a more complex task. Such evidence appears latest around seven months, as manifested in anxiety toward strangers. This phenomenon shows that the infant has categorized most people into a group of "strangers," a feature with negative connotations, versus that of "familiar people," which entails positive connotations. The group of familiar people, however, can encompass a considerable number of persons, each of whom differs according to many dimensions. The infant also differentiates among these familiar people. A hierarchical classification of modifiers, consequently, has to be postulated in order to explain this behavior of the infant.

The second major aspect of the operation-object structure concerns the operations. A multitude of operations, discussed above in connection with the "action" concept, are performed not only by adults in the infant's environment but also by the infant himself. These operations are arranged in spatiotemporal patterns and are repeated very often during the daily routines. Finally, these operations are mostly elements of more complex "syntactic" structures by virtue of their relationships with the subjects performing the operations and with the objects affected by them.

The structures involving the third main aspect, the operator or subject, are also quite varied: The modifier-subject structure corresponds to the modifier-object structure, discussed earlier. The child often observes his mother in spatial relationships to objects or with objects which belong to her, are worn by her, etc. Frequent experiences such as this result in the structure *subject-object.* The infant encounters a similar experience when he perceives the relations of objects to himself.

During the course of the preparation for meals, during other caregiving activities, and with every locomotion, the mother performs many acts that provide models for the subject-action structure. When these activities have a direct and visible impact upon an object, the infant's observations must lead to the more complex mental structure of subject-action-object. Examples of such structures would be: the mother (subject) carrying (action) a bottle (object); the mother (subject) bringing (action) a pillow (object). It is evident that this structure is often amplified by a further element, resulting in the following structure: subject-action-direct object-indirect object. Finally, all of these acts are related to the spatiotemporal dimensions, and in most cases the infant is aware of some of these variables. The mental structures representing these spatiotemporal experiences and acts, consequently, can be quite complex. Factual evidence for the infant's cognitive mastery of these structures has been presented by Moerk and Wong (1976). More observational-analytical research is needed to analyze them fully.

Although current knowledge is incomplete and some conclusions therefore must be considered as preliminary, the following mental structures of the preverbal infant seem to be assured: action-action; action-object; subject-object; object-object; modifier-object; subject-action; modifier-subject-action; subject-action-object; and subject-action-direct object-indirect object and/or other objects in space. No specific assertions are made about the developmental sequence in the appearance of these structures. It is only suggested that the elements of the infant's experience have to be connected systematically into structural units which are at least as complex as described above. That many of these structures may be even more complex is probable when their embedding in the spatiotemporal matrix of experience is considered.

Opportunities for Acquisition of These Structures

The frequency with which these structures are encountered, their biological and psychological importance for the infant, and their attentional salience, together with possible innate predispositions, must lead to their rapid acquisition and secure establishment. The feeding situation was chosen intentionally as an example to stress that some situations are repeated four and more times per day during the first two years of life. Four multiplied by approximately seven hundred and thirty, the number of days in two years, results in at least three thousand repetitions of these structures at a time when the child is especially alert and aware because of his hunger. Because many of the above structures are performed more than once during the feeding situation, a multiple of three thousand is easily attained. Consequently, several tens of thousands of trials permitting the cognitive abstraction and encoding of these structures are experienced before the child starts speaking in sentences composed of several words. Tens of thousands of trials are a respectable number even for the most stringent adherents of learning psychology. Contingent feedback in the form of knowledge of vitally important results, like food intake, makes such pattern abstraction and acquisition even more likely. The following chapter spells out how the above-mentioned structures compare with structures that are found in the first verbal products of the child.

chapter four

Involvement of Innate Propensities and Acquired Cognitive Skills in Language Acquisition and Language Behavior

Preceding chapters presented a selective account of how various functions arise during the preverbal period of child development. The criterion for the selection of these specific functional principles was their probable or at least possible relevance to language behavior. For the convenience of description those principles were subdivided into functions, structures, and meaningful contents. A similar approach is followed in this chapter. The internal structure of the subsections, however, differs in part: Since the development of the preverbal principles has been already summarized, the discussion in this chapter ties in these preverbal with the verbal principles: The contribution of the preverbal developments to the specific forms of verbal behavior is discussed. The criteria for the juxtaposition and the assumption of a relationship between the verbal and preverbal phenomena are twofold: 1) the similarity or identity of the principles underlying both forms of expression, and 2) the gradual and continuous transition of the forms of behavior from a primitive, preverbal level to a verbal level.

When the preverbal roots of verbal behaviors are described, it is not implied that verbal behavior is identical to preverbal behavior. In contrast, the emergent nature of the verbal principles is stressed. This emergence becomes evident partly because many preverbal principles contribute to the appearance of a verbal principle. Furthermore, in this interaction of the preverbal skills, changes occur so that the resulting verbal phenomenon is different from the sum of the preverbal principles. In addition, the verbal forms of behavior do not replace the preverbal ones, but rather the latter continue their functions in other areas on a fully or at least partially unchanged basis. Figure 4.1 suggests the general course of development; specific details probably vary with each emerging verbal principle. The change from the continuous lines to the broken lines is intended to signify a possible change in the preverbal phenomena at the time when part of their function merges into verbal behavior. Reciprocal influences of preverbal and verbal principles have to be expected from this time on. It is also very probable from the study of child development that not all preverbal principles are integrated into the verbal principle at the same time.

The approach chosen in this chapter is still far from the final goal. Ideally, it should be demonstrated how the previously discussed preverbal principles continue in their development and how the integration of some of them necessarily leads to language development and is also sufficient for it. In the future it also will have to be demonstrated why the principles change at certain times and why this change takes place at different times for various children. Such individual differences appear very probable from earlier investigations, as discussed by Leopold (1939-1949), as well as from the discrepancies reported in recent findings, such as those of Braine (1963a) and Miller and Ervin (1964) on the one hand and those of Bloom (1970) on the other.

Although this ideal is fully recognized, at present it cannot be reached. The field which would have to be traversed to attain this goal now remains largely uncharted. Only sketches of the way can be provided, and it is hoped that they may serve as stepping stones either to be rejected as further progress is made or to be incorporated into the

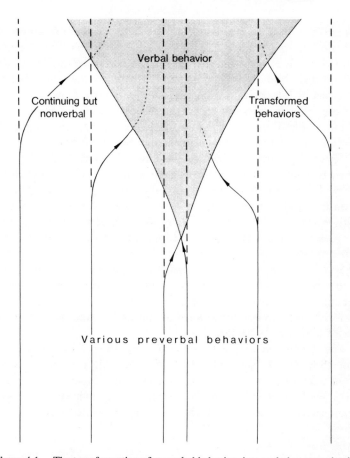

Figure 4.1.   The transformation of preverbal behaviors into verbal communication.

final design of the map. It is reasoned that, if specific antecedents are postulated for every important language principle, then these hypotheses can be relatively easily evaluated by means of experiments or natural observations. The outcome of such studies would prove whether the postulated antecedents are really necessary or even conducive to the development of the specific language principle.

INFORMATION EXCHANGE

Almost all verbal behavior implies information exchange. Yet information exchange is already encountered since birth. Two forms were distinguished in the previous chapter: information exchange with the inanimate environment and information exchange with the animate environment. It is understood that, for the young infant, the borderlines between both types of environments and, therefore, between both types of information exchange are not clearly drawn.

Two other facts are of enormous importance to language behavior. First, the form of the information exchange in language is semiotic, relying mainly upon signs or in a few instance upon symbols. The terms *sign* and *symbol* are used in this context as they were defined by Cherry (1957) in accordance with the Oxford English Dictionary. During his first year of life, the infant progresses gradually but quite rapidly from complete dependence upon objects and the signals emanating from them to increasing dependence upon symbols and signs, as discussed in the preceding chapter under the section on distancing functions.

Second, language is only a code and, therefore, can only transmit information that was conceived prior to and in many respects independently of this code. The content or meaning of a statement, therefore, is of utmost importance to the understanding and explanation of language behavior.

The discussion of the information exchange undertaken by the infant with his environment, of its form as well as content, is subdivided according to whether the source and recipient of the information are the inanimate or the animate-social environment. Special characteristics of the social environment are sketched out in a third section.

Information Exchange with the Inanimate Environment

As previously mentioned, the basis for the information exchange with the inanimate environment lies in the sensorimotor processes and, therefore, in the physical structures and functions of the human body. Similarly, it was demonstrated earlier that even the development of the distancing function is to a large part based upon the shifting predominance of the various sensory organs during the first year of life. It requires only one more step until the infant learns to rely upon secondary representations that stand for the real object. This takes place when the infant recognizes an object not only by means of the stimuli emanating from the real object, but by means of the optical stimuli emanating from a representation, i.e., a toy or picture of the object. That infants in many societies soon become familiar with toys, pictures, or other symbols is commonly observed. Later on, many of these pictures and, therefore, much of the information that the child receives, concerns objects that the infant has never encountered in their real-life form, such as wild animals, faraway places, etc. This detachment from real objects extends so far, that the child becomes familiar with many nonexisting figures, such as those which populate fairy tales, ghost stories, and religious myths.

The following conclusions, consequently, can be drawn with confidence: To a large extent, children learn to rely upon representations for their information intake from the inanimate environment. These representations become progressively more removed from the real object until they consist of pictorial symbols or verbal signs. Connecting links between signals and symbols also can be observed in the acoustic realm in the form of onomatopoetic words. It is common-enough knowledge that the percentage of these words is very high in the vocabulary of young children. The words may be derived from external sounds such as *miau*, *wow-wow*, etc., or they may stem from the child's own expressions of pleasure or satisfaction, such as *ham-ham* or *ba-ba*. In both instances they are generalized to connote many situations and objects that are connected with these experiences. Additional prodding from the environment then leads to the first stable sound forms, which in all language closely resemble the naturally occurring sounds. The acquisition of these and other real words is intimately connected with the animate-social environment and is discussed in the following chapters.

A similar phenomenon is observed in several other forms of the information exchange with the inanimate environment. The progression from sensorimotor acts to internalized operations, which necessarily have to rely upon representations of the objects, has been discussed previously. The transition from direct actions such as grasping and reaching to pointing, as well as the use of the "sound gesture" (de Laguna, 1927), again requires a social and adequately responsive environment. That the unresponsiveness of the social environment can affect negatively the development of symbolic communication is broadly known from clinical cases and was clearly demonstrated in infants of deaf parents who stopped using sounds when crying but nevertheless showed all other signs of crying (Dreikurs et al., 1972).

Information Exchange with the Animate-Social Environment

Many aspects of the above discussion also apply to information exchange with the social environment. The infant orginally experiences the social environment through close physical contact in the feeding situation and whenever he is cared for. In a first process of distancing, he learns to recognize his mother's voice and to differentiate human visual patterns from nonhuman patterns even from a distance. At around seven months of age he also differentiates among the specific faces of familiar people. Through these developments he becomes fully familiar with the fact that some stimulus complexes can stand for or announce other stimuli or experiences. His information exchange therefore proceeds increasingly on the representational-symbolic level. To express the same fact in physiological terms, he has learned to make a large number of intermodal associations consisting of complex configurations of stimuli in each modality. One of these intermodal associations is the association of acoustic stimuli with other meaningful experiences. When adults teach him his first words, exactly the same form of cross-modal association is repeated, and the progress in the infant's reliance upon representation is almost unnoticeable. Qualitatively, however, the symbolic representations start to shade into representation by arbitrary signs. Besides this distancing from the real object, the child in his communication has also progressed in transforming his inborn communication means into social and more flexible means. Crying, smiling, and grabbing become subjected to the intentions of the child and can be used in a means-ends sequence. Grabbing also becomes differentiated. The primitive form of grabbing becomes a subset, and new forms such as reaching, mere pointing, and taking for showing are added.

Effect of the Complexity of the Social Environment

The close physical proximity of the child to other human beings produces an overwhelming need for communication. The wide range of objects with which the infant has become acquainted by the age of one year and the complexity of even the simplest home also demand increasing communication efficiency. The need to communicate is demonstrated by children who invent their own words or word combinations when adult words are not yet available to them. Shortly before the infant becomes aware that his sound complexes can fulfill demonstrative functions, he tries the same on the gestural level through ostensive definitions. He points to objects and tries to attract the attention of the adult to his act of pointing, often through the production of a sound. These facts were discussed by Murchison and Langer (1927). With the development of time awareness in the infant and the planning for the immediate future as well as the memory of the recent past, ostensive definition often cannot fulfill the communication needs arising between the child and the adult, because the objects referred to will not be present in the environment. This discrepancy between intended message and available means of encoding could be one important incentive for the intensification of language learning. Similar hypotheses of K. Bühler were discussed above. The same experience is encountered, of course, by all adults who learn a second language while living in the country where only this language is spoken. These adults first learn those words whose referents are most important for their everyday activities. In a similar vein, Bloom (1970) and Lewis (1951) found that the infant first acquires those words with whose referents he is most familiar.

IMITATION

It would seem that the role which imitation plays in language acquisition would be self-evident. Nevertheless, a controversy exists regarding the degree of importance that should be attributed to imitation. This controversy seems to stem from differences in the use of the term *imitation*. Some authors seem to employ this term in the sense that stimuli which were first observed in the environment are later reproduced by the individual. In this sense, language acquisition has to be based fully upon imitation: otherwise, each infant would have to develop his own unique language. If the term is used in this broad sense, the involvement of other processes, such as a structural analysis of the behavior to be imitated, need not be excluded. Many other cognitive processes could be involved to render imitation more accurate and effective for language learning.

The term *imitation* is employed in a narrower sense when stimuli are presented in an experimental or observational situation, and the *immediate* response of the child is recorded. Only if this immediate response were either fully or at least partly identical would certain authors be willing to call this phenomenon imitation. This approach was used in the studies of Fraser, Bellugi, and Brown (1963) and of Ervin (1964). Often, the latter approach implicitly contains the additional assumption that the memory span of the infant or young child is very short and that, consequently, imitation after a longer time interval would be impossible. Besides the recent findings which have demonstrated that the memory capacity of the infant and young child is considerably greater than was previously believed, logical considerations also lead to the same conclusion. As soon as the infant can utter conventional words or approximations to conventional words, this behavior has to be based upon long-term memory. Since it is based upon memory of previously heard words, it represents one form of imitation. Such "long-interval imitation" would have to be considered important for language acquisition even if there were "not a shred of evidence supporting the view that progress toward adult norms of grammar arises merely from practice in overt imitation of adult sentences" (Ervin, 1964:172). A later chapter demonstrates that the above claim, though probably correct in its extreme form, if the terms *merely* and *adult sentences* were stressed, is wrong in its implied denial of the importance of imitation.

In the broader and common-sense usage of the term, imitation is, without doubt, one of the most important principles involved in language acquisition. The development of this function, therefore, is described more extensively in regard to those aspects that are most relevant for language acquisition.

The almost ubiquitous appearance of imitation in most forms of vertebrates points toward an innate component, which fulfills an important survival function phylogenetically: Behavior that leads to survival will be maintained by the surviving individuals and will serve as a model. A member of the group who is prone to imitate these frequently executed behavior forms has better chances for survival than a person who tries to solve each new problem through trial-and-error procedures. Since logical analysis and planning are not highly developed in many species, including man, imitation of the more experienced individuals of the group would seem to be one of the most efficient means to assure survival in a relatively constant environment. A single genetic code which results in imitative behavior could lead, therefore, to the transmission of an abundance of information that hardly could be stored genetically.

Besides the evidence from comparative psychology and the theoretical considerations, evidence for the innateness of imitation is also found in the human infant. The tendency of neonates to "imitate" the crying of other neonates in hospital wards is generally reported by experienced nurses and was recently reconfirmed by scientific research. It is significant for the present discussion of language development that this first evidence of imitation appears in the vocal realm. Since the mouth together with the lips and the apparatus for crying and breathing are known to attain early a high level of functioning, further imitations centered around these parts can be expected. In accordance with this expectation, Zazzo (1957) reported that the earliest sign of imitation of adult behavior is that of tongue-protrusion, which occurs between ten and twenty days of age. These same parts also play a central role in vocal and verbal imitation. Scubin and Scubin (1907) reported an attempted imitation of the sound *brr* at around one and one-half months of age. Infants of this age seem to be trying very intently to imitate modeled sounds, even if they are unable to utter them spontaneously, as reported by the same author. A similar finding was recently mentioned by Wolff (1969), who observed the first attempted imitation of adult sound models between the sixth to the eighth week. While the infant only succeeds with those vocal patterns that are already at his disposal, he demonstrates imitation in other instances by selecting those which are most similar to the adult model.

From this age on, imitation is progressing and many refinements are added. From a relatively global imitation of behavior, the infant progresses to imitation of specific aspects of behavior, such as specific sounds. This level is clearly attained around six months (K. Bühler, 1930); at nine months the infant is reproducing adult intonation patterns (Nakazima, 1962), and around ten months of age the imitation of full words can be observed. W. Stern (1930) reported that at this age the child responded with the "word" *baba* to the model *dada*. At the same time the infant starts to imitate sounds of the inanimate objects in his environment.

This brief summary provides evidence from several sources that the infant at around the age of ten months is interested and proficient enough in imitation to acquire his first primitive language skills. More complex forms of imitation which develop later are discussed when the interactions between adults and children are analyzed.

TEMPORAL PATTERNS OF BEHAVIOR

Language behavior is pervaded by temporal structures on many levels. Even the smallest unit of sound production, the individual phone, reveals a clear temporal pattern in spectrographic analysis. This temporal pattern becomes more pronounced as the sound product increases in complexity. On the more molecular level, syllables are composed of several phonemes in a specified order. A more complex temporal pattern is already produced by the preverbal child when he reduplicates his babbling syllables, such as *dada* or *mam-mam.* On the more molar level of words and sentences, the temporal pattern is all-important for language production as well as for comprehension. In this final language product many levels of temporal patterns are, consequently, superimposed upon each other. Temporal patterns of similar complexity are found in other areas of infant behavior, and a relationship between the nonlanguage and language patterns has to be proved or at least made plausible, to avoid postulating a language-specific temporal ordering principle.

It does not seem difficult to find many similarities in the temporal structures of preverbal behavior. The bases for word production as well as recognition are laid during the babbling stage, when the infant plays with his mechanisms of sound production and learns to control them. During this same stage, the infant learns to differentiate between the voices of familiar persons and even between the specific intonations of these persons, as discussed above. This provides evidence that he can distinguish temporal patterns accurately on the receptive level. Consonant-vowel patterns and their reduplications are also produced preverbally. On the nonvocal level, similarities in temporal patterns are found quite generally in motor behavior: Lenneberg (1971) has demonstrated that hierarchical orders of temporal structures are one of the basic characteristics of motor behavior. The innervation of the individual muscle is already subjected to a temporal pattern: The movement of a limb represents a temporal pattern on a higher level; and finally global acts, such as walking, are composed of a multilayered temporal hierarchy, which is closely comparable to the hierarchy of temporal patterns as found in language production. The speed of rapid gross motor acts seems to surpass even the speed of coordination involved in language behavior. Nevertheless, infants between one and two years of age generally show more skill in gross motor acts than in enunciation.

In the perceptual realm, the infant continuously encounters temporal structures in the behavior of adults. These structures may be gross motor behaviors exhibited when adults administer to his needs, or they may be fine motor patterns such as those which occur in adult speech or in the common babble dialogues between mother and infant. The infant demonstrates an early understanding of these temporal patterns through his expectations of certain consequences after he has observed the beginning of a behavioral sequence. The previously analyzed feeding situation provides evidence for these expectations.

Another influence producing temporal patterns is directly based upon the innate organization of the human brain and its interaction with the perceptual-motor system. Both systems necessitate a translation of many simultaneous occurrences into temporal sequences. This is partly caused by the narrow attention span but also by the structure of sensory and motor organs. It is evident from tachistoscopic studies that a complex object in the environment is analyzed sequentially. Similarly, a complex plan is realized sequentially in motor behavior. On the central level, only one message is consciously assimilated when two or more messages are presented simultaneously to the same or related brain centers. This was demonstrated when different messages were presented simultaneously to both ears. Studies which attest to the narrow attention span of the infant, and to the development of temporal structures from birth on, have been mentioned in the previous chapters. Therefore, the few selected examples should suffice to demonstrate the point and to arrive at the following conclusions.

Temporal patterns are based partly upon innate principles, such as restrictions of the attention span or the spontaneous production of temporally patterned behavior in vocal and nonvocal acts. The infant often observes temporal structures in the acts of others and in his own behavior. Many of these temporal structures are arranged into complex hierarchical systems. These systems grow in complexity during the first year of life until they reach a high level, as exemplified in walking. Vocal temporal patterns also increase in complexity during the same time period, as exemplified by the ten-month-old infant's babbling with reduplication. Early words and word combinations are just one step more complex in their temporal patterns than the infant's babbling. Yet they are probably less complex than the temporal patterns involved in complex activities such as walking, eating, or breathing. The readiness of the brain to organize hierarchical temporal patterns is consequently established before the patterns actually appear on the vocal-verbal level. On this last level, only a gradual transition from simple to more complex patterns is observable and has been broadly attested.

TRANSFORMATIONS

If the role of transformation in verbal behavior is stressed in this section and in the entire book, it is not implied that the entire theory of generative transformational grammar, as represented in the writings of Chomsky, is adhered to. Independent of this specific theory, transformational processes appear very important in language behavior. Some of the most commonly observed forms of transformations in language are addition, conjunction, deletion, embedding, permutation, and substitution. These transformations are described in more detail in many of the publications of Chomsky and other investigators (Fodor and Katz, 1964) who followed a similar approach. The term *transformational grammar*, as used by these authors, implies that these transformations are employed by the child only when he has started to build more-word sentences. This takes place shortly before the age of two years.

As demonstrated in the preceding chapter, however, transformations on the nonverbal level already appear frequently during the first year of life and become more complex during the second year. A brief summary of how these preverbal developments shade into verbal transformations is presented in the following paragraphs.

The principle of transformation pervades almost all the experiences encountered by the infant, or by the adult for that matter. Just as in language, transformations are performed on the receptive as well as on the productive level. On the receptive level the child observes the actions of adults in their spatiotemporal coordinates and understands the "meaning" of most of these actions in spite of the changed elements in their structures. Similarly, objects are understood as constant and unchanged in spite of changing appearances, when the perspective is modified. The research on object-constancy provides evidence for these conclusions. The same principle also applies in the acoustic realm, which is more pertinent to later language understanding. Recognition of the mother's voice, even if it is intentionally distorted, can be demonstrated at an early age, as documented in Chapter Three. The understanding of intonation patterns is attested by many authors; it appears before the beginning of the second year and is soon followed by an understanding of words. In both cases a variety of voices is encountered, and yet the infant is still able to refer to a "deep-structure," i.e., the invariances underlying the surface patterns.

In the realm of behavioral products, transformations are most evident in nonvocal behavior whenever the infant adapts his reflex-

or action-schemas to the requirements of changing situations. In Chapter Three, Piaget's descriptions of these transformations were elaborated in more detail. The gradual increase in the complexity of these transformations has been described and is amply documented in the literature. In the vocal field, tranformations of sound elements can be broadly observed in the babbling of the infant. A rather complex form of transformations also can be observed during the stage of the one-word sentence, when the infant selects varying verbal means to convey a specific message. The specific selection of the verbal means appears to be related to the variables of the situation. The intended message is, consequently, communicated partly verbally and partly nonverbally. Since the content of the message is not changing in spite of these adaptations, several transformational processes must be involved.

After all these complex antecedents, the grammatical transformations performed by the child when he enters the more-word sentence stage seem comparably simple and elementary. A continuity of the function of transformation in the receptive and productive domain, both for verbal and nonverbal information exchange, is therefore fully evident. Specific finer and systematic descriptions of these preverbal transformations are found in abundance in developmental literature. A systematic and detailed application of these findings to transformations in verbal behavior awaits further research.

PRIMITIVE GENERALIZATIONS, CLASSIFICATIONS, AND FUNCTIONAL EQUIVALENCE

Although the capacity to differentiate between stimuli and stimulus-complexes is important for recognition of objects and acoustic patterns which are regularly associated with these objects, the principle of generalization lies at the heart of labeling. Except in some comparatively few instances when the infant learns proper names for very specific persons and objects, he has to apply one general term to a large variety of objects which fall into the same class. The narrower the vocabulary, the broader the range of these concepts has to be, if the number of different objects to be encoded is held constant. Consequently, the words used by the young infant have to encompass a wide variety of meanings which are clearly distinguished in adult language. In many instances they may even serve only as "sound gestures," similar to "ostensive definitions," without comprising a specific meaning. Further cognitive differentiation between the objects together with adult feedback concerning the distinguishing features of each concept will induce the child to slowly adapt his idiosyncratic concepts to the meanings established in his mother tongue.

The tendency to use terms as a "place-holder" or "attention-getter" with an abstraction from particular meanings is also seen in the language behavior of adults. The word *thing* is often used when a more suitable word with a narrower denotation cannot be immediately recalled. This broad and general label, consequently, serves as an effort-saving substitute when nonverbal variables contribute the necessary information to permit successful communication. Similar evidence can be found in the vernacular expressions of emotions, and this principle may apply even to the use of pronouns in place of nouns. Zipf (1949) demonstrated a similar "principle of least effort" in quite a different realm of language, while Mowrer (1954) found evidence of a "tendency toward economy" even in the communication of rats with the experimenters in the laboratory. Likewise, the infant cannot be expected to be overly concerned with the semantic precision of the terms used, as long as situational variables and parental sensitivity invite him to avoid heightened effort in his communications.

Many examples of overgeneralizations in the first words of infants can be found in the literature on child language development. One instance may suffice to demonstrate this principle. Lewis (1964) described how one child learned to differentiate among different species of quadrupeds in his language behavior and to attach the accepted verbal label to each species. At first a single word was used for cats, dogs, cows, and horses. The range of this concept appeared comparable to the adult concept *quadruped,* though it comprised fewer species. This wide span was thereafter narrowed, though it still included animals belonging to different species. During this second period the child seemed to have hypothesized that size was the distinguishing attribute for verbal differentiation of animals, because he had differentiated between small and large quadrupeds. Finally, after many months of experimentation, the delimitations of the verbal labels as used by the child became the same as those employed in the adult language.

On another level, which appears to be more complex, a similar principle of generalization or perhaps of initial lack of differentiation can be found. This lack of differentiation is most evident when the child communicates in holophrases, but it is still very prevalent on the level which was previously (Braine, 1963a; Miller and Ervin, 1964) described as that of pivot-open grammars. Recent refinements in structural analysis (Brown, 1973) notwithstanding, the evidence from the stage of two-word sentences strongly suggests that children have established several encompassing groups of words as well as specific rules for their combination. With the further development of the child's vocabulary, gradual distinctions in each of these classes are drawn. This was demonstrated by the research of Brown and Fraser (1963). The prolonged environmental instruction, which continues beyond the elementary school years, enables the child to approximate asymptotically the grammatical competence as represented in formal systems of grammar.

When the infant and later the child learns to make these finer distinctions in the semantic as well as in the syntactic field, the old global classes are often not completely discarded but are rather only transformed. Referring to the example provided for the semantic realm, it is obvious that the concept *quadruped* as developed by the child is again used in adult language, since it best describes the objective physical characteristics of a large group of animals. Similarly, the pivot-open distinction is reflected in the adult language which contains two large groups of words: "labels for the things and acts" and "labels for relations between things." These two classes of words have been generally designated as *contentives* and *functors* in recent psycholinguistic research. Although the classes as distinguished by both the child and the linguist are not identical, remarkable similarities can be detected. Consequently, when these older global classes are subdivided into smaller classes, hierarchies of classification have to be developed by the child. Such a differentiation of classes has been described by Brown and Fraser (1963) for the syntactic realm and by Leopold (1948) for the semantic realm.

When Jenkins and Palermo (1964) described the learning of word categories, i.e., classes of words and rules for sentence construction, they used the principle of functional equivalence to explain how the child could acquire word classes. This functional equivalence is evident in the pivot and open combinations. Many open words can be combined with one pivot word, and vice versa. An understanding of functional equivalence is also revealed as soon as the child starts using pronouns to substitute for nouns. Finally, it is implied in every correctly constructed sentence when the various slots in the sentence are filled with the "correct" word classes. Consequently, it cannot be doubted that this principle is of importance in language behavior. Braine (1963b, 1971b) has supported this contention through observational and experimental evidence.

From the above short summary, which is based upon impressive data collections, it should be evident that in the early language products of the child the following four principles are involved: 1) global, relatively primitive generalizations; 2) finer differentiations and classifications; 3) the building of hierarchies of classification; and 4) the principle of functional equivalence of members of classes.

The development of these functions in the nonverbal realm was discussed in previous chapters. It was demonstrated that they start to develop long before the appearance of the first word and that they have already reached a comparatively high level of complexity when the infant is around one year old. A general principle was encountered in various studies and especially in the work of Piaget: The more limited the nervous system is in its functions, the more global the generalizations have to be. With the increasing capacities of the nervous system, the categorizations established also become more sophisticated. This early generalization, which is lucidly described by Piaget (1952) under the term *assimilation*, or by Werner (1940) as a *lack of differentiation*, was found by other authors who described the first steps of language acquisition in children.

Because this principle applies to so many fields and because it functions for a considerable time before language behavior appears, it would seem completely superfluous to postulate that the same principle when it functions in the verbal realm has completely different and autonomous roots. This conclusion becomes even more probable since there is no clearly difined borderline between nonverbal and verbal functions. This gradual transition can be observed in the field of information exchange with the social environment: During the first two years of life the emotional behavior of the infant becomes differentiated into several finer expressions of emotions. Similarly, the infant learns to react differentially to the various emotions expressed by adults. The equivalence of many social stimuli in producing infant babbling has been demonstrated in several recent studies. When the infant demonstrates the first signs of comprehension, global classes are also constructed. He may first differentiate the class of approval versus disapproval, while the specific expressions in each class are equivalent in their effect. Likewise in the infant's own utterances, a global differentiation between request and rejection is generally observed in his directive utterances. Such a differentiation is anticipated on the nonverbal level and appears later also on the verbal level.

Examples of this continuity could be amassed from previous literature and they can be generally observed in interactions with infants. It seems, therefore, that enough evidence exists suggesting or even proving the continuity and identity of the principles involved. If some investigators attempt to prove a different and more redundant hypothesis, then it is their task to refute this evidence and to accumulate a comparable amount of counterevidence. No traces of such attempts, however, can be found in the work of either Chomsky or McNeill.

SYMBOLIC REPRESENTATION AND USE OF WORDS

The real beginning of language, and the most profound factor in language behavior, is generally seen in the use of words as signifiers for something to be signified. Although the characteristics of word use and the way in which words are understood change considerably in the course of development, the important breakthrough in this development already appears with the first understanding of conventional words and with the consistent utterance of a "word" with specific reference. It appears, therefore, that it would be most fruitful to demonstrate the multiple sources and roots of language in connection with the appearance of the first words. Figure 4.2 represents a diagrammatic sketch of the interconnections of probable antecedents and their convergence toward the use of words. Many details in this figure still must be interpreted as hypotheses. Neither has an attempt been made to ascertain the exact temporal sequence of the developments of the individual principles or the time of their convergence. Not enough evidence exists at present to allow such specific conclusions.

The lower end of Figure 4.2 represents the innate structural and functional bases. The individual lines of development can be followed to the top, which represents the end point, the first word. The branchings and convergences cannot be discussed in detail; an intensive discussion of the complex network would require a book in itself. Part of this discussion has been presented in the preceding as well as in the present chapter.

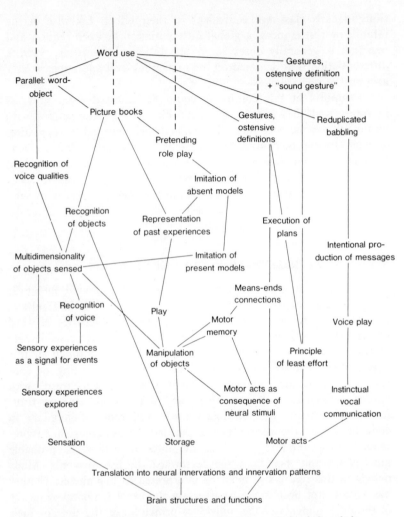

Figure 4.2.   The development of representation and of verbal symbols.

The central basis for every development including language development is, of course, the brain and the nervous system. In considering this central basis, it becomes immediately evident that even in the brain the principle of representation is all pervasive. In the sensory modality as well as in the motor modality or for the storage of experience, the messages have to be transformed and somehow, probably electrochemically, represented in the nervous system. The complexity and the possible manifold of these representations were brilliantly discussed by Pribram (1971) under the title *Languages of the Brain*. It even appears probable that several transformations and representations take place before the sensory stimulus reaches the brain and is analyzed and stored there. The same principle applies to the centrifugal direction, which results in motor output.

First the sensory side of representational development and its interaction with the development in the motor and storage dimensions are discussed. Then the other two topics are shortly summarized.

The infant soon learns that sensory experiences stand for something. Originally this denotatum may be physical satisfaction, as when the infant expects food after being picked up by his mother. It also can be a physical object, which of course is again experienced through other sensory representations. An understanding of the representational function of sensory stimuli is based upon the storage of the original associations among several stimuli, leading to a concept of an external, objective world. The stimuli may be derived from external or internal sources. Many instances where optical or acoustical stimuli serve as representations are mentioned in the preceding chapter. Such instances are also continually encountered in everyday observations of infants. The sociocultural environment specifically contributes to this development of representations through the ample provision of pictures and through the monologues of the mother while she engages in the daily caregiving routines. These principles are discussed in more detail in a later chapter.

While the infant, consequently, is fully familiar with the principle of representation in the acoustical as well as in the optical realm, the structures of his brain continue to develop, leading to more extended memory. Memory itself, however, is based again upon a representation. Present-day theorists (Bruner, 1968; Piaget, 1952) postulate enactive and iconic memories without being concerned about the neuronal form of these memories. Pribram's (1971) ideas on the storage of information as holograms cover also more the iconic aspect of memory. Although evidence about the specific form of the representation in the brain has not yet been unequivocally provided, it is obvious that experiences are somehow abstracted and represented in a transformed state in the brain. Consequently, with increasing memory capacities the infant has to develop increased skills in representing experiences abstractly.

In the realm of motor behavior similar phenomena can be observed. First, as stated above, the motor act itself represents a transformation and therefore a representation of the innervation patterns in the brain. In the later stages of development some of these innervation patterns are experienced as intention and they are then consciously transformed into motor representations. In the field of sensory experience the direction of representation is from concrete to abstract, while in the realm of motor behavior the direction is probably from superordinate-abstract to concrete. The general plan or intention has to be broken down into several subplans, and these molecular plans have to be once again adapted to aspects of the situation before they can be expressed as concrete motor acts. Piaget described a similar principle extensively under the term *accommodation*. A close interaction among motor, perceptual, and memory processes leads to several secondary representations. The child, for example, will be aware of his own behavior and remember it for future reapplication. As soon as the instinctual crying changes to intentional calling, a form of secondary representation is demonstrated in the behavior of the infant. The intentions and wants of the infant also lead to such secondary representations when the principle of means-ends sequences is understood and realized in behavior. The interaction of motor and sensory principles leads to imitation of the behavior of other persons; if memory is added to these two functions, then the imitation of absent models can be observed. Imitation of absent models implies an entire chain of representations: First, the sensory experience is tranformed into neuronal messages. These messages are stored in the brain in probably another form of representation. Then the process is reversed, and the stored information is again transformed into neuronal firing patterns and finally into motor behavior patterns. The infant is conscious of the beginning and end step of this chain of transformations. He is also aware that it is only make-believe, i.e., representation, as is evident from the perceptive descriptions of Piaget (1952). An almost identical chain is found in "pretending" and in the role playing of the child. Both are accompanied by a considerable degree of awareness that representation is involved. No healthy infant, for example, would seriously attempt to eat a mud pie if invited to do so, in spite of the fact that he treats this mud pie in many respects as an equivalent to a real cake or cookie.

In the realm of the expressive function, sounds have acquired during the course of the first year increasingly steady connections with specific states, and they serve as an expression of these states.

As the human environment reacts consistently and meaningfully to these sound productions, the representational function is considerably reinforced. In a similar interaction with the helpful human environment, the role of gestures, another form of intentional representation, is trained. This is mentioned in a previous section of this chapter. Before words are produced, gestures themselves have undergone a process of development. First they have been used in connection with requests and demands, but later the same gestures begin to fulfill referential functions, as when the infant's attention is attracted by some novel stimulus.

Consequently, around the age of one year the infant is fully aware of the principle of representation based upon experiences in several fields; he has actively and passively discovered that sound complexes can represent needs, feelings, and objects in his environment. He has also trained the referential function of representation through the use of gestures either alone or with the addition of sounds to attract attention. It seems, consequently, that besides the combination of these manifold prerequisites, only one influence is needed to lead to the first word: the social and very voluble human environment. That adults guide the child untiringly in his task of language acquisition has been briefly mentioned already. How this guidance interacts, leads to, and builds upon all the hitherto discussed developments is demonstrated in the next chapters. It is argued in these chapters that, once the principle of verbal representation is grasped, the continuous and very intensive instruction provided by adults, together with the increasing need for communication and the steady progress in cognitive development, are sufficient causes for further differentiation and refinement of verbal skills. The great variety of processes involved cannot be given full consideration in this volume since they continue long after the first years of language acquisition.

SPECIFIC CONCEPTS AND MEANINGS

After the contribution of the global functions to language emergence has been discussed, it remains to show how the child expresses the meanings or specific concepts which he has acquired before the beginning of verbal behavior. The period of beginning speech and the more progressed stages when the child enlarges upon his language skills are now considered.

The task would seem to be very simple, since many studies on the acquisition of vocabulary have been published since the beginning of the century. A comparison of preverbal meanings and the increasing vocabulary, therefore, would seem sufficient to conclude this section. The problem is more complex, however.

It is not proved and no logical reason exists to expect that all the concepts which are differentiated also will be expressed in the child's vocabulary. In contrast, it would seem probable that some meanings, which are often expressed preverbally and for which efficient means of communication have been developed, still would be expressed nonverbally for a prolonged period during childhood and perhaps even during the entire life span. Intonation patterns, mimicry, and gestures communicate messages that are not formulated verbally and sometimes could not even be expressed consciously by the speaker. Emotions, desires, or attitudes are types of messages that are often revealed in this way.

Second, it is even less self-evident that the sequence of vocabulary acquisition should be the same as the acquisition of meaning. From the above argument it would follow that just the earliest developed meanings, for which overlearned and perhaps even instinctual nonverbal communication methods exist, would not be expressed in words for a long time. Support for this hypothesis can be found in the work of Leopold (1939) and other authors who reported that the word for *mother* appears relatively late in the vocabulary of many children. A second variable that has to be considered is communicative necessity. If certain facts were self-evident from the situation or through nonverbal communication, it would be redundant to express them in words. This consideration does not imply that the infant has developed means to distinguish exactly between needed information and redundancy. What will probably happen in the everyday interaction between adult and child is that some intentions of the child are always understood without the assistance of words. No need arises, therefore, for the child to refine his encoding abilities. The findings of Luria and Yudovich (1959) concerning the lack of language skills of a pair of identical twins present a clear instance of such a case. If parts of other messages are repeatedly misunderstood, the child probably will be more motivated to try new ways of encoding. This last argument entails the social variables involved in the development of specific words and verbal communication skills generally. This entire topic of the motivation for language acquisition and behavior as well as the specific social interactions contributing to it are discussed in more detail in Chapter Six.

After these general precautions have been duly considered and the dangers of premature parallels and conclusions are taken into consideration, a cautious and preliminary analysis of the semantic world of the child can be ventured upon. In the preceding chapter, surveying the development of meaningful communication, a subdivision into expressive, directive, and referential functions was adopted from previous literature. The same differentiation applies to the functions of language generally. Whether it applies also to early child language is explored in the following section.

Expressive Function

The expressive function is probably phylogenetically and ontogenetically the most primordial communicative function. It differentiates slowly by first adding the directive and finally the referential aspect. Expressive communication is still very prevalent when the child starts to communicate verbally. At this time the global emotion of excitement has been differentiated to result in the expression of many specific feelings. Yet practically no words are found in the early vocabulary of children to express these emotions. Rather they are still expressed almost completely nonverbally during the second year, and the transition to verbal expression takes place only slowly in later childhood. It is, of course, common knowledge that even in adulthood really strong and sudden emotions are expressed mainly by nonverbal means such as screaming, crying, or semiverbal swearing. Enriched and intensive environmental stimulation is required to acquire the skills to express emotions verbally in a differentiated manner. Psycholinguistic and sociolinguistic research has also provided evidence that the ability to express emotions verbally is connected with social class status. Lower social class status, which is often combined with a lack of language stimulation, as proved by the research of Bernstein (1964), Hess and Shipman (1965), and many others, also leads to deficiencies in the verbal expression of emotions.

The greatest proficiency in the expression of emotions is perhaps reached in the arts: poetry, painting, music, drama, and dance. Precisely which specific medium is most successful in expressing the full range of emotions is a moot question. It is significant, however, that other media besides the verbal one have been developed by mankind for emotional expression. In fact, it would appear reasonable to conclude that verbal language is not the optimal means for the expression of human emotions. The skill that is needed to express emotions verbally can be attained through special training and prolonged study, but it requires a relatively high level of cognitive differentiation as a prerequisite. The fact that the young child has developed almost no means, and does not even try to express his emotions verbally, seems to be closely related to these difficulties as experienced by the adult. Both facts are probably the consequence of the above described condition: The inborn instinctive means of the cry, the facial expression, gesture, and intonation in vocal expressions suffice completely and are used for a long time exclusively and still later as an addition to verbal means.

Directive Function

The next category of meanings can be summarized under the term *directive*. This level implies higher cognitive functions. In the case of the expressive function, the child only expresses his own physiological emotional states. The directive function, in contrast, is related to phenomena in the objective environment. While the expressive function is also generally found in lower animals, the directive function is only encountered in a rudimentary form in the higher apes. Even when the child simply requests or rejects an object, he already expresses a relationship between himself and certain outside variables. The main stress, however, still lies on the expressive function. When specific objects are preferred to others, the focus has begun to center upon the object. In these instances the child provides preliminary evidence that he has transcended the limits of his own egocentric experiences and takes specific variables of the objective world into account. This object-attention is admittedly still markedly tinged by the desires or aversions of the individual. A very interesting combination of expressive-instinctive and object-oriented functions is, consequently, encountered in this type of meaningful message. Request and rejection in simple forms are expressed quite early without the use of language as already discussed in the previous chapter. They can be observed even in the neonate. Both are of profound importance to the survival of the organism. Studies of the developmental differentiation of emotional expression have revealed that the negative emotions, such as distress or anger, are expressed earlier than the corresponding positive emotions, such as delight or affection. A similar phenomenon is evident in the development of the verbal expression of directives. As observed by several authors (Leopold, 1939; Lewis, 1964), the word *no* is understood and/or uttered before the word *yes*. Often before the end of the first year of life, specific sound combinations derived from the child's spontaneous babbling repertoire are used consistently to convey requests. Independent of the language community studied and the time when the research was conducted, all investigators have reported that some of the first real words used by the child fulfill a requesting function. These may be words such as the personal or possessive pronoun, a simple verb form, or nouns used as holophrases. It is well known that the investigators working at the turn of the century, especially Meumann (1908) and Stern and Stern (1907), were overly impressed by the emotional-volitional aspect of the beginnings of language. Though they may have underestimated its cognitive aspect, they had observed correctly the high percentage of directive/requesting elements in the early speech of children.

The early requests are still mostly expressed by means of monosyllabic utterances, which are similar to the preverbal consonant-vowel babble forms. Nonverbal means of communication often accompany these verbal expressions of directions.

Closely related to requests are the instances when the infant asserts his possession of an object or tries to persuade others to let him have something. In this instance the verbal expression of this motive is often indistinguishable from a request. Both are expressed in English by the possessive pronoun *mine* or other close equivalents. Even the possessive morpheme *'s* appears relatively early (Brown, 1973; Leopold, 1949). Nonverbal message elements often also accompany the verbal expression of possession until late childhood and even adulthood. In both cases, when the infant names an object by requesting it, as well as when he asserts his possession of it, he is conversing with the adult about this object. The directive function of language has, herewith, evolved into the referential function.

Referential Function

The final category of meaningful expressions has been termed *referential*. This term applies when the infant predominantly *refers* to something in the objective environment. Consequently, a more specific concern for the objects and their relationships in the environment is demonstrated by this function. The environment has acquired its independent stimulus value and is not considered only in respect to the desires of the child. It is also evident that this category will cover a broader range of contents than the previous two categories: Only a relatively small number of emotions is differentiated by human beings, and the dynamic relationship to the environment remains circumscribed by the two basic categories of request and rejection. In contrast, the objects of the environment are much more varied. The larger the number of objects and experiences that are differentiated in the environment, the more conspicuous the relationship between these experiences becomes.

Three main dimensions of relatedness among objects or between persons and objects are experienced: time, space, and causality. A further relationship arises between the child and objects, as soon as the representative function has evolved. This is a cognitive relationship between the child's expectations or memories and actual experiences. It is commonly referred to as ±existence and ±presence.

According to these two main types of designata, the discussion of referential communication is subdivided into two parts: 1) references to persons, objects, or events; and 2) references to relations among these elements in the objective world. The first subcategory potentially contains an infinite number of members. In addition, man with his technological ingenuity is daily adding new members to this class, Since all the objects in his cultural environment are created by man, all of them are potentially meaningful. Consequently, the child, in contrast to most animals, encounters a very large number of meaningful objects which have to be encoded. The second subcategory contains a relatively smaller number of relations. It is, therefore, in some respect similar to the above-discussed topic of directive communication since both deal with relations. However, in early directive communication the child always represents one member of the relationship. This restricts the possible number of relationships to the number of psychological dimensions which the child has established between himself and the environment. In contrast, within the referential category of relations, a theoretically infinite variety of objects can enter into relationships with one another. Several members can be included in each relationship simultaneously on each pole of the dimension, and the relationships, therefore, can become quite complex, even though they are still restricted in number. Then they may tax or surpass the analytical ability of the child.

References to Persons, Objects, and Events   If an attempt were made to analyze the acquisition of the vocabularies of a large number of individual children, the task would be overwhelming and probably not very fruitful. Children come into contact with a large variety of objects, and as a result they acquire an equal variety of labels for these objects. Since each child lives in a different ecological niche, large individual differences in encounters with meaningful objects and in the acquisition of labels can be expected. A complete description, therefore, cannot be attempted. Generally, it has to be concluded from the work of Leopold (1948), from many of the early investigations of language development, and from the recent findings of Bloom (1970), that the child only speaks meaningfully of the objects and relations that he has learned to know intimately through his everyday experiences. This finding, however, does not entail the stronger hypothesis, that all well known objects are also labeled.

Two of the "objects" in the environment of the child with which he is most familiar are his parents. Since the parents sometimes are unavailable, enough negative instances for successful discrimination learning are provided. Consequently, the words for *father* and *mother* should appear very early in all languages. This suggestion has been affirmed consistently by a wide variety of studies. Concepts similar to that of "father" and "mother" are found early and universally. They can refer either to the natural parents only or include one or a few persons performing parental functions. Since the child is lacking in finer articulation skills at this early stage of development, he has to use his well trained babbling sounds to designate these conceptualizations. Variants of the babbling sounds *mama/ nana* or *dada/ baba*, consequently, appear universally as labels for parents and a few close relatives (Jakobson, 1962).

Similar considerations apply to the development of the child's concept of himself as an entity and agent. In the course of the sensorimotor period, the child learns to know himself as an actor and the cause of effects as well as the recipient of many influences from the environment. At the end of the first year he has also integrated his perceptions of his body parts into a more unified concept of bodily self. This concept is also soon expressed verbally. Environmental influences play a part in deciding whether he uses the term *baby* for himself, uses a simplified form of his given name, or uses mainly the pronoun *me* or *mine* to refer to himself. As reported in most protocols, the pronoun *I* appears relatively late. Though no detailed studies exist as to the reasons for this fact, it can be surmised that frequency phenomena and the variety of referents for which this pronoun is used may be the main explanatory variables. It has been reported repeatedly that adults, when speaking to young children, tend to replace the nominative case of the personal pronoun with the name or the label, i.e., *dada, mama,* of the person.

Even in the case of the two relatively simple and straightforward concepts of mother and father, developmental steps are encountered. In the beginning, the child sometimes does not differentiate verbally between the sexes when he refers to adults. This fact was demonstrated by the observations of Leopold (1939). *Dada* therefore can be used for both parents. Or in contrast, when the infant makes a differentiation between the sexes, he uses *dada* for all adult males he encounters, generalizing the term in a different manner. On the other hand, children often have difficulties in understanding that the term for father can apply also to other men, namely, fathers of other children, and not only to their own father. Most longitudinal as well as short-term and cross-sectional studies of children's vocabulary show that a few names of specific persons in the environment of the child are used early and generally in a way that is referentially correct. In addition to the labels for the parents, these may be the names for the nursemaid of previous times, for a sibling, or for a playmate. Sometimes they can be generalized to other persons who are similar with respect to a specific feature to the person originally named. In other cases, the name remains specific for one individual. Underextensions, correct delimitation of the set especially if it has only one member, and overextensions all can be demonstrated in the concepts children connect with labels for persons. The same phenomenon was demonstrated by Anglin (1975) with regard to the child's verbal classifications of objects. From the variety of these concept-label associations it appears that the relationship between the child's perceptual and cognitive discrimination abilities and his establishment of verbal labels for his concepts needs a somewhat more intensive discussion. Although the controversies in this field have by far not yet been resolved, a preliminary analysis can be provided by looking at the attributes of objects and persons that the child differentiates and encodes verbally.

Concepts and categories are formed in accordance with specific features of superficial appearance or with their functional significance for the child. The discussion of the mechanisms of feature detection and their linguistic encoding is therefore indispensable in the study of concept formation. Chapter Three summarized how the infant learns to differentiate between specific qualities of objects. This differentiation is based upon the structure and functioning of the sensory organs and is a prerequisite for the survival of the individual and for effective communication. Although the evidence for early feature detection is strong, its specific relevance for category formation is currently being disputed. The findings and arguments of Rosch (1973, 1975) suggest that categories are formed around prototypes, which are established by a predominantly unconscious averaging of the values of some features. Accordingly, they would not be based upon the logical combination of mutually independent features. These prototypes appear to be similar to the schemas postulated by Piaget or to the global concepts described by Heinz Werner and other psychologists of the cognitively oriented European schools. According to Heinz Werner's orthogenetic law of development, specific features would be only gradually differentiated and articulated in the course of cognitive development. In accordance with the principle that cognitive developments have to precede those in the linguistic realm, it would have to be expected that adjectives, which are mostly employed to express these features verbally, appear somewhat later in the vocabulary of young children. This expectation would be in accordance with the ideas and data profferred by the Clarks. Eve Clark (1973) argued cogently that specific features are gradually added to a concept, a process which leads to the understanding of finer subdivisions within one domain. The polar adjectives of size, length, etc., are the examples most commonly adduced to support this argument. In contrast to the ideas of the Clarks, the prototype hypothesis and the orthogenetic law suggest that the infant does not have partial entries only for his early concepts but a global, undifferentiated whole.

A difficulty for the establishment of straightforward relations between cognitive developments and their verbalization arises, however, from an important differentiation made by Nelson (1974). She stressed the difference between features that are critical for the definition of a concept, i.e., the core characteristics, and those that are only incidental and therefore optional. From a logical standpoint, it would be completely redundant for any speaker to encode in his message the diacritical features together with the label for the concept they help to define. If the child is aware of the information needs of his partner, then it has to be expected that the core features are cognitively differentiated but would not be linguistically encoded in the same context as the concept they define. Exactly this phenomenon is reported in all the discussions of the early development of qualifiers, beginning with Stern and Stern (1907) to the most recent summaries of Brown (1973), Edwards (1973), Bloom (1973), and Bloom, Hood, and Lightbown (1974). The only exception to this principle is found in the case of adjectives that are employed by parents in an interpersonal guidance function. Examples of such uses are, *The knife is sharp* and *The stove is hot*. The child often produces similar constructions though the adjectives describe an inherent attribute of the object. The parental model together with the functional significance of these sentences suffice to explain these exceptions.

A high degree of agreement exists regarding the type of vocabulary appearing earliest and most commonly in child speech. From a survey of the studies published during the nineteenth century and from their own data, Stern and Stern (1907) differentiated three stages of vocabulary development: 1) a substance stage, in which the child principally uses nouns; 2) an activity stage, in which the child adds verbs; and 3) a relations stage, which can be subdivided according to two aspects: when the child adds terms dealing with characteristics of objects and when he expands his vocabulary to include relations among objects. Though the sequence of stages described by the Sterns is not to be taken as absolute and exclusive, the general principle of a sequential, stage-like acquisition of vocabulary was again noted in the literature survey of McCarthy (1954) and in some of the recent detailed analyses such as that of Bloom (1973).

The main objection probably should be raised against the terminology employed by the Sterns. The research of Bower on the early development of the object concept, which was discussed in the previous chapters, studies on perceptual development (E. Gibson, 1963), and those of mother-child interaction (Moerk, 1975c) lead to the following conclusion: The child recognizes, conceptualizes, and labels objects whose substantivity he has never experienced and in many instances could not even experience. Visual perception, figure-ground contrasts, and pictures as presented in children's picture books suffice for the child to conceive of objects and to label them. The reports of one early student of child language development (Chamberlain, 1900) shows that the word *moon* was acquired early and was even generalized to many substantive objects, though the child surely never experienced the substantivity of the moon. Similarly, one of the first words of the writer's own child was *lighty*, em-

ployed for square lights on the ceiling as well as for square air out-
lets of the cooling system. Neither of these objects was ever touched
or handled. It appears, therefore, that object concepts and their
pertinent labels are developed through a broader range of operations
and not only those motor activities that let a child perceive the substantivity of objects.

This conclusion is further supported by the study of the qualifiers that are used most commonly in connection with the early object labels. Independent of whether Leopold's list (1939, I:140-148)
or that of Bloom (1970:245-246) is studied, a large percentage of the
adjectives reported refer to visual characteristics of objects. Brown
(1957) reported similarly that sixty-seven percent of young children's
nouns carry implications of visual contour and eighty-three percent
those of size. Some substantive characteristics of objects admittedly
belong to the core characteristics of any object and therefore need
not be encoded according to the above argument of Nelson (1974).
Other substantive and tactile qualities are encoded verbally, such as
fuzzy, heavy, cold, sticky. The large subsets of adjectives in both
lists refer to visual characteristics, which proves that, when infants
and young children conceptualize objects, they attend to many
characteristics other than substantivity.

It appears that the Sterns' terminology for the second stage, the
activity stage, is also too narrow and therefore partly incorrect. As
argued in detail in Chapter Three, the child is not only active in
the motoric sense, but he is equally engaged in sensory-perceptual
operations and in volitional processes. As previously mentioned,
early authors such as Meumann (1908) were so impressed by this
volitional and emotional aspect of early language that they disal-
lowed the child any objective/referential intentions in his early
words. Although this extreme conclusion has been corrected, it is
generally accepted that the infant has a broad conceptualization of
change/movement/dynamics/efficacy/magical causality before he
differentiates this protoconcept into the various kinds of activities
and events as conceived by adults in Western cultures. Freud, Piaget,
and Werner have demonstrated this undifferentiated conceptualization
of infants in lengthy discussions. If the examples and arguments of
these authors were accepted, then a broader range of concepts would
need to be comprised under the class of *verbs* than only those pertaining to motoric activity. Though this hypothesis is *post hoc,* it is
nevertheless in full accordance with an abundance of data from the

study of language development. It is also self-evident that, at least in the Indo-Germanic languages known to the writer and in the grammars describing these languages, the same broad conceptual realm is subsumed under the grammatical class of verbs. The more refined the scientific grammatical descriptions, the more subsets have been differentiated, as would be expected according to Werner's orthogenetic law. In contrast to the progressive differentiation of this class, linguists such as Fillmore, Postal, and Lakoff recently suggested that adjectives be included in the class of verbs. Though it is not attempted here to analyze their arguments in detail, it appears that developmental and psychological evidence points in the opposite direction. One type of phenomena is transitory, dynamic, and changing, and these are encoded as verbs or at least with labels functioning as verbs. The other type of phenomena is relatively permanent, stable, and consistent. These phenomena are encoded as adjectives or in an equivalent fashion. A good example for this distinction can be found in the case of *waking up* versus *being awake*, *getting scared* versus *being afraid*. The copula *to be* fulfills a completely nondynamic and primarily grammatical function. It is, as generally known, omitted by young children.

The above argument regarding the terminology to be employed for the description of the category of verbs is not so much meant as a refutation of the conceptualization of the Sterns but more as a refinement and supplementation. It is, namely, self-evident from any list of early word classes that a large percentage of the child's verbs refer to motor activities. It is, however, equally clear that a description striving toward completeness has to account for verbs such as *need*, *want*, *see*, *look*, or *watch*. That all these words can express very dynamic experiences is demonstrated by temper tantrums of two-year-olds or the engrossed astonishment with which children handle some new experiences.

The last stage in the classification of the Sterns, the relations stage, has been partially discussed above. The child's encoding of the characteristics of objects has been summarized in connection with the establishment of concepts of objects and the acquisition of labels for them, since objects cannot be conceived and differentiated without attention being paid to their characterizing and incidental features.

A more primitive type of relations, those referring to the primordial directedness of the child toward his environment, has been discussed above in the section on the directive function. The relations discussed in the following section, and which the Sterns referred to, are those existing between objects and events in the environment. They therefore fall under the referential function of language. These relations may include those between the child himself and the environment, if it is probable or evident that the child refers to himself as one object, albeit a special one, which can be related in a manifold number of ways to other objects in the environment.

Structurally Complex References to Relations The references to object relations that are most clearly expressed in the nonverbal and verbal behavior of the young child are summarized below. Because more generality between individual children exists in the relational concepts they develop, the discussion can refer to specific relational structures.

Two of the most basic relationships are those of ± presence and ± existence. The understanding of these relationships leads to the establishment of an object concept and to the gradual construction of the child's understanding of the objective world generally. Piaget has demonstrated through observations of his own children that these two concepts are not differentiated by the very young infant. The distinction between both concepts develops in a rudimentary form only during the course of the first year of life. A wide variety of recent research as quoted in preceding chapters has resulted in the following picture of the sequence of steps leading to the acquisition of this distinction: The neonate reacts with the orienting reflex to suddenly appearing stimuli. Later a searching movement with the eyes and hands is added; the child may request an object by means of crying, or he may show astonishment when he does not see an object where he expected it to be after the removal of a cover. Finally, he may point toward a place where a desirable object is usually kept and name the object (Greenfield and Smith, 1976) although the object is at the moment out of his sight. These last two instances provide evidence for the fact that the infant has already differentiated + existence from − presence. This implies a mental representation of the absent object. One of the first verbal expressions, "all gone," signifying the absence of an object, does not yet contain this differentiation between both types of absence. However, as soon as the child starts asking questions, conveying the message "Where is ——?" or even if he only names an absent object with interrogative or directive intonation, it becomes fully evident that he infers the existence of objects that he does not perceive at the moment. This last cognitive achievement is based upon further development of memory and representation, which allows the child to conceive of goals, objects, and events that he encountered in the past and that will reappear in the future.

A development which has been intensively discussed (Holloway, 1967) in psychological research since Piaget (1952, 1954), and which was summarized in the preceding chapter, is the development of the understanding of spatial structures or relationships. The nonverbal modes whereby the child communicates his insight into these relationships were also previously summarized. What remains to be shown here is how the verbal means supplement and finally supersede the nonverbal means of communication. A crude expression of spatial relationships in the verbal dimension is already found in the infant's use of demonstrative pronouns. The prolocative *there* signifies the specific relationship of one object to the child himself or to other objects. Spatial relations with the self as center are generally conceived and were defined by Kant as some of the primary and basic categories of understanding (Deese, 1969; Piaget, 1952). The child soon associates certain objects with their habitual locations and names either the object when seeing only the location or the location when seeing the object. Piaget (1954) has provided a detailed description of the development of a concept of space, and Greenfield and Smith (1976) have reported on the earliest steps of the encoding of this understanding in verbal form. With the beginning of more-word sentences relations in space are often expressed as noun-noun structures such as *baby highchair, baby room* (Brown, 1970; Brown and Bellugi, 1964; Miller and Ervin, 1964). Brown (1973), in summarizing the appearance of grammatical morphemes, demonstrated that *in* and *on* are, on the average, second in rank order of appearance. Similar early references to location or spatial relations have been reported throughout in the literature. They are often connected with a request, as for example when the child wants to be picked up and says *up. Down, out,* and *in* are several of the other adverbial forms which are used by children instead of verbs and convey a request together with spatial directions. Since physical activity and especially locomotion are intrinsically embedded in the spatial field in which they occur, many action words contain spatial connotations. It was demonstrated by Piaget (1954) and also recently summarized by Flavell (1970) that it takes a long time and considerable cognitive advancement for the child to construct a Euclidian representation of space. The early vocabulary of children refers accordingly only to topological space. Examples of words referring to spatial relationships derived from two children ages twenty-four and twenty-five months are: *at, away, away from, down, here, home, in, off, on, out, there, to, under, up, where.* Most of these terms refer only to topological space, and only primitive roots of Euclidian space appear in some of them.

The close semantic and developmental tie between the deictic gesture, the demonstrative pronouns *that* or *this*, and the prolocatives *there* and *where* has been pointed out by several authors. These locative signs all refer to location only (*at, on, in*), which is the simplest category of locative description (H. Clark, 1973). Signs describing more complex locative relationships, such as direction, negative direction, or path, generally appear later in the early vocabulary of children.

It is not necessary to repeat the description of how an understanding of the temporal dimension develops. This was accomplished to a sufficient extent in Chapter Three. Generally, it can be concluded from the available evidence and especially from the work of Leopold (1949, III:98-99), Lewis (1951), and Piaget (1954) that the infant develops a vague concept of the past and future as differentiated from the present a considerable time before he expresses this distinction in language. This dim awareness of time is first conveyed in an equally undifferentiated way through verbal means.

Even after the child has begun to express temporal relations verbally, the present is still the tense employed predominantly, often morphologically marked as the present progressive *-ing* or with the adverb *now.* These two morphemes appear at the age of approximately two years. Ausubel and Sullivan (1970) reported that on the average the word *today* appears at twenty-four months, *tomorrow* at thirty months, and *yesterday* at thirty-six months.

The *future* orientation of the child, which only extends over a relatively short time span, is mostly still encoded by means of verbs in the present tense or by means of verbs for volition such as *want, need,* etc. Other preliminary forms of expressing future-oriented intentions are reported by Leopold. His child was saying *Mommy bath* when she wanted to express that her mother was getting ready to have a bath. *Lie down* was an announcement that the child was going to lie down, and *ask Papa on* served to express her wish that her father should put something on. Leopold concluded, therefore, that his child was aware of the immediate future but had no trace of a grammatical form for the future tense.

The next temporal dimension that is morphologically clearly differentiated is the past. Forms for the irregular past and somewhat later for the regular past are encountered from around two or two and one-half years on (Brown, 1973). The more complex the temporal relationship, the later its appearance in verbally encoded form (E. Clark, 1970, 1971). Much of the learning on how to encode temporal relationships continues until the school years. During the preschool years the child is still prone to confuse verbally the dimensions of past and future, although the meaning *nonpresent* is clearly expressed. This phenomenon is quite extensively analyzed in the literature on language development. Linguistic research demonstrates that the same phenomenon is found in several older languages and even in modern Hindustani (Nakamura, 1966).

In the case of temporal relations, it is probable that cognitive and language development interact very closely and influence each other. The availability of linguistic differentiations as acquired through formal education may permit the child to order time relations cognitively in a more complex form. A similar phenomenon is currently encountered in several fields of the social sciences, in which the method of time series analysis serves as a prerequisite for a more differentiated analysis of temporal relations and for a better understanding of temporal patterns. This topic, though very fascinating and educationally important, lies outside the realm of the present study.

Finally, a very basic and pervasive relationship that is very salient for the child and is experienced in a very personal manner is the relation of causality. The child encounters cause-effect relations in the most intimate manner when he handles objects and when other persons handle him as an object of their activity. In a less personal way he has much opportunity to observe other persons affecting objects or to see animals as causes of effects. Additionally, in the course of his play and the observation of his surroundings, he observes objects affecting other objects. As summarized in the previous chapters, the latter form of causality may be interpreted by the infant in an animistic way and, therefore, may not be differentiated cognitively from personal efficacy.

These causal relations are predominantly expressed in the English language and in other languages whose acquisition has been studied extensively by means of syntactic structures. As discussed in a previous section, the young child predominantly uses verbs to describe physical acts. Many of these acts are directed toward an object and many of the verbs, consequently, are transitive ones.

Although it is difficult to ascertain how the child structures his perceptual experiences, his behavioral structures can be easily observed, recorded, and analyzed. The same applies to his verbal structures. A study of the homologies between both types of structures is, therefore, possible. Since the behavioral structures appear long before the verbal ones, a forming and molding influence of the former upon the latter would be possible.

PARALLELS BETWEEN THE SYNTAX OF NONVERBAL BEHAVIOR AND THE STRUCTURES OF VERBAL BEHAVIOR

When psycholinguists studied the topic of language acquisition during the last two decades, they applied most of their energy to the exploration of the grammatical development in children. Unfortunately, this interest was often accompanied by the neglect of many other important aspects. Practically no attempt was made to compare the grammatical structures with other nonverbal structures. The linguist Pike and his associates present one important exception to this rule. Explanations of the grammatical structures were, consequently, in most instances restricted merely to linguistic analyses. As a result of this state of affairs, several respected scientists concluded, and correctly so it seems, that linguistic facts alone cannot suffice to explain the acquisition of the syntactic aspect of language. At present the well known way out is to postulate "innate structures." This then exempts the scientist from explaining causally the development of these structures. Whether this is necessary or conducive to the exploration of this question has been discussed already in Chapter Two.

The present approach is different: an analysis of which of the emerging linguistic structures is preceded by an identical or at least a very similar behavioral structure. A complete survey of the literature on linguistic structures is not attempted here. Valuable summaries of data can be found in the publications of Braine (1963b), Brown and Fraser (1963), Brown and Bellugi (1964), and Ervin (1964), as well as in the more recent publications of Brown (1970), McNeill (1970a, b), Menyuk (1971), Cazden (1972), and Brown (1973). The more recent linguistic and especially psycholinguistic analyses of language behavior have also gone one step further in not relying any longer upon merely syntactic descriptions. After the pioneering work of Fillmore (1968) and Chafe (1970) in linguistics, Bloom (1970), Brown (1970, 1973), Schlesinger (1971a, b), and Ervin-Tripp (1971) utilized this semantic approach for the description of the meaningful structure of the child's developing language. Since nonverbal behavior is meaningfully structured, and since the meaningful structure of verbal behavior has been extensively explored during the past five or more years, it should be easy to demonstrate the parallels between both types of structures. Several attempts which relied primarily upon Piaget's approach to preverbal structures have been made to achieve this goal. They can be found in the articles of Edwards (1973), G. Wells (1974), and Moerk (1975a). Moerk and Wong (1976) have also tried to demonstrate this parallel while strictly relying upon observable behavioral structures without any reference to a specific theoretical system to interpret these structures. The findings derived from all these studies provide the basis for the present discussion of the parallels between both types of structures. The development of nonverbal structures was discussed in Chapter Three, where evidence was presented for each of the assertions about the existence of specific structures. Now an integration of these two strands of evidence can be attempted. A tabular survey of the structures is shown in Table 4.1 and explained in more detail in the paragraphs below.

It is commonly observed and acknowledged that most of behavior is composed of holistic acts and not of single atomistic movements. This unity can be observed on the level of the individual muscle movement, on the plane of the movement of one extremity, as well as in the movement of the entire body, or in the completion of one specific goal-directed act. However, only intentional acts generally enter the focus of consciousness. Since full awareness is also a prerequisite for language behavior, only the more global and intentional acts are considered at present.

Act-Sentence

Basic parallels are fully apparent and are therefore only briefly summarized. An "act" of a person which has a clear beginning and end is analogous in this respect to the linguistic unit, the sentence. The main factors constituting an act are an actor, a motor or internal action which is anchored in time, space, and society, and finally the

Table 4.1. Parallels between structures of nonverbal behavior and linguistic structures

Nonlinguistic structures	Linguistic structures
Act	Sentence
Concatenations of actions	Coordinating and subordinating of clauses
Overlapping behavior episodes	Embedding of clauses
Differentiated combinations of cognitive structures	Differentiated combinations of sentence constituents
Person/Object - Object	Noun[a] - Noun
Action - Object	Verb - Noun
Person - Action	Noun - Verb
Person - Action - Object	Noun - Verb - Noun

[a] The noun can be replaced by a proper name or a pronoun.

direction of the act toward one or more objects. The obvious equivalents in sentences are the subject, verb, prepositional phrases or adverbs, plus the direct and indirect objects.

Concatenating of Actions—
Coordinating and Subordinating of Clauses

Individual acts can enter into close relationships with each other, so that it often becomes difficult to draw a precise borderline between them. The same difficulty is generally also encountered in language, where sentences are coordinated or subordinated to each other. The speaker or writer often finds it difficult to decide whether he shall subdivide one statement into two sentences or formulate it as one sentence using coordinate or subordinate clauses. Since the relationships among the units of the larger act or statement can vary widely, different forms of concatenation have been developed. The person who produces an utterance searches for an expression best fitted to what he wants to describe. If he feels that the meaningful units are closely connected, then he will express this connection by means of one sentence with subordinate or coordinate clauses. If, on the other hand, he feels that the facts warrant a separation, he will produce two separate sentences. The relationship between the structure of the acts and actual sentence construction is, consequently, not only one of parallelism but one of dependency: The behavioral cognitive facts constitute the independent variables and the verbal utterances the dependent variables. A structural parallel of both forms, is, therefore, a logical necessity.

Overlapping of Behavior Episodes—Embedding of Clauses

If acts attain even a minimal degree of complexity, they will extend over a considerable time span. It is then easily possible that, during the course of one act, other, shorter acts, which are often subordinated to the main act, are interpolated between the beginning and the end of this main act. Barker and Wright (1955) reported that seventy-three percent (median) of the episodes they observed overlapped simultaneously with one or more other episodes. Since language behavior is often not able to render completely the complexity of nonverbal behavior, a smaller percentage of overlapping descriptions can be expected. Such overlapping descriptions are widely encountered in the form of embedded sentences, and they have also been analyzed by linguists. The more primitive the language skills of a child, the less he will be able to render complex behavioral relationships in complex sentences. Piaget has demonstrated that preschool children still have difficulties in understanding the relationships among motor acts. Consequently, only a few embedded sentences would be expected in the verbal products of this age group. This hypothesis is again fully substantiated by even a cursory analysis of the sentences produced by young children. Although the nonverbal behavioral sequences of young children show some embedding, the embedded actions have to be of short duration or the child cannot grasp the relationships among all of them. Similarly, the adult loses his train of thought if too many subordinate clauses are embedded into the main clause. The same psychological laws, therefore, seem, to apply to embedding in the nonverbal as in the verbal realm, with the only exception that verbal embedding is more difficult than embedding of actions. Consequently, the nonverbal embedding develops earlier and antedates the verbal form of embedding. The identical developmental sequence was repeatedly encountered in other instances, which were discussed previously. A dependency relation, with the nonverbal structures constituting the more basic factors, is therefore again suggested.

Differentiated Combinations of Cognitive Structures and Sentence Constituents

Two types of causal relationships have to be distinguished in considering the single act. They are also differentiated syntactically. The first type of causal relationship could be labeled *reflexive* in that the agent is only the cause of his own activity without directly affecting any object besides him. The spontaneous movement of animate beings is the most basic example of this instance. The second type is the common one, when the agent directly affects an object. Grammatically, the difference between these two types is expressed in the form of intransitive versus transitive verbs, the latter requiring an object while the former does not. The single act in its simplest form consequently has either two or three elements, depending upon whether a reflexive causality or an object-directed act is described. From a syntactic perspective these elements are commonly labeled subject-verb-(object); from a semantic perspective the terms *agent-action-object* are common, though the terminology differs somewhat in the writings of the various semantically oriented authors. These acts are, of course, always performed in a spatiotemporal and social environment. If these latter mentioned aspects are attended to and encoded, the structure of the act and the structure of the verbal description will be considerably more complex. Adverbs, prepositional phrases, and indirect objects are the most common means of expressing these relations verbally.

Though a high degree of agreement exists regarding the basic units of the causal act and of the verbal means with which they are expressed, a controversy has developed about the structural arrangement of these units. Most grammarians and psycholinguists until recently have followed the old tradition, which was also maintained by Chomsky, namely, to subdivide the sentence first into a subject, a noun phrase, and a predicate or verb phrase. Each of the above-mentioned phrases can be subdivided: the verb phrase into a verb and noun-phrase. A two-level hierarchy was therefore postulated for the description of the basic units of the sentence. The data of Bowerman (1973) and of Sinclair-de Zwart (1973) on the speech of young children seem to demonstrate, however, that at least in some cases the subject-verb structure arises prior to the verb-object structure. Levelt (1970), employing a scaling approach and word relatedness data from adult subjects, also found the verb to be more closely related to the subject noun phrase than to the object noun phrase. This sequence of development would suggest that the verb phrase is not the fundamental sentence constituent as it was generally described. Instead of a two-step hierarchy of the simple sentence as described previously in the form:

$$\begin{array}{c} S \\ \diagup \, \diagdown \\ NP \quad VP \\ \diagup \, \diagdown \\ V \quad NP \end{array}$$

a one-level structure of the form:

$$
\begin{array}{c}
S \\
\diagup | \diagdown \\
NP\ V\ NP
\end{array}
$$

or a two-level structure of the form:

$$
\begin{array}{c}
S \\
\diagup\diagdown \\
NP\ \ V\ \ \ \ \ NP
\end{array}
$$

may more adequately describe the syntactic hypothesis, at least for some children and adults. That this fact may be more general than is commonly accepted is suggested by the fact that Leopold's daughter also began with subject-verb constructions before she added verb-object utterances. In the present analysis this developmental perspective is followed; the subject noun phrase and the verb and the object noun phrase are treated as hierarchically equivalent constituents of the young child's sentence; and the postulated intervening node of a verb phrase is omitted.

With three basic elements of the sentence, three two-unit combinations are possible if sequential arrangements of the units in the combination are neglected. These combinations would be subject-verb, subject-object, and verb-object. In addition, one structure combining all three elements is possible, not considering differences in sequential arrangements. As known from an abundance of research on the development of language structures, all four of these structures appear in early speech, with the two-word units generally appearing before the three-word structures. Idiosyncratic differences seem to determine which of the two-unit utterances is used first and which ones are used more often. The fact that all three two-unit constructions appear early in the speech of most children and that they often serve to convey three-element messages suggests that the full three-unit construction is grasped without being immediately expressed in speech. Bloom (1970) postulated a "reduction transformation" to explain this phenomenon, It appears improbable, however, that the child while still in the two-word stage would be able to construct a three-unit linguistic structure and to apply to it an additional linguistic transformation to arrive at the surface structure. The ideas presented in the previous chapter on the gradual establishment of "subroutines" (McKay, 1968) or "modularizations" (Bruner, 1971), which run off more or less automatically and permit the child to build more complex structures by combining two or more subroutines, appear more plausible. According to this hypothesis, the child at the two-word sentence level would not yet have built up subroutines consisting of more-word units and, therefore, would remain restricted to combining, two at a time, those linguistic units that he has already formed, namely, single words. That the child is, nevertheless, communicating the entire message consisting of three or more elements is argued for on the basis of a variety of evidence in the next chapter, when the combination of various communication channels in the process of message transmission is discussed. This explanation is supported by the identical phenomenon encountered in second-language learning, when it is based upon everyday interaction and not upon formal instruction. In this case also the adult second-language learner first communicates with one-word utterances and supplements his meager verbal message by means of nonverbal cues. In this instance it is fully evident that only linguistic processing limitations prevent the formation of longer sentences.

The continuity between the nonverbal behavioral and conceptual structures should become even clearer when the next chapter exhibits how nonverbal or verbal message elements can be substituted almost *ad libitum* when environmental or psychological variables are conducive to it. For the present it remains only to demonstrate the exact parallels between both types of structures by means of a few linguistic examples, which are found in any description of early language.

The first type of causal structure, which was labeled reflexive in the present discussion and which refers to the subject-intransitive verb structure, is exemplified by utterances such as *Adam write, Eve read* (Brown, 1973), or *Airplane bye* (Menyuk, 1971). Locomotory movement is the most common phenomenon described with these structures. Brown (1957) reported that sixty-seven percent of children's verbs name animal or human movement. Yet activities such as reading and writing, which are more "passive" activities, are also referred to. It is evident, therefore, that children at this stage have developed a category of "action" that is relatively broad and abstract, coming closer to a concept of *activity* or *operation* than to *motor movement*. In respect to transitive causality four structures are expected, three partial ones and one consisting of all three elements.

The subject-transitive verb structure is exemplified by the utterances: *Mommy fix, Adam put* (Brown, 1973), *Mommy bounce* (Mommy bounces the child), and *Mommy push* (Bloom, 1970).

The predominance of a human subject acting as a causative agent is seen in these examples as well as in most of the others in the literature. From the context of the communication it is also clear in most cases what the intended object of the action is. The message, therefore, is semantically and structurally complete, even if one element is communicated in a different channel. Since the causative influence upon an object is described in these messages, the causative action is naturally more explicit than in some of the previous examples referring to spontaneous activity and intransitive verbs.

Subject-object constructions have been described extensively by Bloom (1970) and have also been summarized by Brown (1973). A few examples from Brown's summary are presented: *Mommy pumpkin* (Mommy is cutting the pumpkin), *Eve lunch* (Eve is eating lunch), *Mommy sock* (Mommy is putting the child's sock on the child), *Mommy lunch* (Mommy is fixing lunch). Again, it is evident from the situational context that the child had grasped the entire situation, including the activity, and had meant to convey a complete message. It is especially clear in this case how redundant the verbal encoding of the activity is for somebody who shares the contextual information with the speaker. The child, therefore, conveys a message in the most parsimonious way without reducing its informational value. Again, a wide variety of actions are implied in this construction. To subsume the simple physical act of cutting, the more prolonged procedures of eating and dressing, and finally the complex sequence of acts which comprise the preparation of lunch under the same structure, the child has to have formed a broad category of action or operation. The cause-effect relationship pertaining between these agents and objects is, accordingly, also broad and varied.

Verb-object structures occur very commonly in the speech of young children. For the sake of convenience most examples are again taken from Brown (1973): *Hit ball, put light, change diaper.* A clearly observable action upon an object, i.e., a cause-effect relationship, is described in these utterances. In the following instances, however, *hear horn* (Brown, 1973), *see boy, see sock* (Braine, 1963a), the child employs what some linguists call "state verbs." This construction presents an obvious difficulty for the hypothesis that verb-object structures express a causal relationship, with the verb representing the action and the object being the recipient of the action.

At best it could be argued that the object/person or stimulus observed exerts a causal influence upon the person experiencing the sensation. Chafe (1970) accordingly labeled the role of the perceiving person *experiencer.*

This question has not yet been explored in detail and cannot be fully discussed at present. Only a few leads are mentioned, which suggest partial answers: First, it was repeatedly pointed out in the preceding sections that the category of action that the child must have formed appears to be very broad. If he would not have formed such a broad category, he would not treat the various types of action named equivalently, as is demonstrated by distributional evidence. The term *operation* was therefore suggested in place of that of *action* as better representing the breadth of the category. Second, a continuum of activeness can be easily demonstrated in the terms of perception. From the terms *exploring*, to *attending*, to *watching*, and finally to the casual unintended and fleeting perception of a meaningless stimulus, all degrees of active involvement can be implied and expressed. As discussed in Chapter Three in connection with the orienting reflex and as known from the description of the child's "curiosity drive," children are mostly quite intensively involved in their perceptual exploration of the world. The "action" characteristics of perceptual terms, therefore, may be much more vivid for the child than for the adult. Finally, the infant's "omnipotent behavior" (Freud), anthropological research on the "evil eye" and on the assumed impact of the hearing of secret words or magic chants suggest that, on a more primitive level of human cognition, human sensory activity is perceived as much more efficacious/causative. Such a perception could induce the infant and young child to generalize the verb-object construction to cases in which the action as well as the cause-effect relationship are not obvious or even plausible for the adult. The same dynamics could have led to these structures in the course of the evolution of languages.

Though the above suggestions may be more or less plausible, no definitive explanation can be offered at the present. Much more linguistic research on the meaning component of language and more cognitive/psycholinguistic data on the development of meaningful concepts are needed to make more than tentative suggestions.

The last structure that can be derived from the three discussed elements is that of subject-verb-object or agent-action-object (recipient). Because it is more complex, it appears less frequently in the early speech of children. It was argued by several authors before, and it is demonstrated in Chapter Five, that complexity, however, is not always the only reason for the infrequency of this construction. Often some of the basic elements are fully obvious from the context, and the child encodes verbally only the informationally necessary elements. In accordance with these arguments, Brown (1973:174) demonstrated that several children use other three-term relations that mostly include locatives more frequently than the agent-action-object construction. Even more impressive is the evidence offered by McNeill (1966) regarding one of Brown's subjects at an early stage of language development: From forty-nine three-term constructions only four were agent-action-object constructions. Besides linguistic sentence-processing constraints, other variables, such as informational requirements, therefore have to be considered in the explanation of sentences that are incomplete from a purely syntactic/linguistic perspective.

Examples for these basic three-element structures are found relatively rarely in the published literature. Maybe investigators are more impressed by the irregularities in child speech and do not feel the regular expressions deserve closer analysis. Some of the latter are: *I ride horsie*; *I beat drum*; *Adam hit ball* (Brown, 1973). Menyuk (1969) provided two examples that are somewhat different in content though identical in structure: *Daddy wash hands*; *My mommy make eggs*. In these latter examples the child describes other persons and not only himself as the agent performing the action. In addition, while the recipient in these constructions is mostly an inanimate object, *hands* in the sentence *Daddy wash hands* is semantically different. Similarly, *horsie* and *eggs* in two of the other examples are less directly or at least differently affected by the activity described than are *drum* and *ball*. It appears, therefore, that the young child has not only formed a broad category of "action" but also a broad and flexible one of "object of an action."

Problem of Word Order

One problem was left unmentioned during the entire discussion above, that is, the problem of word order. The possible structural combinations mentioned above were discussed as if order were unimportant or random. A wide range of evidence proves, however, that individual children in their utterances at various times and different children from a considerable range of linguistic communities are quite consistent in the word order they employ. Brown (1973:

156–157) provided a wide variety of contradictory evidence on word
order acquisition and use from studies encompassing many cultures
and languages. This evidence does not need to be repeated here.
Only a few preliminary conclusions and suggestions are made. First,
in spite of the wide range of differences attested to by Brown, it
appears that with very few exceptions (Slobin, 1970) children encode
the subject before the other elements of the sentence. This is
logically and communicationally necessary, since the topic has to be
defined before a comment about a topic becomes meaningful. In
accordance with the previous remarks on multichannel communication and its more complete analysis in Chapter Five, exceptions
to these rules have to be expected: In some cases, the topic may be
specified sufficiently by situational evidence or by nonverbal message
elements, so as not to need verbal specification. In some of the
examples quoted by Braine (1971b) the communicational function
seems to have been similar though a little more complex. Braine
mentions that during one stage in Gregory's speech the orders *Fall
down rabbit* and *Rabbit fall down* were seemingly equivalent. A
variety of not yet systematized evidence in the protocols collected by
this writer suggests that this may be a case somewhat similar to that
of topicalization. The full message of the child in the first instance
may have been: *He fell down; the rabbit I mean.* The same interpretation would apply to the equivalence of *Gregory fix it* and *Fix
it Gregory*, i.e., *I fixed it, I myself, Gregory.* Similar constructions
also have been encountered in interactions when it appeared as if the
child had at the last moment doubted whether the topic was clear
enough from nonverbal evidence. In this case, too, the topic or subject was added at the end of the utterance with a barely audible or
inaudible break in the intonation contour. It appears therefore that
both, the rule of stating the subject before the predicate, as well as
the exceptions, make sense logically and communicationally. To prove
this interpretation, very detailed recordings of the vocal expressions,
especially the intonations, together with the nonverbally communicated information would be required.

Although children of various linguistic backgrounds seem to
prefer the verb-object order to that of object-verb, a higher degree
of flexibility is encountered in this case. As evident even from a
comparison of Indo-Germanic languages only, this flexibility is also
encountered in the language structures used by adults. No cognitive
basis for a general preference of either one of these is known at

present. It also would be expected that none will be found, since cognitive bases would come closer to being universal and rigid. This would be in contrast to the observed versatility and flexibility in many languages. Brown (1973) asserted correctly that no reasons are known why individual children seem to prefer specific orders. It is, however, also a fact that until very recently no detailed studies existed of the language input that individual children experience. Even the few studies that have been published to date and that are discussed in Chapter Six do not by far provide evidence detailed enough to establish any cause-effect relationships, which would show how specific forms of the input lead to specific preferred orders. The task of differentiating cognitive and therefore more universal bases for word order from training effects, which are more variable, still lies ahead.

SUMMARY AND CONCLUSION

The pervasiveness of information exchange, which proceeds in a wide variety of channels, has been demonstrated. In the course of this intake and production of information, the child learns to master the world effectively in creating classes of experiences and responses. Functional equivalences across items within each class are established. These equivalences may be established in a single channel of information transmission or they also may be formed across channels. Whereas classifications imply and facilitate transformations, functional equivalences result in symbolic representation, since one experience can stand for, i.e., can mean, something else.

The child not only communicates from birth on, he also starts very early to imitate the behavior of significant adults in his environment. Human beings are much more vocally active than other animal species on a relatively high level of brain development. This vocal activity of adults is predominantly verbal activity; the child through his early and persistent imitation acquires, therefore, the basic vocal skills necessary for later language production. In the course of developing his communicative competence, the child has to make increasingly finer differentiations and specifications as his cognitive mastery of the complex social and natural environment increases. He progresses thereby from purely expressive to directive and finally to referential communication. Since no innate means exist to refer to the large number of social and civilizational artifacts, the child has to rely more and more upon symbols picked up during his imitative play from the social environment. Communication in the verbal channel is herewith established.

However, from birth on, the infant conceives not only single characteristics of objects or single objects, but relationships among characteristics of single objects and between several objects and the social, spatial, and temporal surroundings. In trying to communicate these conceptualizations to his social partners, single gestures, sounds, or words do not suffice. Therefore, the infant needs to employ structured messages. These structured messages are produced for a considerable period and quite successfully by nonverbal means. As his cognitive complexity increases and as he deals increasingly with the man-made and symbolized environment, the child eagerly incorporates the communication system, his mother tongue, which provides structural means ideally suited to express his own structured conceptualizations. Messages expressing the presence, existence, or absence of an object, its membership in a class, *That is a* ——, or its intensional characteristics, *Apple red*, are, consequently, soon expressed in verbal form. The dynamically important relations of requests, rejection, and possession have been conveyed successfully for a long time through nonverbal means. Verbal elements, therefore, are only slowly added to the nonverbal messages, but do not soon replace them. Only when the child becomes more concerned with relations in his environment, and wants to communicate about them, does he have the need to express possession by verbal means only, e.g., *Daddy's hat*.

Nearly from the beginning of his life on, the infant has been actively involved in manipulating objects and persons in his environment. He is, therefore, profoundly aware of his action potential and his effects upon objects. He himself has also been manipulated frequently during the caregiving procedures and has observed other persons manipulating objects or moving in space and performing acts in temporal sequence. He has only a restricted range of nonverbal means to convey all these conceptualizations to social partners. Since he becomes increasingly inclined and nearly forced to convey some of these structured conceptualizations, he is again eager to incorporate some of the means which he finds pre-formed in the adult language system that surrounds him continuously. The vicissitudes of this progress from nonverbal to verbal communication, and the help that the infant receives from adults in his environment, especially from his mother, are described in detail in the following chapters.

chapter
five

Nonverbal Means of Message Transmission and Their Relationships to the Form and Content of Verbal Messages

THEORETICAL PERSPECTIVE

Formulation of the Problem

As implied by the title, the emphasis in this chapter is neither on sentences nor on the more primitive forms of verbal behavior, but on messages. The problem posed in any message exchange is how a communication partner who wants to share a conceptualization or experience with somebody else can achieve this goal. Formulated in this manner, the topic to be analyzed becomes much broader than mere verbal communication and even broader than the combination of verbal and nonverbal communication. Since in most communication situations a considerable part of the conceptualization to be shared is not directly conveyed but has to be extracted from situational and contextual cues, the context becomes an important part in the analysis of message transmission. The more two communication partners are familiar with each other, with the mutually shared context, and with their interpretations of this context, the more they can rely on these shared aspects and the less they need to convey behaviorally to communicate efficiently. This phenomenon is especially obvious in the case of mother and child: A high degree of familiarity with each other and with the relevant situational variables exists. Conceptualizations have to be adapted to the cognitive level of the child, too, and are therefore relatively simple. A high degree of communication efficiency, therefore, can be attained in such a situation even without the use of any verbal means. The first nine to twelve months of each child's life provide abundant evidence for this communication efficiency, since mother and child communicate all this time, although the child neither understands nor produces a single word.

The problem of message transmission so formulated would be too broad and diffuse to be managable in one chapter or even in an entire book. Research on nonverbal communication alone (Birdwhistell, 1970; Duncan, 1969; Hinde, 1972) encompasses a vast array. Research on situational and contextual influences upon message structures and contents has barely begun and is currently discussed primarily from a theoretical perspective under the vague heading "presuppositions." Since this research necessarily has to encompass aspects of meaning and function, it promises to become at least as complex as the domain of nonverbal communicational behavior. A narrower delimitation of the topic therefore has to be found. For the purpose of this book, not all aspects of nonverbal communication and contextual information are of equal importance. Common-sense observations and ample research evidence suggest that much that is encoded nonverbally during infancy and early childhood continues to be encoded in the same channels throughout life, resulting in a wide range of paralinguistic phenomena. Equally, a large proportion of contextual phenomena probably remains presupposed in ordinary conversation, such as the elocutionary aspect of affirmative sentences or aspects pertaining to the basic coordinates of interpersonal communication (see Goffman, 1974). Since much less research has been done on this latter aspect, all statements regarding it must remain preliminary. For the purposes here, only features of nonverbal and contextual information transmission are selected for discussion that are either superficially or formatively influential in language acquisition. Influences that affect the surface appearance of messages but not the underlying message structure are defined as superficial. This is the case, for example, when the context or the nonverbal message fulfills communicative functions by itself leading to abbreviated and apparently incomplete verbal utterances. Contextual and nonverbal features that have become structured on the preverbal level, and are then at a later stage expressed verbally, are designated as formative influences. The resulting semantic and syntactic features reflect these preverbal structures. In accordance with these intentions and delimitations, the discussion in this chapter is mainly restricted to the referential aspects of contextual, nonverbal, and verbal communication, since these aspects are increasingly conveyed verbally and thereby affect language acquisition most profoundly.

Kindred Conceptualizations of Communication

The observation that communication proceeds in several channels is not new. In the nineteenth century, W. von Humboldt asserted that this fact represents one important factor in language development and communication generally. Wundt (1900; see also Sebeok, 1974) wrote a long treatise on the communicational functions of gestures. Malinowski (1923) emphasized in most of his anthropological work the "context of the situation" as a profoundly important aspect. K. Bühler (1934) proceeded to clarify the functions that different channels fulfill in relation to verbal communication. He emphasized that in many instances the main content of the communication is transmitted by the nonverbal action and the environmental variables. When words are added, they often serve as a *diacritical verbal sign* only; this sign consequently does not need a surrounding verbal framework. In the case of the so-called one-word sentences, the single word is surrounded by that for which words are proxy, namely, the situational and behavioral cues that are visible to the receiver of the message. A few years later, Langer (1942), quoting the conclusions of K. Bühler, again emphasized the importance of the context for the understanding of verbal messages. The same theme was broadly expounded in anthropological literature for several decades during the first part of the century. Some authors stressed that some primitive tribes habitually would support their verbal messages by an abundance of gestures, or that they only could understand verbal communication that was supported by nonverbal cues. Although this later view has been proved incorrect in the meantime, it has been generally reaffirmed that nonverbal channels carry a high load of information in many situations. In the realm of philosophy, the role of context has been poignantly asserted in Wittgenstein's (1953) famous description of language as a game that is played in some context for some purpose. Wittgenstein combined contextual and pragmatic-functional aspects in the interpretation of verbal products. Following the lead of the psychologist Karl Bühler, several psycholinguists have accorded considerable attention to this topic. Slama-Cazacu (1961) has devoted an entire book to the exploration of the relationships between verbal utterances and their various contexts. This European tradition is strongly reflected in several publications of Rommetveit and his associates, especially in Rommetveit (1974). Carswell and Rommetveit (1971) as well as Slama-Cazacu (1968) have provided some experimental and observational evidence in support of their theoretical analyses.

Facts of multimodal communication necessarily had to be accorded more attention by investigators interested in social interaction of animals. Detailed analyses are encountered predominantly in the studies of ethologists. Marler (1965) pointed out that in nonhuman higher primates the response to a social signal and therefore, presumably, to its "meaning" depends also upon other variables, especially other accompanying signals in the context of the situation. Similarly, the volume edited by Hinde (1972) comprises a rich array of factual information and theoretical discussions of the modes of communication encountered in many species, including man.

From the above admittedly fragmentary and incomplete citations of previous literature, it can be concluded that the multidimensionality of communication is evident at least in principle. A wide range of factual observations have been discussed in the literature in support of this approach, though much remains to be attained in this respect. Recently, similar considerations have found acceptance in the approaches of the transformationalists in the United States, who discuss one aspect of multichannel communication under the term *presupposition*. Most of the pertinent analyses still deal with the definitional and conceptual problems arising from the enormous expansion of the domain of linguistic studies that resulted from the inclusion of contextual and nonverbal message aspects. Since this chapter is devoted almost exclusively to the relationships between situations and messages, a brief attempt at theoretical clarification of the conceptual questions that are involved appears required. It is intended to provide the necessary basis for the application of these ideas to the development of communicational systems in the infant and especially to the development of verbal communication.

Relationships Between Reality, Its Human
Representation, and Various Forms of Human Behavior

Two types of relationships have to be considered that are profoundly interdependent but nevertheless need to be kept separate conceptually. The first type pertains to the classical question of how man takes account of reality in representing it linguistically. This controversy goes back at least to Plato, who pondered the *physei-thesei* question. It was intensively discussed throughout the Middle Ages and is essentially still unresolved. No attempt therefore can be made to deal with this issue comprehensively. However, the most commonly accepted solution, which Morris (1938:26) termed "the classical tradition," is sketched briefly because it is adopted as the basis for the present analyses.

The second type of these relationships is more specifically pertinent to the present chapter. It concerns how man takes account of reality, physical or social, in not encoding it linguistically but by incorporating it otherwise into a message, namely, how he accounts for shared or presupposed elements of reality in his message structure without translating them into linguistic elements. In this case, reality elements are substituted for linguistic elements.

Language serves to communicate about reality, either the immediate reality as it is observed at a specific place and time by the speaker, or reality as it is remembered or anticipated. All three instances are basically very similar: Regardless of whether it is the immediate reality or some temporally distant aspect of it, human beings only can communicate about it as it is transformed by their perceptual-conceptual system. Saussure's dichotomy of *significant-signifie* therefore needs to be differentiated into a trichotomy to provide a category for the products of these perceptual-cognitive transformations, which in turn form the basis for verbal behavior. Broecker and Lohmann (1948) suggested the terms *Bedeutungsträger-Bedeutung-Bezeichnetes*, which can be rendered as signifier-meaning/concept-signified. Figure 5.1 provides a schematic representation of this relationship between behavior setting, conceptualization, and levels of linguistic encoding.

Since language is a code, it has to be about something whenever it is intended as referential communication. Meaningless babbling or the few instances of rhythmic-rhyming vocal products in songs or rituals which do not serve to communicate specific contents are only antecedents of or derivations from real language. Since language serves as a communication device for speakers, the transformations of and relationships to reality, their internal representations, and their expression in coded form have to be relatively homologous, consistent, and shared. This applies to all steps and variables that intervene between reality and verbal product. Otherwise, indi-

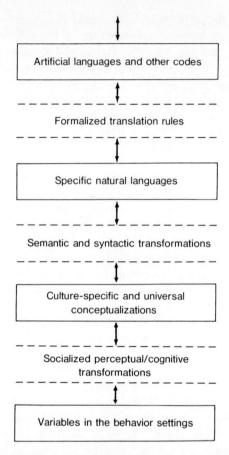

Figure 5.1 Relationship between language and reality: the classical tradition.

viduals could invent their own private language, which would be meaningless or at least misleading for the communication partner. Lewis Carroll's Humpty Dumpty, who assigned meanings to his words according to his momentary and shifting predilections, provides an example of this latter case. Instances of largely private codes that have lost their communicative functions because of this idiosyncracy are encountered in the communication of certain types of schizophrenics. Minor discrepancies from the common norm are encountered in teenage jargons and in languages of certain occupational groups which serve the function of excluding the noninitiate from the community.

Before the elements of Figure 5.1 are discussed more extensively, the overall design deserves a few remarks: The items inside the rectangles are seen as products, while the items between the broken lines are conceived of as "translation" rules and therefore come closer to representing processes. Double arrows are employed to suggest a consistent bidirectionality of cause-effect relations. The arrow at the top of the figure serves to indicate that, in principle, new languages or representational systems could be invented that are more abstract than current artificial languages, such as those of symbolic logic, physics, etc. A few remarks concerning each of the items in the figure should suffice to eliminate possible ambiguities. Since the general conceptualization is so well known, no detailed explanations appear to be necessary.

Variables in the Behavior Setting   Whereas the terminology that is employed by diverse authors differs, the range of phenomena encompassed is relatively similar. Under this aspect are generally considered phenomena of the physical surroundings, with special emphasis placed upon the world of objects and their relationships to each other. The extension of this topic is retained here; however, the emphasis is slightly shifted. For the young child, behavior settings are more restricted and more uniform than for the average adult. They are also more predominantly, and in our technological society almost exclusively, composed of "artifacts," i.e., products of human technology. With one important exception, it may take the city-born infant several years until he becomes somewhat acquainted with objects that are not man-made. Human beings represent the important exception. They attract the attention of the infant most consistently through their nonverbal behavior, their attempts to communicate with him verbally, or even only through their facial features. The aspects of the behavior setting that are relevant for the young child are, therefore, either the properties or the products of human beings. Consequently, the human infant encounters a reality that is already pre-formed and pre-structured by human beings. Since the same human beings and the same cultural heritage shape the nonverbal as well as the language models that are later provided for the child, the conceptual and structural relationships that the child will encounter later in his mother tongue are already formed and trained through this preverbal experience.

Socialized Perceptual/Cognitive Transformations Two aspects have to be differentiated in this domain. First are perceptual/cognitive transformations that are relatively universal for human beings and depend upon the structural and functional properties of the human organism. These result in a considerable number of conceptual universals when they are applied to relatively pervasive aspects of the natural or human environment. As argued in previous chapters, the uniformities may outweigh by far the culturally caused differences in the case of the human infant who grows up in the protection of the nuclear family and experiences universal physical and social needs.

The second aspect centers around the term *socialized* that is employed in the heading. Even if a considerable number of cross-cultural universals have to be expected, differences cannot be neglected. Considerable evidence has been accumulated showing how attitudes, values, and conceptualizations differ in various societies and how these attitudes are transmitted very early to members of the younger generation. Similarly, family structures, the group of persons giving care to the infant, the prevalence and uses of specific objects, etc., differ widely. These diverse cultural phenomena immediately affect the infant and cannot but shape his perception and categorization of the world.

Culture-Specific and Universal Conceptualizations In accordance with the two types of variables in the behavior settings and the two types of transformations discussed above, the conceptualizations established by the young child also should encompass both aspects, universal ones and culture-specific ones. The one point to be reemphasized is that the young child shares both of them, whether universal or culture-specific ones, with the adults in his environment.

Semantic and Syntactic Transformations Even though the Sapir-Whorf hypothesis has been discussed for decades, the pertinent problem is essentially still unresolved, though some recent studies by Rosch (1973, 1975) provide conceptual and methodological refinements for the conceptualization of this question. They also provide valuable data from a cross-cultural perspective. Generally, the findings of various investigators are sufficiently contradictory to justify the retention of the double arrow on the line in Figure 5.1 connecting conceptualizations and natural languages. This implies at least a partial retention of the Sapir-Whorf hypothesis, namely, the belief that linguistic transformation rules produce effects in both directions.

Linguistic transformation rules are a heritage of each cultural community and are transmitted to children. As argued above, consistent and relatively uniform rules have to exist that connect elements in the conceptual domain to those in the language domain. The extension of both domains, however, does not necessarily have to be exactly the same, nor does it need to be assumed that a strict one-to-one relationship exists between the elements of both sets. As soon as disambiguation mechanisms have been established, multiple-to-one relationships can occur in both directions and even can contribute greatly to the parsimony of the translation process.

Specific Natural Languages   In contrast to the similarities and probable universals in the behavior settings and the perceptual/cognitive systems, natural languages appear superficially very heterogeneous. Whereas cultural specificities are self-evident, it has also often been argued that the easy translatability between languages is proof of a high degree of homology between them. A distinction between surface phenomena and base structures, or between grammatical means and semantic intentions, permits the resolution of this seeming contradiction. Slobin's (1973) studies of cross-cultural aspects of first-language acquisition have provided evidence that the content and structures of the early speech of children are astonishingly similar across widely varying linguistic communities. This, too, indicates that there may be more uniformities among languages than are generally recognized. It appears highly improbable that the young child first acquires a more universal language and later abandons it completely and shifts over to the particularistic patterns of his mother tongue.

The same cultural community and the same adults to a large degree shape the child's behavior setting, his conceptual interpretation of this setting, and his means to communicate about it. Close homologies among all three aspects have to be postulated, therefore, to avoid the assumption that adults as well as children live simultaneously in three differently structured worlds: that of perceived reality, that of its cultural interpretation, and that of social communication. Because a high degree of harmony and correspondence are assumed as normal and taken for granted, general semanticists and philosophers have sounded alarm cries when they have encountered discrepancies among the three systems. The level of emphasis accorded these discrepancies must not be equated, however, with the seriousness of their nature.

Formalized Translation Rules and Artificial Languages   Since formalized languages have been fashionable in philosophical circles as attempted improvements on natural languages, and since other forms of formalized languages are being continuously developed in the diverse sciences, they have to be included in a diagram that intends to be encompassing. These codes are currently discussed quite often under the term *metalanguage* and are the object of valuable philosophical scrutiny. The Morse or Braille codes are the simplest examples of artificial languages, which derive from the application of very simple translation rules that do not at all transform the underlying natural language. The scientific systems of physics, chemistry, or even psychology and sociology represent more complex examples whose translation rules are intricate and often controversial.

Neither formalized languages nor their translation rules are relevant for the study of first-language acquisition, and they therefore require no further discussion in the present context. Attention immediately can be directed toward the incorporation of this classical model of the language-reality relationship to the specific purposes and problems of the present analysis. It has been argued in the preceding pages that the human child and the adult, too, are predominantly surrounded by human artifacts. McHale (1974:21) described this fact concisely: "...human artifice is the natural order for human beings." Ethological research leads to one further extension of this argument: Even the environment that is not man made is perceived and conceived according to the function it fulfills in the human order. All the "products" in Figure 5.1 therefore depend upon human conceptualization, and they in turn influence human conceptualization. Instead of a straight-line representation of this relationship, a closed feedback loop therefore would be more appropriate. This is presented in Figure 5.2.

Figure 5.2 suggests that conceptualization leads to behavior, whether nonverbal or verbal, and to the products of this behavior, both of which are important aspects of the behavior setting. The broken line between *artifacts* and *conceptualizations,* as contrasted with the other two continuous lines, is intended to symbolize that artifacts, produced during a specific act, can affect the conceptualizations of their creators or of other persons at subsequent points in time, but they cannot affect the conceptualizations that lead to their existence. An integration of Figures 5.1 and 5.2 suggests how the artificial languages of physics and chemistry lead, after several tech-

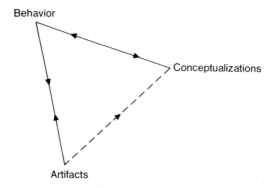

Figure 5.2 Feedback relations between language and reality.

nical translation processes, to the products of everyday use, which represent such a predominant part of technological-man's environment. The closed feedback model, while better representing the interdependencies and feedback processes than a straight line does, brings with it the drawback of suggesting a closure that is evidently in stark contrast to human cultural and civilizational openness. A spiral, combining the symbol for feedback cycles with the evidence concerning the multilayer aspect and the essential openness of human civilization, therefore would constitute the best figural representation of most of the characteristics to be depicted.

Concise Outline of Man's Multidimensional Communicative Space

For the purpose of the following analyses of multichannel communication, a reformulation of the above considerations in set-theoretical terms may be more conducive. The set of "products of human conceptualizations" consists of several subsets, such as material products, cultural objects, and linguistic phenomena. Across these subsets, one-to-one correspondences or other well defined relationships exist. Though a certain predilection may prevail in human conceptual functioning to employ predominantly members of specific subsets in the course of a single activity, the equivalence among members across subsets produces a high degree of flexibility and elements of diverse subsets can be combined in a single process or product. For example, in comic strips, where predominantly pictorial means are employed, verbal elements can be freely added in balloons. Gestures as well as objects can replace words in conversations, such as when the child hands an object to his partner and says, "Hold." Only the most obtuse of partners would grab the hand of the child and hold it instead of the object intended by the child. The evidence on early childhood speech, the phenomenon of comic strips as compared to high level painting and prose, and observations from the study of social class differences in speech suggest another hypothesis: In combining Kurt Lewin's field theory with the present conceptualization of the set and the subsets of products of human conceptualization, it can be suggested that, with less differentiated and more fluid cognitive states, the boundaries between the various subsets are less rigid and the elements from diverse subsets can be more easily combined into one cognitive product. This phenomenon appears to apply in developmental perspective as well as in respect to various levels of sophistication in cognitive functioning. For the present discussion only the developmental perspective is relevant. The three subsets of products of human conceptualization that appear to be most important for the understanding of communicational development and human communication are, therefore, subjected to closer scrutiny.

The subdivision between linguistic and nonlinguistic elements is most obvious and best established. Several approaches could be chosen in the subcategorization of either of these dimensions. A differentiation of linguistic phenomena into prosodic, semantic, and syntactic aspects would appear meaningful from developmental, pathological, and bilingual perspectives. To avoid an overly cumbersome analysis by including too large a variety of variables which then have to be considered separately, the linguistic dimension is not specifically subdivided. The nonlinguistic aspects of messages are subdivided in accordance with established practice and their apparent developmental significance into behavioral aspects, labeled *nonverbal communication,* and into object-related aspects labeled *behavior setting.* Further or different subdivisions may be heuristically fruitful and appear well worth exploring. An investigation into the extent that artifactual objects are employed as communication elements in distinction to natural objects appears, for example, promising. To take into account the literature, only the three dimensions of verbal communication, nonverbal communication, and shared aspects of the behavior setting are considered. The communicative space that is constituted by these three dimensions is sketched out in Figure 5.3.

The conceptualization as represented in Figure 5.3 is obviously not new in its principal aspects. It has been espoused in a very

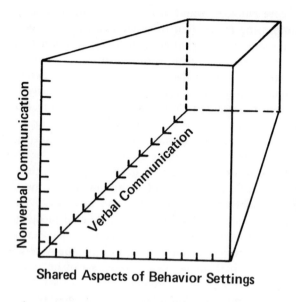

Figure 5.3 Three predominant dimensions of communicative space.

similar form by G. Mead (1934) and by K. Bühler (1934). Kainz
(1960) followed Bühler's ideas and emphasized both channels of nonverbal communication. In the more recent literature, a detailed discussion of this topic has been contributed by Denzin (1971). In
respect to language development, Bloom (1970) and Bowerman
(1970) have employed an approach somewhat similar to the one espoused here, thereby contributing valuable new perspectives on the
principles of language development. Consistent factual applications
of these ideas in the interpretation of developmental data, however,
are still rare. Bates, Camaioni, and Volterra (1975), Moerk (1975b),
Rodgon and Kurdek (1975), as well as Greenfield and Smith (1976)
have recently employed this approach in trying to ascertain the
semantic structure of the messages conveyed by their child subjects.

Since the conceptualization is comparatively well known, only
some brief theoretical remarks on the entire model and the individual
dimensions are required. More attention is devoted to the interrelationships among the three dimensions as they constitute messages at
various levels in ontogenesis.

The representation found in Figure 5.3 implies that communication encompassing fewer than three channels is the exception. Communication events in one channel alone, which would be represented as points on the axes, are quite rare. During the first year of life, communication consists of the shared aspects of the behavior settings in their combination with nonverbal means. This early communication would be represented by means of points in the frontal plane. The lowest horizontal plane would encompass messages that consist only of verbal encodings together with the contextual supports that make their unambiguous interpretations possible. The latter are approximately equivalent to what is discussed in linguistic circles as "presuppositions." This form of messages would be found predominantly in written communication and in cases of highly formal speech, such as certain scientific lectures. The leftmost vertical plane would encompass communication between complete strangers who share no presuppositions and who converse about temporally and spatially distant phenomena. Few instances can be imagined where such communication would proceed very successfully. The overwhelmingly predominant number of messages, however, would lie inside the communicative space delimited by these three dimensions and therefore would encompass all three aspects of communication.

The three coordinates are subdivided into equal intervals to suggest that quantitative and measurable relationships are envisaged. It is well known from common-sense observation and has been reported often in the literature that a high density of information in one channel leads generally to a reduced information load in one or both of the other channels. Evidence for this could be easily amassed. On the one extreme stands the need for explicitness in written communication. This can be contrasted with the frequent omissions of verbal elements in the communication of closely acquainted partners as described by Tolstoy in *Anna Karenina* (pt. V, ch. 18). Tolstoy presents the case of a loving couple who could communicate long and complex thoughts merely by writing the initial letters of each word of the various sentences. Vygotsky (1962) reported that this example was taken from the life of Tolstoy himself, who had proposed to his wife in this manner. Elsewhere (pt. VI, ch. 3) Tolstoy had pointed out in a more theoretical manner that spiritual communality can easily and often does replace orally communicated information. Similar principles, but seen from a different perspective, are encountered when communication in the oral channel is made difficult or impossible. Complex and rich means of nonverbal communication are then developed. Gestures are employed in noisy environments, between partners who do not share a common language, and when verbal communication is completely prohibited or impossible, such as is the case in certain religious orders or among deaf persons. Though these quantitative relationships are commonly recognized, actual attempts at measurement are rare. Some work in the field of information theory is tangentially relevant to this topic, and Moerk (1975b) has made a methodological proposal to ascertain these phenomena in ontogenetic perspective. He has suggested and exemplified the employment of a verbalization quotient which would permit the precise quantitative expression of the percentage of a message expressed verbally.

   Dimension of the Behavior Setting   As suggested by the labeling of the horizontal axis in Figure 5.3, the concern in the present discussion is not directed toward the entire range of the behavior setting but only toward the meaningfully shared aspects of it. In the developmental perspective, the early "sharing" of objects between mother and infant has been recently described by several investigators (Anderson, 1972; Blurton Jones and Leach, 1972; Bruner, 1975). Yeudovitskaya (1971) has explored in detail how adults repetitively present objects in the environment to their infants, beginning this exercise when the infants are only two to three months old. Since adults and children have very similar perceptual and motor systems, many aspects of this shared environment immediately will be perceived and structured by both in the same manner. In other cases the adult has ample opportunity to teach the child the culturally established meaning of specific objects. Not only does the mother show and demonstrate objects to her young child, but the child also directs the attention of the adult to objects or even directly brings objects to his mother for inspection and sharing (Blurton Jones, 1972). On an even more primordial level, the direction of the gaze that is shared by two communication partners represents also a sharing of their perceptions and conceptualizations. Werner and Kaplan (1963:77s) provided a fine analysis of the interaction of "turning-for-looking" and pointing in the development of referential communication that finally results in labeling. Because of this prolonged sharing process, both partners will be able to predict quite well the aspects of the environment to which each partner probably attends. The shared behavior setting therefore can carry a high amount of information for partners who are closely acquainted.

Dimension of Nonverbal Communication   No attempt is made here to deal with the topic of nonverbal communication in a comprehensive manner. Some remarks concerning its relevance to the three-dimensional communicative space as analyzed here have to suffice. The expressive aspect of messages is conveyed nonverbally throughout all of life. In many instances, neither verbal nor situational cues are incorporated by the sender of the message. The receiver, in contrast, often must combine other cues with the message that is conveyed nonverbally in order to more fully understand the meaning of the sender's behavior. Research on the interpretation of infants' cries has shown consistently that adults generally interpret them on the basis of contextual knowledge. The same principle, though in a somewhat lesser degree, applies to the expressive behavior of adults. To fully understand the meaning of crying, anger, or any other emotional expression, the receiver has to know its causes. People cry from happiness as well as from sadness or desperation. Anthropological research has also established that smiling and laughter can have many "meanings."

In directive communication, the sender consistently incorporates contextual cues to convey his intention. The acts of looking toward, reaching, grasping, holding on to, and many other gestures entail their objects in the behavior setting. The receiver of nonverbal directives necessarily has to consider aspects derived from both channels in order to comprehend the message. Traces of such nonverbal and contextual cues can be also observed in the later appearing verbal directions. A close analysis of verbal requests uttered by children and by adults shows that many elements of the request are presupposed, i.e., contributed by the context.

The referential function is obviously most prototypical for verbal behavior. Its roots in nonverbal communication are discussed below in detail when the development of gestures and of the deictic function is analyzed. As the term *referential function* implies, this function is at the same time most closely tied to the environment, i.e., to its referents. It has been often discussed in older psycholinguistic literature, and is summarized by Stern and Stern (1907) and by Werner and Kaplan (1963), that demonstrative pronouns and adverbs, such as *that, there,* etc., may have their roots in the *da* pattern, in which the dental sounds fulfill a deictic function. That both the deictic *da* sounds in the infant's babbling and in demonstrative words require contextual supplementation to constitute a complete message is evident. Similar arguments apply to most pronouns and *pro*-forms. To understand what the word *another* or the expressions *to do, this thing,* etc., really refer to, nonverbal or verbal contextual cues are needed. Deixis is most often encountered in such situations.

On the borderline between nonverbal and verbal communication are two topics that require special discussion. One refers to a function of verbal communication that is neglected in most of the literature. Malinowski (1923) labeled it the function of *verbal communion,* i.e., the fact that verbal behavior sometimes only minimally serves referential and propositional functions and is employed, in a manner similar to mere physical proximity or holding hands, for mere contact purposes. Almost every human being spends countless hours in such verbal communion situations, not finding it worthwhile to remember what the conversation was about. Parents and investigators often report that some children have the habit of bombarding adults with a multitude of questions not for the sake of obtaining information but in order to attract and retain the adult's attention. This aspect of verbal interaction may be important developmentally, as suggested by two lines of studies. Bernstein (1964) and his associates have described in many publications how socioeconomic differences can lead to differences in the habitual employment of language forms that have social-functional significance. Bernstein labeled the two types *elaborated* and *restricted codes.* From another perspective, Nelson (1973) described individual differences in the sequence and emphasis with which children acquire specific language forms and language skills. She differentiated two groups of children, a *referential* and an *expressive* one. The first "seems to be learning to talk about things and the other about self and other people; one is learning an object language, one a social interaction language" (Nelson, 1973:22). Whether the child belongs to the one or to the other group may result in a profound difference in the diachronic and synchronic combination of the various channels. Since research on individual differences in language acquisition generally has been neglected in recent years due to the search for general laws, this brief reference to an important topic has to suffice at present.

The second borderline topic that deserves closer consideration is that pertaining to the *modality* of verbal communication. Linguists have predominantly worked with written corpora and developmental psycholinguists with collections of oral utterances. Both, however, have assumed without hesitation that the material for their studies has to be derived from verbal sources in the strict sense. The relationship between verbal language and other modalities of language communication previously had not been considered intensively. Since the work of the Gardners (1969), who trained a chimpanzee in American Sign Language, the situation has changed, however. Bellugi's research on American Sign Language as it is employed by the deaf (Bellugi, 1972; Bellugi and Klima, 1975) has served to highlight the basic principle that a complex language exists and is employed widely and effectively, though it does not rely on the vocal-phonemic channel. Gestures seem to be one of the most convenient means to usurp the communicative function.

Whereas this quasi-lingual (language-like) communicative mode has attracted scientific attention, and while it is being explored, it may become necessary to reconsider and reinvestigate the gestures that are used for communicative purposes by higher apes and by infants. These gestures follow regular patterns; they can be employed in a variety of situations and therefore can constitute a prelanguage before the development of oral language. If this argument were followed to its logical conclusion, it would mean that the infant could have already developed a nonvocal language before he learns the language of his environment as it is modeled in the vocal channel. The gesture language probably would also build to a large extent upon models provided by adults; i.e., it would be structured according to the same basic principles in respect to semantic and perhaps even syntactic features as the later oral language.

This suggestion may seem to be idle speculation and admittedly cannot be bolstered by strong evidence yet. Some preliminary evidence, however, does exist. The most language-like systems are the sign languages, either the systematized ones, such as American Sign Language, or those invented by deaf persons growing up without any special training. Both can be easily learned and understood by persons fluent in the spoken language. Both are translatable into spoken language. As discussed in later sections of this chapter, gestural elements often serve as substitutes for verbal elements in the speech of children. Slama-Cazacu (1970) has described the same phenomenon in the speech of normal adults, when it accompanies other activities. She labels this phenomenon *mixed syntax*. If elements are so easily substitutable for each other, and if they fit so easily into the same message frames, profound semantic and relational equivalences must exist between them.

Though this topic is not yet defined clearly enough in theoretical perspective, the implications for the understanding of language development are easily seen. The child, in learning his mother tongue, would acquire only new surface structures, while the base structures in their semantic and structural aspect already would have been preformed in a nonvocal-morphemic communication system. Many phenomena that appeared puzzling, such as the learning of deep structures which are never modeled or the relative ease of early language acquisition, would have to be recognized as being somewhat less extraordinary.

Dimension of Verbal Communication   This dimension needs no specific introduction in this context. Suffice it to point out that primarily the communicational aspects of speech are considered. Word play, sing-songs, or strict monologues are less relevant for the understanding of messages.

CHARACTERISTICS OF CHILDREN'S MULTICHANNEL COMMUNICATION

Theoretical Perspective

From birth on, the infant evinces a strong desire and need (McCarthy, 1966) to communicate with others and, therefore, he has much experience with nonverbal communication with adults before verbal communication comes into play (Bates, Camaioni, and Volterra, 1975). Until the age of almost two years, the child has to communicate most of his intentions nonverbally, and he understands the messages conveyed by adults to a large extent by means of nonverbal cues. Brannigan and Humphries (1972) reported that children up to the age of three to four years primarily use gestures, facial expressions, and intention movements to communicate with other children. When children communicate with adults, the verbal channel acquires predominance a little earlier, but the verbal encoding is also accompanied by much nonverbal communicative behavior. Gestures and intention movements largely depend upon situational variables to be communicatively effective. The fact that children and adults communicate relatively well with each other is evidence that both consistently integrate the cues of the environment, the nonverbal, and the verbal behavior of each other in their encoding and decoding of messages.

Adults, too, communicate with their young infants largely without relying upon words. Even when they speak to their infants during the preverbal period, the bulk of the communicative intent is still conveyed through nonverbal messages. Adult speech is probably first perceived by the infant as a pleasant background melody. Frequently repeated elements of this melody soon acquire a distinct character, until the figure-ground relationship between nonverbal and verbal communication becomes reversed in the course of early childhood. Some Continental European scientists (Hörmann, 1967; Weizsäcker, 1959) accordingly stress that language becomes differentiated out of a process of global communication. This conclusion stands in stark contrast to some older associationistic interpretations of language acquisition. Since these two theoretical approaches postulate contrasting psychological principles, the behavioral and cognitive processes that would be assumed as a basis for language acquisition also would have to be different. The essential difference probably lies in the fact that, according to the older European conception, meaning, the structures of meaning, and communicative intentions are seen as primary and as securely established when the process of language acquisition begins. A similar viewpoint is presented in Chapter Four of this book, where the details of these developments are sketched out.

Variety of Communication Channels   To explore communicative behavior in its totality, more than three channels of communication probably should be differentiated. Kogan and Wimberger (1969) enumerated five different means of communication: verbal, visual, tactile, manipulative, and gestural. From a developmental perspective a further subdivision appears meaningful between vocal but preverbal and vocal-verbal communication. Many finer differentiations could be made both in the realm of body language and in regard to voice qualities and patterns. The publications of Birdwhistell (1970), Duncan (1969), and Mahle and Schulze (1964) provide detailed analyses of the entire realm. For the present study, which is aimed at the antecedents of referential language, the somewhat different subdivision of the nonverbal channels that is presented in Figure 5.3 has been chosen. It is similar to that suggested by Austin (1962), who differentiated three nonverbal channels: intonation patterns, the child's motor behavior, and environmental and temporal aspects. Since the present investigation aims mainly at the understanding of the development of referential communication, most of the attention is centered upon the functions of the gestural channel of communication while other motor behavior, e.g., that serving expressive and directive functions, is treated only briefly. Intonation patterns as well are only mentioned incidentally in several sections. Austin's "environmental and temporal aspects" are explored from a psychological perspective as "behavior settings" and "behavior episodes."

The three channels to be studied in detail appear to be employed by the infant and child in a developmental sequence. The behavior setting is attended to almost from birth on, as seen in the orienting reflex. Gestures are understood and employed a good deal later, and verbal comprehension and production appear only toward the end of the first year of life. The amount and type of information received and conveyed in each of these channels must vary accordingly. Even in later childhood and adulthood, when all channels have been mastered, considerable flexibility exists regarding the choice of channels for specific messages and in specific situations. This variety of communicational channels and the flexibility in their employment are factually demonstrated in later sections of this chapter.

Consistency of Communication Content   The previous chapters illustrated how the child's increasing versatility in the use of nonverbal channels permits him to go beyond the reliance upon direct signals and how it finally leads to symbolic and sign behavior. While this previous discussion has been centered on developmental change, an important continuity must not be overlooked. This was already implied by Bertrand Russell (1900). In describing the function of language, he stressed one of its characteristics that applies equally to other forms of communication: All of them share in the structure of the physical world and therefore can express that structure. How these relationships between language and reality are conceived in the present study has been discussed above. The evidence from cross-cultural research on "language universals" (Bach and Harms, 1968; Greenberg, 1963) is in accordance with Russell's argument in that it points to global uniformities in the representations of the physical world. Slobin (1973) reported even more uniform phenomena of infant speech in a wide variety of cultures. When the multimodality of communication and the equipotentiality of the various means of communication are emphasized, the intimate interdependence between communicative structures and objective environmental structures becomes even more obvious. Visual, tactile, manipulative, and to some extent gestural communicative acts cannot but be closely adapted to actual situational variables, mirroring at least the locative relationships, as in the case of visual and gestural communication. In the case of tactile and manipulative communication, e.g., when the child moves the adult's hand toward an object to induce him to open it, specific structural relationships of the objects to be manipulated have to be incorporated into the structure of the manipulative act.

Though the scope of the environment and the child's interpretation of some of its aspects change in the course of development, its basic aspects remain the same. Only on the base of this continuity can the child construct an internalized view of the world. Since the environment, his interpretation of it, and his reaction to it represent the content of the child's communicative acts, this content also has to remain relatively consistent and unchanged.

Developmental Significance of the Combination of Variety of Channels and Consistency of Communication Content   If the above arguments are accepted as valid, several important principles of language acquisition follow: 1) The infant has already learned how the objective world in his immediate environment is structured and what relations exist between these structures. 2) He has learned about these structures and of his personal relationship to them by means of information received through four out of the five channels that were differentiated by Kogan and Wimberger (1969). 3) He has also learned to convey many messages about this objective world by means of the same channels. 4) Since the messages he receives and those he is continuing to convey will change only slightly, his verbal communication will have to resemble in structure and meaning his previous nonverbal communication and thereby indirectly the structure of the objective world. In acquiring verbal skills, the child needs only to match a new symbol system with already mastered message structures. A detailed discussion of the epigenetic relationships between these various channels recently has been presented by Moerk (in preparation-b). Some of these points are summarized in subsequent sections.

Factual Research on the Interdependencies Between Behavior Setting and Expressed Message

The following sections attempt to explore the relationships and interdependencies among the three dimensions depicted in Figure 5.3, with evidence being derived from children's communicative behavior. The analysis, however, has to be preliminary because factual research pertaining to these problems is still sparse. The following discussion therefore, is mainly intended as a basis for future investigations and as an attempt to bring together the hypotheses and findings that are widely dispersed in the literature.

The wording of the title of this section is chosen to emphasize the controversial point of the proposition. By employing the word *interdependencies* it is asserted that the nonverbal environment has direct effects upon verbal behavior. This assertion is in contrast to Chomsky's often repeated pronouncement that verbal behavior is not under the control of external stimuli. Chomsky asserts in *Cartesian Linguistics* (1966:20): "Human language, in its normal use, is free from the control of independently identifiable external stimuli or internal states and is not restricted to any practical communicative function, in contrast, for example, to the pseudo-language of animals." Although a strong case is made here for a dependency upon external stimuli, it is by no means implied that verbal behavior or even the comprehension of verbal messages is completely stimulus controlled. Suggestions on the extent of stimulus control are also provided.

Two topics should be explicated under the above title: 1) the effect of the behavior setting upon communicative nonverbal behavior, and 2) the effect of the behavior setting upon communicative verbal behavior. Data are sparse in both areas. For the second topic a considerable number of theoretical discussions and even some experimental analyses exist. Regarding the first topic the studies of Barker and Wright (1955) on children's behavior in various behavior settings could provide pertinent evidence. The intent and the design of these studies, however, are too remote from the goals of the present discussion, so that they cannot contribute much evidence directly relating to language development. Other ecological/ethological investigations and basically all stimulus-response studies could be marginally pertinent. It is impossible, however, to survey here this enormous range of literature. The discussion to follow therefore centers upon the second topic only. Although it is claimed that similar principles also apply to the first topic, this question has to remain open for the foreseeable future.

Many writers have expressed the belief that the situation or behavior setting has profound influences upon verbal behavior. Wittgenstein's (1953) formulation has already been quoted, i.e., that language is to be interpreted as a game that is played in some context for some purpose. In this overall assertion, influences of the context upon receptive as well as productive aspects of communication are included. The behavior setting, either alone or in connection with the verbal context, strongly influences the interpretations of homonyms and eliminates inappropriate meaning aspects of individual words, as shown by Hymes (1962). The profound influences of the presuppositions of communication partners upon their verbal productions were spelled out repeatedly by psycholinguists (Brown, 1958b; Carroll, 1960; Huttenlocher, Eisenberg, Strauss, 1968; Olson, 1970; Osgood, 1971). These authors demonstrated factually how situational variables affect semantic and syntactic elements of the message that is conveyed verbally. The same fact in the verbal behavior of children was explored by Francis (1969, 1970), Friedlander (1970), Bloom (1970), and Greenfield and Smith (1976). Moerk (1972) provided a relatively detailed analysis of these relationships by demonstrating that the situation or behavior setting has two global types of effects upon the verbal behavior of the child, namely, communicative and formative ones.

Communicative Functions of the Behavior Setting   A shared behavior setting fulfills predominantly communicative functions. This is especially evident in social animals below man that have less fully developed means to communicate about their environments and therefore need to rely predominantly upon their shared perceptions of external stimuli to coordinate their communal and cooperative behavior. Ethologists have provided abundant evidence for this phenomenon. Also in the case of human beings, many facts will be simultaneously apparent to all persons present in a specific behavior setting, so that they need not be conveyed verbally or in any other way. The knowledge that a similarly perceived context is shared by both the sender and receiver of a message permits the sender to specify less in his verbal message. The entire controversy surrounding "egocentric speech" (Piaget, 1926) versus "socialized speech" (Vygotsky, 1962) probably can be resolved by the consideration of situational variables and the child's learned and overgeneralized anticipation that much information can be presupposed. Kohlberg et al. (1968) came to similar conclusions regarding this controversy. Some evidence regarding how the situational influence leads to ellipsis in verbal communication also can be gleaned from past literature, though most authors report only the ellipsis, as in the so-called holophrases or in Bloom's "reduction transformation." Ellipsis is especially evident in the monologues of child and mother while they are in close physical and perceptual proximity. It is even more predominant in what Vygotsky (1962) labeled *inner speech*. Factual evidence for these phenomena is presented in later sections of this chapter.

Formative Functions of the Behavior Setting   A second and very different function of the behavior setting appears to be of even greater importance for the understanding of language acquisition processes. This is its effect upon the content and structure of the verbal utterance. Whereas in the above paragraphs the effect of environmental variables was discussed with regard to what is not encoded verbally, now its effect has to be specified with regard to what is encoded verbally and how this is done. If, as argued in a preceding section, aspects of reality are translated into linguistic structures following certain well defined and shared translation rules, the communicatively important variables of the behavior setting necessarily must have a directly structuring influence upon the verbal product. At least two types of formative functions that the environment exerts upon verbal behavior can be differentiated. In a previous publication (Moerk, 1972), they were labeled *eliciting functions* and *structuring functions*. This terminology is retained here, and the main argument of this previous study is summarized below and supported by examples selected from various authors.

Eliciting Functions   Influences of the behavior setting are summarized under the *eliciting functions,* which lead to the production of previously learned verbal elements or structures but do not result in new structures. *Naming* is the most commonly encountered example of this phenomenon. In the case of naming, a ready-made and previously acquired linguistic element, the single word, is elicited through environmental stimuli impinging upon either child or mother or both. If linguistic changes or innovations are observed, they are due to influences of a communication partner but not to those of the nonverbal aspects of the behavior setting.

Examples of various types of verbal responses are presented in Table 5.1, though all pertain to naming phenomena. Simple naming by the child without any reported evidence of maternal feedback is seen in example one. In examples two and three, the mother provides corrective feedback concerning the child's pronunciation; however, this is done in a somewhat subtle and surreptitious manner. In examples four and five, the caregiver provides obvious corrective and re-

Table 5.1. Eliciting functions of the inanimate environment

Example	Person speaking	Utterance plus context	Source of example
1	M (1,4)[a]	Eyes. (*Touches doll's eyes.*)	Dore (1974)
2	J (1,8)	Bough. (*As she sees a picture of a ball in a magazine.*)	Moerk (1972)
	Mother	Ball? Hm, yes, a little one.	
3	Jeff (2,4)	Ka ka.	Moerk (1972)
	Mother	Is it a good cracker?	
4	J (1,8)	Teaphone. (*As she attends to a tape recorder.*)	Moerk (1972)
	Mother	Telephone? Well, it's like a telephone, but it's a tape recorder. (*After three corrective cycles between mother and child and a subsequent change of topic, the child comes back to the recently learned vocabulary item.*)	
	J	Ta- take(r) corde(r).[b]	
	Mother	That's right, tape recorder, yeah.	
5	A (1,6)	Horse. (*A and caregiver looking at picture book, A pointing to a goat.*)	Edwards (1977)
	Caregiver	No, no, that's not a horse.	
	A	Cats. (*Referring to the same picture.*)	
	Caregiver	No.	
	A	What's that? (*Same picture.*)	
	Caregiver	What is it? That's a goat. Alice, say goat, goat.	
6	Mother	What's that? (*Points to a picture of a dog.*)	Dore (1974)
	J (1,5)	Bau wau.	
7	Mother	What's that? (*Refers to a picture of a bus.*)	Edwards (1977)
	Mk (1,8)	Car.	
8	Mother	What's this? (*Refers to an object the child handles.*)	Moerk (1972)
	J (3,6)	Car box.	
9	Mother	What's that? (*Referring to a picture in a picture book.*)	Moerk (1972)
	P (2,2)	A wing.	————

cont.

Table 5.1   (Cont.)

10	Mother	Yes, a swing.	
	Mother	What's that? (*Putting a toy cow on a chair.*)	Bloom (1973)
	A (1,5)	Pig.	
	Mother	Is that a pig?	
	A	(*Pointing to cow.*)	
	Mother	That's another cow.	

[a] The number in parentheses gives the age of the child in years and months. Dore only provides data for the age range of his subjects, so that an estimate in the form of the mean of this range is only possible.

[b] Parentheses around letters or syllables symbolize that these elements were barely audible.

inforcing feedback for her daughter, thereby helping her to arrive at new semantic/conceptual differentiations. In all these five cases, an object or its representation elicited a naming response by the child. The dependency of this response upon the environmental stimulus is therefore directly evident.

In examples six to ten, the mother invites the child to name an object, by asking a question such as "What's that?". Formulated in learning theoretical terms, she provides a discriminative stimulus in order to alert the child to the fact that verbal behavior is appropriate and desired. The type of verbal behavior the child produces is again directly a function of external stimuli and of his learning history. The mother again can reward the child for his verbal response or correct it if necessary.

Only very few examples of this phenomenon are necessary, since the habit of young children to name the objects they encounter has been discussed intensively during the entire course of the last century. Stern and Stern (1907), who surveyed the extensive previous literature, concluded that the young child goes through a specific naming stage. Almost half a century later Brown (1956) again described these interactions using the term *the original word game*, and as Table 5.1 shows, the same phenomena are reported in corpora collected and published during the most recent years. That such processes may be effective as a form of vocabulary training is highly probable and quite generally accepted. Some anecdotal evidence for this effectiveness has been provided in the older literature. Moerk (1976b) has systematically collected evidence to support this general belief.

Structuring Functions   As discussed in preceding chapters, the infant is keenly aware of environmental structures and relations before he begins to use language. These more complex conceptualizations of the environment require more complex symbolic structures for their encoding and can consist either of combinations of nonverbal and verbal elements or of verbal elements only, i.e., the widely analyzed early more-word structures. The more-word structures have been intensively studied in all grammatical analyses. The structural combinations of nonverbal and verbal elements, however, have been quite consistently misinterpreted until recently, since the nonverbal message elements were not considered in the structural analyses. They are more extensively discussed in the last section of this chapter. Since the evidence for more-word structures is so abundant in all books on early speech, only a minimal number of examples is needed to demonstrate the principles envisaged.

Each of the utterance types shown in Table 5.2 serves to demonstrate a different principle. In utterance one, a very simple case is encountered. In reality a relationship exists between the lady and the ball, and this relationship is also expressed verbally by means of simple juxtaposition of its two elements. As example two, Bloom's (1970) famous instance of *Mommy sock* was chosen to expand upon the principle that is also encountered in example one. As is known from Bloom's discussion, *Mommy sock* can have and did have in Kathryn's communicative behavior several different meanings; i.e.,

Table 5.2. Structuring functions of the environment

Example	Person speaking	Utterance plus context	Source of example
1	J (1,8)[a]	Lady bough.	Moerk (1972)
	Mother	It's a lady's ball. That's right.	
2	K (1,9)	Mommy sock.	Bloom (1970)
3	A (1.10)	Baby ride truck.	Bloom (1973)
		Baby ride truck.	
	Mother	O.K. You ride the truck.	
4	J (3,6)	My hot wheels are under my bed.	Moerk (1972)
5	Mother	What's all over your face?	Moerk (1972)
	C (2,6)	Ice cream on it.	

[a] The number in parentheses gives the age of the child in years and months.

while the elements mentioned remain the same, the relationships among them changed. It is obvious from these two instances that not all elements of the environmental structure necessarily need to be expressed in verbal structures or even by nonverbal message elements. If in the title of the present section a causal relationship between environmental and verbal structures is postulated, then this obviously cannot be meant as implying an exact one-to-one relationship, i.e., that all elements of the environmental structure also would have to appear in the message structure. What has been said about presuppositions and the shared behavior setting can explain to a large degree this lack of isomorphy. Restrictions in the linguistic system of a specific cultural community or of the language-learning child represent a second explanatory factor for this lack of complete congruence.

In examples three and four, relationships are expressed in addition to the elements that are to be related to each other. The type of relationship is obviously very different in these two examples. A more interesting contrast is encountered in the form of both utterances. Example three is an instance of what could be labeled *minimal sufficiency*. Both elements and the relationship between them are expressed by means of one linguistic element each, and nothing else is found in the verbal form of the message. In example four, the child could have conveyed his intended message through the utterance *hot wheel under the bed*. Since *hot wheels* in the child's utterance stands for "racing car" the receiver could have easily reconstructed the object structure from this linguistic structure. The child's utterance surpasses this minimally sufficient formulation in two aspects: First he adds the plural form of the copula, which is only indirectly related to immediate stimulus conditions. Furthermore, he adds the possessive pronoun *my* twice, which does not have any direct equivalent in the environmental structure but is based upon the child's previously acquired knowledge about property relationships.

Two types of nonequivalences between environmental structure and verbal structure are presented in the examples of Table 5.2. In the first type, the environmental structure, even if only its minimally constituent elements are considered, is more complex than the verbal structure. In the second type, as found in example four, the verbal structure has more elements than the environmental structure. Examples three and five represent two cases of equivalences, whereby the minimally sufficient elements are found in both structures.

Example five demonstrates two other phenomena. First, the mother can by means of her question suggest to the child that verbal behavior is appropriate or expected. The child, in his response, relies upon the informational context established by the mother and employs a pronoun only instead of the noun as one of his message elements. The effects of three types of stimuli therefore can be observed in this statement of the child: The mother's question is the reason why the child engaged in verbal behavior; the specific formulation of the mother's question permitted the child to choose a pronoun instead of naming the intended element. Finally, structural relations in the realm of objects, in this case the child's own face, are the roots of the specific elements and structures in the child's message.

A critical reading of the preceding paragraphs and a study of the examples presented show that the hypothesis proposed is a good deal stronger than the more common behavioristic assumption that Chomsky rejected so vehemently. In the general behavioristic arguments on stimulus-response relationships, the response is in principle morphologically and structurally unrelated to the stimulus. Almost any response can be tied to almost any stimulus provided an appropriate learning sequence is established. This principle certainly applies to the learning of labels or other symbols but not in the case of the discussed structuring function of the environment. In the latter case it is posited that structural characteristics of the stimulus situation are reflected in the structural characteristics of the response, though not always in a one-to-one relationship.

The logical basis for this strong assumption has been provided in one of the preceding sections, when the relationships between reality and language were discussed. Factual support can be amply found in everyday observations of speech in context and in some of the experimental studies of psychologists (Glucksberg, 1975; Osgood, 1971). An incidental suggestion of how strong this tie between reality and linguistic structure is for the child, can be found in the fact that prevarication, i.e., intentional lying and pretend language games appear considerably after direct and faithful encodings of environmental givens. If, according to a German proverb, children and fools tell the truth, then it is not because they are especially honest but because they are too stimulus bound to be able to do otherwise.

Verbal structures that are directly influenced by structural relations in the behavior setting appear not only in the verbal behavior of children but also in that of their mothers. Very often instances are found in mother-child interactions when the mother describes her own or the child's behavior while it is still proceeding. She also often encodes static environmental relationships. In this manner she models for her child the pairing of actions/perceptions/conceptualizations and their linguistic codes, while both phenomena hold the attention of the child. Of necessity, she thereby demonstrates the translation rules that relate to both these structural entities. This type of maternal verbal behavior is consequently an excellent form of teaching. Examples of it are presented in the next chapter, when maternal teaching techniques are analyzed. At the present, only the phenomenon needs to be mentioned, together with the fact that the young child's environment is generally stable and that certain routines are performed in this environment thousands of times. Friedlander (1970), who collected extensive evidence for interactional phenomena, emphasized the importance of these routines, and Brown, Cazden, and Bellugi (1969) provided some preliminary evidence for their effects. They found that the frequency and correctness in children's use of prepositions were highly related to the frequency with which those prepositions were modeled and/or expanded by the mothers. Since prepositions are, at least in the case of young children, employed to describe environmental and behavioral phenomena, mostly locative ones, a three-step cause-effect sequence is suggested by these findings: Environmental structures affect the verbal structures of the mothers and the latter in turn affect those of their children. More of these teaching/learning phenomena are presented in the subsequent chapter.

Aspects of Behavior Setting That Affect Its Formative Functions
Ecological and psychological evidence shows that animateness is an important trait for the human infant and for higher species of animals generally. For animals in the wild, it can mean either a social partner, an object of prey, or a predator. The human infant's intense interest in his human environment has been abundantly supported by the recent research literature that was quoted in previous chapters. Piaget (1952) has demonstrated that infants are prone to overextend their concept of animateness and that even preschool children still have difficulties in selecting all those critical features for the categorization of animate versus inanimate objects that are necessary according to adult standards. A behavioral differentiation of these two aspects, however, can be observed from early infancy on. Evidence for a conceptual distinc-

tion along these lines can be found also in the early language products of children. Ingram (1971) has summarized the pertinent evidence from older diary studies, i.e., that transitive verbs are overwhelmingly followed by nouns referring to inanimate objects. Brown (1973) has reported that in early speech almost without exception only animate nouns function as subjects of sentences. Since this differentiation is established in the nonverbal and verbal realm, some of its effects upon language behavior can be described forthrightly.

In the case of younger children the inanimate environment often appears to have only eliciting effects, resulting in mere labeling, while the animate environment is more generally referred to by utterances containing several words. This was found predominantly in several projects (Moerk, 1972, 1974b, 1975b), and it also has been reported in older studies that described the child's naming games. It is not known whether this difference is due to tutoring by the children's parents or whether it is a technique spontaneously adopted by children. Parents could be prone to merely label things, while describing the activities of animate beings by means of more complex propositions. On the other hand, young children could and probably do attend more closely to the few animate beings they know and pay more cursory attention to most of the larger number of inanimate objects they encounter. This difference could lead to a finer perceptual analysis of the characteristics and activities of the former and therefore to more detailed messages relating to them.

Even when the child has reached a stage wherein he encodes both the aspects of the animate and of the inanimate environment in more-word utterances, differences in the resulting messages still prevail. The inanimate environment is encoded mainly by means of noun-noun or noun-adjective structures, with the copula being optional at first, while the animate/human environment is described more often by means of noun-verb and verb-noun or noun-verb-noun structures, i.e., by agent-action or (agent)-action-object structures. The parentheses in the latter structure are employed to suggest that the agent is often omitted, since he is presupposed. If the child employs agent-object structures, an action element is often evidently presupposed or communicated in nonverbal channels. This distinction in the linguistic structures is cognitively meaningful, because aspects in the inanimate environment are mostly static, while those involving animate beings are mostly dynamic. For the encoding of the former, the child consequently employs a categorizing schema, "This is a ———," and an object-and-features schema, "That is ——," whereas for the latter he predominantly employs a human action model, "A is acting" and "A is affecting B." In accordance with man's tendency for physiognomic interpretation of reality, as found in concepts of physics such as *force*, *attraction*, etc., in everyday language, and in the child's special inclination toward physiognomic perception, the borderlines between these types of linguistic description of reality are not always clearly drawn. The categorizing schema, "This is a ——," has been exemplified above in connection with Table 5.1 and with the eliciting function of the environment. As soon as the child names objects, he shows that he has classified them into sets that are described by the labels he gives the objects. In the early stages, the demonstrative pronoun is still replaced by nonverbal deictic elements, and the copula, not being essential for communicative purposes, is omitted. Even if both these elements and other syntactically required morphemes are later added in the child's utterance, these are not due to any direct influences from the behavior setting but to those of the linguistic system that the child has acquired. In these latter cases, the behavior setting also has only eliciting functions.

In contrast, the other models that are employed by the child directly reflect environmental structures. Examples of them are presented in Table 5.3. The object-and-features model is represented in examples one to four as it appears in two different forms. In the first two examples a locative feature is predicated about the object. Whereas the child is probably not yet able to express the type of relationship intended, he mentions both elements of the relationship. At least in the second example, the relationship is also quite evident from the behavioral setting, so that it can be omitted without endangering communicative efficiency. In examples three and four, the feature of the object that caught the child's attention is expressed through a predicate adjective, while the copula is either fully omitted or barely suggested. Those phenomena of the object that are of communicative importance at the specific moment stand in a one-to-one relationship to the two linguistic elements of the utterance.

Examples five to eight reflect the human-action model, either in its intransitive or its transitive form. The relationships between environmental structures and linguistic ones are again quite obvious, since in most cases elements are omitted that are required only syntactically but do not contribute to the content of the message. In later verbal products, content elements may be more often omitted

Table 5.3. Basic types of verbal structures reflecting analogous environmental structures

Example	Person speaking	Utterance plus context	Source of example
1	G (1,7)[a]	Block bag. (*The block was in the bag.*)	Bloom (1970)
2	G (1,8)	Cow mobile. (*The cow was hanging from the mobile.*)	Bloom (1970)
3	E (2,1)	Carriage broken.	Brown and Fraser (1963)
4	N (3,3) Mother N	Louie's spat. Louie's fat? Yah.	Moerk (1972)
5	A (2,6) Mother	Ma-aman came. Mailman came, O.K.	Moerk (1972)
6	G (1,7)	Girl write. (*Describing a picture of a girl drawing.*)	Bloom (1970)
7	S (3,6) Mother	He see baby. He saw the baby.	Moerk (1972)
8	P (2,2)	Mommy bucked the baby off.	Moerk (1972)

[a] The number in parentheses gives the age of the child in years and months.

due to contextually established presuppositions, and purely grammatical elements are added, somewhat concealing the formative effects of the environmental structures. Only the highly educated adult, who habitually employs the distancing function of language, may come close to Chomsky's ideal of a stimulus-free speaker who is only internally guided.

Summary A fourfold cause-effect relationship between environmental structure and language structure has been described and partly substantiated:

1. The structures of the environment serve communicative functions. Verbal means of communication are either not necessary or they convey only parts of the message.
2. In a very simple form of cause-effect relationship between environmental stimulus and language product, the environmental structure only elicits a specific simple linguistic structure according to a learned and relatively fixed bond between both types of structures.
3. On a higher level, complex structures of the environment are rendered in communicative structures consisting either of a combina-

tion of nonverbal and verbal elements or exclusively of verbal elements. The verbal products of child and mother reflect those environmental structures, and the mother models the translation rules.

4. Two overall types of environmental structures, labeled *static* versus *dynamic* structures, are translated into distinct types of linguistic structures in the categorizing and object-and-features schema and the human-action schema.

Besides having informational, eliciting, and structuring functions, the behavior setting also may have restraining functions. Restraint may apply either to speaking generally or only to certain categories of speech. Examples of these restraining functions were presented in the publications of Barker and Wright (1955) and they can be commonly observed. For example, it is not considered proper to engage in casual conversation in a church, or to use colloquial or scatological terms in "good company." These specific restraining functions are only of minor interest for the present topic dealing with language development and therefore they are not considered here. This last function of the behavior setting is more often analyzed under the general headings of "ethnography of speaking" or sociolinguistics," an area which has been extensively explored by Hymes (1962, 1967).

Nonverbal Communication and Its Relationship to Verbal Communication During Childhood

Only one aspect of the three-dimensional communicative space has been spelled out in detail in the preceding chapter: the manner in which aspects of the behavior setting can and do influence message structures. The second aspect has been mentioned several times and has always been implied: that the message structures can be composed of elements conveyed in either the nonverbal or the verbal channel or in a combination of both of them. The relationships between these channels and, more specifically, the effect of nonverbal encoding upon the verbal structures, those that accompany it or will replace it in the course of language development, are analyzed in the present section. After a brief discussion of some pertinent literature and of the theoretically expected relationships, illustrative data on verbal messages and their dependency upon other channels of communication are presented.

In principle, all of nonverbal communication and even noncommunicational behavior could be included in the discussion. It has been argued in two other publications (Moerk, in preparation-b; Moerk and Wong, 1976) as well as in Chapter Four that the structure of the human act in its transitive and intransitive form represents an important mold for later linguistic structures. These considerations, however, already have been presented in Chapter Four and the topic under consideration here would be expanded too far if *communication* were defined so widely. To use the wide range of hypotheses and results that were presented in past literature, the discussion must be restricted to direct social communication and even more specifically to manual gestures. On this topic a considerable number of analyses have been published, and they are surveyed and incorporated into the present argument.

Formative Functions of Nonverbal Communication   A few remarks referring to preceding chapters and preceding sections of this present chapter shall establish connecting links among the various points of the entire argument. It has been expounded that most human behavior is structured. This structured behavior is almost always meaningful for an observer who shares the cultural background and comes from the same interpretative community (*Interpretationsgemeinschaft*, Apel, 1965). G. Mead (1934), building upon Wundt's analyses, described in detail the communicative functions of every social act. It therefore would be justified to include, as do Blauvelt and McKenna (1960), the normal caregiving routines performed by the mother in the set of communicative behaviors. The specific ways of performing these caregiving activities convey to the infant a very basic feeling of security and peace, or tension and danger. In this manner, the child acquires his first experience in interpreting the structured acts of communication partners as meaningful messages. Besides those connotative messages, a second type of meaning that could be labeled *referential* is abstracted by the infant from the observed events. He soon knows that certain preparations mean food, others mean he will be picked up, etc. In this process of learning, the infant establishes a connection between a behavioral/communicative structure and an underlying meaning. This is the same principle that he will have to apply later to understand verbal language. Regarding specific structures, the reader is referred back to the last section of Chapter Four. Since all behavior is informative for the observer, and since the borderline between mere behavior and nonverbal communicative behavior is therefore almost imperceptible, the discussions in Chapter Four apply to a large extent also to the present considerations.

Furthermore, even purely expressive gestures easily become means to direct the behavior of a social partner. The close relationships between, for example, the mere expression of anger and social threat, or the mere expression of a desire and a demand to have it fulfilled by a partner, demonstrates how imperceptible and gradual the transition between these two functions can be. When the mother restrains her infant from some particular activity, or when she prods him into attempting another one, the directive aspect of the gesture has become predominant, even if the mother still employs many expressive features.

It could be asserted with a high degree of justification that every directive message is also referential. Directive messages refer even to two "objects" in most instances: the person who is asked to fulfill a desire and the desired object. Since the person to whom the directive message is addressed is expected to do something, an action and an agent are also implied by the message. It therefore has to be concluded that directive messages contain in their intention structure all three basic elements of the sentence: an agent, an action, and an object.

Only a very minor shift in the action-element is required to lead from the directive message to the purely referential one, as this term is commonly employed. The emphasis in the action-element only needs to shift from a message such as "bring," "give," etc. to that of "look." In accordance with similar considerations, Wundt (1900), Latif (1934), Cassirer (1953), and many others have derived the manual pointing gesture from acts of reaching and grasping. Ontogenetic evidence supports this epigenetic argument, since these functions of nonverbal communication appear in developmental sequence. The expressive gestures are produced and understood earliest and the referential ones last. It appears also that the closer the specific function is in its temporal appearance to the beginning of language, the more it becomes interdependent with the latter. Bühler and Hetzer (1935) reported that infants can respond to and intentionally employ gestures already from the age of six months. Cattell (1940) reported the same phenomenon but only beginning at the age of nine months. Since intentionally employed gestures are referred to in both cases, they probably had either directive or referential functions. How closely gestures are involved in the later appearing directive and referential verbal messages is demonstrated below. Both the temporally contiguous antecedent-consequent relationship and the analytical argument presented above support the conclusion that directive and deictic gestures constitute important molds for the later formulation of verbal messages, the former providing a base structure for the agent-action-object schema, the latter for a deictic categorizing schema, "That is a ———." It need not be shown in detail that the infant is not only producing such messages, but even more often receiving them from his environment. Recent research (Kaye, 1977; Snow, 1975, 1976) on preverbal mother-child interaction has provided some evidence for this.

Before the relationships between nonverbal gestural communication and language as defined by linguists are discussed, another intermediary step that probably serves developmentally as a bridge to the higher linguistic level deserves closer scrutiny. This is the phenomenon that has often been labeled the *vocal gesture*. Even in the case of primates, Marler (1965) and Rowell (1962) emphasized the multimodality of communication and specifically the fact that sounds often have the function of drawing attention to communicative gestures. These authors, and also Hewes (1975), explicated the ecological function of this combination of gesture and sound, especially in the dense leafy environment in which these animals often live. The Sterns (1907), de Laguna (1927), and somewhat later Leopold (1939–1949) described the same phenomenon of vocal gestures in the case of human children. The specific sounds of these vocal gestures are derived first from the babbling repertoire, but their quality changes with the development of *call sounds* (Werner and Kaplan, 1963). It is important to consider separately the functions performed by the messages conveyed in each of the two channels involved. The vocal gesture and even the call sound have only an expressive and at best a directive value. In contrast, the manual gesture of reaching for or pointing to a particular object has a referential function besides its possible directive aspect. The general principle encountered here is that "new forms first express old functions, and new functions are first expressed by old forms" (Slobin, 1973: 184). The new form of the intentionally and instrumentally employed communicative sound complex serves primarily the primitive function of expression, whereas the comparatively older form of gesturing serves the new function of reference. On a somewhat higher level, it is again found that the pointing gesture refers to and specifies one individual object, whereas the word *that* or *this*, while representing a new form, is unspecific and has more of an attention-evoking function. Only with the establishment of a relatively extensive vocabulary of object names, whose meaning is learned when adults "point out" labeled objects, can the verbal channel fulfill the same precise referential functions as gestures have done before.

With these last points of the above discussion one important aspect of the functions of gestures has been touched upon already, i.e., the training value that gestures have for language acquisition. Before the appearance of fitting vocal means, they serve as instruments for the transmission of directive and thereafter referential messages and thereby provide the opportunity to train these new functions. With the employment of vocal means, only one new feature is added in the communicative act, i.e., that the "gesture" in the form of a demonstrative word is now performed orally instead of manually. The fact that, at least in Indo-Germanic languages, the earliest and most primitive deictic words have a dental in their roots has been referred to above. The same "dental gesture" is still found in many of the early referential words of children (Franke, 1899; Stern and Stern, 1907).

Besides forming the structural mold for later appearing vocal functions, gestures also appear commonly in vocabulary training. The Sterns (1907) and many subsequent investigators of early language development agreed upon this one fact, that the meaning of the first words is demonstrated by means of ostensive definition on the part of adults. The same principle applies in a more general sense. It has been insisted upon repeatedly that the communicative function of language arises through the establishment of parallels between environmental and verbal structures. When the mother models for the child a simple verbal structure in order that he may establish this parallel, she cannot assume that the child will know automatically what objects she is referring to. Since almost any environment is of unlimited complexity, if various levels of analysis were considered, the specific units selected for attention would have to be agreed upon before the child can try to match the mother's verbal structures with environmental ones. This is done in two ways: Either the child by means of gestures has made clear to his mother what aspect of the behavior setting he is attending to, or the mother does the same for the child by means of her gestures. Employing the preferred terminology of philosophers of natural language: Before a translational act can be meaningful for the beginning language learner, a definitional act conveyed through gestural channels must have been performed.

The Sterns (1907) had a similar principle in mind when they asserted that the early response of the child to heard speech is fundamentally built upon natural gestures. That gestures in turn can be meaningfully interpreted only on the basis of information from the behavior setting was probably presupposed by them as a matter of fact.

Communicative Functions of Nonverbal Communication   In addition to the formative functions of nonverbal communication and especially of gestures, another influence is predominant in the course of child development. This pertains to the communicative function of gestures, explicated in the following sections.

Substituting Functions of Gestures   That gestures alone can serve communicative functions is supported by the fact that they are also encountered in animals, even in those of relatively low phylogenetic levels. In those instances, gestures together with situational variables necessarily convey the entire message. The "gestures" developed by rats in the experimental situations observed by Mowrer (1960) have been discussed already in a preceding chapter in connection with the principle of economy of effort. On a higher level, it is reported that chimpanzees use gestures and vocalizations in natural communication to indicate locations, demands, etc. This same phenomenon was again substantiated by Jane Lawick-Goodall by means of convincing photographs. The experiment of Gardner and Gardner (1969) provided evidence that a chimpanzee can become quite adept in the artificial gesture language that is also employed by deaf and mute human beings. The general tendency to use gestures as signs is established for several species.

The function of gestures as a language substitute such as the sign language of deaf-mutes is currently being subjected to intensive study. Schlesinger (1970) has presented a challenging account of the grammatical aspect of sign language, and the pertinent endeavors of Bellugi and Klima have been already referred to. From this and much previous work (see Kainz, 1960) it can be asserted that sign language is developed by all persons who grow up without a spoken language, whatever the reason for this lack may be, as long as it is not extreme mental deficiency. According to the accounts of Kainz (1960), the systems of sign language also seem to be more similar across different cultures than do the systems of oral languages. Because these same sign systems are easier to learn than oral languages (Witte, 1930), it may be that sign languages, due to their iconic-figurative roots, are a spontaneously evolving means of communication in species which have evolved a representational function. In the human species, gestures serve as antecedents of vocal language if conditions allow the development of the latter.

Complementing Functions of Gestures   Many authors (Gregoire, 1937; Lewis, 1951; G. Mead, 1934) have remarked on the fact, which can be observed in everyday behavior, that one important function of gestures in the human species is to complement verbal communication. In this respect gestures serve the same function as situational variables in making messages less ambiguous. This form of communicating may be used when circumstances prevent the complete transmission of messages by verbal means. The traveler who does not fully master the language of the host country is perhaps the most ubiquitous example of this instance. Specifically regarding the topic of language acquisition, Lewis (1951) described how adults only slowly replace their gestures and deeds through words in their interaction with children. The same phenomenon was observed by him in children. A similar case was reported for an entire tribe by de Laguna (1927). The Chinook, an Indian tribe, spoke their own Indian language and a lingo containing both English and French vocabulary. They had developed this lingo to communicate with Whites, and it was only insufficiently developed as a linguistic system. Their own language, however, was highly developed, and they did not employ any gestures while conversing in it. Whenever they had to communicate with Whites, however, which involved the use of their special lingo, "the countenances, which had before been grave, stolid, and inexpressive, were instantly lighted up with animation; the low monotone tone became lively and modulated; every feature was active; the head, the arms, and the whole body was in motion, and every look and gesture became distinct with meaning" (de Laguna, 1927: 114–115).

In casual conversation among friends, gestures often replace words or detailed descriptions of situations or objects. This phenomenon is especially found in younger children when they communicate with other children (Brannigan and Humphries, 1972). Children as well as adults, as suggested by means of the above examples, employ the simpler and less effort-provoking means of gestures to complement verbal messages when they have not fully mastered the more complex linguistic system and when situational variables permit such a parsimonious choice, respectively.

Supportive Functions of Gestures   Finally, gestures may fulfill only a supportive function in verbal communication, without carrying any necessary information. As recent research on multichannel communication has shown (Birdwhistell, 1970; Watzlawick, Beavin, and Jackson, 1967), gestures contribute even in this case to the efficiency of communication. They are employed to subdivide the flow of speech more clearly, to add emphasis to certain parts, or to convey in an analogical form what is expressed in digital form through the spoken word. These functions of gestures are still common in the speech of adults and have been in previous times a required feature of public speaking. Though no study that was specifically directed toward this question has been found in the literature survey, it is known from everyday observations that children employ gestures in a similar manner. Examples are quite common in the writer's protocols that have been collected from various dyads. One child (2.8 years) said, "I hit you like this," and made a hitting movement. Another one (2.4 years) described an object as "round like this" and moved both his arms in a circular motion. Descriptions of flying are often accompanied by flapping arm movements, etc. European investigators especially have often stressed how verbal communication grows out of a total communicative act that includes the entire body and the behavior setting. Such supportive gestures are employed involuntarily and are studied for interpretative purposes in most forms of psychotherapy. Though they are employed ubiquitously and are communicatively important, they do not directly contribute to the content and structure of verbal messages. As far as can be discerned at present, they do not have any formative influence upon the verbal message of the young child either. They therefore are not discussed any further in the present context.

Relationships of All Nonverbal Means of Message
Transmission to Verbal Means and to Communication Efficiency
It has been argued and partly substantiated in previous sections of this chapter that both the behavior setting and the nonverbal communicative acts of infants and adults profoundly influence the final form and content of verbal messages. It is also known from common experience and from several experimental studies (S. Asher, 1976; Whitehurst, 1976) that children's communication efficiency generally increases with age. Communication efficiency can be defined as the percentage of intended messages that is correctly understood by the target. It depends upon the channels employed, upon the skills the

sender has acquired in the use of each channel, and upon the sender's evaluation of the receiver's informational needs. Figure 5.4 conveys how this relationship is conceived.

Since means to measure information content in each channel and communication efficiency over all channels have not yet been developed, the numerical values in Figure 5.4 are only estimates and serve only illustrative purposes. Up to the age of one year, the infant conveys all his messages nonverbally. When he begins at this time to employ single words, the message in most instances still can be understood on the basis of nonverbal cues. This fact is also probably the reason why investigators interpreted these single words as sentences,

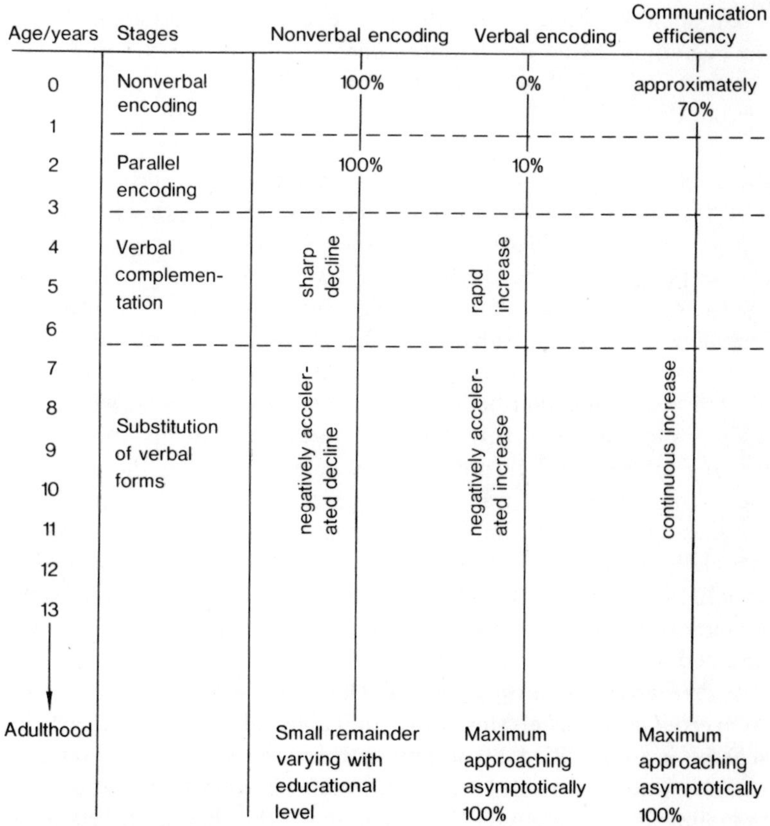

Age/years	Stages	Nonverbal encoding	Verbal encoding	Communication efficiency
0	Nonverbal encoding	100%	0%	approximately 70%
1				
2	Parallel encoding	100%	10%	
3				
4	Verbal complementation	sharp decline	rapid increase	
5				
6				
7		negatively accelerated decline	negatively accelerated increase	continuous increase
8	Substitution of verbal forms			
9				
10				
11				
12				
13				
Adulthood		Small remainder varying with educational level	Maximum approaching asymptotically 100%	Maximum approaching asymptotically 100%

Figure 5.4 Interrelationships between channels of information transmission and the efficiency of communication.

i.e., holophrases. They understood the complete message and equated—incorrectly, it is asserted—this unitary message with the linguistic product, the single word. During this early developmental period, the words represent an addition only to the nonverbal messages, and nonverbal and verbal elements are expressed parallel to each other. The message is therefore partly redundant, a fact which increases its effectiveness though the communication efficiency may still be low. This redundancy is expressed in Figure 5.4 by having the percentages in the second "stage," i.e., parallel encoding, add up to more than one hundred. The specific proportions of messages that are transmitted in each of the diverse channels probably vary from child to child, from situation to situation, and from message to message. It is common knowledge that the efficiency of communication is, in the beginning, below one hundred percent and increases with age and communicative skill of the child. This is illustrated in the right column of the figure.

With further progress in language skills, a larger proportion of the message content is conveyed by means of the verbal channel. The transition between the levels is fluid and continuous; this is represented by the broken lines, which separate the stages. Finally, the verbal part of the messages achieves dominance and becomes increasingly sufficient for effective communication. In principle, language can now be substituted for all the nonverbal channels of communication. The maximum of this substitution is reached in written communication between strangers over distances, where situational variables or other nonverbal message elements cannot convey any information. In normal, oral communication, the nonverbal means of information transmission generally carry a rest-portion of the message. The amount of this portion varies with social class and especially with the education of the speakers, as amply proved by sociolinguistic research. The communication efficiency approaches asymptotically one hundred percent, a goal which is rarely or never attained in ordinary communication.

Preliminary Evidence for the Described Relationships Between Nonverbal and Verbal Messages In Table 5.4, the above theoretical scheme is exemplified by selections from the verbal and nonverbal communication of two two-year-old, male children from middle-class monolingual backgrounds. Evidence about the shared aspects of the behavior setting is included together with nonverbal and verbal message structures. No integration of the partial messages from the diverse

Table 5.4. Interrelationships of nonverbal and verbal communicative acts[a]

Nonverbal communication	Verbal communication
Parallel encoding	
T pulls a vacuum cleaner from D	Mine
C points to something	That
C gives an object to E	Here
C holds a ball	Football
C shows a brush to E	Comb
C sits down on a chair	I sit down
C reaches for a specific book	I want that
C points to lake in which people swim	See water—they swimming
C points to horses in river	Horsie wet
Verbal complementation	
C hands a toy to E	Hold it
C hands a fish puzzle to E	Take fishy
C hands a part of a toy to E	Fix it
C hands a toy to E	Take that off
C points to an opening in a toy	There's broken in there
C hands E shoe to put it on	Shoe came off
C points to a man on a tractor	My daddy driving
C points to a picture	My daddy on it
C points to a picture of a woman	Is that my mommy?
Substitution of verbal forms	
T looks down at D whose diapers are being changed	David pee-pee
C is frustrated because he cannot find a station on the radio	Turn (*imperative*) that radio
C slips down from the chair because it moved	The chair moved over
D asks T	Where did my choo-choo go?
C rubs his behind	I hurt my bottom
C runs into another room	I be back
C fixes a toy	I fixed it
D tells an adult	T broke it
C searching	Where did the pen go?

[a] C stands for child; D and T are two children; E is an observer.

channels is provided, simply because it is not needed. The diverse elements fuse equally automatically for the reader into one unitary and easily comprehended message, as they did this for the hearer.

To substantiate numerically the communicative changes exemplified in Table 5.4, the information content of nonverbal as well as verbal messages would have to be measured together with the meaning intended by the sender and the message actually understood by the receiver. Moerk (1975b) suggested and described a verbalization quotient to express those relationships. For differentiated quantitative analyses, however, the method still needs refinements. The ascription of specific examples to the specific stages is, therefore, not yet definite; the general principle, however, can be demonstrated.

In the first instance, i.e., parallel encoding, the intended message is fully communicated by the nonverbal acts of the children as they are performed in the behavior setting. The verbal part is added for special emphasis, to attract attention, or for other as yet unknown reasons. On the next higher level, as in the case of the examples summarized under the category *verbal complementation,* the message conveyed by the nonverbal act is equivocal. The verbal message serves to clarify whether the partner "shall hold the object," "shall fix it," or "shall put the shoe on again" after it came off. Finally, in the last group of examples, *substitution of verbal forms,* most if not all of the information is conveyed through verbal means, when the child produces a verbal utterance. The nonverbal act contributes only additional but redundant information. This verbal substitution is most evident when children talk about past events, about their plans for the immediate future, or when they search for an object that they specify verbally, i.e., when they begin to employ the distancing function of language.

Although the examples in Table 5.4 serve demonstrative purposes, a detailed analysis of specific effects of the various independent variables is not yet possible, since too many of them remain undifferentiated: Individual differences in language skills or in skills of nonverbal communication are confounded with variables of the behavior setting, especially those of the interaction partners. A second type of analysis is therefore presented in the next section.

Relationships Between Nonverbal and Verbal Messages in Ecological Perspective   To differentiate between the effects of some of these variables upon language performance, it was attempted to keep several of them constant. Complete differentiation will require prolonged experimental work with larger numbers of subjects. A demonstration of the diversity of encoding, when only situational variables change, can be already attempted, however. Individual differences can be accounted for easily by specifying which child produces each utterance. Developmental changes also can be practically eliminated by selecting examples from one single observation session. It cannot be expected that a child could advance much in his cognitive and language skills during the course of merely one hour of casual play. In Tables 5.5 and 5.6, data from one hour of interaction are presented for two children, D and T. At the time of this observation, D was 2,1 and T was 2,2 years old. While the nonverbal communication skills can be assumed as constant for each child during this short time interval, the nonverbal communication effectiveness may vary in interdependence with the type of message and variables in the behavior setting. To reduce the number of variables involved, only two types of meaningful messages, demonstrative messages and requests, were selected for demonstration purposes. Demonstrative messages are presented in Table 5.5 and requests in Table 5.6. Since the semantic dimension partly depends upon variables of the behavior setting, complete constancy on this dimension could not, however, be expected in a free observation situation. After all other subject-related variables have been controlled to a considerable degree, the remaining independent variable, i.e., the type of information conveyed nonverbally, should account for the variations in verbal behavior. The proportional contribution from nonverbal communication in turn must primarily depend upon variables in the behavior setting, which could neither be controlled nor fully recorded.

It is at present almost impossible to provide evidence, in the strictest sense, that the observers perceived the meaning intended by the child. This only could be done convincingly by means of a presentation of a videotape recording of each instance of interaction. Since, however, the examples are part of a full chain of interactions, the communicational intentions of the child could be compared with the observer's interpretations in the ensuing feedback processes. After the communication partner had reacted to the message according to his interpretation of it, the child demonstrated, by means of his satisfaction with the outcome, whether his intention was understood correctly. To further validate the accuracy of the interpretations of the intended meaning, the observations were made repeatedly by two observers simultaneously, so as to check the reliability of the interpretations.

Table 5.5 presents all demonstrative statements of both children. In the course of only one hour, D encoded a demonstrative message, often combined with additional elements, in eleven different ways without repeating the identical form of encoding a single time. T en-

Table 5.5. Examples of encoding of demonstrative messages

Child statement	Alternatives encoded							
	Deixis/Pronoun	Action	Location	Object	Person	Possession	Question	Other
D It isn't there	x		x					Copula
D There go, Trever		x	x		x			
D Choo-choo train				x				
D Here, here			xx					
D Choo-choo train (Bobby)				x	x			
D Do that	x	x						
D Man					x			
D Man in car			x		x			
D What goes in there?		x	x	x				Article
D Here, a choo-choo train			x	x				
D Goes like this	x	x						Comparison
T Look	x							
T Gas				x				
T Hay				x				
T My daddy drinking		x			x	x		
T Shoes				x				
T Him on it	x		x		x			
T Look, look	xx							
T They land on it	x	x	x					
T That one	x			x	x			
T My daddy on it	x		x		x	x		
T My daddy on that	x		x		x	x		
T Open that	x	x		x				
T Is that my mommy?	x				x	x	x	Copula
T Look	x		x		x			
T Him on it	x				x			
T Water, water wash		x		xx				

Table 5.6. Examples of encoding of requests

Child statement	Alternatives encoded					
	Self-reference	Verb requesting	Object	Pronoun	Person addressed	Possession
D I want horsie	x	x	x			
D Clothes, mine			x			x
D Mine						x
D Have a book		x	x			
D I want that	x	x		x		
D I want it	x	x		x		
D Me want	x	x				
D My helicopter			x			x
T Me have it	x	x		x		
T Let me have it (4 times)	x	xx		x		
T Let me have that	x	xx		x		
T Me apple juice (Bobby)	x		x		x	
T Me hold on	x	x				

coded the message "look" sixteen times during the same period and used fourteen different forms of it with only two exact repetitions. In the columns to the right of the statement, the specific elements are marked that the child encoded verbally in formulating the desired message. The diversity of this encoding is self-evident. The causes for such diversity could be discerned through actual observations of the child in the behavior setting. It appeared that the child evaluated the informational needs of the prospective receiver of the message and encoded only those elements that could not be ascertained unmistakably from other variables in the situation. Bloom (1970) observed the same principle in the conversations of her subjects. To provide unequivocal evidence for this assertion, experimental studies that vary single features of the behavior setting will have to be performed. Somewhat pertinent experiments have been undertaken with older subjects by Glucksberg and Krauss (1967), Olson (1970), and Osgood (1971). Although these studies lend support to the above conclusions, they cannot be fully generalized to children who are considerably younger, since age is one of the most important concomitant variables of changes in communicative behavior. Observational evidence for a similar sensitivity of younger children to the requirements of the communication partner has been reported recently by Lewis and Freedle (1973), Shatz (1974), Shatz and Gelman (1973), and several other investigators. These findings and suggestions stand in stark contrast to the previously dominant belief that the young child acts egocentrically in his communicative behavior. Neither the currently available research evidence nor space considerations make it possible to solve this complex question here. Suffice it to suggest that the child's familiarity with the situation and thereby with the various features of the referents, whether diacritical or not, appear to be the decisive factors. According to this interpretation, communicational failures would not be due so much to communicational insufficiencies but to difficulties in the analysis and comparison of complex stimulus situations.

To broaden the basis for these conclusions, the encoding of a second category of messages is presented in Table 5.6: various forms that both children employed to express their requests for an object in the course of one single hour. Cognitive and linguistic skills are again approximately constant, and the basic semantic dimension is also the same. What varies are the details of the behavior setting. D expressed eight requests during this specific hour and he used eight different formulations for these requests. T uttered nine different requests and used six formulations to express them. As far as could be discerned in the present observations, the reasons for this diversity are quite complex. Whereas informational needs seemed to be the decisive criterion for several variations in D's encoding, T seemed to use different formulations more in response to differences in interpersonal relationships. Although this specific problem was not systematically investigated, it appeared that both children often employed more complex and more "polite" forms of request when talking to an adult as compared to the demands that were directed to peers. This preliminary finding is supported by identical evidence that was presented over forty years ago by McCarthy (1930) and Smith (1935). Both scientists could demonstrate that preschool children used longer sentences and more advanced patterns of language when they were conversing with adults than when they were conversing with other children. Recent studies (Shatz and Gelman, 1973; Weeks, 1971) on code switching of young children have confirmed this conclusion. Specific statements are also influenced by the verbal context: A preceding statement uttered by the same child or by another child may have already conveyed some of the needed information. The message that follows consequently can be encoded more parsimoniously.

Though the above examples by no means can be considered as definitely proving the hypothesis of multichannel communication or of the child's sensitivity to the informational requirements of his communication partner, they can serve to demonstrate the type of phenomena that suggests this hypothesis. The same tentativeness is characteristic of most of the details of this chapter, but not of the major lines of argument. These arguments have to be integrated with the reports of many other recent investigators that were quoted repeatedly and with the older findings on human and animal communication. All of them together suggest an approach to the study of language acquisition that is radically different from the recently predominant transformational grammarian approach as well as from a strictly behavioristic learning theoretical one. The conclusions that can be drawn from the above presentations are summarized below to present a concise integration of aspects antecedent to language in the strict sense. These antecedents are viewed as the foundations upon which vocabulary and syntactic skills are built. The aspect pertaining to the learning of verbal skills proper is discussed in the following chapter.

SUMMARY AND CONCLUSION

It has been described on the basis of a wide ranging literature survey in Chapters Three and Four that cognitive and behavioral structures are established by the infant long before he begins to employ language. These structures are derived from and reflect the structures of reality. Many of them are built in close interaction with the social environment and are at first consistently shared and only thereafter intentionally communicated. This communication of cognitive structures is especially evident when directive messages are studied. Referential communication in the form of sharing and showing of objects as well as of pointing is, however, also securely demonstrated before the onset of speech.

Verbal elements are slowly integrated into this variety of complex communicative structures. These processes have been discussed in this chapter. They lead first to one-word utterances, which can be easily interpreted by the receiver of the message who takes into account many other message elements besides the single word. Even before the infant learns to employ verbal symbols, he has learned to choose in a flexible manner from his repertoire of communicative channels those that are most pertinent and effective in specific behavior settings and for specific communication partners. The various communicative surface structures are thereby shaped and formed, while underlying cognitive and intention structures remain relatively stable. When the child begins to employ verbal elements and continues to use them increasingly and more predominantly, he does not need to acquire any profound new principles of communication. He merely employs another part of his body, namely, the vocal tract, as a tool for the purposes of communication and he learns to produce vocal artifacts with it. Since he has already employed this same organ instrumentally in his intentional crying during the second half of his first year of life, the transition to language is quite smooth and "natural" in this respect. The universal babble words *mama, nana,* and similar sound complexes are evidence of this. The second process, i.e., the learning of new articulatory movements in order to approximate the modal sound patterns of the mother tongue, also builds upon a predecessor, but it is more complex and takes a considerably longer period before reaching completion. The predecessor can be found in the infant's learning to adapt his hand and arm movements to the artifacts he encounters in his man-made environment. How close this predecessor is to linguistic skills is seen in the fact that highly developed forms of communication can and quite generally do develop out of this adaptation. Sign language, whether systematically taught to or spontaneously developed by deaf persons, communication by means of drawing and painting, and, of course, written communication, in addition to normal children's and adults' gestural communication, are evidence that manual communication is a close rival of oral communication. The recently reported findings on the predilection of higher primates for manual communication (Fouts, 1973; Gardner and Gardner, 1969) and a variety of reports from anthropological research invite the speculation that only relatively accidental evolutionary variables may have led to the selection of vocal language instead of gestural language as the primary means of human communication. On the other hand, one could assert with justification that all human communities have developed three communication systems: the first encompassing facial expressions, with the exception of those contributing to vocal language; the second as found in manual gestures; and the third as represented by vocal language. There is some overlap among these three major channels; but especially the hands as instruments *par excellence* for cognitive and object-directed behavior can and do often convey many directional and referential messages. The same messages at other times can be expressed in vocal language. Since gestural communication precedes developmentally verbal-vocal communication, it provides one of the most important bases upon which the later evolving oral language can be built. Adults employ this basis consistently in the training of their children's oral language.

chapter
six

Verbal Channel of Communication and Instructional Aspects of Verbal Interactions

SCOPE OF THE INQUIRY

The leading idea that can be traced through all the preceding chapters is that the infant and young child acquire language through interaction with the environment. The child's own dispositions and the environmental constellations may be excellently coordinated to make this acquisition possible, but the child nevertheless has to labor for a prolonged period to master all the prerequisites and to arrive at the end product, language. In previous chapters the establishment of the prerequisites has been described in considerable detail. The present chapter therefore should represent the crowning achievement, by exposing through a fine-grained analysis how the end product is attained. This crowning achievement, however, has to be postponed for the indefinite future, since only partial and very preliminary evidence has been collected that could be employed for such a synthesis. Two approaches have been chosen in the past when investigators approached this topic: The temporally earlier one was that of Brown and associates, who, under the influence of Chomsky's generative system, tried to describe what the actual linguistic competence of the child was at various stages of his development. This aim in its original form and, even more so, the employed methodology, i.e., mere distributional analysis, have been recognized as insufficient and therefore have been replaced by functional and semantic approaches.

The recent change in goals implies a renewed search for a frame of reference before further descriptive attempts can be made.

The second and comparatively recent approach consists of a detailed description of the verbal environment, i.e., of the input that enables the child to acquire the decoding and encoding rules of his mother tongue. With this choice a process-oriented analysis is implicitly accepted as the only valid method. Since the process has at least three aspects, the analysis also should incorporate all three of them: 1) the input provided, 2) the child's handling of this input, and 3) the rules and the knowledge abstracted by the child. The various studies discussed in this chapter rarely included all three aspects simultaneously. Most of them have been devoted to only one of them: the description of the input. Others have dealt solely with children's strategies, while very few have aimed at both of these elements. The third element, the child's linguistic competence, with few exceptions has been studied in isolation. As suggested by the title, this chapter attempts to deal with all three aspects of the problem though the coverage of them necessarily has to be uneven. During the most recent years, a reasonably clear and detailed description of input phenomena has been accomplished. The main emphasis in the present chapter therefore is on the language input that is provided as a model for the child. Remarks on the other two topics are incorporated into this description whenever pertinent evidence exists.

Cognitive/Learning Aspects of Language Acquisition

To deal fully with the child's handling and storage of the input, one obviously would have to integrate much of what was said in Chapters Three and Four with the survey on verbal interactions provided in Chapter Six. Before the child can handle the input cognitively, he has to analyze it perceptually and to store the information in short-term memory. Most of the analyzed elements have to be classified according to their meaning and syntactic functions. While analyzing and classifying, the child also has to establish an abstract representation of the verbal structure, both in its surface form and in its possible underlying base form. If the verbal input contains one element that is unknown to the child, he has to compare this verbal structure with the expected communicative intention of his communication partner to find out what the meaning of the unknown element may have been. He then has to store this hypothesized relation between meaning and symbolic form in order to retain it for later evaluation.

As Bowerman (1976) has recently emphasized, several principles have to be learned by the child in this process of language acquisition. This probably involves several types of learning as well. Vocabulary learning, i.e., the establishment of a relation between verbal symbol and conceptualization, is probably based upon some type of association learning. Even in this case the situation is, however, more complex: With the exception of the relatively rare one-to-one relationships in the case of proper names, words refer mostly to classes of objects or relations. The child therefore has to learn to associate a conceptual class with the sound symbol, which varies across speakers and situations. If he has first assumed a one-to-one relationship, he has to generalize the verbal symbol to many class members.

In contrast to this case of primarily associative learning, one will most often encounter rule learning in language acquisition. Independent of whether it is a question of morphological rules, of syntactic rules, or of the correct employment of intonation patterns, complex cognitive principles are involved. In the case of morphology and intonation patterns, the child can pair linguistic elements or paralinguistic phenomena with cognitive relations. In the case of word order, an abstract principle of serial order is employed to encode a semantic relation. It is highly probable that several levels of learning are involved in language acquisition. Therefore, an application of Gagné's (1968) hierarchical sequence of learning processes to language learning could prove helpful in the clarification of these questions. Not only does the child have to abstract and to master principles and phenomena that differ widely from each other, but parents also must provide their input in a form that makes this possible. That they do provide an optimal linguistic input for their children is argued and partly demonstrated below. The various tasks the child encounters as well as his perceptual and memory propensities therefore must be reflected in the input provided by parents. Pertinent questions about these problems have barely been asked in the available literature. Full answers, therefore, cannot yet be provided, and suggestions and reminders of the problems sometimes have to suffice in the present survey.

Motivational Aspects of Language Acquisition

As these complex cognitive and learning problems are discussed, it might appear as if the carriage were put before the horse. No consideration is given to the problem of what the moving/motivating forces in language learning may be. The question could be and has been asked repeatedly, why the infant should bother to undergo all the labors of acquiring his mother tongue if he fared so well during his first year of life with preverbal means of communication. As is generally known, autistic children do not acquire a functional language in spite of an apparently sufficient level of intelligence. One of the main tenets of learning psychology has been that learning proceeds faster and is more permanent if motivating factors come into play. If prolonged training and exercise are required, such motivational factors become of overwhelming importance, as is well-enough known to every second-language teacher. In the case of the young child, all the phenomena that normally require motivational analyses are encountered: the relatively fast learning of a large amount of material, the prolonged retention of the learned material, and, as seen from the discussion in this chapter, the intensive training and exercise in the interactions between mothers and their children. It is, consequently, not astonishing that the question of motivation has appeared and reappeared in the literature of first-language acquisition. A survey of this topic is, however, somewhat difficult, since various authors have employed widely differing terminology and have probably also aimed at phenomena that are not completely equivalent. Aristotle's and K. Bühler's *organon* model of language appears similar to Skinner's operant aspect. Whether the Wittgensteinian functionalist approach and the recent pragmatic-functional considerations are completely equivalent or only partially overlapping with the *organon*/operant model is not easy to decide. When Humboldt, Langer, and Chase assert that language helps the child to structure and delimit a cognitive world view due to the hierarchical classification of phenomena and relationships that is provided through linguistic structures, they again see language as a tool. It is, however, now considered more as a cognitive and internal tool, contributing to internal information-processing efficiency rather than to pragmatic task solutions. In a different vein, the motivations that mothers experience when they consciously and intentionally teach language and those that they employ to attract and retain their children's attention to the language learning task are certainly different, though they could also be described from a functional perspective.

In the second principal section of this chapter most of the suggestions that were found in the literature on the motivational principles affecting language acquisition and language use of children are summarized and grouped in a preliminary manner. Though it could be argued with justification that logically the motivation for language learning should be explored before the specific learning processes are discussed, the opposite sequence is followed in this chapter. In this manner, the topic for which more substantial findings and theoretical analyses exist is treated first, and the one which necessarily has to remain very preliminary is given less emphasis. It is hoped, however, that the discussion of motivation and the factual evidence that is provided fulfill the valuable function of drawing attention to a neglected area and that it suggests at the same time how many fertile starting points for research already exist.

DELIMITATION OF THE TOPICS

Age Period Under Investigation and the Speed of Language Acquisition

An erroneous assertion that became first famous through Chomsky and Miller (1963), and was widely repeated thereafter, concerns the speed of language acquisition. These two authors argued that children acquire language at an astonishing speed and that they complete most of the tasks of language learning before entering school. According to this argument, only the preschool years would be relevant for the study of our present topic. This argument was reinforced by Lenneberg's (1967) speculations regarding a critical period for language acquisition, which would also fall into the early period of childhood. Many recent studies, such as those of C. Chomsky (1969), of Graves and Koziol (1971), and of Palermo and Molfese (1972) have, however, clearly refuted Chomsky's and Miller's claim. They have shown that children still have considerable problems with even simple language skills during the elementary school years and later on. Evidence to weaken Lenneberg's critical period hypothesis already has been available for a considerable time and more of it has been accumulated recently. As early as 1909, Guillet demonstrated the superiority of adults as compared to children in vocabulary acquisition and retention. In an experimental study, his son learned either the English, French, or German name for specific animals while Guillet himself learned their Japanese counterparts. The father learned the new words almost twice as fast as his son and he retained more than twice as many after a six-week interval. The father relearned the set of words in one-third the number of repetitions that were required by the child. More recently, Asher and Price (1967) subjected eight- to ten-year-old children, fourteen-year-old adolescents, and college students to the same controlled exposure of short commands given in Russian. Both vocabulary and sentence structure had to be learned to complete the experimental tasks successfully. The results demonstrated that the adults were superior to all the children and were doing almost twice as well as the eight-year-olds. The results of the intermediate age groups were in between. Less experimentally controlled but numerically and practically more impressive evidence comes from the speed-language courses, which some military personnel were required to take during and after World War II. Through these programs a considerable level of proficiency in a new language could be attained in a very short period. Evidence exists, therefore, to refute Lenneberg's hypothesis for language learning in general. Whether his hypothesis could be retained for first-language learning currently cannot be decided because of the lack of reliable evidence. The reports on the language learning of the so-called wolf-children are too unreliable to be considered seriously. Luria's and Yudovich's (1959) study, referred to throughout this chapter, seems to partly refute Lenneberg's thesis also for first-language acquisition.

As far as evidence exists, it probably would be best to include all age periods in the study of the principles and motivations for language learning. Research on the parallels between first- and second-language learning (Braine, 1971b; Ervin-Tripp, 1973) also would suggest that, for the understanding of cognitive/learning processes in language acquisition, all ages can and should be studied. The sources and types of environmental input are, however, very different in the case of adult language learning. Certain differences in cognitive and learning processes also must be surmised because of overall cognitive level and interference as well as transfer from the first language. Since the emphasis in this chapter lies on environmental input and on first-language acquisition, and since the goal is to attain some more generalizable descriptions, a limited age period had to be chosen and only the preschool years are covered extensively.

Sources of Input and Their Importance for Language Learning

Adults as Sources   Technical and other sociocultural conditions of society determine largely who will spend the most time with the infant and young child and who, therefore, will be able to provide most of the input. Since most studies on language learning have been performed in Western technologically developed societies, where the husband works outside the home and only commutes home for meals and rest, the conclusions about linguistic input and its effect necessarily must be culturally biased and possibly are not generalizable. The situation that prevails in Western societies, i.e., that mothers spend the most time with their young children, seems, however, to be paralleled cross-culturally. M. Mead (1930) and many other anthropological investigators as well as Lewis (1957), who employed a psycholinguistic perspective, reported on this phenomenon. Probably because of the large amount of interaction and the ensuing satisfaction of primary and secondary needs, stimuli emanating from the mother acquire a special value for the child. Valentine (1930) reported that the child he observed was much more prone to imitate her mother than any other person. Recent research, which is too extensive to be summarized here, has generally affirmed this impression. It has, however, added important new aspects. Friedlander (1970), who performed some of the first and most objective observational studies of language behavior in the home, emphasized that only the most intimate encounters between parent and infant during the care-giving activities may attract the infant's special attention to the verbal stimuli, while much of adult conversation overheard by the infant may have little effect. Leopold (1939) and Delacroix (1930) came to very similar conclusions. These intimate encounters proceed in an environment that is extremely familiar to the child and that allows for a quite accurate prediction of the average expectable message. It is therefore relatively easy for the child to decode a verbal message in this environment and to guess its overall meaning and the meaning of those specific elements that are emphasized by the mother.

With these last considerations the emphasis has shifted somewhat: The length of interaction or the amount of input has not been stressed as much as its attention-evoking value and its semantic transparency. Support for these qualifications comes from several studies. Horner (1968) found that, although children talked most frequently to their mothers, the periods during which mother and child were interacting were relatively brief in each single instance; the rate of conversation, however, was high. White (1972) reported that, although the mothers of his advanced children talked a great deal to their infants, they rarely spent five, ten, or twenty minutes teaching their one- to two-year-olds. Much of the teaching was done "on the sly" and usually at the child's instigation. The importance of these findings is analyzed in later sections when one-trial learning, the active hypothesis formation and testing by the child, and its alert interest verbal input are discussed. However, the foregoing suggests that other persons in the environment, who spend less time with the child, also could be of importance for language acquisition. The question of the father's role therefore comes into the focus of concern.

Very little can be said assuredly in this respect, since the factual reports are few and the reported findings extremely contradictory. On the one hand, the study of Rebelsky and Hanks (1971) is notorious, suggesting that the father spends barely a few seconds per day with his infant child. In contrast, Parke, O'Leary, and West (1972) reported that the father was a very active participant in the care of the newborn infant. Jordan, Radin, and Epstein (1975) explored specifically the father's influence upon intellectual functioning in preschool children and found evidence for such an influence. Most instructive, however, for the present concern is again a report of Friedlander et al. (1972). They described the case of one family in which the father's contribution to the child's verbal input was less than five percent of the total verbal behavior in the home. It was provided in Spanish only, as contrasted to the rest of the input in English. During these short interactions, the father intentionally assumed a teaching role and provided his linguistic input with this instructional goal in mind. Friedlander et al. found that the child's grasp of Spanish at the age of 18 months was comparable to his skills in English. It is hereby suggested that short and rare periods of interaction during which input is provided in an optimal manner can make disproportional contributions to a child's language skills. Similar conclusions are suggested by Nelson's (1973) findings, that the number of adults a child encountered was significantly related to his language development. It could be argued that the more adults the child encounters, the shorter these encounters probably will be, given a fixed amount of waking time. While any final statement would be premature, the possibility obviously exists that the father's input may be of importance and deserves to be studied. That it is more intentionally instructional and systematically different from the mothers' input has been demonstrated recently in very detailed analyses by Blount and Padgug (1976).

Siblings and Peers as Sources   Very little systematic and detailed information exists on the influence of siblings and peers. Some agreement on a few points can be found, however. Earlier investigators (McCarthy, 1930; Smith, 1935) reported that speech among children is considerably simpler than speech between children and adults. Almost the same principle has been discussed recently under the terminology of "code-switching" by Gleason (1973) and Shatz and Gelman (1976). Indirect support for this principle can be found in the negative correlation that Nelson (1973) found between time spent with other children and measures of language level and rate of language acquisition. If children's language is much simpler, then it would provide less advanced models and less challenge and therefore would not be conducive to advanced language development. Evidence for the differential effects of adults versus children upon general cognitive and also language development have been established through research on birth order effects. It is generally found that the single and the oldest child develops cognitively and linguistically faster than later born siblings. As cause of this acceleration is generally postulated the more stimulating and enriching environment provided by adults as compared to that provided by children of the same or of somewhat higher ages (Sutton-Smith and Rosenberg, 1970). The study of Luria and Yudovich (1959) on identical twins who had experienced very little language stimulation from adults and mainly depended upon mutual influences suggests a similar principle. These twins had not yet developed anything that could be labeled a systematic competence of their mother tongue even by the end of the preschool years. The above studies consequently imply that siblings and peers do not normally exert important instructional influences upon language learning.

In partial contrast to this apparent consensus stands Slobin's (1969) cross-cultural evidence that in many less developed societies older siblings take over most of the caregiving functions for their younger siblings and that they soon become almost the only persons to interact relatively frequently on the verbal level with the younger children. These older siblings remain the major source of speech input for the younger ones until the latter reach the age of three to three and one-half years. At this time the larger peer group becomes important for the social and linguistic interactions of the child. At present no data are available about the speed of language development of these children as compared to matched children who would experience primarily adult language input. Since Slobin's informants learned to speak, the effect can be only one of degree. Evidence to support the argument of Slobin that the peer group may be influential for language development was presented by Stewart (1964). He observed that many Black children in Washington, D.C., had adopted the dialect of their peers, while their parents spoke a more or less standard variety of English. In a completely different society and for somewhat older children, M. Mead (1930) also found that teenagers who had worked as domestics in European homes could teach English effectively to their younger peers. The teenage jargon of adolescents prevalent in most societies provides evidence for similar processes of peer group originated teaching. It can be concluded, therefore, that at least for adolescents the peer group can have wide-ranging effects upon language competence and behavior.

The arguments in the above paragraph are derived from other cultures or from children that were considerably older. They therefore cannot be contrasted directly and closely with those in the previous paragraph which dealt with phenomena in Western middle-class groups and with preschool children. Besides the research on code-switching, which deals with communicational and not directly with instructional phenomena, only a few unsystematic remarks were found in the literature. Repeatedly mentioned is the fact that even preschool children of immigrant parents do not speak with such a heavy accent as their parents or that they grow up without any discernible accent. Although the source of this learning is not known, it cannot lie with the parents. The relatively rapid speech acquisition of children coming to foreign countries and having close contacts with a native peer group has also been often casually remarked upon. On a more scientific level, Stern and Stern (1907) argued that younger siblings did not need to ask many *what* questions since older siblings provided labels spontaneously. Vocabulary instruction is thereby attributed to older children. Bar-Adon (1971) emphasized the language-teaching activities of older siblings more generally. He argued on the "basis of [his] observations, that the impact of other children, especially slightly older siblings and somewhat older colleagues, wherever they are available, is of no less importance than that of the parents. Children seem to possess a special sense for 'speech analysis' of their younger siblings or friends . . ." (1971:445). At least the last sentence of Bar-Adon would be supported by research on code-switching. Since Bar-Adon does not give the source of his "observations," their generality cannot be evaluated.

From these casual and conflicting reports on the influences of siblings and peers upon language acquisition, it appears probable that the facts may be equally contradicting. Specific variables, such as the age level of both partners, differences in age and language level between the partners, and closeness of social and emotional ties may be the decisive factors that produce diverse and often contradictory results if they are not taken into account. The findings about the importance of the sensitive calibration of adult speech input, if it shall lead to language learning, would make such an expectation highly plausible.

Mass Media as Sources   Finally, it has to be briefly considered if and to what degree other influences may affect children's language acquisition. The effects of radio and television are often stressed in the literature with the assumption that the large amount of stimulation provided by these two media may be beneficial for language development. Also in regard to this question, no final conclusions can be drawn because the available data are still too sketchy and conflicting. On the one hand, evidence has been accumulated that children develop intellectually earlier and acquire a larger vocabulary at present as compared to the turn of the century (Schramm, Lyle, and Parker, 1961). On the other hand, children from deprived homes who grow up seriously deficient in middle-class language skills often experience a continuous stream of verbal stimulation coming from the television set. Yet this abundance of verbal stimulation has no apparent positive effect upon their language skills. Whitehurst, Novak, and Zorn (1972) described the case of a child who was subjected to abundant television stimulation but deprived of the opportunity of direct verbal exchange with his mother. This child had acquired a vocabulary of only six words at the age of three years and four months. Wachs, Uzgiris, and Hunt (1971) provided supportive evidence and a possible theoretical explanation for this finding. They reported not only a significant negative correlation between the level of ambient noise (television, radio, talking) and performance on a variety of Piagetian tasks, but even more specifically, high amounts of ambient noise were negatively correlated with language development. They concluded that overstimulation leads to habituation of orienting and attentional responses in infants. Nelson (1973) found, too, that the amount of time spent watching television was significantly and negatively related to all language measures. A detailed discussion of the possible effects of television upon language development has been provided by Entwisle (1968). It is not necessary to repeat this analysis here, since no specific investigation of the processes that are involved when the child listens to television was presented.

Wyatt (1969) provided an explanation for this apparent contrast between the amount of stimulation and the amount of learning when she stressed that the linguistic model has to be attuned to the language level of the child. Since the television cannot be attuned to the level of the individual child, the matching between the level of the model and that of the child will be incomplete at best and dependent upon program selection and/or parental guidance. A further aspect pertaining to this question was already explored by Delacroix (1930) before the invention of the television. He emphasized that the child learns more from speech addressed to him than from ambient speech of adults. In the case of most television programs, the speech of the adult characters is even more remote from the child than are conversations between actually present adults. It therefore will be even less conducive to language learning. The discussion in the following sections, of how parents convey linguistic information to their children, often suggests in which respects normal television programs are deficient as language-teaching means. This suggestion that normal television programs have negligible or even negative effects upon language acquisition does not imply, however, that programs that would have positive effects could not be designed. The brief survey, in a later section, of how parents successfully employ the iconic channel of picture books for vocabulary teaching provides some preliminary suggestions on how this could be done.

OVERALL APPROACHES IN RESEARCH ON LANGUAGE INPUT AND LANGUAGE LEARNING

The main body of this chapter surveys studies according to the instructional strategies that are illustrated in each section. Little or no concern, then, is shown for differences in methodological or theoretical approaches. Since, however, a considerable variety of methods and theoretical interpretations are found in the field, a brief systematic discussion of the various approaches that are encountered in the literature appears advisable. The main methodologies of data collection or data generation and the theoretical interpretations of the entire topic and of individual results, therefore, are briefly reviewed in the immediately following sections.

Approaches to Data Collection or Data Generation

The two separate terms *data collection* and *data generation* emphasize one aspect that can be an important problem for research in this field. It was analyzed theoretically, and partly demonstrated in Chapter Five, how situational variables affect verbal output. Whenever the investigator attempts to collect information on language behavior and language learning, he is rarely able to avoid changing the situational context; therefore he may distort the resulting data, i.e., he may generate data instead of merely recording them. This phenomenon is especially obvious in experimental approaches to language training, but it has to be considered in so-called naturalistic observations, too, since many investigators bring a standard set of toys with them, as well as the recording instruments and the observers, which may become the topic of discussion and may otherwise affect the verbal behavior of the children and their mothers. From a logical perspective, a distinction between mere observation and experiment is barely possible. Not only is any act of teaching and training manipulative and therefore experimental in some sense, but even many parental interventions are experiments to see "whether it works." On the other hand, experiments with children have to be relatively "naturalistic" to assure the cooperation of the young subjects, and children often respond to experiments in ways not envisaged in the design of the manipulative procedure. As seen later in the discussion of social class differences in language behavior and language instruction, both semiexperimental and predominantly observational methods have been employed by various investigators. All training programs that are scientifically designed are influenced to a certain degree by the experimental research on human learning, and training is, of course, manipulation in its clearest form.

It is evident, therefore, that any subsets that are formed under this heading cannot be fully and logically exclusive. Also, in the case of the four subsets formed below for the present analysis, the borderlines cannot be clearly and sharply drawn. Some of the studies to be quoted are members of two or even more of these sets, suggesting that two or more dimensions would have to be defined for a complete analysis of this topic. The present ordering is neither final nor exhaustive; it represents only a convenient and helpful way of describing existing research.

Naturalistic Observations in the Home and the Laboratory   Naturalistic observations belong to the oldest methods in child research.

The roots of baby-biographical research go back several centuries, and this method was still employed after the turn of the present century. After a comparatively short eclipse due to considerations of methodological rigor and to concerns with statistical in contrast to psychological significance, the baby-biographical method has again won many followers. It can be predicted with considerable confidence that this trend will continue as long as investigators remain concerned with the whole child and as long as they employ "rich interpretations," which require a knowledge of the shared presuppositions and of the child's system of nonverbally established meanings.

It would take too long to enumerate all the studies that fall under this heading. Suffice it to say that even the early data collection of Brown and associates came close to being baby-biographical. The research of Bloom (1970), Bowerman (1973), and Greenfield and Smith (1976) falls squarely into this category. Several of these authors even reverted to the previously discredited method of studying their own children. Some methodological advances were introduced in these studies such as the addition of other children besides one's own and the provision of standardized play situations. In several cases the entire observation was performed in laboratory settings, which made videorecording possible and also permitted a greater standardization of the environment. A considerable disadvantage of this methodology is that the subject population is not at all representative, being drawn from the investigator's own family and from the circle of his close acquaintances. Middle and upper middle-class mother-child dyads and their language interactions are therefore sampled and the results cannot be generalized to larger and different groups of the population. This restriction in the population, however, could also be seen as an advantage. Since middle- and upper-class dyads are generally successful in their language training/learning endeavors, the resulting descriptions of their interactions will pertain to predominantly successful methodologies, which of course are the main topic of concern.

Studies of Social Class Differences in Language Behavior and Maternal Language Instruction   The research on social class differences offers a valuable counterpart to the select samples that were obtained in many naturalistic observation studies. The recent impetus in this field goes back to the publications of Bernstein (1960, 1962) and to the famous studies of Hess and Shipman (1965, 1967).

Cazden's (1966) review of the field, chapters in Williams' (1970) edited book, and Bruner's (1972b) article have provided surveys of some of the findings and controversies in the field. Much evidence (e.g., Bruck and Tucker, 1974; Francis, 1974a, b; Gay and Tweney, 1975; Skupas and Tweney, 1975; Snow et al., 1976; Zegiob and Forehand, 1975) has been accumulated in the intervening years, affirming the generality of the differences in verbal behavior between the social classes, but falling short of deciding unequivocally whether these overt differences also cause differences in cognitive processes or even cognitive/intellectual capacities.

Since differences in the verbal behaviors of lower-class children are relatively clearly established, and since considerable evidence of parallel differences in the dyadic interactions between mothers and children in this social class have been reported, the opportunity to establish direct cause-effect relationships appears to be high. For this purpose, the differences between middle- and lower-class dyadic interaction patterns have to be compared with the differences in the verbal behavior and comprehension skills of children of both classes.

Experimental Studies of Language Instruction and Language Learning   The methodology of experimental analysis of cause-effect relationships is chosen in most of the natural sciences and is also propounded as ideal in the behavioral sciences. Students of learning psychology have consequently tried to demonstrate language learning on the basis of experimental studies, conducted mostly in the psychological laboratory. Lovaas' (1967) research with autistic children is perhaps best known. Similar principles, however, can be discerned in most of the remedial language training programs employed by speech therapists. Since speech therapy is not discussed in this book, it is not necessary to summarize or evaluate these studies. Although it has been demonstrated beyond doubt that language skills can be learned in this manner, much of the flavor of naturalness that is so clearly felt in the mother's language teaching in the home is missing in the experimenter's teaching attempts and in the subsequent language behavior of the children. The applicability of these studies to normal language acquisition is therefore questionable.

The second paradigm in the experimental study of language learning, that of observational learning, appears to come closer to the natural situation in the home. Especially Bandura and his students (Bandura, 1969, 1971; Bandura and Harris, 1966), and during the more recent years Whitehurst and his associates (Whitehurst, 1971,

1972; Whitehurst and Vasta, 1975), have presented valuable reports on this topic. Details of this research are partly discussed below in connection with the analysis of various theoretical approaches and in a later section that deals with imitation in language learning. The main result that is of interest in this section is that mere modeling can lead to new forms of language behavior in children. The linguistic forms thereby acquired are not produced in a meaningless echolalic manner, nor do they remain restricted to the exact models that were presented by the adult. The child seems to learn not the specific forms only but the rules underlying the production of these forms. Since he has learned the rules, he can generalize them easily to new instances where the rules apply. Formulated in the terminology that was fashionable a few years ago in linguistic circles: The child observes only surface structures but soon produces evidence that he has acquired a knowledge of the deep structures or at least of transformation rules. A wide variety of syntactic and morphological principles have been modeled and learned in this manner in the above-quoted studies. The results therefore are of greatest importance for the analysis of natural language learning, where similar or identical phenomena are observed consistently.

Naturalistic Training Programs Intended to Enhance the Language Skills of Young Children   Two types of training programs have to be differentiated, though both have the same ultimate aim. One type deals with the children directly and therefore represents a direct attempt to reach the goal of increased language competence. The other type aims at the mothers of the children in an attempt to impart to them increased language-teaching competence. Investigators choosing this approach hope to attain the final goal in this indirect manner. Several programs represent combinations or transitional steps between these two types. Mann and van Wagenen (1975), for example, directly instructed children during a few sessions while the mothers watched the interaction. This was done primarily to instruct the mothers and not the children. The principal results were expected through the indirect route with the mother. Other programs similar in intention but predominantly or exclusively employing operant or observational learning methodologies, and pertaining therefore to the previous section, are not included here under a discussion of naturalistic programs. Naturalistic programs contain, as demonstrated in considerable detail below, multiple approaches and methodologies that are very flexibly applied. A distinction between "naturalistic training" and "contrived drill" probably would reflect the distinction intended here. Relatively detailed descriptions of some of these drill methods can be found in the monograph edited by McReynolds (1974). Again it has to be admitted that transitional forms are possible and can be found in the literature.

It appears that investigations of planned interventions were undertaken in Russia before they became common in the United States. Perhaps the most detailed report of the methods and their results was given by Luria and Yudovich (1959:92). These two authors described their methods as "dialogue conversations, verbal analysis of pictures, and relating of stories." This characterization is well worth remembering, since very similar phenomena are again encountered in the analyses of the teaching methods of untrained American mothers presented later. Another Russian description of methodologies is even closer to the phenomena described below. Bronfenbrenner (1970:18–19) quotes in translation the instruction from the official manual of the preschool program for Russian preschools: "The upbringer exploits every moment spent with the child for the development of speech. In order that the infant learns to discriminate and understand specific words, the upbringer speaks to him in short phrases, emphasizes by her intonations the main words in a given sentence, pauses after speaking to the child, and waits for him to do what is asked. It is important that the words coincide with the moment when the child engages in action, or is watching a movement or activity being performed by the adult ..." The reader may compare this description with the following sections of this chapter or even with only the titles of these sections as given in the table of contents. He will find almost complete congruence between the methods prescribed by the Russian educators and those abstracted and described by recent American investigators. Since it is almost certain that both sides arrived at their conclusions and applications independent of each other, a high degree of stability is suggested in the methodologies suited for the teaching of Indo-Germanic languages, even if they are quite different from each other. A comparison of this Russian program with that of Fowler and Swenson (1975), who concentrate upon the labeling of objects and actions, upon the use of little standard games, caregiving situations, and picture books, indicates this same similarity. It is, furthermore, highly suggestive of the value of such multivariate approaches that pre- and elementary school teachers, who have to deal daily with similar problems of language teaching and who receive immediate and continuing feedback about the effectiveness of their methods or the lack of it, have hit upon much the same approach. Evidence of a similar consistency is provided by a variety of authors in the edited book of Stendler Lavatelli (1971); of special note are the descriptions by Cazden (1971) about several English language training programs. A detailed study of the methods employed in these various training approaches and of the results obtained probably would produce a rich harvest of information of how children learn language skills effectively.

Theoretical Orientations
Underlying the Diverse Methodological Decisions

It could appear again that the cart has been put before the horse, when first the operationalizations in the study of language learning are described, whereas their rationale is explained only later. This is indeed the case, and it is also found in most of the reported studies that have been performed in this field. It is often so in human endeavors that practical necessities at first elicit an active behavioral response before the logical bases for them can be fully elaborated. It is evident from the discussion in the next section that these logical bases are not yet very precisely established. Some of them remain even in a very rudimentary form. The classification and the grouping of the various theoretical approaches, as presented here, have been chosen for expositional purposes, and it is not necessarily implied that this procedure would be an optimal system for other purposes.

No-Trial Learning   Perhaps the most important contribution of social learning theory, as propounded by Bandura (1965, 1969), is the establishment of the fact that observational learning is in many cases of equal or even of higher importance than trial-and-error learning. The monolithic restriction to one approach in all behaviorally oriented learning studies thereby has been overcome. Many detailed contributions can be found in Bandura's various publications that appear to be of great importance for the explanation of language acquisition. One of them that may help solve many disputes that arose from analyses of phenomena of normal language acquisition is the distinction between the acquisition of skills and their performance. These two processes may be temporally separated through long intervals. Another important contribution lies in the often repeated demonstration that observational learning is not dependent in each instance upon reinforcement phenomena, but that reinforcement and functional aspects are more complexly related to this type of learning. These findings on observational learning in other settings and with other tasks may make it appear less astonishing that investigators of first-language acquisition could not easily find evidence for motivating and reinforcing variables in all instances of interaction. On the other hand, as demonstrated in the second main section of this chapter, the often encountered complete denial of reinforcement effects in first-language acquisition is not supported by the evidence of mother-child interactions.

It is entailed in Bandura's (1969) analyses that observational learning involves symbolic coding, central organization, and reorganization of stimuli. This learning is therefore highly "cognitive" or "mediational" and therefore is just as easily applicable to aspects of language acquisition that pertain to rules and meaningful responses. Whereas Bandura deals extensively with the symbolic coding of linguistic structures and their representation in memory, another aspect is still being neglected, though it is of utmost importance in psycholinguistic research: The child not only learns and stores linguistic forms, and abstracts their rules, he also abstracts their meanings and he reproduces those forms in meaningful contexts and not in an echolalic fashion. In the process of observational learning the child therefore matches the perceived and abstracted linguistic forms with complex semantic structures and with meaningful intentions. This applies especially to linguistic learning, but it is also pertinent in the case of the learning of aggressive or other nonverbal acts that Bandura studied more intensively. As supported by the pertinent studies of Bandura and his followers, the child later will apply the learned behaviors in meaningful contexts, i.e., to convey one specific type of intended message. He will not, for example, perform aggressive behavior in order to express happiness.

It appears that observational learning theory can make excellent contributions to the explanation of the learning of verbal skills. These theoretical advances are valuable in the following discussion of modeling and imitation in child-mother interactions. The theory, however, is less easily and directly applicable to the understanding of how the child finds out what the learned forms mean and how he should employ them meaningfully in his delayed reproduction.

One-Trial Learning   One-trial learning is quite generally found in studies of concept development. It is based upon a hypothesis-testing approach. Hypotheses are formed about an unsolved problem,

are retained when they lead to correct results, and are discarded in
the opposite case (Ingalls and Dickerson, 1969; Kendler and Kendler,
1967). The theoretical orientation in this type of explanation is clearly
"cognitive," emphasizing active information selection and information processing. Before the child can form hypotheses, he has to
scan and analyze environmental givens. Both the weight attributed
to attentional factors and the emphasis given to cognitive aspects,
which were found in no-trial learning, are also necessary constituents
of one-trial learning. Since it is now almost generally agreed that
much of language learning consists of rule learning, a cognitive
hypothesis-testing approach could be optimally suited to the explanation of language acquisition.

Braine (1971a) rejected such a hypothesis-testing explanation by
arguing that a hypothesis-testing model requires negative instances
and that most research on mother-child interactions provided little
or no evidence for negative feedback, i.e., corrections from the mother.
This judgment of Braine was premature and partly unfounded. First,
it has been shown repeatedly, and is summarized in the following
sections, that much negative feedback in the form of corrections is
provided by mothers. The child therefore has ample opportunity to
utilize negative instances in his decisions about hypotheses. Furthermore, Braine seems to have overlooked that the child could avail
himself of negative instances in a different manner. He could have
formulated hypotheses about specific linguistic forms and could evaluate, from the language input that he receives, whether these hypotheses hold in the speech of the adult. If the linguistically competent
adult employs other forms than those the child expected, this is
clearly a negative instance for the child's hypothesis. In this manner,
hypothesis-testing also could result in many cases in no-trial learning.
It has been recently shown by Shipley, Smith, and Gleitman (1969)
and by Moerk (in press) that children attend quite closely to features
of the input that are not consistent with their linguistic rules, i.e.,
with their hypotheses about what form the input should have. They
selectively imitate features that appear dissonant to them, and they
do this often with a questioning intonation.

The theoretical outlook underlying one-trial interpretations of
language learning also would explain why children often are impervi-
ous to corrections provided by their environment. If children did not
previously form hypotheses about specific linguistic rules, they would
not closely analyze the linguistic input. Without analyzing it, they

often do not perceive discrepancies between their own production and the mother's response and therefore cannot incorporate the corrections provided by the mother. As has been often stressed by philosophers of language, language is mostly employed only as a means to a goal and is thereby transparent. No special attention is devoted to the tool as long as it fulfills its functions without complications. It goes without saying that the child, too, often employs language in this manner. To expect that he would carefully analyze the forms of language most of the time, whether in the input or in the output, would be in complete contrast to what is known about human and infantile information-processing capacities. Only when the tool appears precarious will the child test it again to decide whether to improve it or retain it unchanged. This testing can be done in the form of his own output in order to evoke a parental response (Söderbergh, 1974) or by subjecting the input to a careful and goal-directed scrutiny.

Multiple-Trial and Multiple-Feedback Learning   Multiple trials with feedback that informs the subject about his errors are most commonly encountered in the operant conditioning literature. Multiple trials, however, are not incompatible with cognitively oriented approaches, since the correct hypothesis often can be formulated only after many incorrect ones that lead to unsuccessful trials. As mentioned before, the straight operant conditioning approach as proposed by Skinner (1957) has been consistently rejected in the literature on first-language acquisition. However, it may be worthwhile remembering that it has been applied with considerable success in some operant language training programs. Besides the more ideological reasons, which are often encountered in rationalistically oriented publications, the main reason for the rejection of this approach comes from reports on factual studies. Brown, the leader in the study of first-language acquisition, has continuously asserted that practically no traces can be found in the study of actual parent-child interactions for corrective or reinforcing feedback from parents. This assertion has been widely and often uncritically repeated. It is demonstrated below, and has been shown by Moerk (1972, 1976a, b), that a high density of both corrective and reinforcing feedback is provided by mothers in their verbal interactions with their children. If these findings can be recapitulated with other samples and by other authors, it will have to be concluded that no obstacle exists against reintroducing the operant learning approach at least for the explanation of some phenomena of language acquisition.

While feedback is of greatest importance in this type of learning, in principle it does not matter what the sources of the feedback are. It could be pure communicative effectiveness, i.e., whether or not speech acts lead to the fulfillment of demands; it could be negative reinforcement, such as ridicule, by a critical social environment; or it could be intentional instructional feedback by a concerned adult. A considerable number of authors have concentrated their attention upon this latter phenomenon. Intentional instruction by mothers involves perspectives and influences that differ greatly from those that are assumed as decisive in incidental and operant learning, and is therefore discussed under a new heading.

Training by Mothers   The main difference between the present and the above approach lies in the emphasis upon the locus of intentionality. In the preceding section, only the activity and the intention of the child were considered; the received feedback was somewhat an accidental phenomenon. In contrast, the orientation described in this section focuses on language training and learning as an intentional instructional process, wherein the instructor is at least equally active or even more intentively and goal-directedly involved. This approach to data analysis and interpretation is comparatively new. Unanimous or even overwhelming agreement, therefore, has not yet been reached. Certain linguists and some psychologists propounded up to the early 1970's that mothers' input to children is highly chaotic. This input therefore could not be considered as an important source for the acquisition of language skills. It was considered even less probable that mothers could be intentionally involved in this language-teaching process. Since this time the consensus has changed quite drastically. From the early publications beginning with Drach (1969), Moerk (1972), and Snow (1972), it has become increasingly established that mothers do just that: they provide an almost ideally suited language model for their children, and they do so with considerable awareness and intentionality. Whereas few studies have directly investigated the awareness and intentionality of mothers, it could not be assumed that mothers could make such profound adaptations in the linguistic structure of their single utterances, and in the type of verbal interactions they engage in, without entertaining some ideas about their functional significance. Sociolinguistic/anthropological studies (Harkness, 1975; Voegelin and Robinett, 1954) on the relationship of maternal speech style to society's beliefs about the time and level of children's early linguistic capacities suggest also that maternal input phenomena are a function of a complex set of belief systems, i.e., are a consequence of conscious decisions about what is right and reasonable. Detailed evidence about this maternal language input is provided throughout most of the remainder of this chapter.

One remark on the theoretical and practical implications of the contrast between the approach described in the section on multiple-trial learning and the approach suggested here is in order. A child who would have to acquire his language more or less on his own with only random input from his environment would face an overwhelmingly difficult task. Basically, he would have to construct a linguistic system in a manner comparable to that encountered in the evolution of language. His situation would be analogous to the task of constructing all the insights of science without the help of instruction. What mankind did in thousands of years, he would have to do in a few short years or at best decades. It would be an impossible task and he would fail utterly. In contrast, the child who has scientific insights and discoveries presented in a well-thought-out manner in school can quite easily retrace the explorations of millennia and can arrive after a relatively short period of instruction at the level of know-how and basic understanding of present-day science. Similarly, the child to whom language principles are presented in an optimal manner needs to invest much less time and creative energy. Without such a presentation, language acquisition would be a formidable if not impossible task and would remain the mystery, as McNeill described it. Assuming such a presentation, the young child's achievements are paralleled and surpassed in most instructional settings in school, and the answers to the questions of language acquisition can be found through a comparatively simple analysis of instructional techniques and their effects.

Mutual Regulations Between Mothers and Their Children   All the above approaches still simplify the analytical task in a manner not justified by the actual phenomena. Whenever either the child alone or the mother alone is considered in the explanation of language acquisition, the fact that both partners interact closely and consistently in this process is neglected. One-sided approaches may make the descriptive tasks simpler; however, they distort the phenomena grossly and are not defensible. A double cause-effect relationship exists when mother and child interact. Each partner adapts his own behavior to one or more of the preceding acts of the other.

A descriptive and analytical approach similar to systems analysis (Moerk, 1976b) has to be adopted to do justice to these complex interactions. Simple or even complex correlational methods as they are still employed in many publications can only approximate the phenomena and can also distort them. With correlational methods the data to be correlated are obtained from specified cross-sections of behavior. Frequencies are the aspects that determine degree of relatedness. No avenues are provided to establish contingencies between individual behaviors and even less to establish meaningful contingencies. Frequencies appear to be only of minor importance in language acquisition (Brown, 1973). It is demonstrated below, on the basis of rich data, that meaningful contingencies are decisive. The method of choice, therefore, has to be an interactional contingency approach. The rest of this chapter is devoted to the explication of interactional phenomena.

FORMAL ASPECTS OF LANGUAGE INSTRUCTION AND LANGUAGE LEARNING

Forms and Structures of Interactions

That interpersonal phenomena cannot be described adequately by means of linear patterns, as simple cause-effect sequences, has been already emphasized by Baldwin (1898). He coined the term *circular reaction,* which was adopted by Piaget for the description of cognitive development and by Lewis (1951) for the analysis of verbal interactions. Though the idea was known and its importance acknowledged, its effect on practical research was minimal until the 1960's. In response to parallel considerations and to advanced analyses of feedback processes in the field of cybernetics, psychologists turned to this problem in theoretical studies (e.g., Gewirtz, 1969; Kogan and Wimberger, 1966) and in their practical approaches to data analysis (Bullowa, Jones, and Duckert, 1964; Hess and Shipman, 1967; Slobin, 1968). In these investigations, the authors successfully transcended the two-unit conception of cause and effect and replaced it with a three-unit model: cause-effect-feedback, namely, the circular process. Yet even in the relatively simple cybernetic processes of self-regulating machines, the sequence is almost always longer than three units. The feedback initiates a reaction in the originator of the sequence, and the feedback circle continues. Since psychological processes and interpersonal interactions are more complex than simple mechanisms, the question concerning the length of the chains to be studied and the number of circles to be included arises. No rationale for an arbitrary restriction to three or any other fixed number of units exists. A method to delimit flexibly the size of the units therefore has to be developed.

Valuable bases for this task can be found in the studies of Barker and Wright (1955) and in the summary report of Barker (1968). These authors described "behavior episodes" and established workable rules for their delimitation. Moerk (1972, 1976b) adopted these conceptual foundations and described "verbal behavior episodes" employing criteria of meaningful communication. Based upon these interactionally meaningful delimitations, units for an interactional analysis can be established and instructional phenomena can be explored. The units may vary in length from the simplest case of cause-effect sequences, which Moerk (1972) labeled "linear sequences," to "circular reactions" consisting of three units: remark-response-acknowledgment, to much longer and more complex sequences. After careful analysis of a large number of verbal interactions (Moerk, 1976b), a general description can be attempted.

Certain minimally necessary elements for each specific exchange are encountered as the kernel or nucleus of each specific exchange. They have been labeled and described by Moerk (1976b) as *nuclear interaction patterns*. They can consist, for example, of question-answer-acknowledgment; of request-acknowledgment; or of request-compliance. These nuclear interaction patterns are represented in Figure 6.1 in a straight line in the center extending from the top of the figure to the bottom. Elements and sequences of elements that can be added to these minimally necessary units are described as *subroutines*. These subroutines clarify interaction elements and convey linguistic information. Objective evidence for this differentiation could be found in transitional probabilities. The transitional probabilities between question-answer-acknowledgment are, for example, much higher than those between an answer followed by a question or by any other interaction element. The transitional probabilities between the elements of a kernel, in a top-to-bottom sequence in the center of Figure 6.1, are consequently much higher than those between kernel elements and subroutines. Subroutines are inserted or omitted as the need arises. The general pattern of these interactions is presented in Figure 6.1.

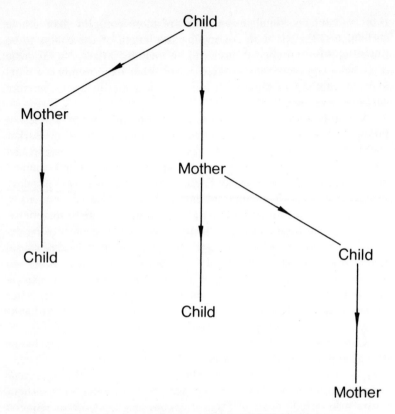

Figure 6.1.   A general pattern of mother-child interactions.

Partly similar conceptualizations have been proposed by Holzman (1974) and by McKay (1972), and the general form of Figure 6.1 will be familiar from other areas of research. Flow charts similar to this one are common in systems analysis and are also employed in the branching programs of programmed instruction as developed by Crowder (1960). Because additional subroutines can be added whenever necessary, either to the nuclear interaction pattern directly or as subroutines of subroutines, infinite recursiveness is theoretically possible, although psychological limitations of the child and the mother restrict the complexity of the verbal interaction episodes.

The processes that can be observed in these verbal behavior episodes can be most advantageously described in terms of the TOTE units of Miller, Galanter, and Pribram (1960): The mother hears an utterance of the child and tests it by comparing it with her standards.

If it is found acceptable, the mother responds to the message according to its content. If it is not acceptable, the mother supplies linguistic information by means of a correction, expansion, etc. From the child's response she can see whether the OPERATION was registered and whether it had the desired effect. If the discrepancy is either eliminated or has been sufficiently diminished, the EXIT mode can be chosen; if not, another subroutine containing an OPERATE and TEST phase can be added. The following section shows that the standards change with the age and the language level of the child. A detailed study of many interaction sequences (Moerk, 1976b) indicates also a differentiation of functional elements into those which serve primarily to introduce an interaction or a subroutine and those that fulfill predominantly terminal functions, signaling the completion of one interaction. For these multiutterance structures, the latter elements fulfill functions comparable to the period in written English or the falling intonation in spoken English, which signify the end of a single utterance. In this manner they fulfill a segmentation function in the extended sequence of turn-taking. The introductory elements are generally questions, spontaneous descriptions of an event or a picture, requests, or commands. The terminal elements employed by mothers are: positive conditioned reinforcement, imitation in agreement, labeling of an object intended as a correction or model, or a simple acknowledging *yes*. The child employs as terminal elements either specific replies to the content of the mother's utterances, a general reply such as *yes* or *yeah*, thereby accepting the mother's model, or nonverbal responses that are adapted to the preceding verbal exchange.

Though the description provided here may seem to be complex, it is too simplistic in two aspects. First, it provides only a very general outline, whereas mother-child dyads are extremely versatile in their mutual adaptations. Every extended protocol contains several sequences that are difficult to fit into a general scheme. More important than individual idiosyncratic forms is the question about the long-term effects of these interactions. Whereas the analysis presented above can demonstrate how and what mothers teach and how the child responds to this teaching, it can at best provide evidence of immediate acquisition on the part of the child and for very short-term retention. To suggest plausibly that the described processes contribute to first-language acquisition, at least intermediate retention has to be demonstrated. Immediate long-term retention may not be required during the early stages of the acquisition of any specific elements, since reinstatements (Campbell and Jaynes, 1966) are very frequent in these interactions between mothers and their children (see also Braine, 1971a). To demonstrate such intermediate-term retention, longer-range time-series analyses will have to be conducted, and the child's production of specific linguistic forms after the mother has taught them will have to be compared with the probability of their occurrence. If Chomsky's assertions concerning the unlimited linguistic productivity of each speaker were taken literally, the probability of occurrence of each specific utterance would be almost zero. Since the child's language repertoire is relatively restricted, and since the topics about which he communicates with his mother are also quite narrow, a higher probability of occurrence for each specific construction has to be assumed. Such an average probability could be easily computed over a comparatively large sample of utterances. If specific forms occur with a higher than expected probability, and if these forms are related either structurally or in content to some previous teaching of the mother, then an effect of this teaching upon the production of the child has to be assumed. In a study of the effects of imitation, Moerk (in press) has recently demonstrated that such longer-range influences of models are highly probable. Whitehurst (1971), in describing the principle of generalized imitation, touched upon similar phenomena. Further points about these studies are presented in the section on imitation below. Suffice it to say here, that the teaching of the mother as well as its effects upon the child can be and have already been demonstrated objectively. Present-day computing facilities make even complex time-series analyses possible. The interpersonal structure of teaching and learning therefore can be demonstrated.

Adaptations of Adult Speech to the Child's Linguistic Level

After several completely unsupported and incorrect assertions by nativists (Chomsky, 1965; Chomsky and Miller, 1963) that the speech input for the child is too chaotic for the learning of anything, the record has been straightened out. Mothers, for whom we have the most information, and also those fathers which have been observed adapt their speech input very carefully to the linguistic and general cognitive level of their children. Since this has been shown beyond controversy, several more specific tasks can be approached immedi-

ately: 1) an encompassing description of the adaptations parents
make has to be provided; 2) the specific calibrations parents attempt
in order to interact most effectively with their individual dyadic partner have to be explored; 3) besides individual differences in interaction styles, differences related to the age and language level of the
child have to be described; and 4) the effects of all these adjustments
have to be explored to discern whether they are conducive to or in-
terfering with language learning.

On the last point, i.e., the effects of parental calibrations, very
little is known yet. The few suggestions that can be made, therefore,
are included in the description of the specific interactional methodologies of parents. The first three topics are comparatively well explored,
and the relevant findings can be briefly and succinctly summarized.

Overall Features of Adult Speech Input to Children   During
the last few years, parental adjustments to child speech have been
repeatedly and excellently described by Newport (1976), Snow (1975),
Thew (1975), and most recently by Cross (1977). These authors have
covered most of previous research in detail and more broadly than
is possible here. Only a brief summary and a supplementation are
therefore needed wherever important contributions have been overlooked. Newport (1976:3) provides the following summary: Mothers
employ a higher and more variable pitch, they speak slower with distinct pauses after each sentence, with few dysfluencies and restricted
and concrete vocabulary. The utterances are short, well formed almost throughout, with few complex or compound clausal structures
and few modifiers or optional constituents. Thew (1975:2–3) gives a
very similar description: Mothers' speech is slower, pitched higher,
recognizable by an exaggerated intonation pattern, strategically marked
by pauses and terminal contours, and shorter in regard to sentence
length. It has a lower type-token ratio, contains mainly concrete
words, many questions and imperatives, few past tenses, few complex or dysfluent constructions. Acoustic clarity is maximized; maternal repetitions and paraphrases make it easier for the child to pick
up a message if he did not manage to do so on the first try. Redun-
dancies provide additional support in his comprehension efforts.
Snow (1975, 1976) emphasizes how mothers create the conversational
context for their children and how they thereby "shape babble into
words" (1975:11). In the same manner they train the turn-taking
skills of the preverbal and barely verbal infant. In regard to conversational context, the semantic relatedness between children's pre-

ceding and the mothers' subsequent utterances deserves attention. Thew (1975) reported fifty-five percent of the mothers' utterances to be so related.

Since most of the studies mentioned above were conducted in Western cultures, the question regarding the universality of this parental speech style has to be raised. Ferguson (1956, 1964) and Hymes (1967) have shown from a cross-cultural perspective that similar forms of baby talk are encountered quite broadly and in highly diverse cultures. Snow et al. (1976:2) concluded, too, from various anthropological studies that "a special register for addressing young children seems to be available in most societies." This register may not be universal, however, since differences in the adaptedness of parental speech have been found (Voegelin and Robinett, 1954).

From these studies, it can be concluded with considerable confidence that baby talk is quite common across cultures and families and that the techniques employed by most parents in Western cultures are similar. This congruence in findings, however, must not overshadow the differences in interpretations that do exist. One controversy is very basic: It pertains to the question whether baby-talk style contributes to language learning. McCarthy (1954), Fodor (1966), and McNeill (1966) emphasized the retarding effects of baby talk. Lewis (1957) and most of the recent investigators asserted in contrast that the described parental adaptations are highly conducive to the child's language acquisition. Cross (1975) provided impressive support for this assertion. However, in the same year, Newport (published as Newport, 1976) came to the conclusion that "motherese" is not a teaching language. Although not enough specific information has been accumulated yet to permit an unequivocal judgment, it can be proposed plausibly that one solution to this controversy can be found in the study of adult calibration and the level of adjustedness to the child's linguistic needs. It is not the absolute form of the input that is decisive, but whether it fits optimally to the receiving system. Depending upon when and how specific feedback is provided, baby talk can have positive effects upon the speed and level of language acquisition. However, it could also have retarding effects if supplied too rigidly and without consideration of the child's linguistic advances.

Another topic of active controversy is whether or not adults provide corrective feedback to the child. This question is of utmost significance in respect to what model of language acquisition can be formulated. As Braine (1971b) has correctly argued, a hypothesis-testing model requires that the child receive information about negative instances. Such information is easiest supplied as corrective feedback. Braine's (1971b) own scanner and storage model would not require such corrections. Since the topic is theoretically important, a more detailed analysis of the evidence for and against negative feedback is provided later in the section on specific interactional phenomena. The possibility, however, has to be considered that the child searches the input for negative instances. Discrepancies between the adult's utterances and the child's actual utterances, or even his expectations of how specific utterances should be formed, could represent such negative instances. If expansions are interpreted as demonstrating that the child's utterance was incomplete and not fully correct, they also could function as signifiers of negative instances.

A final question that has to be raised is whether the hitherto described phenomena represent all forms of adult adaptations to child speech. Some sporadic remarks and a few findings strongly suggest that they do not: Fowler (1962), in referring to older studies, reported that picture books and their accompanying texts have proved to be valuable tools for early language teaching. Since the accompanying texts are mostly in rhythmic and rhyming form, and since these prosodic phenomena have special attentional value and contribute to the ease of storage, the possible effects of rhythmic, rhyming characteristics deserve to be studied as well. Furthermore, as discussed in Chapter Five, the mother must provide a translation of environmental variables into the linguistic code for her language-learning child. Conversations between mother and child, therefore, always have to be based upon a meaningful nonverbal background, so that the child can comprehend unknown elements in the mother's messages on the basis of these contextual cues (McNamara, 1972). That the speech of young children and their parents remains throughout in the here and now often has been emphasized. Only during the course of the preschool and school years do children acquire the ability to use the distancing function (Sigel, 1971) of language. The specific translational adequacy of adult speech input therefore deserves detailed and exact analysis when the child's learning of the linguistic code is to be studied. Some known phenomena are summarized below. Finally, since the period of intensive investigation of parental speech input is still very short, it has to be assumed that several or even many phenomena have not yet been attended to. A consideration of the studies of Blount and Padgug (1976), who rated thirty-four features of maternal and paternal speech, and of that of Van der Geest et al. (1973), who coded one hundred twenty-nine features, gives strong support to this assumption. Much intensive and detailed research on parental input, therefore, still appears to be required before pertinent summaries can be considered to be comprehensive.

Specific Calibrations Between Adults and Their Children   Two aspects have to be considered in regard to specific calibrations. One is quantitative and the other qualitative. The quantitative aspect concerns Hunt's (1961) "problem of the match." Specifically in regard to language acquisition, Brown and Fraser (1963) raised the same question as the problem of the "optimal linguistic lead." Vygotsky (1962) and Söderbergh (1974) observed such an optimal lead when they described that the mother is always one step ahead of the child. Söderbergh also spells out the functional consequences of this lead: The mother models the child's next higher developmental level and thereby elicits more advanced communicative skills. Waxler and Yarrow (1975), in their study on the effects of modeling, found strong suggestions for the importance of a sensitive pacing on the part of the mother. Even though many investigators have noticed this type of quantitative adaptation, only a few seem to have made it the subject of more intensive studies. First appears to be the group around A. and C. Baldwin, especially Frank and Seegmiller (1973). These authors developed a complexity index and reported that mothers were fairly consistently one and one-half to one and three-quarters complexity units (equivalent to two to three years of development) ahead of their children. Moerk (1974a, 1975c) considered individual differences in the adaptations between normal mother-child dyads and found suggestive evidence that such differences exist especially in regard to the tendency of various mothers to tax maximally the linguistic capacity of their children. Similar individual differences were suggested by a preliminary remark of Frank and Seegmiller, that mothers of disturbed children maintain a larger gap in complexity units than do the mothers of normal children. The findings of Hess and Shipman (1965) and Snow et al. (1976) on differences in interaction style between social classes point in a similar direction, although in this case group differences were reported.

Besides these quantitative differences, preliminary reports suggest an almost unrestricted range of specific qualitative differences. Nelson (1973) devoted most attention to this question and reported that she had found two distinct styles: a referential one and an expressive one. Although Nelson concentrated on the characteristics of the children, it is only to be expected that the maternal input somehow must conform to these child styles, otherwise the two would be seriously mismatched. Scattered remarks on individual differences in dyads are found in almost all publications on mother-child interactions. It is too early, however, to attempt any summarizing statement, since no systematic research on this question has been conducted.

Another form of differences deserves attention. The study of Friedlander et al. (1972) on the differential effectiveness of paternal as compared to maternal input in one family, and the recent comparison of input features provided by fathers as compared to those of mothers (Blount and Padgug, 1976), suggest that a very interesting source of individual differences may lie in the comparison of male and female input. Recent studies on speech differences between the sexes would suggest that such differences also would exist in speech addressed to children. Blount and Padgug (1976) reported more baby talk in maternal speech and more serious speech styles modeled by fathers. In a comparison of dyads they also observed a relatively high uniformity in the speech of the diverse mothers, whereas more differences existed in the speech input provided by the fathers. The question, how these input differences affect the diverse aspects of language development, has to be asked and answered. Only some very first glimpses of new areas for research, however, are to be seen in these studies, and only challenging questions can be formulated at present.

Age-Related Changes in Adult-Child Interactions A larger number of investigators have devoted attention to interactional changes with increasing age and language level of the child. Again, quantitative and qualitative data are reported. As would be expected, with increasing linguistic capacity of the child the utterances of the mothers become longer and more complex. The reports of Frank and Seegmiller (1973) as well as of Moerk (1974a, 1975c) suggest how flexibly the mother adapts to the continuous feedback of her child: Over the age range of around two to five years of the child, differences in complexity between maternal and child speech are fairly constant, only showing a very slow and gradual decline as the child approaches the level of almost full colloquial language competence. These regular trends were found, even though Moerk's investigations were cross-sectional, i.e., were subject to the danger of confounding individual differences with age trends. Since Bronson (1974) could not find any trends in mothers' speech patterns when the children were between twelve and twenty-four months old, these age-related trends may be restricted to periods when the child demonstrates advances in grammatical skills and not only in vocabulary.

Qualitative changes are reported more commonly than quantitative ones with increasing age and language competence of children. Broen (1972), Snow (1972), Baldwin (1973), Frank and Seegmiller (1973), Phillips (1973), Moerk (1974a, 1975c), and Cross (1975) discussed these changes. The findings are too complex and diverse to be briefly reported here. Moerk (1975c), for example, studied eight different types of verbal behavior of the mother and nine of the child. He reported four trends: negative relationships with age and/or language level, positive relationships with the same variables, curvilinear relationships, and finally some interaction types that were stable over the period studied. In looking at the intercorrelation patterns he could differentiate a "primitive" interactional pattern, declining with the linguistic level of the child and encompassing forms of both mother and child. A cluster of more mature forms, again consisting of several interaction types of mother and child, increased with age and/or language level of the child. Similar phenomena have been reported by other authors (Cross, 1977; Fraser and Roberts, 1975), and in many instances there was considerable congruence even in the percentages reported. Some of the changes are referred to when specific interaction forms are discussed below.

From this quite diverse evidence it can be concluded with confidence that mothers closely take account of linguistic changes in their children. How the children convey these demands for maternal adaptations, and how the mothers' readiness to adapt herself influences the further language learning of the children, are challenging questions for future research. Cross (1977) suggested that the child's receptive competence is the best predictor of the mother's speech, and Moerk (1974a, 1976b) discussed some of the cause-effect relationships. Such studies also may explain why some children run into serious obstacles in their course of language acquisition, whereas others master this demanding task with comparative ease.

Specific Training Techniques Employed by Adults

This section briefly summarizes a variety of techniques employed by adults in verbal interactions with young children. Two main criteria have been used to select a technique for this discussion: that it had been discussed by several investigators and that it appeared conducive to the child's acquisition of language skills. Of the techniques that involved natural observations, very few have been experimentally evaluated; thus, the second criterion had to be applied somewhat arbitrarily. Whenever either experimental or other types of controlled evaluations on the effectiveness of specific techniques exist, they are also reported.

Because of the restrictions entailed by these two criteria and by the preliminary status of research on the pertinent topics, the enumeration of techniques cannot be considered exhaustive. New phenomena or subdivisions of described phenomena may be found and demonstrated in future studies.

Verbal Encoding of Shared Perceptions and Conceptualizations
It is generally reported in the literature, and is remarked upon in previous chapters, that the conversations between mother and young child are always in the here and now. Chapter Five discusses in detail how language is mapped to reality and how this mapping is accomplished in the course of language development. A description of the actually perceived aspects of the environment and a running commentary on the child's and others' actions would be best fitted to accomplish this mapping. Like many other authors, Phillips (1973) and Snow (1975) reported that, even in the case of the preverbal child, mothers have the habit of talking to themselves aloud while they interact with their children. Since mothers talk about objects and events exactly at the moment when both mother and child share these experiences perceptually, these maternal monologues could have important language-training functions (Moerk, 1972). Leopold (1939, I: 27) demonstrated this teaching function by describing how his child acquired the term *shoe* by means of the mother's monologues while she was dressing him. An almost identical case was reported by Bullowa, Jones, and Duckert (1964), who also remarked upon the similarity of this form of instruction and naming games.

The commonly described naming games seem to appear as the next step in the sequence of language acquisition. Whether the mother merely supplies the label for an object that interests the child at a specific moment, or whether she employs deictic utterances like "This is a ——" or even questions "Is this a ——?" or "Where is the ——?", she provides the name for the object of concern. The simultaneously appearing "What is this?" questions fulfill a similar vocabulary training function, although in the former case vocabulary is taught, while its retention is tested in the latter instance.

In accordance with most authors, Baldwin (1973) reported that mother-child conversations proceed with the age and language level of the child from labeling to conversations about materials and activities. Parental instruction proceeds from one aspect of semantics, namely, vocabulary, to increasingly complex syntactic phenomena. In both cases, parents take care that the child has the opportunity to perceive clearly the mappings and matchings between objective reality and linguistic code. Söderbergh (1974) suggested that mothers and children follow a highly conducive temporal pattern in these instructional activities. First the mother models the mapping of labels to reality, and soon thereafter she tests its effect through "What is it?" questions. Not long afterwards, the child picks up this word game and spontaneously asks "What is this?" questions, specifying thereby for his partner the object and label he wants to have matched. The later appearing "Why ——?" questions require syntactic encoding and therefore provide the opportunity to train this linguistic aspect.

It is also generally reported in the literature that mothers and their children proceed from discussions about the here and now to those about past and future events. In this case, mental representations have to be matched with linguistic codes, which already must have discriminative stimulus value in order to elicit in the child the correct representation. Since the nonverbal experiences of plans are, however, stored at least partially independently of the verbal code, the child still has the opportunity to match representation to code.

Another phenomenon of matching commonly encountered in our culture and seemingly of great value in language teaching deserves special attention. This is the matching between pictures and verbal codes. It is known from a variety of studies that recognition of pictures is encountered at the latest between nine and twelve months (see Stone and Church, 1968). Bower's (1970) research also suggested profound similarities in the processing of visual and verbal material. Bower emphasized, therefore, the need to conceptualize a general cognitive base for both. Piaget's findings and interpretations on the sequential mastery by infants of first the symbolic medium and then that of signs are widely enough known and need not be repeated here. Close scrutiny of the environs of infants in Western societies at least suggests that all three stages of symbolization are quite systematically presented for the infant. Miniaturized and simplified objects, i.e., toys, serve as indices of their real counterparts; pictures represent the objective world on the symbolic level; and parents are, of course, consistently adding the medium of signs, namely, language. Therefore, it could be concluded that parents employ toys and pictures as important tools for language training and that pychologists have intensively studied these processes. The first conclusion is substantiated by common-sense evidence and a few studies, mentioned below. Psychologists, however, have sorely neglected this topic, and the available evidence is therefore quite meager. In the older literature, one short sentence of Latif (1934) referred to the possible parallels between the function of picture books and of ostensive definitions in the acquisition of word meanings. Dawe (1942) described an attempt at language training that involved a considerable amount of viewing and discussing of pictures, and he reported that on nearly all measures the improvement of the experimental group that experienced this treatment was significantly larger than that of the controls. The recent literature includes a report by Snow et al. (1976) showing that children produce more complex speech in book-reading situations. Snow (1976) also spelled out in more detail how parents use this instructional aid: They prod the child with tutorial "What is it?" and "Where is the ——?" questions to test their vocabulary. Moerk (1974a, 1975c) studied the use of picture books in cross-sectional perspective and found that it quickly declines with the age and language level of the child. It is, consequently, a relatively primitive teaching method that is later replaced by discussions about real objects and situations or even of nonpresent experiences. The study of Fowler and Swenson (1975), who employed pictures in a well designed language-training program, supports this conclusion. They reported that pictures are already of importance for language training when the infant is between six and eight months old. A note of contrast is provided by Leonard (1975), however; he found that his subjects, children ranging in age from twenty-eight to forty months, acquired subject-verb utterance forms more readily when these were accompanied by real events instead of merely by pictures. Picture books may be helpful for the training of diverse linguistic skills, i.e., vocabulary versus syntax, and may be employed optimally for the training of either of these at various levels of the child's language development. Topics important for basic research and for practical applications are hereby spelled out and await more intensive investigations.

Utilization of Rhythmic and Rhyming Characteristics of Language In many picture books, the text portions are not written in normal prose style but in rhymed verse. Chukovsky (1963) described in great detail children's passionate delight in nursery rhymes, and Opie and Opie (1959) documented this phenomenon with cross-cultural and cross-temporal evidence. From these publications, and from common-sense experience, the question appears justified as to what the rhythmic and rhyming features that children so often encounter in their input could contribute to language acquisition. The evidence is sparse here, too, but deserves to be summarized because of its possible importance.

Already in 1939, Carroll suggested investigating the hypothesis that learning of rote material is an important factor in speech development. Locke (1971a, b) and Rossi and Wittrock (1971) demonstrated that rhyming qualities of items have a positive effect upon retention. Their subjects, ranging in age from two to five years, retained word lists with rhyming items presented in temporal contiguity better than those presented in random order. In a summary article, Gollin and Moody (1973) also reported strong effects of rhythm upon recall. Martin's (1972) study, though not directly applicable to language development, supports this same general contention, as does, for that matter, abundant common-sense experience.

Directly from the more natural environment of the language-learning child come several reports that substantiate the above considerations. Mussen, Conger, and Kagan (1974) mentioned that eight-month-old boys babble more in response to familiar words read in a normal rhythm than to the same content read monotonously or to nonsense words under both types of intonation.

For younger ages also, Friedlander (1970) reported that his subjects attended to nursery songs three and four times longer than to other kinds of verbal recordings. Two phenomena are demonstrated in the studies quoted above: Rhythmic, rhyming properties attract and captivate the attention of young infants more than mere monotonous verbal stimuli, and they contribute to the retention of the material heard. Fowler (1962: 130) reported the case of a girl who learned to speak, read, spell, and use the typewriter long before the average age. The child's mother used "an endless variety of songs, plays, games, and stories" in her language teaching attempts.

Directly referring to language acquisition are the descriptions of Fowler (1962), Wyatt (1969), and Carlson and Anisfeld (1969). Wyatt (1969) reported cases in which rhythmic, rhyming input accelerated

language development, and Carlson and Anisfeld (1969) discussed
the mechanisms by which this may be achieved. Their subject,
Richard, employed songs and poems as frames for substitution
games. "His spontaneous substitutions of words in song frames and
his completions of the utterances of others showed a higher syntactic
ability than was reflected in his normal speech" (Carlson and Anis-
field, 1969: 569). The principle of employing substitutions in pregiven
constructions as an aid in the child's syntactic progress is encountered
repeatedly below and is then discussed in more detail. In connection with the present topic, two applied programs have to be mentioned. As is generally known, Bereiter and Engelmann (1966) relied
in their language training programs intensively on rhythmic effects, and the DISTAR language program employs rhyming principles very commonly. Both these programs have proven their
effectiveness.

In a brief summary, several points can be made: Rhythmic,
rhyming features of the input attract even very young infants' attention; the same features contribute to better storage and recall in older
children, and they have been shown to be common in homes in which
children acquire language skills precociously. While only a few specific mechanisms are known regarding how the child uses these features in his attempts at language mastery, the principles could be
effectively incorporated in applied language-training programs. Even
from this very preliminary evidence, it seems very likely that these input features contribute not only to vocabulary acquisition but also to
the enrichment of the child's syntactic skills. Rich evidence in the
writer's own protocols of mother-child interactions, which cannot be
presented here, demonstrates that these features are involved when the
child exercises sentence constituents, in the formation of coordinated
clauses, and also in that of complex sentences, containing subordinate
clauses. When employing this tool, the mother often combines it with
that of incomplete sentences, discussed below, and thereby also engages in substitution games, as observed by Carlson and Anisfeld
(1969).

*Modeling and Imitation and Some Teaching/Learning Processes
Involved in Them*   Imitation by children of the language models provided by their adult environment has been discussed in the scientific
literature during the last two hundred years. The factual descriptions
and the theoretical conclusions to which the various authors came are
quite diverse and often contradictory. The topic of imitation has
again attracted lively attention since the studies of Bandura and his

students on observational learning (Bandura, 1971; Bandura and Harris, 1966), which often stand in direct contrast to the conclusions arrived at by developmental psycholinguists. Several good discussions of imitation have appeared during the last few years (Aronfreed, 1969; Ryan, 1973; Sherman, 1971), and it cannot be attempted in the restricted space available to analyze all the available studies or to do justice to all the theoretical positions. For more specialized and comprehensive discussions of the role of imitation in language development, covering most of the pertinent studies, the reader is referred to the recent publication by Ruth Clark (1977) or to that by Whitehurst and Vasta (1975).

In the present context, only problems, findings, and conclusions are described that appear most important for the evaluation of the contribution of modeling and imitation to language acquisition. First some theoretical clarifications appear required: It becomes obvious from the survey of the literature that the unitary term *imitation* has mislead many investigators into assuming automatically that one single and uniform process is described with this term. In contrast to this assumption, a wide variety of research has established beyond doubt that imitation is a complex phenomenon. It can be observed already shortly after birth; phenomena of widely varying complexity are imitated by young children, and the products of these imitations also vary widely. Only one example of such a contrast in the content of imitation is mentioned here, though the dimensions of the contrasts are manifold: Tiedemann (1787) reported that his child subject imitated at an early age not only a few sounds but also entire conversations. To this end the child produced a stream of incomprehensible sounds and accompanied these sounds with gestures. On the opposite pole of this dimension can be found the subjects of Shipley, Smith, and Gleitman (1969) who primarily imitated nonsense words with a questioning intonation "as if they were trying to understand them," or those of Whitehurst (1971) who employed "generalized imitation" by producing new messages on the basis of the syntactic frame that they abstracted from the preceding model. The contrast between these two poles is similar to that between a lay music-lover humming the melody of a song he just heard at the opera and a conductor of the same opera, who may hum the same melody during a rehearsal to prove a point to his orchestra. Superficially both do the same thing, yet nobody would argue that the processes and the understanding involved are the same.

A second problem that has plagued the research on imitation is definitional. To attain methodological purity, investigators often defined as imitation only the quite immediate repetition of a modeled utterance. It is, however, fully established that deferred or delayed imitation of rather complex phenomena already can be observed during the first year of life. For example, Sinclair (1971) reported on a seven-month-old girl who had observed a butterfly flapping against a window during a visit. When she returned to the same house after a week, she went straight to that same window and flapped her arms. Besides the long delay in the performance of the observed phenomenon, the performance itself is of great interest. Considered from the aspect of sensory perceptions, a profound difference exists between the visual stimuli produced by the flapping butterfly and the motoric/kinesthetic stimuli that result from the girl's own arm movements. The child evidently must have abstracted the "deep structure" of flapping from her observation, and she transformed this deep structure into new motoric surface structures. As mentioned above, in Bandura's interpretation of observational learning, acquisition of a skill can be temporally far remote from its applied performance, though the performance is clearly a result of the observation of the model.

Two conclusions can be drawn from the above arguments that pertain to the impact of imitation upon language development: First, many types of imitation must be considered, surface imitations as well as imitations and reconstructions of base structures. Also, imitations of the entire model utterance as well as of only parts of it are common. Furthermore, it cannot be assumed that the child is not employing imitation if he produces a construction that is not similar to the immediately preceding model. Long delays between the observation of the model and the imitation are possible. Before a conclusive answer can be provided about what the effects of imitation are, the *how* of imitation has to be reconceptualized. The positive findings that exist about the consequences of the modeling-imitation interaction can be generally accepted as valid, especially if they have been reported by several authors who studied different samples and employed varying methodologies. Whenever denials of possible effects of imitation are encountered, they may result from operational restrictions of the term employed and not from factual limitations.

Whitehurst (1973) has provided convincing evidence from his own work, and from a survey of the social learning approach, that imitation training often results in the acquisition of new grammatical rules. Bloom, Hood, and Lightbown (1974) have demonstrated the same principle for spontaneous imitation in the normal home situation of their observed children. The findings of Shipley et al. (1969), of Bloom, Hood, and Lightbown (1974), and of Moerk (in press) make inevitable the conclusion that modeling and imitation lead to vocabulary acquisition. This same phenomenon was already encountered above in the naming games played in connection with picture books and with objects of the environment. Bloom, Hood, and Lightbown (1974), who employed a longitudinal approach, suggested several cognitive processes by which imitation becomes progressive in respect to vocabulary and syntactic structures. Moerk (in press) combined such a longitudinal approach with a detailed time series analysis and analyzed the learning processes within single observation sessions and across sessions. He not only demonstrated the function of selective or generalized imitation (Whitehurst, 1971, 1973) in the acquisition of a variety of syntactic constructions, he also described the processes by which the child generalizes from the model. A hitherto overlooked phenomenon that he reported may deserve special attention: It appeared several times as if a specific construction modeled only once would not elicit an imitation by the child. If, however, several structurally identical or similar utterances were modeled in a short interval, the child was more prone to attempt to imitate the model. Something like a threshold value, then, seems to have been reached that is conducive to the application of a comprehended construction in the child's active production. This threshold probably can be attained either by means of special motivational phenomena, to be described below, or by means of simple repetition. The repetitiveness of maternal speech therefore would be advantageous in this perspective also.

A last point must be mentioned in this abbreviated discussion of the process of imitation: It has been often reported in the literature that, at least during certain periods, mothers imitate their children more often than children repeat their mothers' utterances. Slobin (1968) has demonstrated well how these maternal imitations with expansion often lead to enriched utterances of the child, since the child in turn imitates the mother's expanded utterance. Since the mother's expansion often contains corrections or at least more advanced structures, this circular process also leads to more advanced utterances on the part of the child. Cross (1975) demonstrated this fact statistically.

Moerk's (1976b) process analysis of mother-child interaction suggested that such circular double feedback processes are extremely common, and that they lead to fine calibrations between the utterances of the mother and those of the child. Since the mother is always ahead of the child by several complexity units, and since her verbal output serves as a standard, this calibration automatically results in the child using more complex and more advanced linguistic forms.

Mothers not only employ the principle of imitation intentionally in correcting and expanding their children's utterances, they also employ modeling and elicited imitation as a teaching technique. Liiamina (1960) reported the result of an experimental study that illustrates the principle: Children produce more adequate pronunciation responses when they are prodded to "Say ——," with the word being specifically modeled after the invitation to repeat it. Moerk (1974a) encountered the same phenomenon in a considerable number of the dyads he observed in the course of naturalistic interactions. The child's obedient imitation in turn can be either corrected or affirmed/rewarded by the mother (Moerk, 1976b).

After the progressive function of imitation has been asserted and partly demonstrated, at least by references to the pertinent literature, one possible limitation regarding this conclusion has to be mentioned. The literature is almost unanimous that imitation on the part of the child is a relatively primitive phenomenon and declines steeply with age (Moerk, 1974a, 1975c; Nelson, 1973; Nicolich and Raph, 1975; Shipley, Smith, and Gleitman, 1969). The same fact seems to apply to maternal expansions (Cross, 1975). Whereas this high level of agreement among different investigators is impressive, it has to be kept in mind, however, that all of them worked with relatively restricted operational definitions of imitation. If long-delayed imitations and more abstract ones are included in the definition of imitation, this conclusion may have to be changed. That considerable openness is required in this field is suggested by the spread of children's rhymes, teenage jargon, or even by the impact of school upon the language performance of children. If older children would not imitate their new models in the wider sense of the word *imitation*, they could barely incorporate so rapidly many new elements in their speech patterns.

A further oversimplification has to be dealt with before the topic of modeling and imitation can be concluded. In the same manner as imitation is too often taken as a uniform process, so also does the single word *modeling* often conceal the large variety of forms that modeling can take. It has been repeatedly demonstrated since the studies of Snow (1971) and Broen (1972) that mothers model often highly informative build-up and break-down sequences in which word and word-phrase boundaries are delimited and specified as unitary constituents. One informative example from Snow (1971) may be quoted here since it is brief but nevertheless instructive: Mother: "Pick up the red one. Find the red one. Not the green one. I want the red one." Whereas the predicate noun phrase is primarily specified in this construction, the child also has the opportunity to notice the boundaries within the noun phrase, such as that between adjective and anaphoric pronoun or between article and adjective. The child also could abstract several rules about verb use and when a subject of a sentence is needed or has to be omitted. Many and more complex examples of modeled sequences are described in the literature. Although the frequency of such modeling has not yet been investigated, this is of minor importance since a single model could suffice for a child who is just at the point of testing and accepting/rejecting a hypothesis. It may be informative to compare these observations from naturalistic interactions between mothers and their children with the experiment reported by Razran (1961). In this experiment it was demonstrated that varied linguistic formulations pertaining to the same content lead to faster progress in the acquisition of language skills than other combinations of verbal and nonverbal input.

Future analytically oriented investigations may persuade the scientific community to abandon both global terms, that of imitation and of modeling, in order to establish more differentiated antecedent-consequent relationships.

Question and Answer Interactions and Their Training Functions
Many conversational skills are involved in question-answer interactions whose establishment is discussed here in the sequence in which they probably appear developmentally. Although all conversation is based upon the principle of turn-taking, this phenomenon is most evident in question-answer interactions. Normal conversations can include relatively prolonged monologues by either partner, but questions have to be phrased quite briefly for clarity's sake and children reply to them even more laconically. Recent research on preverbal interactions between mothers and children (Snow, 1975; Stern, 1975) has shown that mothers train the turn-taking skills

needed for this type of interaction almost from the time of birth on. Since the baby at this time is an utmost unskilled turn-taker, the mothers construe any act of his as a turn and provide their own turns in response to it. At the time of around eighteen months, when the child shows some skills in question-answer interactions, he has consequently already been trained in turn-taking for almost one and one-half years.

Snow (1975, 1976) performed a special study on another instructive phenomenon: Mothers are already quite actively engaged in asking questions when their babies are only three months old. It is self-evident that mothers cannot expect a verbal reply at this age so that their asking of questions therefore must have different functions. Mothers deal with this situation by not only asking the question but by immediately providing the required answer or by using some other techniques to construe a turn for the baby. In the case of the mother providing both questions and answers, the baby not only learns turn-taking skills but has the opportunity to learn verbal turn-taking techniques and specifically question and answer techniques. Since mothers continue these types of behavior long into the verbal period, when their children will understand at least part of the verbal input, the children thus have the chance to analyze semantic and syntactic aspects of this type of conversational exchange. Gleason (1973) reported that parents still provide this form of input when their children are between four and eight years of age. Although the exact and specific steps in the learning process have not yet been explored, it cannot be doubted that in the course of eight years of quite intensive teaching many and complex aspects of question-answer conversation could be learned.

Besides the training in general turn-taking skills, evidence on more specific teaching techniques of mothers exists. Broen (1972) and Snow (1975, 1976) exemplified in some detail how mothers resort to reformulations of their questions and to sophisticated break-down or build-up sequences in their questioning, when they expect an answer from their child but do not see it forthcoming after the first formulation of the question. Such sequences can provide information on syntactic boundaries and on the elements admissible in various frames. In addition, since mothers often end up by also providing the answers to their questions after having reformulated the question several times, they thereby also model the transformations that differentiate questions from affirmative sentences. Depending upon the content of the questions and answers, semantic information also can be transmitted in these instances.

Another means employed by mothers to simplify for their children the comprehension of questions are the "occasional questions" described by Brown, Cazden, and Bellugi (1969). As Moerk (1976b) has shown, these questions follow mostly after a statement of the child and serve to clarify for the mother specific constituents of the child's utterance. Brown et al. differentiated two subtypes: the "say constituent again" and the "constituent prompt" questions. Whereas both specify for the child the element that the mother would like to have repeated from the child's previous utterance, the constituent prompt questions narrow down the possible response mostly to one word only and thereby make the task clearer for the child. In selecting one specific word in the frame of a sentence constituent, the mother again invites the child to approach his own utterances with an analytical orientation. The reader will remember similar sentence-parsing exercises from his school days. Besides specifying constituents for the child, the mother, in introducing a question-answer exchange, sets the stage for adding further information or corrections if needed. A very similar interactional function is encountered when the mother repeats verbatim but with interrogative intonation the child's putative utterance, if she is not fully sure whether she understood it correctly. In repeating the utterance, she provides phonetic, syntactic, and morphological corrections when necessary. Since she asks the child in this manner something like, "Is it this you wanted to say?", she contrasts her correct version with the child's faulty one. Since the child has to reply to the mother's question, he has to analyze the mother's formulation and to compare it with his intention, in order to answer "yes" or "no." Much grammatical learning could result from such an exchange.

One specific type of training, which appears shortly after the child is one year old, deserves special mentioning. This is the often discussed "What is this?" question, first asked by the mother and around one to two years later also by the child. Snow (1975, 1976), in agreement with many previous authors, reported that these questions are especially common when mother and child look together at pictures or browse through picture books. The mother thereby tests the child's vocabulary knowledge and she provides the correct answer if the child "fails" the test. Not only can the child learn new words, but he can also establish the semantic boundaries of his concepts, since in the form of real objects, and even more in the form of their pictorial representations, many and diverse exemplars of each concept are encountered. In studying interactional sequences, it is very often found that in the course of this original word-game (Brown, 1956) children provide the incorrect label and thereby give their mothers the chance to clarify the extension of a specific concept. In delimiting the extension, they often explain to the child why the element does not fall under the specific set, thus also spelling out for him the relevant aspects of the intension of the concept.

Since it is argued in the above discussion, as well as by most authors who studied this topic, that questions and answers can serve important training functions, a brief consideration regarding their frequency may be advisable. The findings are not always in full congruence, and conclusions therefore have to be preliminary. Seegmiller (1973) emphasized that large differences exist between dyads in the frequency of question-answer exchanges. Moerk (1974a) has suggested that one reason for these differences may lie in the reaction of the mothers to being observed. Tense mothers seem to take refuge in more questions more often than do relaxed mothers, who employ many different means to get their children to converse. That questions are a more primitive form of interaction is also suggested by the fact that most authors detected a decline in maternal questioning with higher language levels of the child. For the ages between two and one-half and three years the given percentages range between the twenties up to the fifties. For the age level of around five years, the commonly reported percentage lies between less than ten and around twenty. Snow (1976) and Moerk (1975c) described curvilinear trends in question frequencies of the mothers of children between three and twenty-four months and two to five years old, respectively. These partial differences in estimates of averages and the large individual differences suggest that it is too early to rely upon any exact percentage given. Brown's (1968) more detailed analyses, suggesting that different types of questions become dominant at various levels of the child's linguistic development, would provide a preliminary explanation for the differences in frequencies found.

Although not very closely relevant to the present topic of maternal training strategies, questions asked by children deserve a few remarks. First, the child's questions demonstrate that he has profited from the models provided so persistently by the mother. Second, the answers to his questions can provide him with much semantic and syntactic information. Britton (1970), in accordance with other authors, reported that infants already "ask questions" before they can speak. They do this by means of intonation patterns, by pointing, and through other gestures. The commonly discussed *what* questions follow soon thereafter. Nelson's (1973) finding, that the frequency of questions asked by children at the age of two years is positively related to all indices of language acquisition and especially to vocabulary acquisition, provides some evidence for some of the effects of these questions. During the later years, children's questions become a good deal more complex and are aimed at many topics besides the identification or labeling of objects. *Why* questions have most often been described for the three- to four-year period, but many other forms are employed (Meyer and Shane, 1973) that help the child to cognitively master his environment whose complexity he more and more perceives. That questions and answers also can contribute to memory storage and retention has been shown recently by Ross and Balzer (1975). Since all the needed information is provided in verbal form in the answer, and since the child is interested in receiving the information, i.e., to decode the answer, it follows that he must at least be training his linguistic skills. Since by his very question the child defines the general topic, he probably will be able to guess the meaning and function of single unknown elements of the answer. In this manner, answers given for their content's sake can lead to the learning of new linguistic forms as well.

Interactional/Instructional Potential of Incomplete Sentences Incomplete sentences are generally employed by mothers in two varieties, as questions and as statements. Formulated as questions, they are almost identical in form and function to the constituent prompt questions discussed above. The only difference is that in the case of constituent prompt questions an interrogative pronoun, mostly *what*, replaces the constituent, whereas in incomplete sentences a long and meaningful pause fulfills the same function. The training potential of this form of incomplete sentences therefore should be similar to that discussed in connection with occasional questions; i.e., they demonstrate the parsing of sentence constituents.

The principles in affirmative sentences are somewhat similar but probably more complex. A brief example of an only partially successful and a successful interchange will best serve to demonstrate a variety of phenomena: The first partially successful maternal attempt is taken from Snow (1975:13):

Mother: Oh, yes. He's [Titus] on the floor. Titus is . . .
Child: Floor.
Mother: Yes, Titus is on the floor.

It is quite evident from this interaction that the mother had expected the child to supply the entire prepositional phrase, and because this did not materialize she modeled it again. The second example, more typically encountered, is taken from Moerk (1976a:73) (almost identical phenomena are described by Wilkinson (1971) and Söderbergh (1974) taken from English and Swedish dyads, respectively):

Mother: We put flowers in . . .
Child: Vase.
Mother: We put flowers in a vase.

The difference between these two instances is that, in the second case, the child could supply almost everything the mother had omitted. The mother had to add only a relatively minor element, the indefinite article. This was because she had supplied in her incomplete sentence the most critical element, the preposition. Söderbergh (1974) especially emphasized that mothers provide mostly just the difficult and normally unstressed elements, such as prepositions and conjunctions, as final elements in their incomplete sentences. Since children follow the principle of specially attending to the last element in the modeled utterance (Slobin, 1973), the method of incomplete sentences should prove ideal for the training of the more complex functors, while at the same time permitting the testing of the child's vocabulary. The child's success or failure in his attempted completion, of course, also provides the mother with information on the child's mastery of a specific linguistic construction. Because Stern and Stern (1907) described the same phenomenon for German dyads that was reported by Bloom (1970) for dyads from the East Coast, by Moerk (1972, 1976a) for those from the West Coast, by Söderbergh (1974) for mothers and children in Stockholm, and by Wilkinson (1971) for their counterparts in England, it can be concluded that incomplete sentences are employed by mothers quite broadly. Regarding their effectiveness for language training, it may be of interest that Risley and Wolf (1967) reported "partial prompts," e.g., Therapist: "Out . . ." Child: "Out the door," to be effective in establishing functional speech in echolalic children. In sample interactions collected by this writer (see Moerk, 1972, 1976a), the child almost always attained the goal set by the mother, even if he had to supply consecutive subordinated clauses. This speaks for the power of the method.

Maternal Corrections of Children's Utterance   Since the pronouncements of Brown, Cazden, and Bellugi (1969), the preconception is dominant that mothers do not provide grammatical corrections but only respond to the truth value of the child's utterance or to its social acceptability. This assertion was so often repeated in the literature, mostly without the provision of any additional evidence, that it is almost accepted as common knowledge. It appears that only Horner (1968) and some students in Slobin's cross-cultural language project, as quoted by Slobin (1975), have adduced additional data to support this belief. This question is of great theoretical importance in respect to the two models of language learning discussed by Braine (1971b), i.e., the hypothesis-testing model versus the perceptual-learning model. It appears advisable, therefore, to check closely the findings of authors, particularly those who approached their data independent of the preconceived idea that corrections are rare or nonexistent. Meumann (1908) asserted that many examples of semantic corrections were encountered in the literature he surveyed. Bullowa, Jones, and Bever (1964) stressed the mother's role as a provider of corrective feedback. Hess and Shipman (1967:445) reported: "The mother regularly provides immediate affirmation or negation after each response, although her responses to errors are problem-centered and informative rather than critical." The last words of this formulation are important in the resolution of the controversy in the reports, and the reader is therefore invited to retain them in his intermediate memory. Moerk (1974a, 1975c) reported on age trends in corrective feedback provided by mothers and specified that this corrective feedback included phonetic, semantic, and syntactic information. Snow (1975) offered an example of a semantic correction, and Snow et al. (1976) found phonological corrections. An example of a morphological plus phonological correction taken from Lentin (1973:39) may provide a clue for the evaluation of the contradictory reports in the literature:

> Child: Ca c'est un zoi.
> Father: Oui, c'est une oie.
> Child: Une oie, un zoi.
> Father: Une oie, oui.

Whereas it is evident that the father provides both phonological and morphological corrections in this short exchange, it may be less evident that the father is concealing the corrective force of his reply or at least softening the emotional impact of his corrections through the repeated *Oui*, which normally serves as a conditioned positive reinforcer. Moerk (1976b) contributed further to the clarification of this question: Mothers mostly camouflage the corrective force of their reply by providing the correction as imitation with corrections or as imitation with expansion. In addition, they also often simultaneously provide conditioned positive reinforcement. It appears that mothers were so effective in their attempts to camouflage that they deceived several investigators, but not their own children. As interactional analyses show, for example, the ones presented by Moerk (1976b), children are well aware that the mother provides linguistic information and they often incorporate it in their imitations of the mother's correction. Moerk (1976a), in his study of the motivational use of discrepancies, has spelled out the principles involved: If, in her reply to an utterance of the child, the mother establishes a discrepancy, whether phonetic, semantic, or grammatical, both partners of the interaction seem to agree on the following two principles: If a discrepancy exists between the child's and the adult's statement, then the adult's utterance is correct or at least more acceptable and that of the child needs to be changed. Since parents formulate their responses to be informative/accepting and not critical/rejecting, the possible negative effects of negative feedback, which often have been found in experimental studies, are avoided.

How acutely parents attend and react to their children's mistakes was impressively demonstrated for this writer in a recent casual observation. For one-half hour this writer was able to observe parents and their approximately three-year-old child in a public waiting room. The child made two clear linguistic mistakes, besides some minor slips in his pronunciation. The first one was a morphological mistake with the child using an incorrect form of the past:

Child: Hab' hingreift.
Mother: Hinge*griff*en (with clear enunciation of all syllables and emphasis on the third syllable).

In this example, the mother immediately corrected the mistake. The second mistake the child made was semantic:

Child: Die Mutti soll Dir sagen, wie die Weste geht.
Mother: *Wie's Stricken* geht, meinst Du.

In this discussion, dealing with the knitting of a sweater and how to learn it, the child could not express his intention fully. He wanted to say, "Die Mutter soll Dir sagen, wie das Stricken der Weste geht."

The mother, in providing the correction, encoded his intention and told him also that she did this ("meinst Du"). Only one of many examples, showing how effective these corrections are, is provided from the writer's own interaction with his daughter. At the time of this conversation, she was three years, three months old and had been overgeneralizing the regular past to irregular forms:

> Child: She teached me.
> Father: She taught you?
> Child: Yes, she taught me.

About one minute later the following sequence occurred:

> Child: . . . She teached me.
> Father: She taught you.
> Child: She taught me.

Since this time, the child has correctly and spontaneously used the irregular past *taught* several times. Intermediate-term acquisition is therefore demonstrated as a consequence of these corrections. No evidence regarding the long-term consequences of these two interactions has been observed yet. In the case of other corrected and correctly repeated forms of the irregular past, the child was, however, observed after several days employing the incorrect, i.e., overgeneralized, form again.

Space limitations do not allow a detailed analysis of the exact interactional processes that involve maternal corrections. This has been done in considerable detail by Moerk (1976b). Suffice it to say, that in the overwhelming number of cases the child either imitates the mother's correcting utterance or at least accepts it through a "yes" or an equivalent response. Both in accepting and even more in imitating it, he must have analyzed it and he thereby had the opportunity to compare and contrast his faulty utterance with the correct one modeled by the adult.

After the phenomenon has been analyzed and established, that mothers correct often and effectively, further research will probably soon produce more detailed information on all the principles involved and on the effects upon the child's language learning.

Conclusions

The research on parental language teaching and training is still in its beginning stages, and the time is not yet ripe for final statements. As mentioned repeatedly in the above survey, contradictory findings are reported and controversies about their interpretations abound. The conclusions drawn here, therefore, necessarily reflect only the available research and a somewhat personal evaluation. They may have to be adjusted in the future.

In contrast to the doubts that have been expressed recently (Newport, 1976) about the instructional value of maternal speech input, it has been argued throughout that maternal techniques are almost optimally fit for the instruction of all types of linguistic skills. This conclusion applies only to the mother-child dyads studied, i.e., those from predominant middle- and upper-class backgrounds. As the studies by Bernstein (1960, 1962) and by Hess and Shipman (1965, 1967) suggest, the situation may be radically different for lower-class mother-child dyads. Middle-class mothers seem to be alert most of the time to their children's linguistic output. They seem to be able to remember its main characteristics, so that they can spontaneously adjust their utterance complexity to the child's level. By first providing the child with single labels and later with clear delimitations of the sentence constituents and their hierarchical patterning, they help the child match the linguistic code with his perceptual and conceptual structures. Although mothers make language learning an overwhelmingly pleasant experience, they have nevertheless found ways to provide corrective feedback and have developed techniques to emphasize the more difficult elements of constructions so that the child can perceive them clearly and can analyze and store them. Besides providing the necessary information for language acquisition, mothers also intermittently test their children's knowledge by means of questions, incomplete sentences, or directly by prodding: "Can you say ——?" If the child does not pass the test, the mother has learned about one of his weaknesses and provides, mostly in an inconspicuous manner, the needed linguistic teaching and training. In addition, though it could not be discussed in detail here, it may be mentioned in conclusion that specific mother-child dyads develop idiosyncratic means of interaction and they differ from one another widely in regard to the frequency with which they employ some of the general principles. Since language learning is probably highly overdetermined, rigid restrictions to a few principles are not needed. Considerable openness in the approaches used in research is also required so that some of the more rare techniques can be perceived and correctly conceptualized.

A concluding remark should tie in the findings and conclusions presented in this chapter with some of the discussions in earlier chapters. Since mothers appear so ingenious in their teaching techniques, the children acquiring language under the guidance of such teachers need neither be endowed with detailed inherited linguistic knowledge, nor need they be intellectually or conceptually precocious. Cognitive feats that the child accomplishes in other areas of non-verbal functioning appear to suffice also in principle to explain the child's linguistic progress. That the results can be quite disastrous if mothers are neither expert nor ingenious, has been a daily experience of many elementary school teachers in schools serving economically deprived areas. That decreased emphasis upon basic language teaching can have profound negative effects during middle childhood and adolescence is also evident, unfortunately, in high schools and even on the college and university levels.

DYNAMIC ASPECTS OF DYADIC INTERACTIONS

It is with considerable trepidation that this section on the dynamic or determining aspects of dyadic mother-child interactions is added. There are two reasons for this hesitation. First, the concept of *motivation* and research on motivation have been the object of intensive metatheoretical criticism recently, and the entire problem is not yet settled. Second, discussions of motivation are currently almost taboo in the field of psycholinguistics. As is commonly known, Skinner (1957) attempted to explain language behavior from a behavioristic point of view and employed the principles of reinforcement and control extensively. Shortly thereafter, Chomsky (1959) vehemently attacked this conceptualization, and since that time a highly critical—or perhaps an uncritically negative—response has to be expected whenever the term *motivation* in language behavior and acquisition is mentioned.

The reasons that outweighed these justified hesitations were briefly mentioned in Chapter One. On the one hand, common-sense experience, which is also supported by an abundance of research evidence, proves that variables which have been commonly labeled *motivational* can contribute profoundly to the speed of acquisition and to the length of retention of the material to be learned. The second reason is found in the literature on language acquisition itself: On the one hand, the term *motivation* is either generally eschewed or, if the topic is mentioned at all, authors insist that no motivational variables can be detected in mother-child interactions. On the other hand, motivational considerations are creeping into the analyses under the guise of many different terms. The currently predominant ones are *pragmatics* and *functionalism*. It is, however, also not uncommon that authors speculate about the intentions the child may have when he employs language or that they discuss the practical or cognitive benefits the child may derive from language mastery. Many of these considerations would be subsumed in behavioristic terminology under an operant approach and therefore would be counted under motivational phenomena.

Based upon these considerations, it was decided to include this section on the dynamic controlling aspects of dyadic interactions, though it has to be admitted that the discussion by no means can be considered final. Rather, it must fulfill the function of breaking the ground, or rather the ice, so that fruitful work on the topic can be begun. A brief overview over the theoretical situation is presented first.

Theoretical Perspective of the Problem

Two topics have to be considered. First, the question arises whether hypothetical constructs as encountered in motivational terms contribute to the clarification and explanation of behavior and specifically of language behavior. Only if such constructs are judged conducive to the explanation of human behavior can the second topic be approached. This is the search for specific determining influences upon language acquisition and behavior. Both these topics only can be discussed briefly here, and the sources quoted will have to be consulted for more extensive analysis.

Motivation in Metatheoretical Perspective   Although the concept of motivation is very old and well founded in the lay interpretation of behavior, recently it has become controversial. Cofer and Appley (1964) concluded, after a thorough survey of all existing research, that "it is clear that a comprehensive, definitive psychology of motivation does not yet exist." In a more extreme reaction both Littman (1958) and Guilford (1965) concluded that it would be best either to abandon the label *motivation* or to discontinue research on motivation while concentrating only upon observable behavior. Gewirtz (1969) also demonstrated the danger inherent in the use of motivational terms, since it could lead to a relapse into gratuitous labeling exercises and to a retardation in the scientific exploration of the problems. On the other hand, many attempts have been made during the same period to describe new motivational principles which were previously completely overlooked or neglected. Montgomery (1951) discussed an "explanatory drive," Harlow (1953) an "exteroceptive and curiosity drive," Berlyne (1955) also stressed the "curiosity drive," and R. White (1959) added the concept of "competence motivation" to this list of motivating forces. Considering this profusion of new terms, it is understandable that scientists who prefer conceptual parsimony feel challenged to fight the danger of relapsing into the empty labeling exercises as found, for example, in the lists of instincts formulated by McDougall (1915).

An integration of these two seemingly incompatible approaches appears possible, however, if the intended function of the employed terms is clearly spelled out. The terms to be suggested in the present survey are not conceived as having explanatory value in the sense that they would contribute to the understanding of the neurological mechanisms that lead to the behavior of interest here. However, they do fulfill an important function for descriptive purposes in helping to classify and order the diversity of phenomena under observation. They also can contribute to empirical or functional explanations in E. R. Guthrie's or B. F. Skinner's sense. In this latter function they serve as short-hand representations of complex interactional processes, they specify antecedent-consequent relationships, they contribute to their taxonomy, and they may even contain preliminary elements of a physiological/neurological explanation. In the same manner, the terms *hunger* or *thirst* fulfilled important descriptive/communicative/explanatory functions long before the physiological mechanisms underlying these motives were known. When, for example, Harlow and Berlyne describe the "curiosity drive," they not only subsume a large variety of behavioral phenomena under a term that effectively conveys the main characteristics of all these behaviors; they also imply that these behaviors are related to principles of information intake and to the degree of the subject's familiarity with this information. If these descriptive and hypothesis-forming aspects of the terms are made explicit, they can serve as valuable guidelines for factual-experimental or observational testing of the proposed conceptualizations. In a similar vein, Miller (1963) has argued eloquently that functional relations among variables can be studied and described effectively and productively, even if the specific reasons for the relationships are not yet understood.

To enhance the value of the suggested terms and descriptions, two precautions are maintained: Terms are chosen for which the criteria for inclusion and exclusion are clear and unambiguous, so that the term in itself will represent an operational definition. Furthermore, the terms chosen are significantly related to conceptualizations that have been established in other domains of psychological research and/or they are based upon demarcations that occur in the natural habitat of the species.

Motivation in Language Training/Learning and Verbal Behavior Generally   The studies enumerated and described in the preceding sections of this chapter demonstrate that adults, when they interact with young children, manifest verbal behavior patterns that are different from their normal verbal behavior. In these interactions they engage in rather systematic teaching activities. How much motivation on their part may be required perhaps can be estimated from the reinforcement, i.e., the salary a foreign language teacher receives over the course of three to four years. This is the time it takes the child to acquire most of the basic rules and vocabulary of his mother tongue.

Staats (1971) briefly mentioned as a possible source of motivation that mothers may experience pride and satisfaction when their child acquires language relatively early. This statement, however, is too global and lacks specific evidence to serve more than the function of directing attention to an area where research is needed. That very strong motivating forces are at work in the adult was already observed by Brown and Bellugi (1964). They pointed out (1964:140): "Indeed we found it very difficult to withhold expansions. A reduced or incomplete English sentence seems to constrain the English-speaking adult to expand it into the nearest properly formed complete sentence." It has to be remarked that Brown and Bellugi were not the parents of the observed children and that the design of the study called for detached observations by the investigators. The motivating variable which was postulated by Staats, consequently, was excluded in this situation. Nevertheless, the adults felt "constrained" to provide corrections. A similar conviction was expressed by Slobin (1968: 439): "The speech of very young children has a peculiar force in eliciting these sorts of expanded imitations from adults." Similarly, Thew (1975:13) reported that "adults ... seem to be compelled to disambiguate young children's expressions." A similar observation can be made easily by every person who interacts with young children, whether they be his own or those of strangers.

Another form of motivation for vocal interaction seems to be experienced by the parents during the babbling stage. Stone and Church (1968) pointed out that conversation-like exchanges of nonsense sounds between parents and their baby begin at two to three months and become a stable pattern before the age of one year. Neither the argument of Staats nor the observations of Brown, Slobin, and Thew seem to apply to the babbling conversations between adults and their infants.

Since the form of parental verbal behavior changes considerably with the language level of the child, a considerable variety of motivational variables could be involved. The prevalence of specific variables may change as the child progresses from the babbling stage to complete language mastery. Since very few investigators have even considered the motivational bases of the verbal behavior of the parent and especially the mother, the topic cannot yet be analyzed in all its details. At least two subaspects, however, can and will be differentiated: one pertaining to the adult's fine adaptations to the child's changing language level, and the other to the specific training and teaching behaviors that are performed by the parent.

Similarly, the large variety of and the changes in the vocal-verbal behaviors of young children suggest that it may be too simplistic to assume only one or a few variables that would control all aspects of language acquisition. Various forms of vocal behaviors may be based upon equally varied motivations. Common sense and currently available observations seem to suggest two main aspects that should be studied in the course of the child's language learning: 1) the motivations underlying the baby's vocal communication with adults generally and his receptive preference for the human voice (Wolff, 1966), and 2) the motivations underlying the many changes in the child's vocal behavior as he progresses from crying to cooing and babbling and later to the mastery of his mother tongue. This last topic encompasses several subtopics: the increase in the infant's babbling when he receives social feedback (Rheingold, 1956; Rheingold, Gewirtz, and Ross, 1959); the infant's "training" of his vocal skills even when he is alone (Weir, 1962); the infant's motivation to imitate heard sounds and to adapt his babbling to the sounds of his mother tongue (Fry, 1966; Lieberman, 1967); and the infant's motivation to learn the meaningful words and all the complicated rules and exceptions in the grammar of his mother tongue, although he had discovered earlier that he could get by easily with much more primitive baby talk or even with mere crying and gesticulating.

No attempt can yet be made to explore all these topics in detail. However, it will be seen in the course of the following literature survey that diverse authors presented speculations and some findings that touch upon many of the specified aspects.

Kindred Conceptualizations of the Dynamics of Language Acquisition

The first task in a historical overview of hypotheses on the reasons for language behavior and language development is a conceptual one: how to order the diverse observations and suggestions into a meaningful hierarchical system of nonoverlapping but optimally inclusive sets and subsets. The arrangement employed in the following discussion is a preliminary systematization which will have to be revised with growing theoretical and conceptual advances in the field. In accordance with the prevalent conceptualizations ranging from Aristotle's *organon* approach to K. Bühler's revival of this interpretation and Skinner's *operant* function of language, it can be concluded that language is normally used as a tool. This appears to apply equally from the developmental perspective. The largest number of suggestions on the motivation of language acquisition falls, accordingly, under this general set, which is labeled in the present survey the *operant function*. Two major subsets of phenomena soon become apparent when the literature and corpora of interactions are studied. In one subset, language behavior is encountered that leads to immediate and tangible benefits, such as food, a toy, physical help, etc. Until a better term is suggested, this subset is here described as *utilitarian operant*. In another set of phenomena, language is employed as a tool to explore and order the environment cognitively. This subset is therefore designated as *cognitive operant*. Both subsets are further subdivided in the following sections.

In contrast to the instances in which language is employed as an instrument to attain something outside its realm, another group of phenomena can be differentiated wherein utterances are intended only to elicit language products. A few examples may contribute to the clarification of the conceptualization and the underlying phenomenon: When a teacher questions his students about their assignments or when she requests specific information about a topic that she has previously explained, she engages in this type of behavior. The phenomena of language behavior that reflect this principle are described as *interaction/communication immanent*. As suggested by the above examples, these phenomena are especially common in teaching situations, and they are also encountered frequently in the situation of language teaching in the home.

It is not implied that these three headings encompass all types of dynamic aspects that lead to language behavior. It seems, however, that a large percentage of utterances encountered in normal mother-child interactions fall under one of these sets. Other groupings may be more advantageous for the study of other settings or other inter-action partners.

Utilitarian Operant Function   As briefly mentioned above, the belief in the *organon* aspect of language spans the period from Aristotle to Skinner and the present. As a minor curiosity in historical perspective, though it had a major impact upon research approaches during the last two decades, may be mentioned the fact that Austin (1962) published his famous book, *How To Do Things with Words,* only three years after Skinner's (1957) operant explanation of language had become discredited through Chomsky's (1959) philosophically motivated attack. Austin's book symbolized the acceptance of Wittgenstein's functional approach in the Anglo-Saxon literature, and it was also the beginning of the pragmatic/functional analyses of speech that are just coming into fashion. It therefore could be said that Skinner, after being refuted by a linguist-turned-philosopher, was almost immediately vindicated by a philosopher of language. While the refutation attracted everybody's attention and was religiously adhered to, the vindication worked on a subsurface level and emerged after more than a decade triumphant. At present, Skinner's and with it Aristotle's conceptualizations have been again accepted though under the terminology of natural language philosophy, whereas Skinner's system and his terminology are still mostly refuted. In the following discussion not only the operant function of language is described, but Skinner's and the learning theorists' contributions are accorded the attention they deserve.

Skinner (1957), relying upon more general principles of learning psychology, suggested the *mand* and the *tact* as two phenomena that could explain basic aspects of language acquistion. In the case of the *mand*, the verbal expression of the speaker functions as operant and reinforcement is provided in most cases by the listener who fulfills the child's wish. In contrast, when the child produces a verbal utterance in the form of a *tact*, a response of the listener provides generalized vicarious reinforcement for the association of the referent and the verbal response.

Mowrer (1952, 1960) had something in mind that is very similar to Skinner's *tact* when he developed his "autism theory." In combining principles from learning psychology and from psychoanalysis, he endeavored primarily to explain the phenomenon of imitation, whereas imitation as a generalized response tendency was employed to explain language acquisition. The infant would try to reproduce sound complexes of his parents because of their comforting value. This value is derived from the association of parental speech or sound play with the comforting experience of being cared for. A considerable number of behavioristically oriented psychologists accepted Skinner's theoretical approach and many practitioners applied it in their language-training programs. A brief evaluation of the evidence pertaining to it therefore appears required. No encompassing literature survey is attempted, since it is neither feasible nor necessary in the present context. Some of the studies to be quoted do this well and encompassingly.

Primary Reinforcement Contingent upon Vocal Behavior For the preverbal period, Rheingold (1956) and Rheingold, Gewirtz, and Ross (1959) demonstrated that babbling increases remarkably when infants receive social reinforcement contingent upon their babbling. The supportive value of this finding for the learning theoretical position, however, is restricted not only by the fact that it applies only to the preverbal period but also because it accounts only for the increase of already mastered vocalizations and not for changes in vocal behavior. This last phenomenon has been demonstrated by Routh (1969), who found that contingent reinforcement of the vocalizations of two- to seven-month-old infants not only increased the overall production of sounds but also the particular class of vocalizations being reinforced. Considering primary reinforcement for language behavior itself, in contrast to mere babbling, the literature and the extended protocols of mother-child interactions collected by the writer were searched intensively. Both these sources suggest that parents almost never respond to specific verbal behaviors with primary reinforcement in the manner that Skinner's *tact* would suggest. However, it is reported below that much conditioned reinforcement is given for such verbal behavior. In addition, most verbal interactions proceed in a pleasant atmosphere and therefore could be associated with comforting experiences as Mowrer conceived it in his autism theory.

Conditioned Reinforcement Contingent upon Verbal Behavior and Language Learning   A considerable number of investigators tested this conception in experimental settings in the laboratory, following the traditions of learning psychology. Barely pertinent are the studies showing increases in specific verbal elements during interviews or therapy sessions, when they were followed by conditioned reinforcement, such as *hmm, yes,* etc. A summary and evaluation of these studies have been provided by Salzinger (1959). For the present purposes, however, only those studies are of interest that deal with the acquisition of new skills. Most of these latter investigations dealt with the effect of imitation combined with reinforcement upon the acquisition or enhancement of language skills. Bandura and Harris (1966), in one of the earlier studies, demonstrated that subjects exposed to a combination of syntactic modeling and reward for imitation of the model showed a greater increment in the production of rare constructions than did a control group. Even before this American study, Popova (1956), as quoted by Elkonin (1971), found that the establishment of gender agreement between verbs and nouns was only accomplished successfully after a reward was added to the modeling procedure. In the intervening ten to fifteen years, the principle has become fully affirmed. Waxler and Yarrow (1975) reported, for example, impressive correlations, in the range of .60 to .70, between the frequency of reinforcement and that of imitation. Sherman's (1971) review has demonstrated in an encompassing manner the value of reinforcement for producing imitation of speech and even for generativity in language production. Wiegerink et al. (1974) therefore could state summarily that modification of infant vocal behavior by operant procedures has been well documented. Leonard (1975) added more specifically that recent studies demonstrate also unequivocally that children can produce novel and grammatical utterances through reinforcement contingencies. Other authors reached the same conclusion, and it therefore can be taken as established that reinforcement can contribute effectively to verbal learning, at least as far as experimental situations are concerned.

In order to build a bridge between the laboratory and the home, where most language learning proceeds, the experimental findings have to be compared with observational ones. Here also the evidence is reassuring, even if less extensive and detailed. Hess and Shipman (1967), in an observational study performed in the laboratory, described how mothers relied on praise and encouragement to motivate their children. This was especially observed in middle-class mothers. Similarly, Nelson (1973) reported that mothers dispense positive reinforcement specifically for language behavior. In accordance with Hess and Shipman, she noted that this reinforcement was not very frequent. Bee et al. (1969) and Feshback (1973) explored social class differences in this form of feedback. Middle-class mothers are much more prone to rely upon positive reinforcement, while lower-class mothers employ negative reinforcement more frequently. Moerk (1976b) provided detailed examples of how mothers use conditioned reinforcement in shaping language behavior and rewarding successful trials. He also analyzed in detail the complex routines and subroutines to show where reinforcement is provided in natural interactions and which functions it fulfills in them. Whereas conditioned reinforcement that is provided by the mother has been securely established, the frequency of it seems quite low. In a quantitative study, Moerk (in preparation-a) found on the average only two instances of direct conditioned reinforcement, such as praise, per hour of mother-child interaction. This result, however, is partially misleading, being based upon too narrow a definition of conditioned reinforcement. As evident from Moerk's (1976b) analysis of the patterns of interaction, a simple "yes" on the part of the mother, or an agreeing imitation of the child's preceding utterance, serve the same function as praise. Furthermore, mothers respond to and amend quite consistently the child's utterances if they do not conform to the standards they have set. No response of the mother serves as signal for the child that his utterance was acceptable, i.e., "correct." In normal mother-child interactions, a type of imitation, a simple "yes," or even a lack of response may therefore fulfill the same function as direct praise, namely, that of conditioned reinforcement. If interactions are analyzed in this functional perspective instead of by only looking at the superficial structures, it must be concluded that the frequency of conditioned reinforcement is high, indeed.

It can be asserted, therefore, that the occurrence of conditioned reinforcement has been demonstrated in the home as well as in the laboratory. It is more often employed by middle-class mothers, who are also more effective in their instructional attempts, than by lower-class mothers. It encompasses, as Moerk (1976b) has shown, a cue function as well as a motivational function. From this varied evidence, though still preliminary in scope, it can be concluded with a considerable degree of confidence that conditioned reinforcement is an important variable in language training and learning.

Skinner's Mand *and Behavioral Evidence*   In employing a more common terminology, Skinner's *mand* could be translated as a *request* or *wish* uttered by the child. Osgood (1957), Mowrer (1960), Staats (1971), and basically all learning theorists emphasized the value of words as a means of instrumental and social control. In developmental perspective, Stone and Church (1968) remarked upon the early use of bedtime screaming for social control. The human baby quickly learns to employ effectively the meager means for control that are at his disposal, since he is otherwise quite helpless. Lewis and Goldberg (1969) argued that the tendency to and the means for social control could be acquired equally rapidly and retained as permanently as the feeling of helplessness. In agreement with this, Rodgon, Jankowski, and Alenskas (in preparation) describe how children discover that they can exert verbal control over their environment and how they employ this discovery. The recent studies of Bates, Camaioni, and Volterra (1975) and Bates (1976a, b) provide similar evidence about the "performative aspects" of prespeech and early speech. Halliday (1975), in describing developmental functions of speech, expounded in part the same ideas. Several studies of children's verbal requests are in process, and the evidence is therefore securely established that vocal/verbal behavior is employed by the child to attain need gratification or wish fulfillment. Also, past investigators of child language, such as Leopold (1946) and Lewis (1957), have emphasized this functional use of language by the infant and child. As mentioned above, the basic conceptualization of language as a tool, *organon,* goes back to Aristotle. Brown and Hanlon (1970) asserted, however, that all this evidence is not pertinent. They argued that this principle could not conceivably contribute to the acquisition of new and more complex skills if the forthcoming reinforcement were not contingent upon selective communication effectiveness. They then categorically denied that any communication pressure favors more mature constructions by children, and they supported this assertion by several examples showing that mothers understand their children's messages even though their grammatical constructions are quite incorrect by adult standards.

If this assertion were accepted at face value, then the entire argument about Skinner's hypothesis would have arrived at a dead end. There are, however, several theoretical and methodological flaws in the argument of Brown and Hanlon, which when spelled out change the picture considerably. Three problems with the Brown and Hanlon argument are considered: 1) Without a doubt the child has to attain a minimum level of communication efficiency to have his wishes fulfilled. If his adult partner does not understand him, the probability that his wishes are fulfilled will be dependent only upon the adult's ability to guess the child's needs. Therefore, the child learns to communicate, even if not always verbally. The more complex his wishes become, and the more he converses about absent referents, the more complex and accomplished his messages will have to become. 2) Mothers often repeat the verbal utterance of the child in an expanded form and with a questioning intonation. They also may employ in this context the occasional questions which were described by Brown himself. In this manner, they question the child to see whether they understood his wish correctly. The child, in order to respond adaptedly, must analyze the mother's utterance and compare it with his own intention. Considerable language skills could be acquired in this situation. 3) A clear methodological shortcoming lies in the fact that Brown and Hanlon considered only the verbal interactions, neglecting all the information transmitted through nonverbal channels. This was done although their dyads always communicated in a face-to-face situation and therefore had unlimited access to each other's nonverbal messages. It is, consequently, not astonishing that Brown and Hanlon could not find any evidence for differential communication effectiveness dependent upon the level of linguistic complexity of the message. As discussed in Chapter Five, communication effectiveness is consistently high when all communication channels are freely employed. As is known from a considerable number of experimental studies, the situation is radically different when some channels are blocked, such as when a screen is erected between the communication partners, which prevents them from seeing each other's gestures and the variables in the behavior setting. In these cases, the reward resulting from efficient communication is highly dependent upon verbal communication effectiveness. Since Brown and Hanlon did not keep constant the amount of information transmitted in nonverbal channels, they had no basis to judge the differential communication effectiveness of purely verbal messages. As argued under (1) and (2) above, a close observation of mother-child interaction provides abundant evidence for such differential communication effectiveness if the contributions of other channels are considered or eliminated, as, for example, in the conversation about past events and absent referents.

On the basis of these three considerations the Brown and Hanlon argument against the importance of the operant aspect of verbal behavior for language acquisition can be discounted as invalid. In addition, Moerk (1976b) has provided detailed and quantitative evidence concerning how mothers consistently seized the opportunity to add a considerable amount of language instruction when the child made a demand. Direct questions, occasional questions, reformulations with and without expansions, and corrections are only some of the means that mothers employ in response to a request from the child if they are not satisfied with his linguistic formulations. Several subroutines can intervene between request and wish fulfillment, and these subroutines serve the function of language training and learning. Although more studies are needed to establish broader foundations for this conclusion, it already appears justified to declare that Skinner's principle of *mand* is factually supported. Since mothers provide much linguistic information before fulfilling the child's demands, the operant function could be important in linguistic progress.

It can be only briefly mentioned here, and is more extensively demonstrated in Moerk (1976a; in preparation-a), that language is used in the same manner to fulfill the needs and wishes of the mother. She gives the child directions and guides him in tasks that are too difficult for him to solve on his own. Shipley, Smith, and Gleitman (1969) remarked on the frequency of this phenomenon. In order to accomplish this, the mother has to adapt her linguistic constructions to the level of the child's comprehension. Bernstein and Henderson (1969) reported that mothers are aware of their functional use of speech and that they are convinced that it would be more difficult to guide their children without the use of language. It appears therefore that Skinner's principle of *mand* shapes the verbal behavior not only of the child but also that of the mother. Each of these behaviors is altered in a different direction, the utterances of the one become more sophisticated, those of the other more simple; and in this manner mother and child arrive at the close calibration that is described in one of the preceding sections. Although important, this principle is certainly not the only one that affects both partners.

Cognitive Operant Function   An intensive and extensive literature survey showed that this second topic, how language contributes to the cognitive exploration and ordering of the world, has been mostly overlooked during the last decades. In contrast, authors during the nineteenth century and into the first half of the twentieth century attributed much weight to this function. The following survey, therefore, relies more upon this older literature; suggestions in the more recent literature indicating that this topic deserves more attention are added as warranted.

In the beginning of the nineteenth century, Wilhelm von Humboldt postulated a "need to speak" as the source of language behavior. This need, according to Humboldt, is closely related to the main function of language, the transformation of experiences into cognitive property of the individual. The child as well as the adult, according to this interpretation, would employ language as a means, an *energeia* in the words of Humboldt, for the cognitive conquest of the world. Around a century ago, Steinthal said: *"Es muss sprechen, um zu denken"* (1871:360): To think discursively, the child needs linguistic tools. This statement also expresses the conviction that speaking is indispensable for cognitive functioning. When Stern and Stern (1907) discussed the *Symbolverlangen* (desire for symbols) of the child and described his continuing search for symbols, they explained the reason for this search in a similar way. The same thought is found in the work of Langer (1942). She postulated a "need for symbolization" and defined the symbol-making function as one of man's primary activities, which he has to exercise of necessity. The same conviction was again expressed by Cassirer (1944) when he described the child's "hunger for names." Cassirer expanded his ideas and added a functional explanation of this need: He asserted that the child's eagerness and enthusiasm in the acquisition of names do not originate in a mere desire for learning or using names, but that they mark the desire for the detection and conquest of an objective world. Cassirer's suggestion and Langer's (1942:113) belief that "the transformation of experience into concepts, not the elaboration of signals and symptoms is the motive of language" are in close accord with the ideas propounded during the nineteenth century.

More recently, de Vos (1961) specified as one of four functions of symbolic communication its contribution to the establishment of a precise conceptual economy, and Chase (1966) expressed a similar idea with special reference to the child. He hypothesized that the child's interest in naming might at an early age serve to differentiate the organism from the rest of the physical environment. A structuring, conceptualizing function of language is again implied in this suggestion. Since the child would notice this tool-aspect of language, he would become highly motivated to attain mastery of this tool. When E. Gibson (1971:353) expounded upon "a built-in need to get information about one's environment,...a search for invariance,...the reduction of uncertainty and the discovery of an economical distinctive feature..."she referred only to the motivation and reinforcement value underlying perceptual learning; her ideas, however, are in close congruence with those of the above authors who discussed the advantages of the learning of linguistic skills. Since perceptual learning leads to representation, as do language skills, the diverse authors really discussed the same underlying process, i.e., representation that entails these advantages in conceptual functioning.

Hunt (1965) employed a somewhat more complex two-step approach toward the acquisition of language skills. He agreed with the above authors that the child, in learning labels for objects, attempts to master the novel experiences he encounters. He explains, however, that the common *what* questions of the child derive from the fact that the child has developed a task-standard that all things and actions have names. Whenever the child does not know the name of specific objects or actions, he would experience an incongruity, and this incongruity would lead to the asking of questions. The child's discovery of the cognitive value of language would be more of a secondary consequence of this intrinsically based motive for language acquisition. When K. Bühler (1934) emphasized *Funktionslust* (function pleasure) as one of the main causes for language acquisition and for the training of language skills, he also referred to an intrinsic cognitive reason, such as R. White's (1959) "competence motivation." Weir's (1962) reports on her son's pre-sleep functional exercises point toward a similar underlying principle.

The determiners suggested by the various authors, however, do not need to be applied exclusively of one another in the explanation of language development. The child may go through a three-step process in regard to what controls his language learning, in a manner similar to that encountered in many activities of adults. First a skill is laboriously learned in order to attain extrinsic goals. Then the mastery of the skill and its perfection becomes an autonomous motive, as is most obvious in artistic productions whether in primitive pottery or in modern abstract painting. This highly refined skill can be then employed again in the discovery and the mastery or even in the forming of new realities. The last phenomenon could be paralleled by the child's enjoyment of fairy tales, wherein remote or unreal worlds are generated or discovered through language.

Quite clear evidence for an exploratory use of language is found in the child's *why* questions toward the end of the preschool years. A similar motivation very probably also contributed to the earlier *what* questions. Stern and Stern (1907) discussed these questions quite extensively in their survey of the older literature on language acquisition. In the protocols of interactions between present-day children and their mothers, this phenomenon is readily apparent, too. The child requests information about a topic that concerns him, and the mother, at least the middle-class mother, provides this information as accurately as she can. Moerk (1973) discussed in more detail than is possible here that this question-answer interaction is in principle similar to the orienting reflex as explored by Zaporozhets (1965): A new aspect of one's experience requires exploration, nonverbal or verbal, and this almost reflexive need to explore is only satisfied after the phenomenon is understood. Many levels of understanding are, of course, possible.

The mother and the child have to encode and decode often quite complex messages in these interactions. The verbally encoded messages refer to aspects of the behavior setting and are therefore "translations" of it. The mother and the child also cooperate skillfully and eagerly to make certain that the messages are received and understood correctly by the partner. Much refinement of verbal skills is not only possible in these interactions but almost absolutely necessary. These interactions and the dynamics underlying them therefore will contribute to the progress in the child's language competence.

Interaction/Communication Intrinsic Motivations A broad heading has been chosen for this section and the term *intrinsic* is intended to orient the reader toward the conceptualizations developed by researchers on "intrinsic motivation." Since a considerable variety of phenomena that would fall under this general heading have been described by diverse authors, this section may fulfill the function of delimiting the set and suggesting several subsets.

Striving for Communicative Clarity Stern and Stern (1907) postulated a "language-shortage" or a "speech-need" (*Sprachnot*) to account for the child's search for new means to convey his conceptualizations. Leopold (1949) mentioned an "urge for greater clarity" in the verbal behavior of children, and Cromer (1968) concluded that the child actively searches for new forms and structures to express newly understood relationships. Later, Cromer (1974) even asserted that the child invents words for the things he wants to communicate. Sachs (1971:394) referred to the same phenomenon when she stressed that "often there is evidence in the child's speech of the search for a form to express an idea." Luria (1975) added a principle that he labeled *-cept* to Skinner's *mand* and *tact* in order to emphasize such a communication intrinsic motivation. Every person who uses a not-fully-mastered second language for communicational purposes will be very familiar with this search for forms to express an idea. This search sometimes can take a long time and can involve several dictionaries and handbooks of grammar. Besides the desire for communicative clarity in the production of utterances, E. Gibson (1971) reported that she observed a similar desire in the child to clearly comprehend utterances addressed to him. In both cases, such a striving would be conducive to advances in language mastery. The latter type of desire is described below as it applies to the mother as well.

Attention-Maintaining Techniques Friedlander (1970) wondered whether parents reward children for their listening or how the child's often obvious attention to spoken language should be explained. Blount and Padgug (1976) may have provided one answer to this question by demonstrating how many and diverse discourse features parents employ to make their utterances acoustically attention provoking. Shipley, Smith, and Gleitman (1969) described the parent's concern to hold his listener's attention, and Snow (1975) referred to the mother's attempts to get her child to take his turn in the interaction process. If the child shall know when to take his turn, he has to listen and to analyze the discourse features signifying that his turn is coming up. It appears from this still very preliminary evidence that middle-class parents are quite concerned to retain the child's attention and to present him with a distinct input which allows him to see and abstract order in the utterances. In this manner, the parental attention-maintaining techniques and the child's desire to comprehend clearly messages addressed to him converge harmoniously in contributing to the fuller reception and decoding of parental models.

Uncertainty Reduction   Not only the child appears to have this need to clearly comprehend utterances addressed to him, the mother and every adult have it as well, perhaps even to a higher degree. Moerk (1976a) described an interaction pattern which he labeled "uncertainty reduction as a motive for the mother's language behavior." This pattern can be seen every time a child's message is not clearly enough formulated. The mother employs a variety of means: either normal questions, Brown's "occasional questions," an imitation with expansion and questioning intonation, the technique described below as *Zeigarnik effect*, and others. All are intended to assure the mother's understanding of the child's message. It has been mentioned above that in this process the mother encodes the supposed messages in her own words and thereby provides an advanced linguistic model for the child. The child, in analyzing and responding to the mother, can and must learn something about this more accomplished reformulation of his message. He may even compare his imperfect and the mother's more perfect utterance in ascertaining exactly what the source of the problem is. This uncertainty-reducing technique of the mother has not only been described by Brown and Moerk, but also by Söderbergh (1974), Snow (1975), Thew (1975), and Cross (1977); it is therefore common for a wide variety of dyadic partners. Similar phenomena are, of course, well known from normal conversations among adults; from introspection the reader may even remember the motivation or tension often arising in such situations, tension which only subsides after communication has been reestablished.

Question-Answer Standard   In many interactions the above phenomenon cannot always be easily and clearly differentiated from maternal questions that only have the function of involving their children in conversation, keeping the conversation going, or inducing the child to provide a better formulation, although the mother understood the incorrect one. In this latter instance, the transition from merely conversational phenomena to those of "instructional conversation" has been made. If it is assumed with Snow (1975) that the child has already acquired early in life a task-standard that a question requires an answer, such a learned motivation could account for this common phenomenon and the interactional success of questions. Snow (1975) has recently described in detail how mothers train this task-standard of question-answer interactions from the time their babies are three months old. That the child at the age of two to three years would have acquired such a standard would not be astonishing considering the length and intensity of training. Lewis (1937) already emphasized that adults always attempt to evoke from the child not merely any response, but a spoken response to their verbal input. Questions are one of their means to do this. McKay (1968) provided a sensitive informational and dynamic analysis of question-answer interactions from a systems-theoretical point of view, which expounds the present conceptualization in more detail.

Prodding A similar phenomenon is encountered in what Moerk (1976a) labeled *prodding*. The mother mostly formulates a question of the kind: "Can you say ——?" and also models the word or phrase she wants repeated. The child, knowing that this is a request for verbal imitation or even a "test" of his competence and not a question, repeats the word or phrase modeled by the mother. Two types of task-standards are encountered in this interaction. The first consists of the interactional conventions that a request should be honored. That parents invest much energy over many years to get their children to comply with their requests is common knowledge, although the exact learning history has not yet been explored. How profoundly effective middle-class parents can be, may be seen from the recent trends in assertiveness training for adults, wherein the clients again have to learn not to comply with requests.

The second task-standard is found in the mother's modeled utterance, which the child is challenged to imitate as closely as possible. The motivational aspect of this second task-standard is discussed immediately below, after one more closely related phenomenon is described, for which the term *Zeigarnik effect* has been chosen.

Zeigarnik Effect The term *Zeigarnik effect* is intended to remind the reader of dynamics studies by Zeigarnik (1927) and Ovsiankina (1928). Zeigarnik found that uncompleted tasks are better remembered than completed ones. Ovsiankina showed that persons who fail to complete an activity tend to wish to resume it when there is an opportunity to do so later, whereas those who have completed the activity most often will choose something new. Mothers seem to employ a combination of both principles in their verbal interactions with their children. They begin a sentence but leave one important part of it uncompleted. This incomplete sentence or statement, demanding completion, seems to represent a strong incentive for the child. The term *incomplete sentence* will also evoke the recollection of a very similar method that is employed in clinical psychology. The evidence from clinical experience and similar formulations of Gestalt psychology concerning the "law of closure" suggests the generality of the underlying principle. Contextual givens make it easy for the child to complete the sentence. A detailed study of instances of these interactions, as presented in Moerk (1976a), shows that other motivational variables can contribute in the same situation. Often the incomplete sentence is formulated in question form or at least with a questioning intonation. Some mothers use the rhythmic and rhyming properties of stories in picture books to make it easier for the child to fill in the missing elements. In this case, larger sentence constituents or even entire subordinate sentences can be omitted from the mother's incomplete sentence.

Discrepancy/Cognitive Dissonance A final technique of inducing the child to improve his verbal skills can be abstracted from another type of interaction: When the child has said something in a less than perfect manner and the mother has noticed the incongruity of this utterance with her established phonetic, semantic, or grammatical rules, she repeats the child's utterance in an improved or corrected form. The child in turn notices the discrepancy between his own initial statement and the mother's repetition and attempts to bring his own repetition of the mother's model into closer congruence with his mother's utterance. For this last step of the multicircle interaction sequence, another principle, discussed earlier, has to be postulated, one which seems to be acknowledged by both partners: If a discrepancy between the child's and the adult's utterance exists, then the adult's version is correct and that of the child needs to be adapted.

The description of the phenomenon clarifies clearly why the term *discrepancy/cognitive dissonance* was chosen in a previous publication (Moerk, 1976a) in order to characterize it. Discrepancy, cognitive dissonance, or incongruity was postulated as an important motivational principle by several authors (Festinger, 1957; Hebb, 1949; Kelly, 1955; Piaget, 1952) and it continues to be investigated. As evident from the above description, the principle affects both mother and child. In the case of the former, it would explain the peculiar urge described by Brown and Bellugi (1964) and Slobin (1968) to imitate the child's utterance with expansions. Not only the mother attempts to eliminate the discrepancy but also the child. He does this by attempting to bring his own statement in closer agreement with the mother's model.

Slobin (1968) calculated that children add something to their original statements in around fifty percent of these types of imitation. This discrepancy appears to be an excellent example of a principle that motivates both mother and child to engage in verbal behavior that leads to advancement in the child's linguistic skills. Since discrepancy/ dissonance has been reported to affect higher animals, newborn infants, as evident from their heart rate response and their orienting reflexes, as well as adults in a wide variety of social situations (Festinger, 1957), a powerful controlling principle appears to be herewith at the disposal of the parent. Since a discrepancy can be demonstrated by the mother in the phonetic, semantic, and grammatical realms, the principle is also versatile as a technique for language teaching.

Multiple Motivational Variables Since the above dynamic principles have been described separately, the reader may have gained the impression in the course of this description that they are mutually exclusive. This, however, would be an unwarranted conclusion. Mothers are skillful in combining several principles sometimes even in one single utterance and more often in one interaction sequence. When, for example, in one instance the child pronounced the word *soldier* as *soldgineer,* the mother responded with the utterance: "Can you say *soldier*?" In this case, she asked a question which required a response, she prodded the child to do something, and she also spelled out clearly the discrepancy between the child's and her own correct pronunciation. Thereafter she continued her corrective action until the child produced a satisfactory performance. If entire interaction episodes are studied with all their subroutines, multiple causation (Skinner, 1957) is quite often encountered. Since motivation is interpreted as a dynamic principle, it would be expected that an accumulation of such dynamics is experienced if several motivating principles are combined by the mother. The phenomenon observed in this respect is comparable to that described by Blount and Padgug (1976) in the case of intonation features. Parents combine a multitude of intonation features to attract and hold the infant's attention. In language training, mothers seem to apply a multitude of motivating features to get the child to interact verbally and to proceed thereby to higher levels of competence. The techniques used by mothers are many-sided in another aspect as well. As J. Brown (1949) has spelled out, feedback can be informational, rewarding, and motivating. In many of the motivating attempts described above, the mother provides simultaneously with the motivation also the information on what has to be improved. Whether it is a discrepancy, prodding, a question, or the Zeigarnik effect, the linguistic information provided through these techniques is easily apparent.

SUMMARY AND CONCLUSION

It is by no means denied that the above section on dynamic/motivational variables in language acquisition is still very preliminary. It could not be otherwise at the present state of the field. An area had to be delimited and described. A survey and review of previous speculations, hypotheses, and factual reports had to be attempted. It is hoped that this preliminary task, which is needed in any area of research, has been accomplished to a satisfactory degree.

The double aspect of motivation, i.e., the motivation of the mother for her teaching behavior and that of the child for his learning, has been spelled out. For both partners, a variety of specific phenomena have been described and arranged in a preliminary hierarchy of classes and subclasses. Parallels between the phenomena observed in early dyadic verbal interactions and those studied in a variety of psychological fields have been remarked upon. This communality of the underlying principles and their wide applicability across ages and species may add to the persuasiveness of some of the descriptions. Substantiating data could not be presented here, but references were quoted frequently, and the writer has provided in some of his other publications (Moerk, 1976a, in preparation-a) substantiating evidence for his classifications. Whereas almost all of the above considerations are only qualitative, a quantification of some of these phenomena on a sample of American middle-class dyads has been presented recently (Moerk, 1975d, in preparation-a). Whether qualitative or quantitative, all the above suggestions can be subjected relatively easily to observational or experimental evaluation. Such evaluations certainly will lead to some reformulations and improvements in conceptualizations. It is hoped that the present outline, together with the improvements to be expected, will lead also to a better understanding of the language-training and language-learning processes.

In contrast to the often extremely preliminary considerations concerning the dynamic and motivational principles in language acquisition, the ground is more secure in regard to the informational techniques employed by mothers that have been analyzed in the first main section of this chapter. Based upon the wide variety of evidence summarized, which is derived by diverse authors from widely different samples of dyads, a rather strong conclusion appears justified from the discussion presented in this chapter: Even after a very brief period of research into the instructional methodologies of mothers and the learning strategies employed by children, the findings make it appear highly plausible that these techniques can account for the acquisition of surface structures or code characteristics as encountered in diverse languages. In accordance with previous arguments by linguists, it is agreed that no base structure learning in the strict sense is needed, since base structures evolve from semantic intentions of child and adult and from the cognitive reconstructions of environmental givens that the child makes in the course of his first two years of life. The establishment of some of these intention structures has been illuminated in Chapters Two to Five. If the contributions of all these chapters are integrated, an overall but encompassing picture of early language acquisition may begin to evolve. Many details will have to be filled in during the coming years and decades.

References Cited

Aaronson, D. R. 1976. Psycholinguistics since the turn of the century. In: D. R. Aaronson and R. W. Rieber (eds.), Developmental Psycholinguistics and Communication Disorders. The New York Academy of Sciences, New York.

Allport, F. H. 1924. Social Psychology. Houghton-Mifflin, Boston.

Ament, W. 1899. Die Entwicklung von Sprechen und Denken beim Kinde. Wunderlich, Leipzig.

Anderson, J. W. 1972. Attachment behavior out of doors. In: N. G. Blurton Jones (ed.), Ethological Studies of Child Behaviour. Cambridge University Press, London.

Anglin, J. M. 1975. On the extension of the child's first terms of reference. Paper presented at the Biennial Meeting of the Society for Research in Child Development, April, Denver.

Apel, K. O. 1965. Die Entfaltung der 'sprachanalytischen' Philosophie und das Problem der 'Geisteswissenschaft'. Philos. Jahrb. 72: 239–289.

Aronfreed, J. 1969. The problem of imitation. In: L. P. Lipsitt and H. W. Reese (eds.), Advances in Child Development and Behavior. Academic Press, New York.

Aronson, E., and S. Rosenbloom. 1971. Space perception in early infancy: perception within a common auditory-visual space. Science 172: 1161–1163.

Asher, J. J., and B. S. Price. 1967. The learning strategy of total physical response: some age differences. Child Dev. 38: 1219–1227.

Asher, S. R. 1976. Children's ability to appraise their own and another person's communication performance. Dev. Psychol. 12: 24–32.

Austin, J. L. 1962. How to Do Things with Words. Oxford University Press, London.

Ausubel, D. P., and E. V. Sullivan. 1970. Theory and Problems of Child Development. Grune & Stratton, New York.

Babska, Z. 1970. The formation of the conception of identity of visual characteristics of objects seen successively. In: Cognitive Development in Children. Five Monographs of the Society for Research in Child Development. University of Chicago Press, Chicago.

Bach, E., and R. T. Harms (eds.). 1968. Universals in Linguistic Theory. Holt, Rinehart and Winston, New York.

Baldwin, A., and C. Baldwin. 1973. Information exchange in mother-child interaction. Paper presented at the Biennial Meeting of the Society for Research in Child Development, March, Philadelphia.

Baldwin, C. 1973. Comparison of mother-child interactions at different ages, and in families of different educational level and ethnic backgrounds. Paper presented at the Biennial Meeting of the Society for Research in Child Development, March, Philadelphia.

Baldwin, J. M. 1898. Mental Development in the Child and the Race. Macmillan, London.

Ball, W., and E. Tronick. 1971. Infant responses to impending collision: optical and real. Science 171: 818–820.

Bandura, A. 1965. Vicarious processes: a case of no-trial learning. In: L. Berkowitz (ed.), Advances in Experimental Social Psychology. Academic Press, New York.

Bandura, A. 1969. Principles of Behavior Modification. Holt, Rinehart and Winston, New York.

Bandura, A. 1971. Analysis of modeling processes. In: A. Bandura (ed.), Psychological Modeling. Aldine-Atherton, Chicago.

Bandura, A., and M. B. Harris. 1966. Modification of syntactic style. J. Exp. Child Psychol. 4: 341–352.

Bandura, A., D. Ross, and S. Ross. 1963. A comparative test of the status envy, social power, and secondary reinforcement theories of identificatory learning. J. Abnorm. Soc. Psychol. 67: 527–534.

Bar-Adon. A. 1971. Primary syntactic structures in Hebrew child language. In: A. Bar-Adon and W. F. Leopold (eds.), Child Language: A Book of Readings. Prentice-Hall, Englewood Cliffs, N.J.

Barker, R. G. 1968. Ecological Psychology. Stanford University Press, Stanford, Cal.

Barker, R. G., and H. F. Wright. 1955. Midwest and Its Children. Harper & Row, New York.

Bates, E. 1976a. Pragmatics and sociolinguistics in child language. In: D. Morehead and A. Morehead (eds.), Normal and Deficient Child Language. University Park Press, Baltimore.

Bates, E. 1976b. Language and Context. The Acquisition of Pragmatics. Academic Press, New York.

Bates, E., L. Camaioni, and V. Volterra. 1975. The acquisition of performatives prior to speech. Merrill Palmer Q. 21: 205–226.

Bee, H. L., L. F. van Egeren, A. P. Streissguth, B. A. Nyman, and
M. S. Leckie. 1969. Social class differences in maternal teaching
strategies and speech patterns. Dev. Psychol. 1: 726-734.

Bell, R. Q. 1968. A reinterpretation of the direction of effects in
studies of socialization. Psychol. Rev. 75: 81-95.

Bell, S. M., and S. M. D. Ainsworth. 1972. Infant crying and maternal responsiveness. Child Dev. 43: 1171-1190.

Bellugi, U. 1972. Studies in sign language. In: T. J. O'Rourke (ed.),
Psycholinguistics and Total Communication: The State of the
Art. American Annals of the Deaf, Washington, D.C.

Bellugi, U. 1975. Sign language of the deaf as a clue to the "roots"
of language. Paper presented at the Conference on Origins and
Evolution of Language and Speech, The New York Academy of
Sciences, September, New York.

Bellugi, U., and E. S. Klima. 1975. Aspects of sign language and its
structure. In: J. Kavanagh and J. E. Cutting (eds.), The Role of
Speech in Language. MIT Press, Cambridge, Mass.

Benedict, H. E. 1976. Language comprehension in 10- to 16-month-
old infants. Unpublished doctoral dissertation, Yale University,
New Haven, Conn.

Bereiter, C., and S. Engelmann. 1966. Teaching Disadvantaged
Children in the Preschool. Prentice-Hall, Englewood Cliffs, N.J.

Berko, J., and R. Brown. 1960. Psycholinguistic research methods.
In: P. H. Mussen (ed.), Handbook of Research Methods in
Child Development. John Wiley & Sons, New York.

Berlyne, D. E. 1955. The arousal and satiation of perceptual curiosity
in the rat. J. Comp. Physiol. Psychol. 48: 238-246.

Berlyne, D. E. 1965. Structure and Direction in Thinking. John
Wiley & Sons, New York.

Berlyne, D. E. 1969. The reward value of light increment under
supranormal and subnormal arousal. Can. J. Psychol. 23: 11-23.

Berlyne, D. E. 1970. Children's reasoning and thinking. In: P. H.
Mussen (ed.), Carmichael's Manual of Child Psychology. John
Wiley & Sons, New York.

Bernstein, B. 1960. Language and social class. Br. J. Soc. 11: 271-
276.

Bernstein, B. 1962. Social class, linguistic codes and grammatical
elements. Lang. Speech 5: 221-240.

Bernstein, B. 1964. Elaborated and restricted codes: their social
origins and some consequences. Am. Anthropol. 66(2):55-69.

Bernstein, B., and D. Henderson. 1969. Social class differences in the relevance of language to socialization. Sociology 3: 1-20.

Bever, G. 1961. Pre-linguistic behavior. Unpublished honors thesis, Department of Linguistics, Harvard University, Cambridge, Mass.

Bever, G. 1970. The cognitive basis for linguistic structures. In: J. R. Hayes (ed.), Cognition and the Development of Language. John Wiley & Sons, New York.

Birdwhistell, R. L. 1970. Kinesics and Context. University of Pennsylvania Press, Philadelphia.

Blauvelt, H. H., and J. McKenna. 1960. Capacity of the human newborn for mother-infant interaction. II. The temporal dimensions of a neonate response. Psychiatr. Res. Rep. 13: 128-147.

Bloom, L. M. 1970. Language Development: Form and Function in Emerging Grammars. MIT Press, Cambridge, Mass.

Bloom, L. M. 1973. One Word at a Time. Mouton, The Hague.

Bloom, L. M., L. Hood, and P. Lightbown. 1974. Imitation in language development: if, when, and why. Cog. Psychol. 6: 380-420.

Blount, B. G., and E. J. Padgug. 1976. Mother and father speech: distribution of parental speech features in English and Spanish. Paper presented at the Stanford Child Language Research Forum Conference, April, Stanford, Cal.

Blumenthal, A. L. (ed.). 1970. Language and Psychology. Historical Aspects of Psycholinguistics. John Wiley & Sons, New York.

Blurton Jones, N. G. 1972. Non-verbal communication in children. In: R. A. Hinde (ed.), Nonverbal Communication. Cambridge University Press, London.

Blurton Jones, N. G., and G. M. Leach. 1972. Behaviour of children and their mothers at separation and greetings. In: N. G. Blurton Jones (ed.), Ethological Studies of Child Behaviour. Cambridge University Press, London.

Bouveresse, J. 1974. In: H. Parret (ed.), Discussing Language. Mouton, The Hague.

Bower, G. 1970. Imagery as a relational organizer in associative learning. J. Verb. Learn. Verb. Behav. 9: 529-533.

Bower, T. G. R. 1967. The development of object permanence: some studies of existence constancy. Percept. Psychophys. 2: 411-418.

Bower, T. G. R. 1971. The object in the world of the infant. Sci. Am. 225: 30-38.

Bowerman, M. F. 1970. Learning to talk: a cross-linguistic study of early syntactic development, with special reference to Finnish. Unpublished doctoral dissertation, Harvard University, Cambridge, Mass.

Bowerman, M. F. 1973. Early Syntactic Development. Cambridge University Press, London.

Bowerman, M. F. 1974. Learning the structure of causative verbs: a study in the relationships of cognitive, semantic and syntactic development. Pap. Rep. Child Lang. Dev. 8: 142-178.

Bowerman, M. F. 1976. Semantic factors in the acquisition of rules for word use and sentence construction. In: D. Morehead and A. Morehead (eds.), Normal and Deficient Child Language. University Park Press, Baltimore.

Boyd, E. F. 1975. Visual fixation and voice discrimination in 2-month-old infants. In: F. D. Horowitz (ed.), Visual Attention, Auditory Stimulation, and Language Discrimination in Young Infants. Monogr. Soc. Res. Child Dev. 39. (Nos. 5-6, Serial no. 158).

Brackbill, Y. (ed.). 1967. Infancy and Early Childhood. The Free Press, New York.

Braine, M. D. S. 1963a. The ontogeny of English phrase structure: the first phase. Language 39: 1-13.

Braine, M. D. S. 1963b. On learning the grammatical order of words. Psychol. Rev. 70: 323-348.

Braine, M. D. S. 1971a. The acquisition of language in infant and child. In: C. E. Reed (ed.), The Learning of Language. Appleton-Century-Crofts, New York.

Braine, M. D. S. 1971b. On two models of the internalization of grammar. In: D. I. Slobin (ed.), The Ontogenesis of Grammar. Academic Press, New York.

Brannigan, C. R., and D. A. Humphries. 1972. Human non-verbal behavior, a means of communication. In: N. B. Jones (ed.), Ethological Studies of Child Behavior. Cambridge University Press, London.

Bransford, J. D., J. R. Barclay, and J. J. Franks. 1972. Sentence memory: a constructive versus interpretative approach. Cog. Psychol. 3: 193-209.

Bridges, K. M. 1932. Emotional development in early infancy. Child Dev. 3: 324-341.

Britton, J. 1970. Language and Learning. University of Miami Press, Coral Gables, Fla.

Broecker, W., and J. Lohmann. 1948. Vom Wesen des sprachlichen Zeichens. Lexis 1: 24–33.

Broen, P. A. 1972. The verbal environment of the language-learning child. ASHA Monogr. 17.

Bronfenbrenner, U. 1970. Two Worlds of Childhood. Russell Sage Foundation, New York.

Bronson, W. C. 1974. Developments in behavior with agemates during the second year of life. Paper presented at the ETS-sponsored Conference, Origins of Behavior: Peer Relations and Friendships, October, Princeton, N.J.

Brown, J. S. 1949. A proposed program of research on psychological feedback (knowledge of results) in the performance of psychomotor tasks. (Mimeograph). University of Oregon Medical School, Portland.

Brown, R. 1956. Language and categories. In: J. S. Bruner, J. J. Goodnow, and G. A. Austin (eds.), A Study of Thinking. John Wiley & Sons, New York.

Brown, R. 1957. Linguistic determinism and the parts of speech. J. Abnorm. Soc. Psychol. 55: 1–5.

Brown, R. 1958a. Words and Things. The Free Press, Glencoe, Ill.

Brown, R. 1958b. How shall a thing be called? Psychol. Rev. 65:14–21.

Brown, R. 1968. The development of wh-questions in child speech. J. Verb. Learn. Verb. Behav. 7: 279–290.

Brown, R. 1970. Psycholinguistics. The Free Press, New York.

Brown, R. 1973. A First Language. The Early Stages. Harvard University Press, Cambridge, Mass.

Brown, R., and U. Bellugi. 1964. Three processes in the child's acquisition of syntax. Harv. Educ. Rev. 34: 133–151.

Brown, R., C. Cazden, and U. Bellugi. 1969. The child's grammar from I to III. In: J. P. Hill (ed.), The 1967 Minnesota Symposium on Child Psychology. University of Minnesota Press, Minneapolis.

Brown, R., and C. Fraser. 1963. The acquisition of syntax. In: C. N. Cofer and B. S Musgrave (eds.), Verbal Behavior and Learning. McGraw-Hill, New York.

Brown, R., and C. Hanlon. 1970. Derivational complexity and order of acquisition in child speech. In: J. R. Hayes (ed.), Cognition and the Development of Language. John Wiley & Sons, New York.

Bruck, M., and G. R. Tucker. 1974. Social class differences in the acquisition of school language. Merrill Palmer Q. 20: 205-220.

Bruner, J. S. 1967. The ontogenesis of symbols. In: To Honor Roman Jakobson. Essays on the Occasion of his Seventieth Birthday. Mouton, The Hague.

Bruner, J. S. 1968. The course of cognitive growth. In: N. S. Endler, L. R. Boulter, and H. Osser (eds.), Contemporary Issues in Developmental Psychology. Holt, Rinehart and Winston, New York.

Bruner, J. S. 1969. Eye, hand and mind. In: D. Elkind and J. S. Flavell (eds.), Studies in Cognitive Development: Essays in Honor of Jean Piaget. Oxford University Press, Toronto.

Bruner, J. S. 1971. The growth and structure of skill. In: K. J. Connolly (ed.), Motor Skills in Infancy. Academic Press, New York.

Bruner, J. S. 1972a. Nature and uses of immaturity. Am. Psychol. 27: 687-708.

Bruner, J. S. 1972b. Poverty and childhood. In: R. K. Parker (ed.), The Preschool in Action: Exploring Early Childhood Programs. Allyn & Bacon, Boston.

Bruner, J. S. 1973. Organization of early skilled action. Child Dev. 44: 1-11.

Bruner, J. S. 1974. The organization of early skilled action. In: M. P. M. Richards (ed.), The Integration of a Child into a Social World. Cambridge University Press, London.

Bruner, J. S. 1974/75. From communication to language: a psychological perspective. Cognition 3: 225-287.

Bruner, J. S. 1975. The ontogenesis of speech acts. J. Child Lang. 2: 1-19.

Bühler, C., and H. Hetzer. 1928. Das erste Verständnis für Ausdruck im ersten Lebensjahr. Z. Psychol. 197: 50-61.

Bühler, C., and H. Hetzer. 1935. Testing Children's Development from Birth to School Age. Farrar & Rinehart, New York.

Bühler, K. 1926. Les lois générales d'évolution dans le langage de l'enfant. J. Psychol. 25: 597-607.

Bühler, K. 1930. The Mental Development of the Child. Routledge & Kegan Paul, London.

Bühler, K. 1934. Sprachtheorie. Fischer, Jena.

Bullowa, M., L. G. Jones, and T. G. Bever. 1964. The development from vocal to verbal behavior in children. In: U. Bellugi and R. Brown (eds.), The Acquisition of Language. Monogr. Soc. Res. Child Dev. 29. (Serial no. 92).

Bullowa, M., L. G. Jones, and A. R. Duckert. 1964. The acquisition of a word. Lang. Speech 7: 107–111.

Burtt, H. E. 1967. The Psychology of Birds. Macmillan, New York.

Butler, S. R., and U. Norrsell. 1968. Vocalization possibly initiated by the minor hemisphere. Nature 220: 793–794.

Campbell, B. 1970. The roots of language. In: J. Morton (ed.), Biological and Social Factors in Psycholinguistics. University of Illinois Press, Urbana.

Campbell, B. A., and J. Jaynes. 1966. Reinstatement. Psychol. Rev. 73: 478–480.

Campbell, B. A., and N. E. Spear. 1972. Ontogeny of memory. Psychol. Rev. 79: 215–236.

Carlson, P., and M. Anisfeld. 1969. Some observations on the linguistic competence of a two-year-old child. Child Dev. 40: 569–576.

Carpenter, G. C., and G. Stechler. 1967. Selective attention to mother's face from week 1 through week 8. Proceedings of the 75th Annual Convention of the American Psychological Association. 2: 153–154.

Carroll, J. B. 1939. Determining and numberating adjectives in children's speech. Child Dev. 10: 215–229.

Carroll, J. B. 1960. Language development. In: C. Harris (ed.), Encyclopedia of Educational Research. 3rd Ed. Macmillan, New York.

Carroll, J. B. 1964a. Language and Thought. Prentice-Hall, Englewood Cliffs, N.J.

Carroll, J. B. 1964b. Words, meanings, and concepts. Harv. Educ. Rev. 34: 178–220.

Carswell, E. A., and R. Rommetveit (eds.). 1971. Social Contexts of Messages. Academic Press, London.

Cassirer, E. 1944. An Essay on Man. Yale University Press, New Haven, Conn.

Cassirer, E. 1953. The Philosophy of Symbolic Forms. Yale University Press, New Haven, Conn.

Cattell, P. 1940. Measurement of Intelligence in Infants. Psychological Corp., New York.

Cazden, C. B. 1966. Subcultural differences in child language: an interdisciplinary review. Merrill Palmer Q. 12: 185–219.

Cazden, C. B. 1971. Language programs for young children: notes from England and Wales. In: C. Stendler Lavatelli (ed.), Language Training in Early Childhood Education. University of Illinois Press, Urbana.

Cazden, C. B. 1972. Child Language and Education. Holt, Rinehart and Winston, New York.

Chafe, W. L. 1970. Meaning and the Structure of Language. University of Chicago Press, Chicago.

Chamberlain, A. F. 1900. The Child: A Study in the Evolution of Man. Charles Scribner's Sons, New York.

Chambers, W. G. 1904. How words get meanings. Ped. Sem. 11: 30.

Chase, R. A. 1966. Evolutionary aspects of language development and function. In: F. Smith and G. A. Miller (eds.), The Genesis of Language: A Psycholinguistic Approach. MIT Press, Cambridge, Mass.

Cherry, C. 1957. On Human Communication. MIT Press, Cambridge, Mass.

Chomsky, C. S. 1969. The Acquisition of Syntax in Children from 5 to 10. MIT Press, Cambridge, Mass.

Chomsky, N. 1957. Syntactic Structures. Mouton, The Hague.

Chomsky, N. 1959. Skinner: Verbal Behavior. Language 35: 26-57.

Chomsky, N. 1965. Aspects of the Theory of Syntax. MIT Press, Cambridge, Mass.

Chomsky, N. 1966. Cartesian Linguistics. Harper & Row, New York.

Chomsky, N., and G. S. Miller. 1963. Introduction to the formal analysis of natural languages. In: R. D. Luce, R. R. Bush, and E. Galanter (eds.), Handbook of Mathematical Psychology. John Wiley & Sons, New York.

Chukovsky, K. 1963. From two to five. University of California Press, Berkeley.

Church, J. 1961. Language and the Discovery of Reality. Random House, New York.

Clark, E. V. 1970. How young children describe events in time. In: G. B. Flores d'Arcais and W. J. M. Levelt (eds.), Advances in Psycholinguistics. American Elsevier, New York.

Clark, E. V. 1971. On the acquisition of the meaning of before and after. J. Verb. Learn. Verb. Behav. 10: 266-275.

Clark, E. V. 1973. What's in a word? On the child's acquisition of semantics in his first language. In: T. E. Moore (ed.), Cognitive Development and the Acquisition of Language. Academic Press, New York.

Clark, H. H. 1973. Space, time, semantics, and the child. In: T. E.

Moore (ed.), Cognitive Development and the Acquisition of Language. Academic Press, New York.

Clark, R. 1977. What's the use of imitation? J. Child Lang. In press.

Cofer, C. N., and M. H. Appley. 1964. Motivation: Theory and Research. John Wiley & Sons, New York.

Cowan, J. L. 1970. The myth of mentalism in linguistics. In: J. L. Cowan (ed.), Studies in Thought and Language. University of Arizona Press, Tucson.

Critchley, M. 1939. The Language of Gesture. Longman, New York.

Cromer, R. F. 1968. The Development of Temporal Reference during the Acquisition of Language. Unpublished doctoral dissertation, Harvard University, Cambridge, Mass.

Cromer, R. F. 1974. The development of language and cognition: the cognition hypothesis. In: B. Foss (ed.), New Perspectives in Child Development. Penguin Books, Baltimore.

Cross, T. 1975. Some relationships between motherese and linguistic level in accelerated children. Pap. Rep. Child Lang. Dev. 10: 117-135.

Cross, T. 1977. Mother's speech adjustments: the contributions of selected child listener variables. In: C. Ferguson and C. E. Snow (eds.), Talking to Children: Language Input and Acquisition. Cambridge University Press, Cambridge.

Crowder, N. A. 1960. Automatic tutoring by intrinsic programming. In: A. A. Lumsdaine and R. Glaser (eds.), Teaching Machines and Programmed Learning. National Education Association, Washington, D.C.

Culp, R. E., and E. F. Boyd. 1975. Visual fixation and the effect of voice quality and content differences in 2-month-old infants. In: F. E. Horowitz (ed.), Visual attention, auditory stimulation, and language discrimination in young infants. Monogr. Soc. Res. Child Dev. 39. (Serial no. 158).

David, E. E., and P. B. Denes (eds.). 1972. Human Communication: A Unified View. McGraw-Hill, New York.

Dawe, H. C. 1942. A study of the effect of an educational program upon language development and related mental functions in young children. J. Exp. Educ. 11: 200-209.

Deese, J. 1969. Behavior and fact. Am. Psychol. 24: 515-522.

Delacroix, H. 1930. Le Langage et la Pensée. 2nd Ed. Alcan, Paris.

de Laguna, G. A. 1927. Speech: Its Function and Development. Indiana University Press, Bloomington.

Denzin, N. K. 1971. Childhood as a conversation of gestures. Paper presented at the Meeting of the American Sociological Association, Denver.

De Vos, G. 1961. Symbolic analysis in the cross-cultural study of personality. In: B. Kaplan (ed.), Studying Personality Cross-culturally. Row, Peterson, Evanston, Ill.

Dimond, S. J., and J. G. Beaumont (eds.). 1974. Hemisphere Function in the Human Brain. Halsted Press, New York.

Dore, J. 1974. A pragmatic description of early language development. J. Psycholing. Res. 3: 343–350.

Dore, J. 1975. Holophrases, speech acts and language universals. J. Child Lang. 2: 21–40.

Drach, K. M. 1969. The language of the parent: a pilot study. In: K. M. Drach, B. Kobashigawa, C. Pfuderer, and D. Slobin (eds.), The Structure of Linguistic Input. Unpublished manuscript, University of California, Berkeley.

Dreikurs, R., B. Grunwald, and F. C. Peppter. 1972. Never underestimate the power of children. Intell. Digest 11(10): 54–66.

Duncan, S. 1969. Nonverbal communication. Psychol. Bull. 72: 118–137.

Edwards, D. 1973. Sensory-motor intelligence and semantic relations in early child grammar. Cognition 2: 395–434.

Edwards, D. 1977. The sources of children's early meanings. In: I. Markova (ed.), Language and Social Context. John Wiley & Sons, New York.

Eimas, P. D., E. P. Sigueland, P. Jusczyk, and J. Vigorito. 1971. Speech perception in infants. Science 171: 303–306.

Eisenberg, R. B. 1967. Stimulus significance as a determinant of newborn responses to sound. Paper presented at the Biennial Meeting of the Society for Research in Child Development, March, New York.

Eisenberg, R. B. 1970. The organization of auditory behavior. J. Speech Hear. Res. 13: 461–464.

Elkind, D. 1967. Piaget's conservation problems. Child Dev. 38: 15–27.

Elkind, D. 1971. Cognition in infancy and early childhood. In: Y. Brackbill (ed.), Infancy and Early Childhood. The Free Press, New York.

Elkonin, D. B. 1971. Development of speech. In: A. V. Zaporozhets and D. B. Elkonin (eds.), The Psychology of Preschool Children. MIT Press, Cambridge, Mass.

Entwisle, D. R. 1968. Subcultural differences in children's language development. Int. J. Psychol. 3: 13-22.

Ervin, S. M. 1964. Imitation and structural change in children's language. In: E. H. Lenneberg (ed.), New Directions in the Study of Language. MIT Press, Cambridge, Mass.

Ervin-Tripp, S. M. 1971. An overview of theories of grammatical development. In: D. I. Slobin (ed.), The Ontogenesis of Grammar. Academic Press, New York.

Ervin-Tripp, S. M. 1973. Author's postscript. In: A. S. Dil (ed.), Language Acquisition and Communicative Choice. Essays by Susan M. Ervin-Tripp. Stanford University Press, Stanford, Cal.

Fagan, J. F. 1971. Infant's recognition memory for a series of visual stimuli. J. Exp. Child Psychol. 11: 244-250.

Fantz, R. L. 1958. Pattern vision in young infants. Psychol. Rec. 8: 43-47.

Fantz, R. L. 1961. The origins of form perception. Sci. Am. 204: 2-8.

Fantz, R. L. 1966. Pattern discrimination and selective attention as determinants of perceptual development from birth. In: A. H. Kidd and J. L. Rivoire (eds.), Perceptual Development in Children. International Universities Press, New York.

Fantz, R. L., J. M. Ordy, and M. S. Udelf. 1968. Maturation of pattern vision in infants during the first six months. In: N. S. Endler, L. R. Boulter, and H. Osser (eds.), Contemporary Issues in Developmental Psychology. Holt, Rinehart and Winston, New York.

Ferguson, C. A. 1956. Arabic baby talk. In: For Roman Jakobson. Mouton, s'Gravenhague.

Ferguson, C. A. 1964. Baby talk in six languages. Am. Anthropol. 66: 103-114.

Feshbach, N. D. 1973. Teaching styles of Israeli four-year-olds and their mothers. Paper presented at the Meeting of the American Educational Research Association, February, New Orleans.

Festinger, L. 1957. A Theory of Cognitive Dissonance. Harper & Row, New York.

Fillmore, L. J. 1968. The case for case. In: E. Bach and R. T. Harms (eds.), Universals in Linguistic Theory. Holt, Rinehart and Winston, New York.

Flavell, J. H. 1963. The Developmental Psychology of Jean Piaget. D. Van Nostrand, Princeton, N.J.

Flavell, J. H. 1970. Concept development. In: P. H. Mussen (ed.),

Carmichael's Manual of Child Psychology. Vol. 1. John Wiley & Sons, New York.

Flavell, J. H., P. T. Botkin, C. L. Fry, J. W. Wright, and P. E. Jarvis. 1968. The Development of Role-Taking and Communication Skills in Children. John Wiley & Sons, New York.

Fodor, J. A. 1966. How to learn to talk: some simple ways. In: F. Smith and G. A. Miller (eds.), The Genesis of Language. MIT Press, Cambridge, Mass.

Fodor, J. A., T. G. Bever, and M. F. Garret. 1974. The Psychology of Language. An Introduction to Psycholinguistics and Generative Grammar. McGraw-Hill, New York.

Fodor, J. A., and J. J. Katz. 1964. The Structure of Language: Readings in the Philosophy of Language. Prentice-Hall, Englewood Cliffs, N.J.

Fouts, R. S. 1973. Acquisition and testing of gestural signs in four young chimpanzees. Science 180: 978-980.

Fowler, W. 1962. Cognitive learning in infancy and early childhood. Psychol. Bull. 59: 116-152.

Fowler, W., and A. Swenson. 1975. The influence of early stimulation on language development. Paper presented at the Biennial Meeting of the Society for Research in Child Development, April, Denver.

Francis, H. 1969. Structures in the speech of a 2½-year old. Br. J. Educ. Psychol. 39: 291-302.

Francis, H. 1970. Linguistic competence and natural language. La Linguistique 6: 47-51.

Francis, H. 1974a. Social background, speech and learning to read. Br. J. Educ. Psychol. 44: 290-299.

Francis, H. 1974b. Social class, reference and context. Lang. Speech 17: 193-198.

Frank, S. M., and M. S. Seegmiller. 1973. Children's language environment in free play situation. Paper presented at the Biennial Meeting of the Society for Research in Child Development. March, Philadelphia.

Franke, C. 1899. Sprachentwicklung der Kinder und der Menschheit. In: W. Rein (ed.), Encyklopädisches Handbuch der Pädagogik. Beyer, Langensalza.

Fraser, C., U. Bellugi, and R. W. Brown. 1963. Control of grammar in imitation, comprehension, and production. J. Verb. Learn. Behav. 2: 121-135.

Fraser, C., and N. Roberts. 1975. Mothers' speech to children of four different ages. J. Psycholing. Res. 4: 9–16.

Freedman, D. G., C. B. Loring, and R. M. Martin. 1967. Emotional behavior and personality development. In: Y. Brackbill (ed.), Infancy and Early Childhood. The Free Press, New York.

Friedlander, B. Z. 1970. Receptive language development in infancy: issues and problems. Merrill Palmer Q. 16: 7–51.

Friedlander, B. Z., A. C. Jacobs, B. B. Davis, and H. S. Wetstone. 1972. Time-sampling analysis of infants' natural environments in the home. Child Dev. 43: 730–740.

Fry, D. B. 1966. Development of the phonological system. In: F. Smith and G. A. Miller (eds.), The Genesis of Language. MIT Press, Cambridge, Mass.

Gagné, R. M. 1968. Contributions of learning to human development. Psychol. Rev. 75: 177–191.

Gardner, R. A., and B. T. Gardner. 1969. Teaching sign language to a chimpanzee. Science 165: 664–672.

Gay, J., and R. D. Tweney. 1975. Development of linguistic comprehension and production in lower-class Black children. Paper presented at the 83rd Annual Convention of the American Psychological Association, September, Chicago.

Gazzaniga, M. S., and R. W. Sperry. 1967. Language after section of the cerebral commissures. Brain 90: 131–148.

Geschwind, N. 1964. The development of the brain and the evolution of language. Monogr. Ser. Lang. Ling. 17: 155–169.

Geschwind, N. 1965. Disconnection syndromes in animals and man. Brain 88: 237–294, 585–644.

Geschwind, N. 1967. The neural basis of language. In: K. Salzinger and S. Salzinger (eds.), Research in Verbal Behavior and some Neurophysiological Implications. Academic Press, New York.

Geschwind, N. 1970. The organization of language and the brain. Science 170: 940–944.

Geschwind, N. 1972. Language and the brain. Sci. Am. 226: 76–83.

Geschwind, N. 1974. The anatomical basis of hemispheric differentiation. In: S. J. Dimond and J. G. Beaumont (eds.), Hemisphere Function in the Human Brain. Halsted Press, New York.

Gewirtz, J. L. 1969. Levels of conceptual analysis in environment-infant interaction research. Merrill Palmer Q. 15: 7–48.

Gibson, E. J. 1963. Perceptual development. In: H. W. Stevenson (ed.), Child Psychology. Sixty-second Yearbook, National Society for the Study of Education. Part I. Ch. 4. University of Chicago Press, Chicago.

Gibson, E. J. 1969a. Perceptual Learning. Prentice-Hall, Englewood Cliffs, N.J.

Gibson, E. J. 1969b. Principles of Perceptual Learning and Development. Appleton-Century-Crofts, New York.

Gibson, E. J. 1971. Perceptual learning and theory of word perception. Cog. Psychol. 2: 351–368.

Gibson, J. J. 1966. The Senses Considered as Perceptual System. Houghton Mifflin, Boston.

Gleason, J. B. 1973. Code switching in children's language. In: T. E. Moore (ed.), Cognitive Development and the Acquisition of Language. Academic Press, New York.

Glucksberg, S. 1975. The development of referential communication skills. In: F. D. Horowitz (ed.), Review of Child Development Research. Vol. 4. University of Chicago Press, Chicago.

Glucksberg, S., and R. M. Krauss. 1967. What do people say after they have learned to talk? Studies of the development of referential communication. Merrill Palmer Q. 13: 309–316.

Goffman, E. 1974. Frame Analysis: An Essay on the Organization of Experience. Harvard University Press, Cambridge, Mass.

Goldstein, K. 1948. Language and Language Disturbances. Grune & Stratton, New York.

Gollin, E. S., and M. Moody. 1973. Developmental psychology. In: P. H. Mussen and M. R. Rosenzweig (eds.), Annual Review of Psychology. Vol. 24. Annual Reviews, Palo Alto, Cal.

Graves, M. F., and S. Koziol. 1971. Noun plural development in primary grade children. Child Dev. 42: 1165–1173.

Greenberg, J. H. (ed.). 1963. Universals of Language. MIT Press, Cambridge, Mass.

Greenfield, P. M., and J. Smith. 1976. The Structure of Communication in Early Language Development. Academic Press, New York.

Greeno, J. G., and R. S. Bjork. 1973. Mathematical learning theory and the new "Mental Forestry." In: P. H. Mussen and M. R. Rosenzweig (eds.), Annual Review of Psychology. Vol. 24. Annual Reviews, Palo Alto, Cal.

Gregoire, A. 1937. L'Apprentissage du Langage les deux Premières Anneés. Vol. 1. Université de Liege, Liege.

Grewel, F. 1959. How do children acquire the use of language? Phonetica 3: 193–202.

Guilford, J. P. 1965. Motivation in an informational psychology. In: D. Levine (ed.), Nebraska Symposium on Motivation. University of Nebraska Press, Lincoln.

Guillet, C. 1909. Retentiveness in child and adult. Am. J. Psychol. 20: 318–352.

Hall, E. T. 1959. The Silent Language. Fawcett, New York.

Halliday, M. A. K. 1975. Learning how to mean. In: E. H. Lenneberg and E. Lenneberg (eds.), Foundations of Language Development. A Multidisciplinary Approach. Vol. 1. Academic Press, New York.

Harkness, S. 1975. Cultural variation in mother's language. Word 27: 495–498.

Harlow, H. F. 1953. Motivation as a factor in the acquisition of a new response. In: Current Theory and Research on Motivation: A Symposium. University of Nebraska Press, Lincoln.

Harris, D. B. (ed.). 1957. The Concept of Development. University of Minnesota Press, Minneapolis.

Hayes, C. 1951. The Ape in our House. Victor Gollancz, London.

Hebb, D. O. 1949. The Organization of Behavior. John Wiley & Sons, New York.

Hediger, H. 1961. The evolution of territorial behavior. In: S. L. Washburn (ed.), The Social Life of Early Man. Aldine, Chicago.

Heidbreder, E. 1958. Woodworth and Whorf on the role of language in thinking. In: G. S. Seward and J. P. Seward (eds.), Current Psychological Issues. Holt, New York.

Hess, R. D., and V. Shipman. 1965. Early experience and the socialization of cognitive modes in children. Child Dev. 36: 869–886.

Hess, R. D., and V. Shipman. 1967. Cognitive elements in maternal behavior. In: J. P. Hill (ed.), Minnesota Symposia on Child Psychology. Vol. 1. University of Minnesota Press, Minneapolis.

Hess, W. R. 1962. Psychologie in biologischer Sicht. Georg Thieme, Stuttgart.

Hewes, G. W. 1975. The current status of the gestural theory of language origin. Paper presented at the Conference on Origins and Evolution of Language and Speech, September, New York.

Hinde, R. A. (ed.). 1972. Non-verbal Communication. Cambridge University Press, London.

Hiorth, F. 1974. Noam Chomsky, Linguistics and Philosophy. Universitetsforlaget, Oslo.

Hirschman, R., and E. S. Katkin. 1974. Psychophysiological functioning, arousal, attention, and learning during the first year of life. In: H. W. Reese (ed.), Advances in Child Development and Behavior. Vol. 9. Academic Press, New York.

Holloway, G. E. T. 1967. An Introduction to the Child's Conception of Space. Humanities Press, New York.

Holzman, M. 1974. The verbal environment provided by mothers for their very young children. Merrill Palmer Q. 20: 31–42.

Hook, S. (ed.). 1969. Language and Philosophy. New York University Press, New York.

Hörmann, H. 1967. Psychologie der Sprache. Springer Verlag, Berlin.

Horner, V. M. 1968. The Verbal World of the Lower Class Three-year-old: A Pilot Study in Linguistic Ecology. Unpublished doctoral dissertation, University of Rochester.

Hulsebus, R. C. 1973. Operant conditioning of infant behavior: a review. In: H. W. Reese (ed.), Advances in Child Development and Behavior. Vol. 8. Academic Press, New York.

Hunt, J. McV. 1961. Intelligence and Experience. Ronald Press, New York.

Hunt, J. McV. 1965. Intrinsic motivation and its role in psychological development. In: D. Levine (ed.), Nebraska Symposium on Motivation. University of Nebraska Press, Lincoln.

Huttenlocher, J., K. Eisenberg, and S. Strauss. 1968. Comprehension: relation between perceived actor and logical subject. J. Verb. Learn. Verb. Behav. 7: 527–530.

Hymes, D. 1962. The ethnography of speaking. In: T. Gladwin and W. C. Sturtevant (eds.), Anthropology and Human Behavior. Anthropological Society of Washington, Washington, D.C.

Hymes, D. 1967. The functions of speech. In: J. D. DeCecco (ed.), The Psychology of Language, Thought, and Instruction. Holt, Rinehart and Winston, New York.

Ingalls, R. P., and D. J. Dickerson. 1969. Development of hypothesis behavior in human concept identification. Dev. Psychol. 1: 707–716.

Ingram, D. 1971. Transitivity in child language. Language 47: 888–910.

Irwin, O. C. 1948. Infant speech: development of vowel sounds. J. Speech Hear. Disord. 13: 31–34.

Jakobson, R. 1941. Kindersprache, Aphasie und allgemeine Lautgesetze. Almquist & Wiksell, Uppsala.

Jakobson, R. 1960. Concluding statement: linguistics and poetics. In: T. A. Sebeok (ed.), Style in Language. MIT Press, Cambridge, Mass.

Jakobson, R. 1962. Why "mama" and "papa"? In: R. Jakobson (ed.), Selected Writings. Mouton, The Hague.

Jakobson, R., and M. Halle. 1956. Fundamentals of Language. Mouton, s'Gravenhague.

Jeffrey, W. E. 1968. The orienting reflex and attention in cognitive development. Psychol. Rev. 75: 323–334.

Jenkins, J. J., and D. S. Palermo. 1964. Mediation processes and the acquisition of linguistic structure. In: U. Bellugi and R. Brown (eds.), The Acquisition of Language. Monogr. Soc. Res. Child Dev. 29. (Serial no. 92).

Jerison, H. J. 1973. Evolution of the Brain and Intelligence. Academic Press, New York.

Jordan, B. E., N. Radin, and A. Epstein. 1975. Paternal behavior and intellectual functioning in preschool boys and girls. Dev. Psychol. 11: 407–408.

Kagan, J., and R. E. Klein. 1973. Cross-cultural perspectives on early development. Am. Psychol. 28: 947–961.

Kagan, J., and M. Lewis. 1965. Studies of attention. Merrill Palmer Q. 11: 92–127.

Kainz, F. 1960. Psychologie der Sprache. Vol. 2. Ferdinand Enke, Stuttgart.

Kaplan, G., and E. Kaplan. 1971. The prelinguistic child. In: J. Eliot (ed.), Human Development and Cognitive Processes. Holt, Rinehart and Winston, New York.

Katz, J. J., and J. A. Fodor. 1963. The structure of semantic theory. Language 39: 170–210.

Kaye, K. 1977. Thickening thin data: the maternal role in developing communication and language. In: M. Bullowa (ed.), Before Speech. Harvard University Press, Cambridge, Mass.

Kearsley, R. B. 1973. The newborn's response to auditory stimulation: a demonstration of orienting and defensive behavior. Child Dev. 44: 582–590.

Kelemen, G. 1949. Structure and performance in animal language. Arch. Otolaryngol. 50: 740–744.

Kellog, W. N., and L. A. Kellog. 1933. The Ape and the Child: A Study of Environmental Influence upon Early Behavior. McGraw-Hill, New York.

Kelly, G. A. 1955. The Psychology of Personal Constructs. Norton, New York.

Kendler, T. S., and H. H. Kendler. 1967. Experimental analysis of inferential behavior in children. In: L. P. Lipsitt and C. C. Spiker (eds.), Advances in Child Development and Behavior, Vol. 3. Academic Press, New York.

Kogan, K., and H. C. Wimberger. 1966. An approach to defining mother-child interaction styles. Percept. Mot. Skills 23: 1171–1177.

Kogan, K., and H. C. Wimberger. 1969. Interaction patterns in disadvantaged families. J. Clin. Psychol. 25: 347–352.

Kohlberg, L., J. Yaeger, and H. Hjertholm. 1968. Private speech: four studies and a review of theories. Child Dev. 39: 691–736.

Kohler, E. 1929. Kindersprache und Begriffsbildung. Ein Beiträg zur Problemgeschichte. In: Beiträge zur Problemgeschichte der Psychologie. Festschrift zu Karl Bühler's 50 Geburtstag. Gustav Fischer, Jena.

Kravitz, H., and J. J. Boehm. 1971. Rhythmic habit patterns in infancy: their sequence, age of onset, and frequency. Child Dev. 42: 399–413.

LaBarre, W. 1954. The Human Animal. University of Chicago Press, Chicago.

Lakoff, G., and J. R. Ross. 1967. Is Deep Structure Necessary? (Published by the authors, Cambridge, Mass.)

Langer, S. K. 1942. Philosophy in a New Key. The American Library, New York.

Lashley, K. S. 1951. The problem of serial order in behavior. In: L. A. Jeffress (ed.), Cerebral Mechanisms in Behavior. John Wiley & Sons, New York.

Latif, I. 1934. The physiological basis of linguistic development and of the ontogeny of meaning. Psychol. Rev. 41: 55–85, 153–176, 246–264.

Lenneberg, E. H. 1962. Understanding language without ability to speak: a case report. J. Abnorm. Soc. Psychol. 65: 419–425.

Lenneberg, E. H. 1966. The natural history of language. In: F. Smith and G. A. Miller (eds.), The Genesis of Language. MIT Press, Cambridge, Mass.

Lenneberg, E. H. 1967. Biological Foundations of Language. John Wiley & Sons, New York.

Lenneberg, E. H. 1971. The importance of temporal factors in behavior. In: D. L. Horton and J. J. Jenkins (eds.), Perception of Language. Charles E. Merrill, Columbus, Ohio.

Lentin, L. 1973. Interaction adultes-enfants au course de l'acquisition du langage. Et. Ling. Appl. 9: 9–50.

Leonard, L. B. 1975. The role of nonlinguistic stimuli and semantic relations in children's acquisition of grammatical utterances. J. Exp. Child Psychol. 19: 346–357.

Leontiev, A. A. 1970. Social and natural in semiotics. In: J. Morton (ed.), Biological and Social Factors in Psycholinguistics. University of Illinois Press, Urbana.

Leontiev, A. N., and A. A. Leontiev. 1959. The social and individual in language. Lang. Speech 2: 193–204.

Leopold, W. F. 1939–1949. Speech Development of a Bilingual Child. 4 vols. (I, 1939; II, 1947; III & IV, 1949). Northwestern University Press, Evanston, Ill.

Leopold, W. F. 1948. Semantic learning in infant language. Word 4: 173–180.

Levelt, W. J. M. 1970. A scaling approach to the study of syntactic relations. In: G. B. Flores d'Arcais and W. J. M. Levelt (eds.), Advances in Psycholinguistics. American Elsevier, New York.

Levy, J. 1974. Psychological implications of bilateral asymmetry. In: S. J. Dimond and J. G. Beaumont (eds.), Hemisphere Function in the Human Brain. Paul Elek, London.

Lewis, M. M. 1937. The beginning reference to past and future in a child's speech. Br. J. Educ. Psychol. 7: 39–56.

Lewis, M. M. 1951. Infant Speech: A Study of the Beginnings of Language. Humanities Press, New York.

Lewis, M. M. 1957. How Children Learn to Speak. George G. Harrap, London.

Lewis, M. M. 1964. Language, Thought and Personality. Basic Books, New York.

Lewis, M., and K. Freedle. 1973. Mother-infant dyad: the cradle of meaning. In: P. Pliner, L. Krames, and T. Alloway (eds.), Communication and Affect. Language and Thought. Academic Press, New York.

Lewis, M., and S. Goldberg. 1969. Perceptual-cognitive development in infancy: a generalized expectancy model as a function of the mother-infant interaction. Merrill Palmer Q. 15: 81–100.

Lewis, M., and S. Lee-Painter. 1974. An interactional approach to the mother-infant dyad. In: M. Lewis and L. Rosenblum (eds.), The Effect of the Infant on its Caregiver. John Wiley & Sons, New York.

Lieberman, P. 1967. Intonation, Perception, and Language. MIT Press, Cambridge, Mass.

Lieberman, P. 1968. Primate vocalizations and human linguistic ability. J. Acoust. Soc. Am. 44: 1574–1584.

Liiamina, G. M. 1960. Development of speech comprehension in children in the second year of life. (English translation.) Voprosy Psikhol. 3: 106–121.

Lilly, J. C. 1967. Dolphin vocalization. In: C. H. Millikan and F. L. Darley (eds.), Brain Mechanisms Underlying Speech and Language. Grune & Stratton, New York.

Littman, R. A. 1958. Motives, history and causes. In: M. R. Jones (ed.), Nebraska Symposium on Motivation. University of Nebraska Press, Lincoln.

Locke, J. L. 1971a. Acoustic imagery in children's phonetically mediated recall. Percept. Mot. Skills 32: 1000–1002.

Locke, J. L. 1971b. Phonetic mediation in four-year-old children. Psychonom. Sci. 23: 409.

Lorenz, K. 1965. Evolution and Modification of Behavior. University of Chicago Press, Chicago.

Lorenz, K. 1966. On Aggression. Harcourt, Brace & World, New York.

Lorenz, K. 1969. Innate bases of learning. In: K. H. Pribram (ed.), On the Biology of Learning. Harcourt, Brace & World, New York.

Lovaas, O. I. 1967. A program for the establishment of speech in psychotic children. In: J. K. Kind (ed.), Childhood Autism. Pergamon Press, Oxford.

Luchsinger, R., and G. E. Arnold. 1965. Voice, Speech and Language. Constable, London.

Luria, A. R. 1965. Higher Cortical Functions in Man. Basic Books, New York.

Luria, A. R. 1975. Basic problems of language in the light of psychology and neurolinguistics. In: E. H. Lenneberg and E. Lenneberg (eds.), Foundations of Language Development. A Multidisciplinary Approach. Vol. 2. Academic Press, New York.

Luria, A. R., and F. I. Yudovich. 1959. Speech and the Development of Mental Processes in the Child. Staples Press, London.

Mahle, G. F., and G. Schulze. 1964. Psychological research in the extralinguistic area. In: T. A. Sebeok, A. S. Hayes, and M. C. Bateson (eds.), Approaches to Semiotics. Mouton, The Hague.

Malinowski, B. 1923. The problem of meaning in primitive languages. In: C. K. Ogden and I. A. Richards (eds.), The Meaning of Meaning. Harcourt, Brace & World, New York.

Mann, M. E., and R. K. van Wagenen. 1975. Alteration of joint mother-child linguistic styles, involving procedures of extension, elaboration, and reinforcement. Paper presented at the Biennial Meeting of the Society for Research in Child Development, April, Denver.

Marler, P. 1965. Communication in monkeys and apes. In: I. DeVore (ed.), Primate Behavior. Holt, Rinehart and Winston, New York.

Martin, J. G. 1972. Rhythmic (hierarchical) versus serial structures in speech and other behavior. Psychol. Rev. 79: 487–509.

Mayers, K. S., R. T. Robertson, E. W. Rubel, and R. F. Thompson. 1971. Development of polysensory responses in the association cortex of kittens. Science 171: 1038–1040.

McCarthy, D. 1930. The Language Development of the Preschool Child. University of Minnesota Press, Minneapolis.

McCarthy, D. 1952. Organismic interpretations of infant vocalizations. Child Dev. 23: 273–280.

McCarthy, D. 1954. Language development in children. In: L. Carmichael (ed.), Manual of Child Psychology. John Wiley & Sons, New York.

McCarthy, D. 1966. Affective aspects of language learning. In: A. H. Kidd and J. L. Rivoire (eds.), Perceptual Development in Children. International Universities Press, New York.

McCawley, J. D. 1968. The role of semantics in grammar. In: E. Bach and R. T. Harms (eds.), Universals in Linguistic Theory. Holt, Rinehart and Winston, New York.

McDougall, W. 1915. An Introduction to Social Psychology. Luce, Boston.

McHale, J. 1974. Futures critical: a review. In: The Rome World Special Conference on Futures Research 1973. Human Futures, Needs, Societies, Technologies. IPC Business Press, Guilford, Surrey, U.K.

McKay, D. 1968. The informational analysis of questions and commands. In: W. F. Buckley (ed.), Modern Systems Research for the Behavioral Scientist: A Sourcebook. Aldine, Chicago.

McKay, D. 1972. Formal analysis of communicative processes. In: R. A. Hinde (ed.), Non-Verbal Communication. Cambridge University Press, London.

McNamara, J. 1972. Cognitive basis of language learning in infants. Psychol. Rev. 79: 1–13.

McNeill, D. 1966. Developmental psycholinguistics. In: F. Smith and

G. A. Miller (eds.), The Genesis of Language. MIT Press, Cambridge, Mass.

McNeill, D. 1970a. The development of language. In: P. H. Mussen (ed.), Carmichael's Manual of Child Psychology. Vol. 1. John Wiley & Sons, New York.

McNeill, D. 1970b. The Acquisition of Language. The Study of Developmental Psycholinguistics. Harper & Row, New York.

McNeill, D. 1970c. Explaining language universals. In: J. Morton (ed.), Biological and Social Factors in Psycholinguistics. University of Illinois Press, Urbana.

McReynolds, L. V. (ed.). 1974. Developing systematic procedures for training children's language. ASHA Monogr. 18.

Mead, G. H. 1934. Mind, Self and Society. University of Chicago Press, Chicago.

Mead, M. 1930. Growing up in New Guinea. W. Morrow, New York.

Menyuk, P. 1969. Sentences Children Use. MIT Press, Cambridge, Mass.

Menyuk, P. 1971. The Acquisition and Development of Language. Prentice-Hall, Englewood Cliffs, N.J.

Menzel, E. W., and M. K. Johnson. 1975. Communication and cognitive organization in humans and other animals. Paper presented at the Academy of Sciences Conference on Origins and Evolution of Language and Speech, September, New York.

Meumann, E. 1908. Die Entwicklung der ersten Wortbedeutungen beim Kinde. Engelmann, Leipzig.

Meyer, W. J., and J. Shane. 1973. The form and function of children's questions. J. Genet. Psychol. 123: 285-296.

Miller, G. A. 1956. The magical number seven plus or minus two: some limits in our ability for processing of information. Psychol. Rev. 63: 81-97.

Miller, G. A., E. Galanter, and K. H. Pribram. 1960. Plans and the Structure of Behavior. Holt, Rinehart and Winston, New York.

Miller, N. E. 1963. Some reflections on the law of effect produce a new alternative to drive reduction. In: M. R. Jones (ed.), Nebraska Symposium on Motivation. University of Nebraska Press, Lincoln.

Miller, W., and S. Ervin. 1964. The development of grammar in child language. In: U. Bellugi and R. Brown (eds.), The Acquisition of Language. Monogr. Soc. Res. Child Dev. 29. (No. 1, Serial No. 92).

Milner, B. 1962. Laterality effects in audition. In: V. B. Mountcastle (ed.), Inter-hemispheric Relations and Cerebral Dominance. Johns Hopkins University Press, Baltimore.

Moerk, E. L. 1972. Principles of dyadic interaction in language learning. Merrill Palmer Q. 18: 229-257.

Moerk, E. L. 1973. Specific cognitive antecedents of structures and functions in language acquisition. Child Study J. 3: 77-90.

Moerk, E. L. 1974a. Changes in verbal child-mother interactions with increasing language skills of the child. J. Psycholing. Res. 3: 101-116.

Moerk, E. L. 1974b. A design for multivariate analysis of language behavior and language development. Lang. Speech 17: 240-254.

Moerk, E. L. 1975a. Piaget's research as applied to the explanation of language development. Merrill Palmer Q. 21: 151-170.

Moerk, E. L. 1975b. The multiple channels of the young child's communicative behavior. Linguistics 160: 21-31.

Moerk, 1975c. Verbal interactions between children and their mothers during the preschool years. Dev. Psychol. 11: 788-794.

Moerk, E. L. 1975d. A cross-sectional study of determiners and reinforcers for specific verbal behaviors of young children and their mothers. Paper presented at the 55th Annual Convention of the Western Psychological Association, April, Sacramento, Cal.

Moerk, E. L. 1976a. Motivational variables in language acquisition. Child Stud. J. 6: 55-84.

Moerk, E. L. 1976b. Processes of language teaching and training in the interactions of mother-child dyads. Child Dev. 47: 1064-1078.

Moerk, E. L. Processes and products of imitation: additional evidence that imitation is progressive. J. Psycholing. Res. In press.

Moerk, E. L. Determiners and reinforcers of verbal behaviors of young children and their mothers. In preparation-a.

Moerk, E. L. Piaget's concept of horizontal and vertical décalage as applied to the understanding of language development. In preparation-b.

Moerk, E. L., and N. Wong. 1976. Meaningful and structured behavioral antecedents of semantics and syntax in language. Linguistics 172: 23-39.

Montgomery, K. C. 1951. The relation between exploratory behavior and spontaneous alternation in the white rat. J. Comp. Physiol. Psychol. 44: 582-589.

Moore, K. M., and A. N. Meltzoff. 1975. Neonate imitation: a test of existence and mechanism. Paper presented at the Biennial Meeting of the Society for Research in Child Development, April, Denver.

Morehead, D. M., and A. Morehead. 1974. From signal to sign: a Piagetian view of thought and language during the first two years. In: R. L. Schiefelbusch and L. L. Lloyd (eds.), Language Perspectives—Acquisition, Retardation, and Intervention. University Park Press, Baltimore.

Morris, C. W. 1938. Foundations of the theory of signs. In: O. Neurath, R. Carnap, and C. W. Morris (eds.), International Encyclopedia of Unified Science. Vol. 1, no. 2. University of Chicago Press, Chicago.

Morris, C. W. 1946. Signs, Language and Behavior. Prentice-Hall, Englewood Cliffs, N.J.

Morton, J. 1970a. What could possibly be innate? In: J. Morton (ed.), Biological and Social Factors in Psycholinguistics. University of Illinois Press, Urbana.

Morton, J. (ed.). 1970b. Biological and Social Factors in Psycholinguistics. University of Illinois Press, Urbana.

Moss, H. A. 1973. Communication in mother-infant interaction. In: L. Krames, P. Pliner, and T. Alloway (eds.), Advances in the Study of Communication and Affect. Vol. 1: Nonverbal Communication. Plenum Press, New York.

Mowrer, O. H. 1952. The autism theory of speech development and some clinical applications. J. Speech Hear. Disord. 17: 263-268.

Mowrer, O. H. 1954. The psychologist looks at language. Am. Psychol. 9: 660-692.

Mowrer, O. H. 1958. Hearing and speaking: an analysis of language learning. J. Speech Hear. Disord. 23: 143-152.

Mowrer, O. H. 1960. Learning Theory and the Symbolic Processes. John Wiley & Sons, New York.

Murai, J. 1960. Speech development in infants. Psychologia 3: 27-35.

Murchison, C., and S. Langer. 1927. Tiedemann's observations on the development of the mental faculties of children. Ped. Sem. 34: 205-230.

Mussen, P. H., J. J. Conger, and J. Kagan. 1974. Child Development and Personality. Harper & Row, New York.

Nakamura, H. 1966. Time in Indian and Japanese thought. In: J. T. Fraser (ed.), The Voices of Time. George Braziller, New York.

Nakazima, S. 1962. A comparative study of the speech development of Japanese and American English in childhood. Stud. Phonol. 2: 27-39.

Nelson, K. 1973. Structure and strategy in learning to talk. Monogr. Soc. Res. Child Dev. 38. (Nos. 1, 2, Serial no. 149).

Nelson, K. 1974. Concept, word, and sentence: interrelations in acquisition and development. Psychol. Rev. 81: 267–285.

Nelson, K. E., G. Carskaddon, and J. D. Bonvillian. 1973. Syntax acquisition: impact of experimental variation in adult verbal interaction with the child. Child Dev. 44: 497–504.

Newport, E. L. 1976. Motherese: the speech of mothers to young children. In: N. J. Castellan, D. B. Pisoni, and G. R. Potts (eds.), Cognitive Theory. Vol. 2. Lawrence Erlbaum, Hillsdale, N.J.

Newport, E. L., L. R. Gleitman, and H. Gleitman. 1975. A study of mothers' speech and child language acquisition. Pap. Rep. Child Lang. Dev. 10: 111–116.

Nicolich, L., and J. B. Raph. 1975. A longitudinal study of representational play in relation to spontaneous vocal imitation and development of multiword utterances. Paper presented at the Biennial Meeting of the Society for Research in Child Development, April, Denver.

Oettinger, A. G. 1972. The semantic wall. In: E. E. David and P. B. Denes (eds.), Human Communication: A Unified View. McGraw-Hill, New York.

Ogden, C. K., and I. A. Richards. 1923. The Meaning of Meaning. Harcourt, Brace & World, New York.

Olson, D. R. 1968. Language acquisition and cognitive development. Paper presented at the International Conference of Social-Cultural Aspects of Mental Retardation, Nashville.

Olson, D. R. 1970. Language and thought: aspects of a cognitive theory of semantics. Psychol. Rev. 77: 257–273.

Opie, I., and P. Opie. 1959. The Lore and Language of Schoolchildren. Oxford University Press, London.

Orne, M. T. 1973. Communication by the total experimental situation: why it is important, how it is evaluated, and its significance for the ecological validity of findings. In: P. Pliner, L. Krames, and T. Alloway (eds.), Communication and Affect. Language and Thought. Academic Press, New York.

Osgood, C. E. 1957. Motivational dynamics of language behavior: In: Nebraska Symposium on Motivation. University of Nebraska Press, Lincoln.

Osgood, C. E. 1971. Where do sentences come from? In: D. Steinberg and L. Jakobovits (eds.), Semantics: An Interdisciplinary

Reader in Philosophy, Linguistics and Psychology. Cambridge University Press, London.

Ovsiankina, M. 1928. Die Wiederaufnahme unterbrochener Handlungen. Psych. Forschung 6: 302–379.

Palermo, D. 1970. Research in language development: do we know where we are going? In: L. Goulet and P. Baltes (eds.), Lifespan Developmental Psychology. Academic Press, New York.

Palermo, D. 1976. Semantics and language acquisition: some theoretical considerations. Paper presented at the Psychology of Language Conference, June, University of Stirling, Scotland.

Palermo, D., and D. L. Molfese. 1972. Language acquisition from age five onward. Psychol. Bull. 78: 409–428.

Parke, R. D., S. E. O'Leary, and S. West. 1972. Mother-father-newborn interaction: effects of maternal medication, labor, and sex of infant. Paper presented at the Annual Convention of the American Psychological Association, September, Washington, D.C.

Penfield, W., and R. Roberts. 1959. Speech and Brain Mechanisms. Princeton University Press, Princeton, N.J.

Phillips, J. R. 1973. Syntax and vocabulary of mother's speech to young children: age and sex comparisons. Child Dev. 44: 182-185.

Piaget, J. 1926. The Language and Thought of the Child. Harcourt, Brace, New York.

Piaget, J. 1952. The Origins of Intelligence in Children. International Universities Press, New York.

Piaget, J. 1954. The Construction of Reality in the Child. Basic Books, New York.

Piaget, J. 1964. Development and learning. In: R. Ripple and V. Rockcastle (eds.), Piaget Rediscovered. Cornell University Press, Ithaca, N.Y.

Piaget, J. 1970. Genetic Epistemology. Columbia University Press, New York.

Piaget, J. 1971. Biology and Knowledge: An Essay on the Relations between Organic Regulations and Cognitive Processes. University of Chicago Press, Chicago.

Pike, K. L. 1954, 1955, 1959. Language in Relation to a Unified Theory of the Structure of Human Behavior. Parts I, II, III. Summer Institute of Linguistics, Glendale, Cal.

Porter, R. J. Jr., and B. I. Berlin. 1975. On interpreting developmental changes in the dichotic right-ear advantage. Brain Lang. 2: 186–200.

Premack, D. 1975. Mechanisms of intelligence: preconditions for language. Paper presented at the Conference on the Origin and Evolution of Speech, New York Academy of Sciences, September, New York.

Preyer, M. I. 1882. Die Seele des Kindes. Fernau, Leipzig.

Pribram, K. H. 1971. Languages of the Brain: Experimental Paradoxes and Principles in Neuropsychology. Prentice-Hall, Englewood Cliffs, N.J.

Pribram, K. H., and W. E. Tubbs. 1967. Short-term memory, parsing and the frontal cortex. Science 156: 1765-1767.

Ramsay, D. S., and J. J. Campos. 1975. Memory by the infant in an object notion task. Dev. Psychol. 11: 411-412.

Razran, G. 1961. The observable unconscious and the inferable conscious in current Soviet psychophysiology: interoceptive conditioning, semantic conditioning, and the orienting reflex. Psychol. Rev. 68: 81-147.

Rebelsky, F., and C. Hanks. 1971. Fathers' verbal interaction with infants in the first three months of life. Child Dev. 42: 63-68.

Reese, H. W. (ed.). 1973, 1974. Advances in Child Development and Behavior. Academic Press, New York.

Rheingold, H. L. 1956. The modification of social responsiveness in institutional babies. Monogr. Soc. Res. Child Dev. 21. (No. 2, Serial no. 63).

Rheingold, H. L., J. L. Gewirtz, and H. W. Ross. 1959. Social conditioning of vocalizations in the infant. J. Comp. Physiol. Psychol. 52: 68-73.

Risley, T. R., and M. M. Wolf. 1967. Establishing functional speech in echolalic children. Behav. Res. Ther. 5: 73-88.

Rodgon, M. 1976. Single-Word Usage, Cognitive Development, and the Beginnings of Combinatorial Speech. Cambridge University Press, London.

Rodgon, M., W. Jankowski, and L. Alenskas. A multifunctional approach to single-word usage. In preparation.

Rodgon, M., and L. A. Kurdek. 1975. Vocal and gestural imitation in children under two years old. Paper presented at the Annual Convention of the American Psychological Association, August, Chicago.

Rommetveit, R. 1968. Words, Meanings, and Messages. Academic Press, New York.

Rommetveit, R. 1974. On Message Structure: A Framework for the

Study of Language and Communication. John Wiley & Sons, New York.

Rosch, E. 1973. On the internal structure of perceptual and semantic categories. In: T. E. Moore (ed.), Cognitive Development and the Acquisition of Language. Academic Press, New York.

Rosch, E. 1975. Universals and cultural specifics in human categorization. In: R. Brislin, S. Bochner, and W. Lonner (eds.), Cross-cultural Perspectives on Learning. Halsted, New York.

Ross, H. S., and R. H. Balzer. 1975. Determinants and consequences of children's questions. Child Dev. 46: 536–539.

Rossi, S., and M. C. Wittrock. 1971. Developmental shifts in verbal recall between mental ages two and five. Child Dev. 42: 333–338.

Routh, D. K. 1969. Conditioning of vocal response differentiation in infants. Dev. Psychol. 1: 219–226.

Rowell, T. E. 1962. Agonistic noises of the rhesus monkey (*Macaca mulatta*). Symp. Zool. Soc. Lond. 8: 91–96.

Russell, B. 1900. A Critical Exposition of the Philosophy of Leibnitz. Allen & Unwin, London.

Ryan, J. F. 1973. Interpretation and imitation in early language development. In: R. Hinde and J. S. Hinde (eds.), Constraints on Learning: Limitations and Predispositions. Academic Press, London.

Ryan, J. F. 1974. Early language development: towards a communicational analysis. In: M. P. M. Richards (ed.), The Integration of the Child into a Social World. Cambridge University Press, London.

Sachs, J. 1971. The status of development studies of language. In: J. Eliot (ed.), Human Development and Cognitive Processes. Holt, Rinehart and Winston, New York.

Salzinger, K. 1959. Experimental manipulation of verbal behavior. J. Gen. Psychol. 61: 65–94.

Salzinger, K., and S. Salzinger. (eds.). 1967. Research in Verbal Behavior and Some Neurophysiological Implications. Academic Press, New York.

Satz, P., D. J. Bakker, J. Teunissen, R. Hoebel, and H. Van der Vlugt. 1975. Developmental parameters of the ear asymmetry: a multivariate approach. Brain Lang. 2: 171–185.

Schachtel, E. G. 1947. On memory and childhood amnesia. Psychiatry 10: 1–26.

Schank, R. C. 1972. Conceptual dependency: a theory of natural language understanding. Cog. Psychol. 3: 552–631.

Schlesinger, I. M. 1970. The grammar of sign language and the problems of language universals. In: J. Morton (ed.), Biological and Social Factors in Psycholinguistics. University of Illinois Press, Urbana.

Schlesinger, I. M. 1971a. Production of utterances and language acquisition. In: D. I. Slobin (ed.), The Ontogenesis of Grammar: A Theoretical Symposium. Academic Press, New York.

Schlesinger, I. M. 1971b. Learning grammar: from pivot to realization rule. In: R. Huxley and E. Ingram (eds.), Language Acquisition: Models and Methods. Academic Press, New York.

Schramm, W. A., J. Lyle, and E. B. Parker. 1961. Television in the Lives of our Children. Stanford University Press, Stanford, Cal.

Scubin, E., and G. Scubin. 1907. Bubis erste Kindheit. Grieben, Leipzig.

Sebald, H. 1968. Adolescence. A Sociological Analysis. Appleton-Century-Crofts, New York.

Sebeok, T. A. (ed.). 1974. Wundt: The Language of Gesture. Mouton, The Hague.

Seegmiller, B. 1973. The norms and patterns of mother-child interaction in free play. Paper presented at the Biennial Meeting of the Society for Research in Child Development, March, Philadelphia.

Semmes, J. 1968. Hemispheric specialization: a possible clue to mechanism. Neuropsychologia 6: 11–26.

Shatz, M. 1974. Beyond syntax: the influence of conversational rules. Paper presented at the Social Science Research Council on Language Input and Acquisition, September, Boston.

Shatz, M., and R. Gelman. 1973. The development of communication skills: modifications in the speech of young children as a function of listener. Monogr. Soc. Res. Child Dev. 38. (No. 5, Serial no. 152.)

Shatz, M., and R. Gelman. 1976. Beyond syntax: the influences of conversational constraints on speech modification. In: C. Ferguson and C. Snow (eds.), Talking to Children: Language Input and Acquisition. Cambridge University Press, London.

Sherman, J. A. 1971. Imitation and language development. In: H. W. Reese (ed.), Advances in Child Development and Behavior. Vol. 6. Academic Press, New York.

Shipley, E. F., C. S. Smith, and L. R. Gleitman. 1969. A study in the acquisition of language: free responses to commands. Language 45: 322–342.

Sigel, I. 1971. Language of the disadvantaged: the distancing hypothesis. In: C. S. Lavatelli (ed.), Language Training in Early Childhood Education. University of Illinois Press, Urbana.

Siklossy, L. 1975. Problem solving approach to first language acquisition. Paper presented at the Conference on Origins and Evolution of Language and Speech, The New York Academy of Sciences, September, New York.

Sinclair, H. 1971. Sensorimotor action patterns as a condition for the acquisition of syntax. In: R. Huxley and E. Ingram (eds.), Language Acquisition: Models and Methods. Academic Press, New York.

Sinclair-de Zwart, H. 1973. Language acquisition and cognitive development. In: T. E. Moore (ed.), Cognitive Development and the Acquisition of Language. Academic Press, New York.

Skinner, B. F. 1957. Verbal Behavior. Appleton-Century-Crofts, New York.

Skupas, R. S., and R. D. Tweney. 1975. Performance in a grammatical task as a function of race, social class, and dialect: difference, deficit, or response bias? Paper presented at the 83rd Annual Convention of the American Psychological Association, September, Chicago.

Slama-Cazacu, T. 1961. Language and Context. Mouton, The Hague.

Slama-Cazacu, T. 1968. L'étude du Roumain parlé, un aspect négligé—"l'indicatio ad oculos." Résumé in Actes du XIIe Congrès Internationale de Linguistique et Philologie Romanes (Bukarest) 1: 591-599.

Slama-Cazacu, T. 1970. The dynamic-contextual method in sociolinguistics. Paper presented at the World Congress of Sociology, September, Varna.

Slobin, D. I. 1966. Comments on "Developmental Psycholinguistics." In: F. Smith and G. A. Miller (eds.), The Genesis of Language. MIT Press, Cambridge, Mass.

Slobin, D. I. 1968. Imitation and grammatical development in children. In: N. S. Endler, L. R. Boulter, and H. Osser (eds.), Contemporary Issues in Developmental Psychology. Holt, Rinehart and Winston, New York.

Slobin, D. I. 1969. Questions of language development in cross-cultural perspective. Working paper no. 14, Language-Behavior Research Laboratory, Berkeley, Cal.

Slobin, D. I. 1970. Universals in grammatical development in children. In: G. B. Flores d'Arcais and W. J. M. Levelt (eds.), Advances in Psycholinguistics. American Elsevier, New York.

Slobin, D. I. 1973. Cognitive prerequisites for the development of grammar. In: C. A. Ferguson and D. I. Slobin (eds.), Studies of Child Language Development. Holt, Rinehart and Winston, New York.

Slobin, D. I. 1975. On the nature of talk to children. In: E. H. Lenneberg and E. Lenneberg (eds.),. Foundations of Language Development. A Multidisciplinary Approach. Vol. 1. Academic Press, New York.

Smith, M. E. 1935. A study of some of the factors influencing the development of the sentence in pre-school children. J. Genet. Psychol. 46: 182-212.

Snow, C. E. 1971. Language acquisition and mothers' speech to children. Unpublished doctoral dissertation. McGill University, Montreal.

Snow, C. E. 1972. Mothers' speech to children learning language. Child Dev. 43: 549-565.

Snow, C. E. 1975. The development of conversation between mothers and babies. Unpublished manuscript.

Snow, C. E. 1976. The conversational context of language acquisition. Paper presented at the NATO Conference on the Psychology of Language, June, University of Stirling, Scotland.

Snow, C. E., A. Arlman-Rupp, Y. Hassing, J. Jobse, J. Joosten, and J. Vorster. 1976. Mothers' speech in three social classes. J. Psycholing. Res. 5: 1-20.

Söderbergh, R. 1974. Barnets Sprackutveckling och dess konsekvenser foer pedagogiken. Institutionen foer Nordiska Spraok, University of Stockholm.

Spears, W. C., and R. H. Hohle. 1967. Sensory and perceptual processes in infants. In: Y. Brackbill (ed.), Infancy and Early Childhood. The Free Press, New York.

Sperry, R. W., and M. S. Gazzaniga. 1967. Language following surgical disconnection of the hemispheres. In: C. H. Millikan and F. L. Darley (eds.), Brain Mechanisms Underlying Speech and Language. Grune & Stratton, New York.

Staats, A. W. 1971. Child Learning, Intelligence and Personality. Principles of a Behavioral Interaction Approach. Harper & Row, New York.

Staats, A. W., and C. K. Staats. 1963. Complex Human Behavior:

A Systematic Extension of Learning Principles. Holt, Rinehart and Winston, New York.

Steinschneider, A. 1967. Developmental psychophysiology. In: Y. Brackbill (ed.), Infancy and Early Childhood. The Free Press, New York.

Steinthal, H. 1871. Abriss der Sprachwissenschaft. I. Einleitung in die Psychologie der Sprachwissenschaft. Dümmler, Berlin.

Stemmer, N. 1973. An Empirist Theory of Language Acquisition. Mouton, The Hague.

Stendler Lavatelli, C. (ed.). 1971. Language Training in Early Childhood Education. University of Illinois Press, Urbana.

Stern, C., and W. Stern. 1907. Die Kindersprache: Eine psychologische und sprachtheoretische Untersuchung. Barth, Leipzig.

Stern, D. N. 1975. Infant regulation of maternal play behavior and/or maternal regulation of infant play behavior. Paper presented at the Biennial Meeting of the Society for Research in Child Development, April, Denver.

Stern, W. 1930. Psychology of Early Childhood. Holt, New York.

Stevenson, H. W. 1972. Children's Learning. Appleton-Century-Crofts, New York.

Stewart, W. A. 1964. Foreign language teaching methods in quasi-foreign language situations. In: W. A. Stewart (ed.), Non-standard Speech and the Teaching of English. Center for Applied Linguistics, Washington, D.C.

Stone, J. L., and J. Church. 1968. Childhood and Adolescence. A Psychology of the Growing Person. 2nd Ed. Random House, New York.

Stone, J. L., H. T. Smith, and L. B. Murphy. (eds.). 1973. The Competent Infant. Research and Commentary. Basic Books, New York.

Sullivan, E. V., and D. E. Hunt. 1967. Interpersonal and objective decentering as a function of age and social class. J. Genet. Psychol. 110: 199–210.

Sutton-Smith, B., and B. G. Rosenberg. 1970. The Sibling. Holt, Rinehart and Winston, New York.

Teuber, H.-L. 1967. Lacunae and research approaches to them. In: H. Millikan and F. L. Darley (eds.), Brain Mechanisms Underlying Speech and Language. Grune & Stratton, New York.

Thew, C. 1975. Theories about linguistic input. Paper presented at the Western Conference on Linguistics, October, Calgary.

Thorpe, W. H. 1967. Animal vocalization and communication. In: C. H. Millikan and F. Darley (eds.), Brain Mechanisms Underlying Speech and Language. Grune & Stratton, New York.

Thorpe, W. H. 1974. Animal Nature and Human Nature. Anchor Press/Doubleday, Garden City, N.Y.

Tiedemann, D. 1787. Beobachtungen über die Entwicklung der Seelenfähigkeiten bei Kindern. Bonde, Altenburg.

Tinbergen, N. 1952. Instinktlehre. Paul Parey, Berlin.

Trevarthen, C. 1974. Prespeech in communication of infants with adults. J. Child Lang. 1: 335–337.

Turnure, C. 1971. Response to voice of mother and stranger by babies in the 1st year. Dev. Psychol. 4: 182–190.

Valentine, C. W. 1930. The psychology of imitation. Br. J. Psychol. 21: 105–132.

Van der Geest, T., R. Gerstel, R. Appel, and B. Tervoort. 1973. The Child's Communicative Competence: Language Capacity in Three Groups of Children from Different Social Classes. Mouton, The Hague.

Vetter, H. J., and R. W. Howell. 1971. Theories of language acquisition. J. Psycholing. Res. 1: 31–64.

Voegelin, C. F., and F. M. Robinett. 1954. Mother language in Hidatsa. Int. J. Am. Ling. 20: 65–70.

Vygotsky, L. S. 1962. Thought and Language. MIT Press, Cambridge, Mass.

Wachs, T. D., I. C. Uzgiris, and J. McV. Hunt. 1971. Cognitive development in infants of different age levels and from different environmental backgrounds: an exploratory investigation. Merrill Palmer Q. 17: 283–317.

Wada, J. 1974. Morphological asymmetry of human cerebral hemispheres: temporal and frontal speech zones in one hundred adult and one hundred child brains. Paper presented before the American Academy of Neurology, San Francisco.

Washburn, S. L., and I. DeVore. 1961. The social life of baboons. Sci. Am. 204(6): 62–71.

Watson, J. S. 1966. Perception of object orientation in infants. Merrill Palmer Q. 12: 73–94.

Watzlawick, P., J. H. Beavin, and D. D. Jackson. 1967. Pragmatics of Human Communication. Norton, New York.

Waugh, N. C., and D. A. Norman. 1965. Primary memory. Psychol. Rev. 72: 89–104.

Waxler, C. Z., and M. R. Yarrow. 1975. An observational study of maternal models. Dev. Psychol. 11: 485-494.

Weeks, T. E. 1971. Speech registers in young children. Child Dev. 42: 1119-1131.

Weir, R. 1962. Language in the Crib. Mouton, The Hague.

Weizsäcker, C. F. 1959. Sprache als Information. In: Die Sprache. Vortragsreihe der Bayrischen Akademie der schönen Künste. Darmstadt, Germany.

Wells, G. 1974. Learning to code experience through language. J. Child Lang. 1: 243-269.

Wells, R. 1969. Innate knowledge. In: S. Hook (ed.), Language and Philosophy. New York University Press, New York.

Wells, R. 1970. Comprehension and expression. In: J. L. Cowan (ed.), Studies in Thought and Language. University of Arizona Press, Tucson.

Werner, H. 1940. Comparative Psychology of Mental Development. International Universities Press, New York.

Werner, H., and B. Kaplan. 1963. Symbol Formation. John Wiley & Sons, New York.

White, B. L. 1971. Human Infants. Experience and Psychological Development. Prentice-Hall, Englewood Cliffs, N.J.

White, B. L. 1972. Fundamental early environmental influences on the development of competence. Paper presented at the Third Western Symposium on Learning: Cognitive Learning. Western Washington State College, Bellingham, Wash.

White, B. L., and R. Held. 1966. Plasticity of sensorimotor development in the human infant. In: J. S. Rosenblith and W. Allinsmith (eds.), The Causes of Behavior: Readings in Child Development and Educational Psychology. 2nd Ed. Allyn & Bacon, Boston.

White, R. 1959. Motivation reconsidered: the concept of competence. Psychol. Rev. 66:297-333.

Whitehurst, G. J. 1971. Generalized labeling on the basis of structural response classes by two young children. J. Exp. Child Psychol. 12: 59-71.

Whitehurst, G. J. 1972. Production of novel and grammatical utterances by young children. J. Exp. Child Psychol. 13: 502-515.

Whitehurst, G. J. 1973. Laboratory studies of imitation and language acquisition: is there an interface with the normal environment? Paper presented at the Biennial Meeting of the Society for Research in Child Development, March, Philadelphia.

Whitehurst, G. J. 1976. The development of communication: changes with age and modeling. Child Dev. 47: 473–482.

Whitehurst, G. J., G. Novak, and G. A. Zorn. 1972. Delayed speech studies in the home. Dev. Psychol. 7: 169–177.

Whitehurst, G. J., and R. Vasta. 1975. Is language acquired through imitation? J. Psycholing. Res. 4: 37–59.

Wiegerink, R., C. Harris, R. Simeonsson, and M. E. Pearson. 1974. Social stimulation of vocalizations in delayed infants: familiar and novel agent. Child Dev. 45: 866–872.

Wilkinson, A. 1971. The Foundation of Language. Talking and Reading in Young Children. Oxford University Press, London.

Williams, F. (ed.). 1970. Language and Poverty. Perspective on a Theme. Markham, Chicago.

Witte, O. 1930. Untersuchungen über die Gebärdensprache. Z. Psychol. 116: 225–308.

Wittgenstein, L. 1953. Philosophical Investigations. Macmillan, New York.

Wolff, P. H. 1965. The development of attention in young infants. Ann. N.Y. Acad. Sci. 118: 815–830.

Wolff, P. H. 1966. The Causes, Controls and Organization of Behavior in the Neonate. Psychological Issues. International Universities Press, New York.

Wolff, P. H. 1969. The natural history of crying and other vocalizations in early infancy. In: B. M. Foss (ed.), Determinants of Infant Behavior. Vol. 4. Methuen, London.

Wundt, W. 1900. Völkerpsychologie. Engelmann, Leipzig.

Wyatt, G. L. 1955. Speech and Interpersonal Relations in Childhood. The Free Press, New York.

Wyatt, G. L. 1969. Language Learning and Communication Disorders in Children. The Free Press, Glencoe, Ill.

Yeudovitskaya, T. V. 1971. Development of attention. In: A. V. Zaporozhets and D. B. Elkonin (eds.), The Psychology of Preschool Children. MIT Press, Cambridge, Mass.

Zaporozhets, A. V. 1965. The development of perception in the preschool child. Monogr. Soc. Res. Child Dev. 30. (No. 2, Serial no. 100).

Zazzo, R. 1957. Le problème de l'imitation chez le nouveau-né. Enfance 2: 135–142.

Zegiob, L. E., and R. Forehand. 1975. Maternal interactive behavior as a function of race, socioeconomic status and sex of the child. Child Dev. 46: 564–568.

Zeigarnik, B. 1927. Über das Behalten von erledigten und uner-
ledigten Handlungen. Psychol. Forsch. 9: 1-85.
Zipf, G. K. 1949. Human Behavior and the Principle of Least Effort.
Addison-Wesley, Reading, Mass.

Index

Abstraction, 70
Accommodation, 118
Act, 90
  analagous to the sentence, 136
  with regard to behavior, 6
Action structures, 93
Active orientation, toward outside stimuli, 43
Active-passive alternations, 94
Activity category, 141
Adaptations of adult speech to child's linguistic level, 230
Adjectives, included in verb class, 130
Adolescents, effect of peer group on language competence and behavior, 212
Adults
  different verbal behavior of, with children, 259
  interacting verbally with children, 14
  language learning, compared to children, 208
  motivating forces at work in, 259
  speech input, specific translational adequacy of, 233
  underlying structures of behavior in, 51
Adverbs of place, and communication of spatial relationships, their use with verbal function, 132
Affective qualities of various frequencies of the sound spectrum, 80
Age-determined bases for remembering, 78
Age-related changes in adult-child interactions, 235
Age-related trends, survey over previous research, regularity of, 236ff.
Alloplastic process, 47
Ambient noise, high amounts of,

negatively correlated with language development, 213
American Indian, use of gesture to communicate with Whites, 189
American Sign Language, 21, 33
Amnesia, in adults, concerning childhood experiences, 77
Analysis of language acquisition and training, present "global-diffuse" approach, 20
Analytical approach to mother-child interactions, bases for, 227
Anatomic description of individual organs, 34
Antecedents of language behavior, 19, 32, 55ff.
Arbitrary signs, representation by, 104
Aristotle, 24
Artificial languages, 158
Artificiality of the child's environment, 49
Arts, high degree of proficiency in expression of emotion in, 121
Assimilation, 114
"Association area of association areas," peculiar to the human brain, 40
Attention, definition, 65
"Attention getter," 112
Attention-maintaining techniques, 272
Automatic translation, 20
Awareness of thoughts and feelings of others, 75

Babble and chatter, tendency of higher apes, 35
Babbling, 65
  increase in, contigent on social reinforcement of, 263
"Babbling dialogues," 51
  fine motor patterns, 108
  between mother and infant, 35

Babbling drift, 65
Babbling—listening—babbling, circular process of, 50
Baby-biographical approach, advantage of, 5
Baby talk, 232
  effects on child, 232
  encountered broadly in diverse cultures, 232
Bandura, 10, 220
Bases, biological, 13
Behavior
  syntax of, 2
  with regard to acts and pragmatics, 6
Behavior setting, 163
  effect on communicative behavior, 171
behavioral structures, development of, 90
Behavioristic approach, 7
  basic principle of, 7
  cognitive approach, more behavioral than, 4
  motivation and reinforcement, 259–264
Bipedalism, impact on language development, 47
Brain
  central basis for language development, 116
  localization, 40
  relations between language and the, 37
  size and capacity, 37
Brain research, relevant findings regarding conceptualization and communication, 17
Braine
  scanner and storage model, 233
  as supporter of factual/behavior position, 6
Bruner, 17
Bühler, 10
  insight into completeness of one-word utterances, 21

Calibrations between adults and their children, 234
Capacities of the infant, nativistic assumption in contrast to what is known of, 31
Categories of structure, differentiable, 92
"Causal chains" leading from innate structures and physiological function to actual language behavior, 32, 36
Causality, 124, 134
Cause-effect-feedback process, 226
Cause-effect principle, 44
Central organization in observational learning, 221
Channels of information transmission, interrelationships with efficiency of communication, 191, 149ff.
Child
  effects on mother, 23, 62, 225
  use of language to explore world, 271
  formulating and testing hypotheses and rules, 23
  instigating teaching, 210
  process of observational learning, 221
  questions of, 249
Chomsky, 8, 16, 110
Circular reactions, 226, 227
Classification, 69
Code-switching, 211
Cognitive analysis as link in causal chain, 48
Cognitive approach, advantage of, 4
Cognitive basis for linguistic structures, 18, 65–97, 110–120
Cognitive development, 7
  and language learning, 20
  relationship to verbalization, 127
Cognitive operant, 261
Cognitive structures
  analyses of, 90
  definition, 57
Cognitive-learning theoretical frame of reference, 10

Cognitive-Piagetian approach in language development, 18
Cognitive-semantic approach, 6
Cognition, 3, 32
Communality, 13
Communication
  and conceptualization, cross-species perspectives, 17
  efficiency, 82
  exchange, global function of, 59
  nonverbal and environmental, 151
Communicative behavior, context of, 6
Communicative clarity, child's striving toward, 271
Communicative competence, 9
Communicative space, dimensions of, 161
Competence, vagueness as a term, 9
Competence motivation, 270
Competence-performance dichotomy, 8
Complex network of neurons, interconnection between in the human brain, 38
Complex object, sequential analysis of, 109
Complex plan, sequential realization of, 109
Complexity of social environment, effects of, 104
Complexity index, 234
Concatenating of actions, 137
Concept, features relevant to definition of, 127
  dissimilarity to those held by adults, 85
Concept development, in children of past and future, 133
  previous to word comprehension or utterance, 83
  in situations ecologically significant to the subject, 84
Conceptual development, 3
Conditioned reinforcement

frequency of, 265
  of verbal behavior, 264
Consonant-vowel patterns, 108
Contentives, 113
Contents, 2
Contrasting approaches to pragmatic and semantic aspects of early language, 15
Cooing stage, 65
Coordinating and subordinating of clauses, 137
Corrective feedback, adult provision of, 232
Correlational methods of analysis, fallacies in, 226
Cross-modal association formed through adult teaching of first words, 104
Cross-species perspective, Premack's analytic approach, 20
Culture-specific code in language development, 22
Curiosity drive, 43, 143
Curvilinear relationships, 236

Data collection, inadvertently affecting data generation, 215
Data generation, 215
Deaf parents, infants of, non-use of sound when crying, 103
Decontextualization, increase in, 76
Decreased emphasis on basic language teaching, profound negative effects of, 256
Deictic gesture, 104, 133
Demonstrative, 181
Demonstrative messages, examples of encoding, 196
Demonstrative pronouns, 133
Dependency, prolonged and profound in infancy, impact upon human cognitive development of, 49
Deprivation experiments, 58
Derived function as link in causal chain, 48

Desire to communicate
and language development, 33
strong, in infant, 167
Development
of emotions, outline of, 86
of representation and of verbal
symbols, 116
as term employed in European
tradition, 8
of vocalization, 64
Developmental psycholinguistics,
current activity in, 1
Diachronic approach to ontogenetic
establishment of language skills,
11-12
Diachronic/epigenetic perspective, 13
Dichotomic approaches, 12
Differential communication effectiveness, 267
Differentiation, infant
between the voices of familiar
persons, 108
use of acoustic features for, 68
Directive functions, 121
description of development of, 85
developments in the first year
resulting in, 61
and relating to phenomena in the
objective environment, 122
Disambiguation mechanisms, 3, 157
Discrepancy/cognitive dissonance,
275
Discrimination ability, as a prerequisite for communication,
67-69
Discrimination accuracy, 82
Dissonant features in input, children's imitation of, 222
Distancing function, 76
development of, 102
first stages in, 104
process of, built into play activities of the child, 50
Distinction between the acquisition
of skills and their performance,
220
Distributional analysis, 203
Dolphin, size and structural com-

plexity of brain, compared to
man, 37
Dyadic relationship, between infant
and adult, 23, 62, 225
Dynamics of language acquisition,
kindred conceptualizations of,
261
Dynamic aspects of dyadic interactions, 256

Early communicative development, 6
Early language, volitional and emo-
tional aspect of, 129
Early language products, principles
of, 114
Ears, structured especially for voice
reception, 35
Ecological exploration of animal and
human behavior, 21
Egocentric experiences, transcending
limits of, 122
Embedded clauses, comprehension
of sentences with many, 91
Embedding of sentences, 138
Embryogenesis, with regard to de-
velopment of knowledge, 7
Emotions, differentiation into finer
expression, 114
Enactive level, 41
Enactive memories, 117
Entropy, 60
Environmental influences, interac-
tion with inborn structures, 28
Environmental structure and cause-
effect relationship with language
structure, 182
Environment-organism-symbol
system continuum, 91
Epigenesis, 8
Equilibration, 12, 15
Equivalence class, formation of, 70
Ethological investigations, 21
Events, categories of, 69
Evolution by prosthesis, 47
Existence, 124
of objects momentarily not per-
ceived, 132

Experimental analyses regarding functions involved in specific linguistic acts, 19

Experimentalists, teaching attempts, questionable applicability of, to normal language acquisition, 84, 217

Exploratory drive, 43, 143

Expressive differences between adults and their children, 234–235

Expressive function of communication, 61
description of development of, 85
performed by nonverbal channels, 63
and transition to verbal communication, 121

Expressive gestures, 185

Extension
of a term, 5
versus intension, 3

Father
in dyads, differences existing in speech input provided by, 235
small children's misunderstanding of meaning of, 126

Feature detection
and linguistic encoding, 126
relevance for category formation, 127

Feature notation, 86

Feedback, 224
omnipresence of the physical environment, with the infant, 60
from parents, Brown's assertion of nonexistence of corrective and reinforcing feedback, 223
provided by mothers, existence of, 223
relating to multiple-trial learning, 223

Feeding situation, 94, 98
as learning trials of the infant, 45
temporal structure of, 93

Fetus, reaction to loud sounds, 79

First words
first age of understanding, 67
and requesting function, 123
vocal antecedents of, 71

First language acquisition, widely contradictory theoretical approaches, 24

Forgetting and relearning, with respect to vocabulary of language-learning children, 18

Formal descriptions of human competence, 8

Formalized translation rules, 158

Formative function exerted upon verbal behavior by environment, 173

Formative functions of nonverbal communication, 184–188

Forms of transformations in language, 110

Functional analyses, 7

Functional definitions as example of childhood perception of the meaning of objects, 82

Functional equivalence, 113

Functioning
enactive, iconic, and symbolic, 95
of human children, 11

Functions
definition of, 57
pertaining to realm of pragmatics, 2
socio- and psycholinguistic concept of, 24

Functors, 113

Future orientation of the child, 33

Generalization
development based upon the ability to abstract, 69
from locative to social relationships, 96

Generative transformational grammar, 110

Genome, 28

Genetic bases and environmental givens, interaction of, 13

Gestalten, 89
Gesture
  functions of, 188–190
  vocal, 186–188
Goals of the present study, 10
Grasping reflex, 61

Hemisphere dominance, flexibility
  during early childhood years, 42
Hemispheric asymmetry, contrast of
  prenatal anatomical establishment with slow functional realization, 39
Hierarchical classification, 69
  of objects and events, 41
Hierarchical orders of temporal
  structures, 108
  readiness of brain to produce, 109
Hierarchy, instructional complexity,
  91
Holistic acts, most behavior composed of, 136
Holistic approach, 11
Holograms, 117
Holophrases, 113, 123
Human conceptualization, 160
Human interpretations of natural
  environment, 50
von Humboldt, Wilhelm, "need to
  speak" postulation, 269
Hypothesis testing, attentional be-
  havior shift toward, 67
Hypothetical constructs, 257

Iconic level, 41
Iconic memories, 117
Iconic representation in newborn
  animal, 73
Imagery as one of the basic functions of vertebrates, 73
Imitation, 74
  of absent models, 118
  of adult language models by children, 241
  of adults, 52
  as a complex phenomenon, 242

as declining primitive phenomenon, 245
defined, 243
earliest signs of, 107
important survival function of, 106
neurological basis of, 41
as one of main tools of language
  acquisition, 75
role in language acquisition, 105,
  244
types of, 243
Imprinting, 73
Imputation of structure into unstructured sequences of events,
  90
Inanimate environment, eliciting
  function of, 174
Inborn reflexes and perceptual
  mechanisms, development into
  behavioral and cognitive
  schemes, 92
Inborn structures, interaction with
  environmental influences, 28
Induction, insufficient to explain
  acquisition of language, 31
Infant, production of structures,
  89–90
Information as holograms, 117
Information exchange, 11, 59, 101
  with animate social environment,
  59, 104
  with inanimate environment, 59,
  102
Information transmission, 4
Innate basis of behavior, exploration
  of, approaches to, 29
Innate components of a living system, 29
Innate propensities, 13
Innate structures as part of causal
  chain, 48
Innately programmed critical period
  for development of linguistic
  skills, 33
Input
  adult versus peer and sibling, 211
  emphasis on its attention-evoking

value and its semantic transparency, 209

features, provided by fathers as compared to those by mothers, 235

mass media as sources of, 213

short and rare periods of, ability to make disproportional contributions to child's language skills, 210

technical and sociocultural conditions as determinants of, 208–209

television as source of, 213

Intelligence, higher forms of, development from inborn reflexes, 29

Intension
of a concept, 5
versus extension, 3

Instruction by mothers, 224

Instructional potential of incomplete sentences, 250

Integrative, 12

Interaction
patterns in relation to child's language level, studied by Moerk, 236
sequences, 229
structures, complexity in, developed relatively early, 94

Interest span, increase in course of first year, 66

Intermediate-term retention, method of demonstrating, 230

Intermodal associations, 70, 104
made possible by human "association area of association areas," 40

Internal cue-selection component, 66

Intersubjectivity, primacy of in information exchange, 60

Intonation patterns, 64
early age of ability to discriminate, 68
infant reproduction of adult's, 107
understanding of, 110

Intuitive stage, 95

Investigations of spontaneous language teaching versus Russian planned interventions, 219

Lack of differentiation, 114

Language, 8
antecedents of, 32, 55ff.
as code to transmit preconceived information, 102
employed by mothers, fitness for acoustical and grammatical analysis, 22
mapped to reality, development of, 237
multiply overdetermined, 53
and reality, relationship between, 154
as a tool, 206, 223
use as intersubjective behavior, 6
use of term in present context, 9
Wittgensteinian description of, 151

Language acquisition
cognitive/learning aspects of, 101ff., 204
end product, how attained, 203–204, 226–256
father's role in, 210
through interaction with environment, 203
motivational aspects of, 205–206
necessary principles learned by child for, 205
principles of, 170
siblings and peers as sources of, 210
speed of, 207–208
suitability of hypothesis-testing cognitive approach to, 222

Language acquisition device
characteristics of, 29
development of, 48

Language behavior, importance of content or meaning to the understanding and explanation of, 102

Language development, prerequisites for, 32

Language shortage, 49
Language skills
    antecedents of, 10
    how acquired by child, 23
    predecessor of multifactorial, 32
    taught by mothers to their children, 23, 203ff.
Language training and learning
    experimental studies of, 217–218
    as an intentional instructional process, 224
Languages of the Brain, 117
Lawick-Goodall, Jane, 188
Law of minimum effort, 52
Learning set, 18
Learning theoretical approach to language acquisition, 15
Lenneberg, ambiguity on innate structures, 56
Lenneberg's hypothesis concerning a critical period, 208
Linear sequences, 227
Linguistic encoding as link in causal chain, 48
Linguistic information supplied by mother, 229
Linguistic structures, parallels with structures of nonverbal behavior, 137
Linguistic universals, roots of, 55
Localization
    as consequence of learning, 42
    of language centers in the brain, 40
Long-interval imitation, 106
Lorenz, K., 10, 16

Mand, 266
Manipulation, infant, of his environment, 45
Maternal correction of children's utterance, 252
Maternal input, necessity of conformation with child styles, 235
Maternal input phenomena as function of a complex set of belief
systems, 225
Maternal monologues, 51
    language-training functions of, 237
Maternal speech, simplification, situation-adaptedness, and repetitiveness, 23, 230–236
Maternal verbal behavior, 179
Matrix algebra, 5
Meaning
    definition of semantic scope of, 82
    development of, 84
    preverbal development of, 11, 81
    and reference, distinction between, 3
The Meaning of Meaning, 81
Meaningful world for the infant, development of, 85
Meaningless versus meaningful behavior, 2
Means of communication, enumerated, 168
Memory
    based upon representation, 117
    development, and language acquisition, 37
    model, 78
    span, of the infant or young child, 105–106
    unresolved questions regarding, 76
Mentalistic approach, 3
    advantage of, 4
Message exchange, 149
Message transmission, 14
Methodologies, Russian description of, 219
Modeling, 246
    leading to new forms of language behavior in children, 218
Modifier-object structure, based upon differentiation, 96
Modifier-subject structure, 96
Monologues of children, 51
Monologues of mothers, 51
More-word structures, 176
Mother
    adapting to continuous feedback of child, 235

adjusting to child's speech, 231
of disturbed children, 234
in dyads, uniformity in speech of,
235
input to children, 224
input as stimuli with special value
to the child, 209
tendency to tax children to
their linguistic maximum, 234
word for, relatively late appearance in child's vocabulary, 120
Mother-child conversations
based upon meaningful nonverbal
background, 233
their development with the age
and language level of the child,
238
Mother-child interaction, 225
analytical approach, 226
preverbal, 186
Motivation, 256–277
factors in first-language instruction and learning, 23, 256–277
Motivational terms, 257
Motivational variables
in language acquisition, 24, 120
variety of, 260–277
Motor act as transformation, 118
Mowrer's autism theory as explanation of the phenomenon of imitation, 263
Multichannel communication, 21,
149ff.
Multidimensional communicative
space, outline of, 159
Multimodal association, ability of
human brain, 40
Multimodal communication, 152
Multiple motivational variables, 276
Multiple-trial learning, 223
compatibility with cognitively ori-
ented approaches, 223

Naming games, 180, 237
Naming stage, 175
Nativistic claims, support or refuta-
tion of,on neurological basis, 27
Nativistic conceptions, 16

Nativistic hypothesis, rejection and
acceptance of, 55
Nativistic stance, tendency toward in
intelligence testing, 28
Natural language philosophy, 3
Naturalistic observation
methodologies discussed, 216
as research, 215-216
Naturalistic training programs, 218
Need for communication of the child,
104
Negative feedback, mother's, in relation to language development of
the child, 222
Negative instances, requisition for
hypothesis-testing model, 232-
233
Neonatal response to patterned sound
stimuli, 35
Neurological brain research, lack of
cross-fertilization with psycholinguistic speculation, 27
New terms to describe new motivational principles, 258
"No," understood and uttered before
"yes," 122-123
Nonverbal behavior
meaningfully structured, 136
syntax of, parallels to structures of
verbal behavior, 135
Nonverbal communication
of adults, extensive studies of, 21
effectiveness of, 33
relevance to three-dimensional
communicative space, 164
Nonverbal interactions of infants and
their mothers, intensive analyses
of, 21
Nonverbal language, 14
Nonverbal and verbal communicative
acts, interrelationships of, 193
Nuclear interaction patterns, 227, 228

Object concept, 129
development of, 48

Object concept—*Continued*
establishment of, 131
in infants, 87
Objects as items of common interest
between mother and infant, 63
Observational-analytical research, 97
Observational experimental study,
217-218
Observational learning, of equal or
higher importance than trial-
and-error learning, 220
Occasional questions, 248
One-trial learning as cognitive process, 221-222
One-word sentence, 91
complete message character of, 21
as result of complex transformational processes, 111
Onomatopoetic words, 71, 80
combining human and nonhuman
sound models, 65
as connecting links between signals
and symbols, 103
of infants, 74
Operant function, 24, 261
Operation category, 141
Operation-object, as structure basic
to infant's environment, 95
Operational stage, 95
Optimal linguistic lead, 234
Optimal manner of presentation of
linguistic system versus random
input, 225
Organon approach to language, 24
Orienting reflex, 42, 66, 131
"Original word game," 175
Orthogenetic law of development,
20, 127, 130
"Ostensive definitions, " 112

Parallels between structures of nonverbal behavior and linguistic
structures, 137
Parental input
adjustments to child speech, 231
corrections of children's utterance,
252-254

provided to help child master
language learning tasks, 205
Parental language teaching
conclusions about, 254
contradictory findings about, 254
controversies about, 255
Past tense
forms for, 134
and future, verbal confusion, 134
Performance, 8-9
Personal relationships, subgroups of,
95
Perspectivism, 75
Phonemes, 108
Phonetic aspects of linguistic phe-
nomena, 25
Piaget, 6, 8, 10
Pictorial symbols, 103
Picture books, 239
Pivot-open grammars, 113
Place-holder, use of terms as, 112
Positive relationship, between age
and language level, 236
Pragmatics, 7
aspect of language development, 6
defined, 7, 29
with regard to behavior, 6
Preschool period, establishment of
linguistic system, 25, 207-208
Presence, 124
Present tense, predominant tense
employed, 133
Pretending, 118
Preverbal behaviors, transformation
into verbal communication, 101,
183-200
Preverbal channels of communica-
tion, related to verbal communi-
cation, 7, 159-167, 167-203
Preverbal experience, infant's
private way of categorizing the
world, 84
Preverbal language systems, 9
Preverbal meanings, comparison to
increasing vocabulary, 120
Principle of generalization, at the
heart of labeling, 111
"Private" speech, 62, 75

Process-oriented analysis
aspects of, 204
as only valid method, 204
Prolocatives, 133
Prodding, 274
Products, 2
Psycholinguistic speculation, lack of
cross-fertilization with neuro-
logical brain research, 27
"Public" language, 63

Qualitative calibrations between
adults and their children, 234
Quantitative calibrations between
adults and their children, 234
Quasi-lingual communicative mode,
167
Question-answer interaction
with environment, 43
of mothers with their preverbal
babies, 247
training functions of, 246
Question-answer standard, 273

Random input versus optimal manner
of presentation of linguistic system, 225
Reacquired words, 18
Reality
of human infant, preformed and
prestructured by human beings,
155
question of linguistic representation of, 153
Reciprocal influences of preverbal
and verbal principles, 100
Reduction transformation, 91, 140
Redundancy, 11
of verbal encoding of activity for
small child, 142
Referential function, 121, 123–135
description of development of,
49, 61, 85
differences between adults and
their children, 234
and main dimensions of reference,
123–124
Reflex chains in the neonate, 47
Reflex stage and origin of cognitive

development, 32
Reflexive type of causal relationship,
139
Regulatory mechanisms provided by
heredity, 2
Reinforcement
denial of existence severely enforced, 24
phenomena, as related to observational learning, 220–221
of verbal behavior, 24, 258–265
Reinstatement, phenomena of, 77
Relatedness, main dimension of, 124
Relations, child's skill in dealing
with, 71
Remembering, age-related strategies
for, 78
Reorganization of stimuli in observational learning, 221
Representation
enactive, 73
iconic, 73
symbolic, 73
reliance of children upon for information intake from the inanimate environment, 103
and verbal symbols, development
of, 116
Representational function of sensory
stimuli, 117
Representational meaning, infant's
first encounter with, 76
Requests as examples of encoding,
197
Retention, necessity of demonstration of, 229
Rhyming
characteristics, 233
qualities, positive effect on retention, 240
Ritualization, 52
Rule learning in language acquisition, 205
Rule-governed behavior, 9
Rule-governed speech, antecedents,
33
Russian and American methodologies, congruence between,
219

Sapir-Whorf hypothesis, 156
Second-language learning, 141
Semantic developments, definition of, 57
Semantic features, 3, 5
Semantic-pragmatic distinction, disappearance of, 1
Semantic and structural aspects of linguistic phenomena, 25
Semantic and syntactic transformations, 156
Semantics, excluded by linguists, 2
Semiotics, 29
  and information exchange through language, 102
Sensorimotor processes as basis for information exchange with inanimate environment, 102
Sensorimotor stage, 95
Sensorimotor structures, of the child, as steps to cognitive structures, 46
Serial order, principle of, 46
Sexes, verbal differentiation between, 126
Sign
  definition, 102
  origins, 7
Signals
  reliance of senses of sight and sound upon, 76
  symbols and signs, efficiency of, 53
Situational and contextual influences on message structures and contents, 150
Skinner, 24
Social class differences in language behavior, studies of, 216-217
Social environment, negative effect of unresponsiveness on development of symbolic communication, 103
Social and symbolic behavior, 52
"Sound gesture," 103, 111-112
Sound patterns associated with other experiences, 79
Space, 124
Spatial concepts, early development

of, 87
Spatial or locative structures, 92
Spatial structures or relationships, development of the understanding of, 132
Species-specific innate language bases, 40
Specific qualitative differences between adults and their children, 234
Specific training techniques, 236
Speech acts, 6
Speech among children, simpler than between children and adults, 211
Speech motivation, hypothesis of Skinner versus that of Brown and Hanlon, 267
Spontaneously created words, 62
Stages of vocabulary development, 128
"State" verbs, 142
Stimuli from human beings, newborn and infant specific reaction to, 86
Stimulus complexes, substitution of some for others, 104
Storage processes, development of necessary prerequisites of, 79
Strangers, infantile categorization of most people into group of, 96
Strategies of language learning and retention, 18
Strong universals, definition of, 55
Structures
  as all-pervasive phenomena, 89
  of nonverbal behavior, parallels with linguistic structures, 137
  types occurring in early speech, 140
Subject-action-object structure, models for, 97
  parallel with infant cognitive structures, 46
Subroutines, purpose of, 227
Substantivity 128-129
Sufficiency, as applied to language acquisition, 10
Symbol, definition, 102

Symbolic coding in observational learning, 221
Symbolic level, 41
Symbolic nature of human environment, 50
Symbolic representations, 73-74, 104
Symbolization, increasing process of, built into play activities of child, 50
Synchronic considerations of language skills, 11
Syntax
    of behavior, 90, 93, 136-146
    of language, 136-146
Synthesis, 12
"Systemic ambiguity," 8

Television, negatively correlated with language development, 213-214
Temporal patterns, 46
    importance for language production, 108
Temporal sequences, translation of simultaneous occurrences into, 109
Temporal structures, 93, 107
"Tendency toward economy," in communication, 112
Terminal elements employed by mothers in interaction sequences, 229
Terminal elements employed by child in interaction sequences, 229
Theory of mass action, applicability to language acquisition and performance, 42
Theory of relationship regarding learning, cognitive development, and language development, 17-18
Thing, as broad and general effort-saving substitute label, 112
"Thingness," infant's understanding of, 69
Time, 124
    awareness of, development in infant, 105
Time series analysis, 134
Tone of voice, meaningful to infant, 64

Tools as essential cause of culture, 49
Topological space, 133
TOTE units, 228
Train of thought, loss of, 138
Transformations
    familiarity first attained on preverbal level, 45
    mastery of, 44
    principle of, 72
    role in verbal behavior, 72, 110
Transformational model, experimental evaluation of, 19
Transitional probabilities, 227

Uncertainty reduction as motive for mother's language behavior, 273
Univariate design, analogy between the infant with one-word sentence and the scientist, 91
Universal cognitive structures, 51
Universal primary group experience, 51
Utilitarian operant, 261

Vanishing words, in vocabulary of language-learning children, 18
Variety of communicational functions, 11
Verb
    closer relation to subject noun phrase than to object noun phrase, 139
    predominantly used to describe physical acts, 135
Verbal behavior, 6, 23
    differences between the social classes, 217
    structures of, parallels to syntax of nonverbal behavior, 135
Verbal communication, 165
Verbal complementation, 194
Verbal expression of emotions
    deficiencies in, 121
    undeveloped in young child, 122
Verbal principles tied to preverbal, 99
Verbal signs, as tools for representation, 103
Verbal transformations, preverbal developments shaded into, 110
Vertical décalages, 76

Videotape, for recording situational contexts and nonverbal behaviors, 21
Vocabulary
  acquisition of, 120
  appearing earliest and most commonly, 128
  instruction as attributed to older children, 212
  learning, 205
Vocal mechanisms
  preprogramed to acquire speech, 34
  refined structural arrangement in man, 34
Vocal nature of human environment, 50
Vocal temporal patterns, 109
Vocal/verbal behavior employed by child to attain need gratification, 266
Voice recognition, study on, 68
Voluntary production of utterances, 65

Washoe, 33
Werner, Heinz, 127
Wernicke's area of the human brain, involvement in language comprehension, 41
"What is this?" question, 248
Wittgenstein, 10
Words
  invention of, when labels not yet available, 104
  order of, consistency in, 144
  use of as signifiers, 115

Zeigarnik effect, 274